PACK THE COURT!

PACK THE COURT!

A Defense of Supreme Court Expansion

STEPHEN M. FELDMAN

TEMPLE UNIVERSITY PRESS
Philadelphia • Rome • Tokyo

TEMPLE UNIVERSITY PRESS
Philadelphia, Pennsylvania 19122
tupress.temple.edu

Library of Congress Cataloging-in-Publication Data

Names: Feldman, Stephen M., 1955– author.
Title: Pack the court! : a defense of Supreme Court expansion / Stephen M.
   Feldman.
Description: Philadelphia : Temple University Press, 2021. | Includes
   bibliographical references and index. | Summary: "Challenges the
   argument that court-packing will politicize the Court and undermine its
   institutional legitimacy, arguing that the "law-politics dichotomy" is a
   myth because politics always has and always will influence Supreme Court
   decision-making"—Provided by publisher.
Identifiers: LCCN 2021058733 (print) | LCCN 2021058734 (ebook) |
   ISBN 9781439921586 (cloth) | ISBN 9781439921593 (paperback) |
   ISBN 9781439921609 (pdf)
Subjects: LCSH: United States. Supreme Court—History. | Law—Political
   aspects—United States. | Separation of powers—United States. |
   Judges—Selection and appointment—United States. | United
   States—Politics and government.
Classification: LCC KF8742 .F45 2021 (print) | LCC KF8742 (ebook) | DDC
   347.73/262—dc23
LC record available at https://lccn.loc.gov/2021058733
LC ebook record available at https://lccn.loc.gov/2021058734

Printed in the United States of America

9 8 7 6 5 4 3 2 1

To my partner, Laura

CONTENTS

ACKNOWLEDGMENTS

This book is partly derived from numerous articles. Many people helped along the way with comments on the various article manuscripts (sometimes on more than one of the manuscripts). I thank Charles Barzun, Marty Belsky, Jim Delaney, Richard Delgado, Deb Donahue, Stanley Fish, Howard Gillman, Sam Kalen, Ken I. Kersch, Sandy Levinson, C. J. Peters, Tamara Piety, Scot Powe, Joel Selig, Cass Sunstein, Alex Tsesis, Mark Tushnet, and Evan Zoldan. My gratitude goes to the two anonymous Temple University Press reviewers and especially to Greg Goelzhauser for his penetrating comments on the full book manuscript. The Housel/Arnold endowment provided financial assistance for the work. The librarians at the University of Wyoming College of Law provided sterling support, as always. And finally, I thank Dean Klint Alexander for his support of my work. Please note that Election Day, November 3, 2020, arrived during the production of the book. The book was updated to account for changes as of November 7, 2020. For instance, as of that date Joe Biden was president-elect; President Donald Trump was raising unsubstantiated legal challenges and refusing to concede; and control of the Senate remained in doubt because of runoff elections in Georgia.

I used (and modified) parts of the following articles:

Court-Packing Time? Supreme Court Legitimacy and Positivity Theory,
    68 Buff. L. Rev. 1519 (2020).
Free-Speech Formalism and Social Injustice, 26 Wm. & Mary J. Race,
    Gender & Social Justice 47 (2019).

Free-Speech Formalism Is Not Formal, 12 DREXEL L. REV. 723 (2020).

Having Your Cake and Eating It Too? Religious Freedom and LGBTQ Rights, 9 WAKE FOREST J.L. & POL'Y 35 (2018).

The Politics of the Law-Politics Dichotomy, 33 B.Y.U. J. PUB. L. 15 (2019).

Nothing New under the Sun: The Law-Politics Dynamic in Supreme Court Decision Making, 2017 PEPP. L. REV. 43.

Missing the Point of the Past (and the Present) of Free Expression, 89 TEMPLE L. REV. ONLINE 55 (2017).

Fighting the Tofu: Law and Politics in Scholarship and Adjudication, 14 CARDOZO PUB. L., POL'Y & ETHICS J. 91 (2015).

Is the Constitution Laissez-Faire? The Framers, Original Meaning, and the Market, 81 BROOK. L. REV. 1 (2015).

Supreme Court Alchemy: Turning Law and Politics into Mayonnaise, 12 GEO. J.L. & PUB. POL'Y 57 (2014).

Chief Justice Roberts's Marbury Moment: The Affordable Care Act Case (NFIB v. Sebelius), 13 WYO. L. REV. 335 (2013).

The Interpretation of Constitutional History, or Charles Beard Becomes a Fortuneteller (With an Emphasis on Free Expression), 29 CONST. COMMENTARY 323 (2014).

Unenumerated Rights in Different Democratic Regimes, 9 U. PA. J. CONST. L. 47 (2006).

The Rule of Law or the Rule of Politics? Harmonizing the Internal and External Views of Supreme Court Decision Making, 30 LAW & SOC. INQUIRY 89 (2005).

PACK THE COURT!

1

—

INTRODUCTION

The Court-Packing Controversy

Should Democrats add justices to the Supreme Court if given the chance, whether in 2021 or afterward? Or would Democratic court packing destroy the Court as an apolitical judicial institution? During the summer of 2019, a pending Supreme Court gun-rights case thrust the court-packing issue to the forefront of political and constitutional debate, where it is likely to remain for several years, regardless of the Court's decision.[1]

A New York City regulation banned licensed handgun owners from transporting their weapons anywhere other than a shooting range within the city. Even if a gun was unloaded and locked in a storage case, the owner could not take it to a second home or shooting range outside the city. A gun owners' association and three city residents sued, challenging the constitutionality of the regulation under the Second Amendment. The Second Circuit Court of Appeals upheld the regulation, and the gun owners sought to appeal to the U.S. Supreme Court. In January 2019, the Court granted review in the case, *New York State Rifle & Pistol Association, Inc. v. City of New York, New York*.[2] At the time, the case portended the Court's first major statement regarding gun rights since 2008 and 2010, when it concluded in two cases that the Second Amendment protects an individual's right to own firearms against unreasonable federal, state, and local regulations.[3]

After the Court accepted review, New York City eliminated its regulation prohibiting the transport of licensed handguns. Moreover, the State of New York enacted a statute that will prevent cities and other localities from adopting any similar bans on licensed handgun transportation. In light of these changes in the law, the city asked the Court to dismiss the case as moot. There is no longer a live case or dispute for the Court to decide, the city argued. The changes in the law gave the gun owners "everything they have sought in this lawsuit."[4]

The gun owners disagreed. They had not received everything they sought. Their response, filed with the Court, requested a judicial decision: The current Supreme Court should elaborate gun rights protected under the Second Amendment, they urged.[5] The case then took an unusual turn. On August 12, 2019, Democratic Senator Sheldon Whitehouse of Rhode Island and four other Democratic senators filed a friends of the court (amici curiae) brief asking the Court to dismiss the case for mootness, as requested by New York City.[6] But this was no run-of-the-mill legal brief. It argued that the gun owners and the powerful National Rifle Association want the Court to decide the Second Amendment issues because the Court's five conservative justices are their partners in a political "project" to expand gun rights and "thwart gun-safety regulations." Politics should not determine the Court's decision making, the senators' brief proclaimed. But the conservative justices consistently issue conservative decisions: "With bare partisan majorities, the Court has influenced sensitive areas like voting rights, partisan gerrymandering, dark money, union power, regulation of pollution, corporate liability, and access to federal court, particularly regarding civil rights and discrimination in the workplace. Every single time, the corporate and Republican political interests prevailed." Indeed, as the brief underscored, polls show that a majority of the public believes politics rather than law currently shapes the Court's decisions. The brief concluded with a remarkable challenge: "The Supreme Court is not well. And the people know it. Perhaps the Court can heal itself before the public demands it be 'restructured in order to reduce the influence of politics.' Particularly on the urgent issue of gun control, a nation desperately needs it to heal." To spell this out, these U.S. senators forewarned of potential political reprisal: If the conservative justices do not stop pushing a conservative political agenda with their judicial decisions, then the Democrats—with public support—will change the structure and makeup of the Court whenever the Democrats gain the opportunity.[7]

The senators, in short, threatened court packing. If the Democrats win control of both congressional branches and the presidency in 2021 or subsequently, they could pass a statute adding new justices to the Court. The Court has numbered nine justices for the past 150 years, but the Constitution does not fix the number. In fact, before 1869, Congress had enacted statutes changing the Court's size seven times, often for political reasons. During one politically volatile decade, Congress increased the Court to ten seats, dropped it to seven, then settled on nine. If the Roberts Court sufficiently angers the public and Democrats gain the political power, what would stop the Democrats from expanding the Court and appointing new justices? The Democrats would need to add four more justices, increasing the Court to thirteen, to shift the balance of power. A Democratic president would nominate four progressives, who would be confirmed by the Democratic-controlled Senate. The progressives would then hold a seven-to-six majority on the Court, the first progressive or liberal majority in decades, even though the Democrats have won the popular vote in seven out of the last eight presidential elections.[8]

As extraordinary as the senators' brief was, the response from Senator Mitch McConnell of Kentucky, the Republican majority leader, was even more surprising. He did not bother filing a brief or other official legal document in the case. On August 29, 2019, he sent a letter to the Court, signed by all of his Republican senate colleagues. The Democrats' threat to pack the Court outraged McConnell. The Court, he wrote, must remain "independent" of politics. The justices must follow the rule of law: "Americans cannot trust that their constitutional rights are secure if they know that Democrats will try to browbeat this Court into ruling against those rights." The justices should know that the Republicans "will brook no threats" to the Court's neutrality.[9]

So there it is. The Democrats accuse the conservative justices of deciding one case after another in accord with the Republican political agenda. If the justices do not stop and instead follow the law, then the Democrats will have no choice but to pack the Court. In response, the Republican senators in effect said to the Court, "Don't worry, we've got your back."[10] Progressive political commentators echoed the Democratic call for court packing, provoking backlash from conservative commentators. More significant, during the 2019 presidential campaign season (leading up to the 2020 election), at least two Democratic hopefuls, Senator Elizabeth Warren and Senator Kamala Harris (who would become vice president-elect), supported the possibility of court packing. And former Attorney General Eric Holder recommended that Democrats "should consider expanding the Supreme Court."[11] Yet other Democrats then campaigning for the presidential nomination (as well as some progressive commentators) remained more circumspect. They acknowledged that something must be done about the Court, but please: no court packing. Pete Buttigieg and Beto O'Rourke supported adding justices but only in a way that would supposedly "depoliticize" the Court, while Senator Bernie Sanders suggested that the current justices could be demoted to lower federal courts. Most important, the eventual Democratic president-elect, Joe Biden, opposed court packing (more on that at the end of this chapter).[12]

When it comes to Supreme Court decision making, both sides—Republicans and Democrats—subscribe to a law-politics dichotomy: the idea that law and politics must remain separate and independent. The justices must decide cases by neutrally applying the rule of law. Politics is a disease that threatens the health of the judicial process. If politics infects Supreme Court decision making, then Court decisions are tainted. In an interview given soon after McConnell sent his letter, Chief Justice John Roberts reiterated the law-politics dichotomy: "We will continue to decide cases according to the Constitution and laws without fear or favor. That's necessary to avoid the politicization of the Court." His message was unambiguous: Politics corrupts adjudication, and the justices will have none of it.[13]

The most common criticism of court packing is that it will undermine the law-politics dichotomy. Republicans and Democrats alike profess to worry that court packing will destroy the legitimacy of the Supreme Court as a judicial institution. The Court must be kept clean of politics so that its decisions are based on the rule of law.[14] And nowadays, some Democrats worry that if they seize an opportunity to pack the Court, the Republicans will respond tit-for-tat, repacking the Court with new conservative justices when they get the opportunity. Once the Court is politicized, there will be no going back.[15]

The law-politics dichotomy, though, is a myth, propagated over the years for professional and political reasons. Contrary to this myth, law and politics dynamically interact in Supreme Court decision making. Law is neither the handmaiden of politics nor mere window-dressing, hiding political machinations. But law should never be understood as being separate and independent from politics, at least in Supreme Court decision making. In most cases, the justices sincerely interpret the relevant legal texts—the Constitution, statutes, executive orders, and so on—but interpretation is never mechanical. No algorithmic method reveals the correct meaning of the text.[16] Constitutional interpretation, in particular, is never merely two plus two equals four. Instead, the justices' political ideologies always influence their interpretations of the Constitution and other texts, so law and politics always intertwine in the adjudicative process. If politics writ large is the purposeful and overt pursuit of political goals—think of members of Congress trying to enact a statute— then Supreme Court decision making is typically politics writ small. Politics shapes the justices' interpretive conclusions even though the justices focus on the law. Politics writ small inheres in legal interpretation—or, to put it conversely, legal interpretation is politics writ small. Unsurprisingly, then, the justices' legal interpretations and judicial conclusions ordinarily coincide with their political preferences.

If the Court decides cases pursuant to a law-politics *dynamic*—and the law-politics *dichotomy* is a myth—then the primary criticism of court packing vanishes. If Supreme Court decision making is not and never has been apolitical, then court packing cannot undermine the legitimacy of the Supreme Court as an apolitical institution. Court packing cannot infect the Court with politics because the law-politics dynamic is already (and always) inherent in legal interpretation and Supreme Court adjudication. Whether or not Democrats pack the Court, Supreme Court decision making will continue to be simultaneously partly legal and partly political.

Once we put aside the specious concern about preserving a law-politics dichotomy, then we can consider the crucial normative question: Should the Democrats add justices to the Court if they have the opportunity? The unequivocal answer: Yes. Pack the Court!

History reveals that Congress has repeatedly changed the number of justices based largely on political grounds—seven times by express statute. The Court has fluctuated between a minimum of six and a maximum of ten seats. Nothing in the Constitution precludes Congress from enacting statutes changing the Court's size. Most recently, for more than a year from February 2016 to April 2017, McConnell and a Republican-controlled Senate Judiciary Committee de facto reduced the Court to eight justices when they refused to open confirmation hearings for Democratic President Barack Obama's nominee Merrick Garland (nominated to fill the seat of the deceased Justice Antonin Scalia). After the Republican Donald Trump was elected president, McConnell and the Republicans returned the Court to its nine-justice size by confirming President Trump's substitute nominee, Neil Gorsuch.[17]

If history does not preclude Democratic court packing, the politics of the Roberts Court cements the need for it. Despite claiming to follow the rule of law, the Roberts Court has consistently decided cases in accord with a conservative political agenda. Corporations and the wealthy usually win; the poor might not even get into court.[18] Employers win; unions and employees lose.[19] Whites win; people of color lose.[20] Men win; women lose.[21] Christians win; non-Christians lose.[22] Republicans with entrenched political power win; Democratic voters lose.[23] Gun owners win; everybody else loses.[24]

Political science empirical studies underscore the political tilt of the Court. Ever since the conservative Clarence Thomas replaced the liberal Thurgood Marshall in 1991, conservative blocs of justices have controlled the Rehnquist and Roberts Courts.[25] On the Rehnquist Court, the bloc of Chief Justice William Rehnquist and Justices Scalia, Thomas, Sandra Day O'Connor, and Anthony Kennedy consistently voted together to issue conservative decisions.[26] On the early Roberts Court—Roberts became Chief Justice in 2005—the bloc of Chief Justice Roberts and Justices Scalia, Thomas, Kennedy, and Samuel Alito likewise voted together and reached conservative conclusions.[27] With the conservatives Neil Gorsuch and Brett Kavanaugh recently replacing the conservative Scalia and the moderately conservative Kennedy, respectively, the current Roberts Court is likely to become even more conservative; the addition of Amy Coney Barrett after Ruth Bader Ginsburg's death cemented a six-justice conservative bloc. The early Roberts Court already ranked as the most pro-business Supreme Court since World War II. The five conservatives ranked among the top ten justices most favorable to business from the 1946 through the 2011 terms. Alito and Roberts stood first and second on the list.[28] In free-expression cases, the conservative justices supported the First Amendment claims of conservative speakers far more strongly than those of progressive speakers. Progressive justices also showed an in-group bias toward progressive speakers, but not as strong as that of the conservative justices.[29] And as one might expect, the conservative justices shaped the Court's docket in accord with their political concerns. For instance, a study focusing on the period from May 19, 2009, to August 15, 2012, concluded that the U.S. Chamber of Commerce, representing business, filed more amicus briefs supporting petitions for certiorari (requesting Supreme Court review) than any other organization. The chamber had the second-highest success rate. Compared with a similar study conducted five years earlier—partially during the Rehnquist Court years—the new study underscored that the top sixteen filers of certiorari-stage amicus briefs are now "more conservative, anti-regulatory, and pro-business" than the previous top sixteen, which already were strongly pro-business. The findings also showed that these briefs influence the justices' decisions when shaping the Court's docket. A pro-business Court responds positively to pro-business petitioners.[30]

If the Democrats were to gain control of both houses of Congress and the presidency in 2021 or later, they would undoubtedly begin enacting statutes implementing a progressive agenda. They might pass laws creating universal health care, strengthening environmental protections and fighting climate change, combatting structural and unconscious racism, protecting public health from pandemics (such as the novel coronavirus), restricting gun ownership, restoring and fortifying voting rights, and protecting documented and undocumented immigrants.[31] The Roberts Court, with its current personnel, could invoke and construct constitutional barriers that would threaten all of these laws. In the fall of 2019, conservative political commentators began laying the seeds for such a judicial backlash, arguing that Elizabeth Warren's progressive agenda, for example, showed "open contempt for legal and constitutional boundaries."[32] But with control of both houses of Congress and the presidency, the Democrats could also enact a statute adding justices to the Supreme Court. And even the Roberts Court might find it difficult to find such a law unconstitutional, given the long history of congressional adjustments to the Court's size.

This book presents a historical, analytical, and political argument justifying court packing in general, and Democratic court packing more specifically whenever the Democrats gain sufficient control over the national government. Chapter 2 traces the numerous changes that Congress made to the size of the Court over the nation's first century. The chapter begins by explaining the constitutional provision establishing a Supreme Court and its lack of guidance regarding the Court's size. It then concentrates on political disputes that engendered congressional enactments changing the number of justices. Key time periods were the early national years, particularly when the election of 1800 transferred political power from the Federalist administration of John Adams to the Republican administration of Thomas Jefferson, and the Civil War and Reconstruction era. From 1861 to 1869, politically driven Congresses changed the number of authorized Supreme Court seats from nine to ten to seven to nine.

Chapter 3, also historical, focuses on the most famous attempt at court packing: President Franklin D. Roosevelt's court-packing plan of 1937. During the 1930s, the nation's form of democratic government transformed. The United States had long been a republican democracy, emphasizing the virtuous pursuit of the common good. But because of a variety of economic, social, and cultural forces, pluralist democracy supplanted republican democracy. As manifested in FDR's New Deal, pluralist democratic government emphasized a process open to a diversity of values and interests. Widespread political participation became paramount. Throughout much of the 1930s, however, conservative justices on the Court resisted this transition and continued to apply republican democratic principles, which led the Court to invalidate multiple New Deal statutes. In 1936, FDR was reelected in a landslide. With this popular affirmation of the New Deal, he introduced a court-packing plan that would have increased the size of the Court from nine to a maximum of fifteen justices. If the Court insisted on blocking the New Deal, he would change the structure and makeup of the Court. While Congress debated FDR's court-packing plan, the Court shifted its position, accepting pluralist democracy and upholding all types of New Deal legislation.

Chapter 4 follows the history of the law-politics dichotomy itself. The chapter emphasizes three key periods in the development of the dichotomy. The first is the early national period. Judicial and legislative functions initially overlapped; law and politics were not sharply separated. A legislature, for instance, might review a court decision. But during the 1790s and early 1800s, judicial and legislative functions became more distinct, with courts starting to carve out a realm of law ostensibly separate and independent from politics. The second key period was after the Civil War, when university-based law schools first emerged. To justify a position in the postbellum universities, law schools needed to teach and study a pure science of law, distinguished from other university disciplines such as history, sociology, economics, and political science (or government). The third key period was the 1930s and 1940s, after the Court accepted the nation's transition from republican to pluralist democracy. With that transition, the Court needed to wrestle with its own function or role when exercising judicial review, adjudicating the constitutionality of legislative and executive actions. Ultimately, the historical development of the law-politics dichotomy underscores that political and professional forces engendered and sustained the dichotomy. Lawyers, judges, and law professors trace, justify, and protect a realm of power—legal-judicial power—by distinguishing that realm from politics. Supposedly, within the legal-judicial realm, only legal professionals are trained and equipped with sufficient knowledge to understand and resolve *legal* issues and disputes.

Chapter 5 analytically critiques the law-politics dichotomy. While legal scholars (and other legal professionals) tend to insist that the Court decides cases apolitically pursuant to the rule of law, some (though not all) political scientists argue the opposite: that Supreme Court decision making is purely political. Justices vote according to their political ideologies; legal principles and doctrines are irrelevant. Drawing on both legal and political science scholarship, the chapter aims for a middle ground: Neither pure law nor pure politics determines Supreme Court votes and decisions. Both disciplines, law and political science, are partly correct: Law and politics together dynamically shape Supreme Court adjudication. This analysis exposes the law-politics dichotomy as a myth. In Supreme Court decision making, law and politics cannot be separate and independent. Delving deeply into legal interpretation, the chapter explains how a law-politics dynamic animates Supreme Court adjudication. Always. Politics cannot be banished from the Court's interpretation and application of legal texts, whether the Constitution, a statute, or otherwise. But despite the importance of politics, a distinction between politics writ small and politics writ large underscores that, in most cases, the justices sincerely interpret and apply the relevant legal texts. While this chapter focuses on legal interpretation and Supreme Court decision making, it has important implications for court packing. Namely, if the law-politics dichotomy is a myth and the Court always decides pursuant to a law-politics dynamic, then court packing cannot undermine the legal purity of the Court. The Court was never a pristine legal-judicial institution in the first place; it was never bereft of political influence.

Chapter 6 further explores the implications of the law-politics dynamic. Ironically, recognizing the law-politics dynamic is unlikely to change Supreme Court decision making in any significant manner. The justices will continue doing as they have always done: They will sincerely interpret and apply legal texts as they decide cases. And in doing so, they will continue deciding pursuant to politics writ small, at least in most cases, (and politics writ large in the rare case). For this reason, the justices' sincere legal judgments will almost always correspond with their political ideologies. When the conservative Justice Alito disagreed with the progressive Justice Ginsburg on the interpretation of the First Amendment free-speech clause, to take one example, neither justice was lying or being disingenuous. Most likely, they both sincerely interpreted the constitutional text, but they did so from distinct political horizons. They could each attempt to persuade the other of the correct interpretation, but they were unlikely to do so—partly because no mechanical method can prove the right answer, and partly because their opposed political ideologies informed their respective interpretive judgments.[33]

Chapter 6 next explains the implications of the law-politics dynamic for politicians, commentators, and citizens, all of whom should dismiss the claims of justices and would-be justices (Supreme Court nominees) to be apolitical in applying the rule of law. Laypeople should realize that the Court paradoxically justifies and increases its political power by denying its political power. The justices are empowered to decide cases in accord with their political views partly because they maintain that they are rigidly following the law. Originalism, a favored interpretive method of many conservative jurists and scholars, is discussed as an example. Originalism ostensibly uncovers a fixed and objective (and therefore apolitical) meaning for the Constitution by requiring the justices to discover the original public meaning of the constitutional text. But, of course, originalism, no more than any other interpretive approach, does not cleanse politics from Supreme Court adjudication. Instead, originalism facilitates conservative conclusions by conservative justices—a predictable outcome once one recognizes that politics writ small is inherent to the Court's decision making.

Given the extent to which law and politics intertwine in Supreme Court interpretation and adjudication, presidents unsurprisingly choose, and Congresses typically confirm (or reject), Supreme Court nominees based heavily on political considerations, despite the usual insistence by all involved that politics must be irrelevant to the Court's business. Contrary to conservative claims that Democrats politicized and ruined the appointment process in

1987 when they refused to confirm Robert Bork, presidents starting with George Washington have seen Congress shoot down their nominees for political reasons. Throughout American history, nearly one-fourth of the Supreme Court nominees have failed. The list of those seriously challenged at least partly on political grounds includes John Rutledge (a key constitutional framer), Louis Brandeis, Felix Frankfurter, John Marshall Harlan II, Thurgood Marshall, and Abe Fortas. (All of these individuals ultimately served at least some time on the Court, though Rutledge served less than a year on a recess appointment.) Chapter 6 concludes by briefly exploring the ramifications of the law-politics dynamic for legal scholars.

Chapter 7 explores one final important implication of the law-politics dynamic: While consistently emphasizing that they neutrally follow the rule of law, the conservative Roberts Court justices have issued numerous conservative judicial decisions. Focusing primarily (though not exclusively) on constitutional cases, the chapter demonstrates that the conservative justices protect an undemocratic society in which wealthy white Christian men predominate and hold power. The cases are organized into the following categories: the Court's denigration of democratic government; the Court's protection of wealth and the economic marketplace; the Court's failure to protect women; the Court's protection of whites and disregard for people of color; and the Court's protection of mainstream Christianity but not non-Christian religions. Of course, since politics is always part of Supreme Court decision making, these conservative decisions are predictable—when a conservative bloc of justices controls the Court. Given this, the best remedy for the Court's conservatism is court packing. If given an opportunity, Democrats should add as many justices as necessary to create a progressive majority. While the first six chapters articulate a historical and analytical argument justifying court packing in general, Chapter 7 presents a political argument, based on the Roberts Court decisions, justifying Democratic court packing in particular. And undoubtedly the determination to pack the Court will be made politically; no specific set of criteria must be satisfied. The Court's failure to protect and strengthen democracy will certainly loom large in political calculations, but it will ultimately be the corpus of the Roberts Court's decisions that will determine the public and political sentiment. Chapter 7 concludes with a section analyzing counterexamples: the Roberts Court's seemingly liberal or progressive decisions that an opponent of court packing might emphasize. Based on this handful of decisions, the opponent of court packing might declare that the Court is not conservative enough to justify Democratic court packing. But, as will be demonstrated, most of these decisions contain substantial conservative elements.

Chapter 8, the Conclusion, summarizes the book's historical, analytical, and political argument and recommends that Democrats pack the Court whenever they gain the opportunity, whether in 2021 or later. Rather than viewing history as establishing a norm against court packing, as some have suggested, we should understand history as showing the Court engaged in a type of dialogue with Congress, the president, and the public about the scope of judicial power. If and when the Democrats electorally sweep Congress and the presidency, the Court will be pressured to respect Democratic political power. Perhaps John Roberts and other conservative justices will shift in a progressive direction, but given the current polarization in American politics, such a shift seems improbable.[34] As the chapter discusses, the Roberts Court's conservatives and their legal-constitutional doctrines are likely to derail progressive Democratic enactments and policies. Almost certainly, the Democrats will need to add progressive justices to the Court to avoid lengthy pitched legal-political battles against the conservative justices. Finally, Chapter 8 considers one last objection to court packing. Even if this book's argument is valid—that is, that not only is court packing in general justifiable, but that Democratic court packing is justified in our current circumstances—what if court packing will nonetheless undermine the Court's legitimacy in the eyes of the people? In other words, even if the law-politics *dichotomy* is a myth, even if the Court always decides pursuant to a law-politics *dynamic*, what if court packing by Democrats causes many people to lose faith in the Court's authority? The chapter answers this question by drawing on political science research demonstrating a positivity bias. The Court has developed a sufficient reservoir of goodwill so that court packing would be unlikely to diminish its legitimacy; any focus on the Court (even because of court packing) is likely to reinforce the public's positive perceptions of the institution.[35]

Court packing is not the threat to the Supreme Court's institutional legitimacy that many fear. To be sure, court packing would wield political power against the justices in an effort to influence the Court's decision making. But politics has always pervaded the Court and its processes. The historical chapters of this book—Chapters 2 to 4—demonstrate that politics has always been part of the nomination process, the confirmation process, and, significantly, the process of setting the number of justices on the Court. The analytical chapters—Chapters 5 and 6—demonstrate that politics is always part of legal interpretation and the Court's decision-making process. To pretend that politics infects and corrupts the judicial process is to deny the obvious.

Together, then, the historical and analytical chapters justify court packing in general. Because politics pervades the Court's makeup and adjudicative process, court packing cannot destroy the Court's institutional purity—the Court's decisions always and already combine law and politics. But even if court packing is sometimes justifiable—the subject of Chapters 2 to 6—that does not necessarily mean that court packing is justified in our current circumstances. Should the Democrats, in other words, pack the Court when they have the opportunity? Chapter 7 answers this political question: The conservative politics of the Roberts Court demands a political response by Democrats. The Republicans' rushed confirmation of Barrett barely a week before Election Day in 2020—after refusing in 2016 to consider Garland, nominated more than seven months before Election Day—only reinforces the Democrats' political position.

But here we should pause. Democrats can consider a multitude of political responses to the Court's conservatism. Recall that in 2019, some of the Democratic presidential candidates advocated changing the Court without packing it. Potential changes other than court packing fall into two general categories. First, dozens of times throughout American history Congress has attempted to limit or reduce the scope of the Court's power. The specifics of these court-curbing efforts typically reflected the particular contemporary political disputes. For instance, during the Progressive era of the early twentieth century, Congress considered a bill that would have required at least a two-thirds majority of the justices to invalidate congressional (presumably Progressive) legislation.[36] More frequently, Congress has considered bills that would carve away part of the Court's subject matter jurisdiction—for all cases involving abortion, to take one example, or for all cases involving national security, to take another.[37] If these court-curbing bills had been enacted into law, then the Court would have been precluded from hearing and deciding cases in the designated areas. The most extreme of these proposals would completely remove the Court's power to decide constitutional issues.[38]

Second, particularly in recent years, commentators have suggested changes to the Court's size and makeup that would ostensibly "save" or "preserve" its institutional role as an apolitical, "nonpartisan," or "neutral" judicial decision maker.[39] These proposals can be subdivided into two basic types. First, some recommend term limits for the Supreme Court justices. While the specifics can vary, the typical proposal suggests staggered eighteen-year terms so that each president appoints a justice every two years.[40] Second, several commentators propose expanding the number of justices in some stylized fashion so the expansion does not amount to straightforward court packing (simply adding justices to shift the partisan balance on the Court). For instance, Tracey George and Chris Guthrie recommend increasing the Supreme Court to fifteen justices who would function more like judges on a federal Circuit Court of Appeals. That is, randomly selected panels of three justices would decide most cases, while all the justices sitting en banc would decide the unusual or special case.[41] Daniel Epps and Ganesh Sitaraman have developed two alternative schemes also based on a stylized Court expansion. One they call the "Supreme Court Lottery": Every judge currently on a federal Circuit Court of Appeals would literally become a Supreme Court justice (there are currently 179 circuit court judges). Out of this pool, random panels of nine would decide cases. Panels, though, would be politically restricted: "[E]ach panel would be prohibited from having more than five Justices nominated by a President of a single political party (that is, no more than five Republicans or Democrats at a time)."[42] The second scheme they call the "Balanced Bench." It would increase the Court to fifteen justices, including five Republicans and five Democrats: "These ten Justices would then select five additional Justices chosen from current circuit (or possibly district) court judges. The catch? The ten partisan-affiliated Justices would need to select the additional five Justices unanimously (or at least by a strong supermajority requirement)."[43]

These potential changes to the Court—whether a court-curbing measure, an imposition of term limits, or a stylized expansion—are all problematic. Most, if not all, of them are of questionable constitutionality.[44] Given this, one might expect the Roberts Court to invalidate any enacted change: After all, these proposals would diminish the power of either the current justices or the Court as a whole. As Chapter 7 discusses, the Roberts Court (and the Rehnquist Court before it) has been wary of congressional enactments, so the justices would likely be hostile to any congressional tampering with the Court itself. Some of the proposals have problems unique to them. For example, any court-curbing reduction of the Court's subject matter jurisdiction would only dent the Court's power. If Congress were to attempt to eliminate the Court's power to adjudicate the constitutionality of race-based affirmative action programs, to take one illustration, the Court would still be empowered to protect the wealthy and the economic marketplace, to protect mainstream Christians rather than religious minorities, and to protect men but not women. Historically, such court-curbing measures have rarely been enacted and have achieved only "relative success," with that limited success typically arising only because one or more justices shifted their judicial positions in response to the court-curbing threat.[45] In the words of the political scientist David O'Brien, if Congress seeks to control a recalcitrant Court, "[c]ourt-curbing legislation is not a very effective weapon."[46] To be sure, as suggested above, in these highly polarized times we cannot reasonably anticipate a court-curbing threat to induce one of the conservative justices to shift leftward. Finally, any change to the Court that would ostensibly return it to apolitical or neutral decision making will necessarily fail. As Chapters 5 and 6 explain, the Court always decides cases pursuant to a law-politics dynamic. Apolitical Supreme Court adjudication is a myth. At best, some of the proposed stylized expansions of the Court will leave us with a plethora of five-to-four or eight-to-seven decisions in politically salient cases (or some other partisan split, depending on the total number of justices). In fact, even supposedly neutral decisions are likely to be conservative because polarization has pushed Republican justices more rightward than it has pushed Democratic justices leftward.[47]

From the Democratic standpoint, when straightforward court packing is compared with the possible alternative changes to the Court, it is superior in two important ways.[48] First, the constitutional arguments recognizing Congress's power to change the size of the Court—without any of the stylized alterations suggested by other commentators—are overwhelmingly strong. Even the current Court, consistently hostile to congressional enactments, would find it difficult to invalidate a statute simply adding justices to the Court.[49] Second, only court packing would ensure that an altered Court—a newly progressive Roberts Court—would be able to counter the conservative legacy of the current Roberts Court. As described in Chapter 7, the Roberts Court's conservatism is deep and wide. The Court has handed down numerous conservative decisions and constructed conservative constitutional doctrines that, if left untouched, can lead to conservative results in the Supreme Court and the lower courts for decades. Democrats can guarantee a change in direction only by establishing a progressive majority on the Court. In fact, if the current Roberts Court were to feel threatened, whether by a court-packing or a court-curbing bill, the conservative justices might be motivated to imminently construct even more and deeper conservative doctrines before it is too late. For instance, the conservative justices might reach for an abortion case that would allow them to overturn *Roe v. Wade* and eliminate a woman's right to choose abortion, or they might reach for a Second Amendment case that would allow a strengthening of gun rights.[50] Only outright Democratic court packing could overcome the current Court's substantial conservative legacy.

In sum, to stop the Roberts Court from issuing one conservative decision after another, to prevent the Roberts Court from thwarting a future progressive legislative agenda, the best Democratic approach is to change the makeup of the Court. More specifically, the Democrats should pack the Court by adding at least four progressive justices.[51] But what happens when

Democratic President-elect Joe Biden is sworn into office in January 2021 (as of this writing, on November 7, 2020, he was president-elect, though President Trump was raising unsubstantiated legal challenges and refusing to concede; control of the Senate remained in doubt because of Georgia's runoff elections)? Biden has previously opposed court packing, so is the possibility already dead? No, for four reasons. First, Democrats in Congress might pass a court-packing bill, and Biden, when confronted with the bill, might acquiesce to the wishes of his party. Second, and related to the first point, Vice President-elect Harris (and other presidential advisers) might persuade Biden to change his position and support court packing. Third, the death of Justice Ginsburg and the Republicans' rushed confirmation of Justice Barrett changed the political calculus surrounding court packing, as Biden himself acknowledged. (He suggested the possibility of creating a commission to study potential Court changes.) Finally, if (or when) the Roberts Court, as currently constituted, starts invalidating Democratic statutes passed under Biden's watch, the Court itself might provoke him to recognize the need for court packing.

2

THE SIZE OF
THE SUPREME COURT

A History

Congress changed the number of justices on the Supreme Court seven times over the course of the nation's first century. In most instances, the changes arose at least partly from partisan political motivations.[1] The ideological alignments (or misalignments) among Congress, the president, and the Court prompted the alterations to the Court's size. When Congress is ideologically aligned with the president while being misaligned with the Court, it is more likely to increase the number of justices, empowering the president to nominate and Congress to confirm new justices. But if Congress is ideologically opposed to the president, it is more likely to shrink the Court, assuming Congress can overcome presidential resistance to the change. Simultaneously, the justices themselves sometimes recognize political threats and adjust their judicial stances in response. The justices, in other words, have shifted their legal positions to defuse potential confrontations with Congress and the president.[2]

The Constitution established a national judiciary but left ambiguous its precise makeup and, to a lesser degree, the scope of its jurisdiction (the judiciary's power to decide specific types of cases). Article III, in its first sentence, states: "The judicial power of the United States, shall be vested in one supreme Court, and in such inferior Courts as the Congress may from time to time ordain and establish." And that's it. The constitutional text provides no other guidance about the size or makeup of the Supreme Court, though it adds that all federal judges "shall hold their offices during good behaviour, and shall . . . receive . . . a compensation, which shall not be diminished during their continuance in office."[3]

During the Constitutional Convention in Philadelphia, the framers said little that might clarify the meaning of these particular provisions. As a topic of deliberation, the judiciary took "a backseat to other issues."[4] Early in the convention, on June 4, 1787, the delegates unanimously agreed "that a national judiciary be established . . . to consist of One supreme tribunal, and of one or more inferior tribunals."[5] The establishment of one supreme tribunal, the Supreme Court, would not be reconsidered, though the creation of the lower federal courts and the method for appointing federal judges would be further debated. In The Federalist No. 81, Alexander Hamilton explained: "That there ought to be one court of supreme and final jurisdiction is a proposition which has not been, and is not likely to be contested."[6]

The framers left it to the first Congress to flesh out the makeup of the Supreme Court (as well as the creation of the lower federal courts). The Judiciary Act of 1789 was the twentieth statute passed by Congress. It established that the Supreme Court would have a total of six justices, "a chief justice and five associate justices."[7] The act also created two types of trial courts: district courts and circuit courts, each assigned distinctive types of cases. The three circuits—the eastern, the middle, and the southern—did not have their own judges. Rather, a district court judge and two Supreme Court justices would hold court in each of the circuits. Consequently, the act linked the number of Supreme Court justices with the number of circuits: two justices per circuit. The justices would need to devote substantial time to arduous travel for their circuit duties.[8]

The number of justices established by the first Judiciary Act would endure for barely a decade. The framers had designed the constitutional system to combat the effects of political factions and had opposed the formation of political parties. From the framers' perspective, institutionalized political parties would corrupt republican government.[9] Regardless, during the 1790s various political disputes led to the emergence of two "proto-parties": the Federalists, led by Alexander Hamilton and John Adams, and the Republicans, led by Thomas Jefferson and James Madison.[10] The Federalists and the Republicans vehemently disagreed about many issues, ranging from the creation of a national bank to relations with France and England. Both sides accused the other of being a political party bent on corruption and the destruction of the United States. The Federalists maintained control of both houses of Congress, as well as the presidency, through the 1790s, though George Washington attempted to remain above the factional imbroglios.[11]

Toward the end of the decade, the Federalists under President Adams made several serious political miscalculations, including the passage of the Alien and Sedition Acts and subsequent prosecutions of Republican officeholders and publishers. These political missteps fueled a Republican sweep of the elections of 1800. Faced with the impending loss of presidential and congressional power, the lame-duck Adams administration and Federalist Senate sought to stock the federal judiciary with as many Federalist judges as possible within the brief time remaining before the Republicans took control. The first order of business for President Adams was the appointment of a new chief justice. Chief Justice Oliver Ellsworth had already sent a letter of resignation to the president on October 16, 1800. Adams offered the position to former Chief Justice John Jay. When Jay declined, Adams turned to Secretary of State John Marshall, who accepted the position and took the oath of office on February 4, 1801.[12]

The Federalists were not yet finished, though only a month remained before Thomas Jefferson would be sworn in as the new president. The Federalist-controlled Congress had, in truth, been discussing for several years modifying the organization of the federal judiciary. Circuit riding by the Supreme Court justices was an ongoing and significant problem under the first Judiciary Act. Justice James Iredell described the "duty [as] severe," and Jay resigned from his position as the first chief justice because, in his words, it "takes me from my Family half the Year." Partly for this reason, on February 13 Adams signed into law the Judiciary Act of 1801, which eliminated the original federal judicial circuits while creating six new circuits and expanding their jurisdiction. Significantly, the act terminated the justices' circuit-riding duties. The result was the establishment of sixteen new federal judgeships. Because Adams rushed to nominate and the Senate confirmed Federalists for these positions only days before Jefferson's inauguration, the appointees became known as the midnight judges.[13]

While practical reasons supported the enactment of the new Judiciary Act—namely, remedying problems from the 1789 act, including the justices' circuit-riding duties—the Federalists also unequivocally sought to retain power in at least one branch of the national government. After losing Congress and the presidency, they viewed "a firm, independent, and extensive Judiciary" as their refuge.[14] An additional provision in the new act underscored its partisan nature. This provision would, in the future, eliminate by attrition one position from the Supreme Court itself. Justice William Cushing had been chronically ill for years and, in the event of his feared death, Federalists did not want President Jefferson appointing a replacement (as it turned out, Cushing remained on the Court until his death in 1810).[15]

The Federalists had one more card to play. They enacted the Organic Act of the District of Columbia on February 27, 1801, less than a week before Jefferson's inauguration, set for March 4. This statute authorized forty-two positions for new justices of the peace in the district, which Adams sought to fill with Federalists. The Senate confirmed the appointees on March 3, and Adams's still acting Secretary of State John Marshall set forth to deliver all of the commissions before March 4. He delivered most but not all of them. Jefferson and James Madison, his new secretary of state, refused to deliver the remaining ones. William Marbury was an appointee who did not receive his commission, so he sued in the Federalist-controlled Supreme Court for a writ of mandamus that would order Madison to deliver the commission. Jefferson and Madison spurned the Court, not even participating in the proceeding. The dispute eventually led to the landmark decision, *Marbury v. Madison*, which established that the Court had the power of judicial review over executive and congressional actions.[16]

Once in office, Jefferson and the Republicans mounted a more sustained resistance to the Federalists than the mere refusal to deliver a few commissions for justices of the peace. Jefferson condemned the Federalists for retiring "into the judiciary as a stronghold [where] all the works of republicanism are to be beaten down and erased."[17] He viewed repeal of the 1801 Judiciary Act to be of the highest priority, so the Republican-controlled Congress promptly took up the matter. The remaining Federalist members of Congress reasonably insisted that Article III mandated that federal judgeships were lifetime appointments: Federal judges "shall hold their offices during good behaviour."[18] Republicans replied that repeal would permissibly eliminate the offices of the judges rather than removing the Federalist judges themselves (though the judges would no longer have their judgeships). In March 1802, Congress passed the Repeal Act, which abolished the new circuit courts and the concomitant judgeships and therefore restored the Supreme Court justices' circuit-riding duties. The jurisdictional reach of the remaining lower federal courts was narrowed to the pre-1801 parameters.[19]

For a brief time, Marshall and the other Federalist Supreme Court justices considered resisting the Repeal Act by refusing to resume circuit riding (though Marshall, as the most recent appointee, had himself never before engaged in circuit riding). The justices' disgruntlement did not deter the Republicans. By the end of April, they had enacted the Judiciary Act of 1802. It reinstated the Federalists' idea of having six (rather than three) federal circuits but now with one Supreme Court justice assigned to each circuit, so the number of authorized justices was returned to six. Once again, then, the number of justices became linked to the number of circuits. The act also eliminated the Court's next two sessions (scheduled for June and December 1802), significantly delaying the Court's opportunity to rule on the constitutionality of the Repeal Act—remember, the Court remained in the control of John Marshall and other Federalists. Even so, the Court subsequently rejected a challenge to the Repeal Act in *Stuart v. Laird*, decided in 1803. To be sure, the Court avoided explicitly holding that Congress could remove federal judges, which would have enhanced Republican power while being difficult to square with the constitutional text. Skirting this issue, the Court instead reasoned that the congressional transfer of cases from one federal court to another was constitutional.[20]

In light of the Court's prior proclamation, in *Marbury*, of its power of judicial review over Congress and the president, *Stuart v. Laird* manifested a substantial acquiescence by the Court. Marshall and his colleagues implicitly acknowledged that the other branches more directly represented the people and could wield political power to control the judiciary. In fact, even in *Marbury* Marshall's ultimate decision gave an implied nod to political realities. Marshall prudently tempered the challenge to Republican President Jefferson and the Republican-controlled Congress by holding that the Court lacked jurisdiction over Marbury's claim. Despite boldly establishing the Court's power of judicial review, Marshall declined to use it to confront any specific congressional or executive action. He instead handed Jefferson and the Republicans the final outcome they wanted: Marbury lost the case and would not receive his commission. Basically, Marshall allowed the Republicans to win on a legal technicality: Marbury had sought to invoke the Supreme Court's original rather than appellate jurisdiction by bringing the suit directly to the Court.[21]

The Republicans went beyond their restructuring of the federal court system in their attempt to diminish entrenched Federalist judicial power. Recognizing that the further termination of judgeships might face constitutional obstacles, the Republicans seized on impeachment as the best means for eliminating Federalist judges. The Republicans first targeted a partisan Federalist district court judge, John Pickering, an easy target because of his alcoholism and apparent insanity. The House of Representatives impeached him in February 1803. Then, despite disagreement over whether alcoholism and insanity constituted an impeachable offense—"Treason, Bribery, or other high Crimes and Misdemeanors"—the Senate voted along party lines to convict Pickering in March 1804.[22]

After convicting Pickering, the Republicans immediately turned their sights on the Supreme Court. Justice Samuel Chase had been notoriously partisan while conducting several Sedition Act trials of Republicans in 1800.

Later, while riding circuit, Chase charged the Republicans with leading the nation toward "mobocracy," and purportedly denigrated President Jefferson during an 1803 grand jury charge. Seeking retribution, House Republicans impeached Chase in early 1804 on eight counts. Republicans at the time held twenty-one of the thirty-four Senate seats, but they could not muster the two-thirds supermajority needed to convict on any count (a slight majority supported conviction on two of the counts). If the Senate had convicted, some Republicans were supposedly ready to attempt to remove Marshall from office, too.[23]

In subsequent years, the nation's growing population and steady expansion westward created pressure to add new federal circuits. This pressure also led to calls for additional Supreme Court justices, since the number of circuits remained linked with the number of (circuit-riding) justices. In response, a Republican-controlled Congress added a circuit and another justice in 1807, enabling Jefferson to appoint his third justice. (His first two appointments resulted from a death and a resignation.) Over the next three decades, different presidents asked Congress to increase the number of circuits. Members of Congress repeatedly refused to comply because they did not want to empower the sitting president to appoint additional justices. In 1837, however, on the last day of Andrew Jackson's presidency, a Democratic Congress solidified Democratic control of the Court by passing a Judiciary Act that added two circuits and two justices while reorganizing the boundaries of the various circuits. Jackson immediately nominated John Catron and William Smith. Both were confirmed, though Smith declined the appointment. The next president, the Democrat Martin Van Buren, nominated John McKinley, and the Senate confirmed.[24]

After this expansion to nine justices, Congress did not change the Court's size until the Civil War. When the war began, early in 1861, a fraught relationship existed between the Court, on one side, and Republican President Abraham Lincoln and the Republican-controlled Congress, on the other. The primary source of the tension was the Court's 1857 proslavery decision, *Dred Scott v. Sandford*. Chief Justice Roger Taney's opinion had declared that Congress lacked the power to restrict slavery and that even free black Americans were not citizens.[25] In the 1860 election, Lincoln and the Republicans had run in direct opposition to *Dred Scott*. Their disdain for the Court was so great that Lincoln left three seats empty for more than a year and a half while a Republican senator proposed abolishing the Taney Court and creating a new one.[26]

Taney, for his part, openly confronted Lincoln at the outset of the war. The border state of Maryland was a political key to the balance of power between the Union and the secessionist states. If Maryland seceded, it would present an imminent threat to the national capital in Washington, DC, which Maryland bordered on three sides. When violent protests erupted in Baltimore, Lincoln imposed martial law and suspended habeas corpus in the city, as well as in other parts of Maryland. Before long, the Union Army arrested John Merryman, a wealthy Baltimorean advocating for secession while organizing a Confederate military unit. Merryman petitioned for habeas corpus in a Baltimore federal court, where Taney (a Maryland native) was the circuit judge. Taney ordered Merryman's release, which the military commander refused, citing Lincoln's order. Taney responded by issuing a second writ ordering Merryman's release. Taney threatened to summon a posse comitatus and held that Lincoln's suspension of habeas was unconstitutional. Taney concluded with a direct rebuke of Lincoln: "[The court decision should] be laid before the president, in order that he might perform his constitutional duty, to enforce the laws, by securing obedience to the process of the United States." Lincoln ignored Taney's order and explained the suspension of habeas as necessary to preserve the Union.[27]

When Lincoln finally began nominating justices in January 1862—Noah Swayne was first—he of course sought pro-Union and antislavery candidates. In the meantime, Congress took two wartime actions to shift the Court in a Republican direction. First, during the summer of 1862, Congress reorganized the nine federal circuits, incorporating several states that had not belonged to any circuit while also, most importantly, decreasing the number of southern circuits from five to two. Since the justices were still burdened with circuit-riding duties, appointments remained geographically based. Let's say a seat opened for the justice responsible for riding circuit in New England. A president would then nominate an individual from that geographical location. When Congress reduced the number of southern circuits, it justified Lincoln's nomination of more northerners (or, at least, fewer southerners). Second, in March 1863, Congress added a new (tenth) Supreme Court seat to account for the previous creation of a tenth circuit, centered in California. Not incidentally, this additional seat empowered Lincoln to nominate another pro-Union, antislavery justice.[28]

Partly because of the new justices and partly because of the practical demands of wartime, the Court mostly avoided challenging Lincoln during the remainder of the war, despite Taney's intransigence. The *Prize Cases* provide a prominent example. On April 19, 1861, soon after the outbreak of hostilities—but before any congressional declaration of war—Lincoln proclaimed a blockade of Confederate ports. After the Union Navy seized numerous southern ships and their cargoes, several shipowners sued, alleging that the president, without congressional authorization, lacked constitutional authority to impose a blockade and take their property. When the case was argued, Lincoln's first three appointees sat on the Court, but of the remaining six justices, five (including Taney) had been in the *Dred Scott* majority, voting for the proslavery position. Moreover, the shipowners presented a reasonable argument based on international law. Nevertheless, the Court sided with Lincoln and the Union in a slim five-to-four decision. Justice Robert Grier, a northern Democrat who had sided with Taney in *Dred Scott*, wrote a majority opinion that emphasized the president's practical need to act in response to southern secession and aggression. The nation was at war, a civil war, even if Congress had not officially said as much. "The President was bound to meet it [the civil war] in the shape it presented itself, without waiting for Congress to baptize it with a name; and no name given to it by him or them could change the fact." The shipowners were asking the "Court to affect a technical ignorance of the existence of a war, which all the world acknowledges to be the greatest civil war known in the history of the human race, and [which would] cripple . . . the Government and paralyze its power by subtle definitions and ingenious sophisms." The politics roiling the *Prize Cases* were stark for the nation and for the Court. The Judiciary Act of 1863, adding a tenth justice, went into effect the same day the justices handed down the decision. Even so, the dissenters were ready to condemn Lincoln and his "personal war" as illegal.[29]

After the war, with Lincoln's assassination and Andrew Johnson's assumption of the presidency, the political context for the Court changed dramatically. Johnson, a Democrat from Tennessee, opposed Republican plans for Reconstruction. Consequently, the Republican-controlled Congress did not trust him to appoint any new justices to the Court. When Justice John Catron died on May 30, 1865, Johnson nominated Attorney General Henry Stanberry for the vacant seat. Congress responded with the Judiciary Act of 1866, which reduced by attrition the size of the Court, from ten to seven justices, and reorganized the federal circuits, reducing the number from ten to nine. Chief Justice Salmon P. Chase supported the legislative change because he hoped that, with fewer justices, Congress might raise the salaries of the remaining justices (it did not happen).[30]

At that point, nine active justices remained, but Justice James M. Wayne died on July 7, 1867, leaving eight living justices. For more than two years, the Court operated with eight justices. In April 1869, one month after the Republican Ulysses S. Grant was inaugurated as president, Congress (still in

Republican control) passed a new Judiciary Act, adding two more seats to the Court, for a total of nine. The act also reduced (but did not eliminate) the justices' circuit-riding duties while providing for a retirement pension at full pay (an incentive for resignations). With only eight justices currently living, Grant had the opportunity to nominate a new justice imminently. When the seriously ill Justice Grier announced his retirement in late 1869, effective January 31, 1870, Grant had a second open seat to fill. In fact, Grant's two Republican appointees, William Strong and Joseph P. Bradley, promptly joined the three dissenters from the recently decided *Hepburn v. Griswold* to overrule that decision and uphold the Legal Tender Act of 1862, which allowed the Union to issue paper money (greenbacks) not redeemable in gold or silver, crucial for the Union's financing of the war.[31]

From the beginning of the Civil War in 1861 to the beginning of President Grant's first term in 1869, politically driven Congresses changed the number of authorized Supreme Court seats from nine to ten to seven to nine. Moreover, during those years of war and Reconstruction, Congress tinkered with the Court's jurisdiction for political purposes. In one noteworthy case, the Mississippi newspaper editor William H. McCardle attracted Republican ire by publishing articles harshly critical of Reconstruction. The Union Army, operating under a Reconstruction statute, prosecuted him for libel, among other charges, after he condemned northern generals for being "each and all infamous, cowardly, and abandoned villains, who, instead of wearing shoulder straps and ruling millions of people, should have their heads shaved, their ears cropped, their foreheads branded, and their persons lodged in a penitentiary."[32] After the lower federal courts denied McCardle's petition for habeas corpus, he appealed to the Supreme Court pursuant to a jurisdictional statute enacted in 1867. Fearing the Court might use the case to undermine Reconstruction, the Republican-controlled Congress repealed the 1867 statute and stripped the Court of jurisdiction over the appeal. The Court nonetheless decided *Ex parte McCardle* in 1869. Unanimously upholding the congressional repeal, the Court concluded that it lacked the jurisdictional power to decide the merits of McCardle's petition.[33]

Since 1869, Congress has not passed any legislation changing the size of the Court. Regardless, the Republican Senate Majority Leader Mitch McConnell de facto reduced the Court to eight justices for more than a year after Justice Antonin Scalia's death in February 2016. President Barack Obama nominated Judge Merrick Garland (of the U.S. Court of Appeals for the District of Columbia) to fill the seat, but McConnell, with the cooperation of all eleven Republican members of the Senate Judiciary Committee, refused even to open hearings on Garland's possible confirmation. When the Republican Donald Trump was elected president in November 2016, McConnell's partisan gambit paid off, as Trump nominated and the Senate confirmed the conservative Neil Gorsuch (in April 2017), returning the Court to its prior size of nine.[34]

Putting aside (for the moment) the Republicans' de facto reduction of the number of justices in 2016, the lack of legislation changing the Court's size since 1869 has not been for lack of effort. Rather, it has been for lack of consensus. Over the past 150 years, members of Congress have repeatedly advocated to change the Court's size (and jurisdiction) for partisan purposes.[35] The most serious attempt to change the makeup of the Court, though, originated with a president, Franklin Delano Roosevelt. FDR's court-packing plan is the focus of the next chapter.

3

FDR'S COURT-PACKING PLAN

Franklin Delano Roosevelt's court-packing plan is best understood within the context of broad changes in the practice and theory of American government. From the early twentieth century until approximately the beginning of World War II, the United States was in the throes of a sustained political struggle over the meaning of democratic government. While the nation finally transformed from a republican to a pluralist democracy in the 1930s, the Supreme Court resisted the change. The Court continued enforcing the principles of republican democracy even as FDR and the New Dealers were passing statutes in accord with the new pluralist democracy. The clash between these two contrasting forms of democratic government ultimately led to FDR's court-packing plan.[1]

REPUBLICAN DEMOCRACY

From the framing of the Constitution through the early twentieth century, American government had always been understood to be republican democratic. The democratic element of republican democracy arose from popular sovereignty. Government ostensibly rested on the consent of the governed, so sovereignty was grounded in the people. Citizens and elected officials were supposed to be virtuous: In the political realm, they were to pursue the common good or public welfare rather than their own partial or private interests.[2] When citizens or officials used government institutions to pursue their own interests, then the government was corrupt. Groups of like-minded citizens who corrupted the government were deemed factions, whether constituted by a majority or a minority of citizens. James Madison described a faction as "a number of citizens, whether amounting to a majority or a minority of the whole, who are united and actuated by some common impulse of passion, or of interest, adverse to the rights of other citizens, or to the permanent and aggregate interests of the community."[3] By definition, then, a factionally controlled government pursued "partial interests" or "private passions" rather than the common good.[4]

Founding-era Americans believed they were especially well suited for this form of government. An agrarian economy in which many white Protestant men were freeholders engendered a rough material equality unknown elsewhere in the world, and this material equality in turn engendered a culture of political equality. "I think our governments will remain virtuous for many centuries," Thomas Jefferson wrote in 1787, "as long as they are chiefly agricultural; and this will be as long as there shall be vacant lands in any part of America."[5] Sixteen years later, the Virginia judge and legal scholar St. George Tucker echoed Jefferson. "[S]cenes of violence, tumult, and commotion" that had destroyed earlier republics, Tucker explained, "can never be apprehended [in America], whilst we remain, as at present, an agricultural people, dispersed over an immense territory."[6] Moreover, with an overwhelming number of Americans being committed to Protestantism and tracing their ancestral roots to western or northern Europe, the people seemed sufficiently homogeneous to join together in the pursuit of the common good.[7]

Two aspects of republican democratic government, as understood by the framers, are worth underscoring.[8] First, although not all Americans were wealthy white Protestant Anglo-Saxon men, political exclusion preserved at least a surface homogeneity. For example, while the framers of the national Constitution sought to construct a republican democratic government, they readily accepted severe state government restrictions on suffrage. At the time, more than half the population was barred from voting. Property and wealth qualifications disqualified some white men, while women, Native Americans, and African American slaves were typically excluded from voting through the Civil War era and afterward.[9] Such exclusions from the polity—from "the people"—were justified in the name of republican democratic principles: These societal groups were deemed insufficiently virtuous to understand or to contribute to the common good. When large numbers of Irish Catholic immigrants began coming to the United States in the mid-nineteenth century, Protestant nativists unsurprisingly condemned them as "unfit for citizenship."[10] Catholics, the nativists charged, lacked the civic virtue necessary for participation in American republican institutions. "Protestantism favors

Republicanism," stated Samuel Morse, "whereas 'Popery' supports 'Monar-chical power.'"[11] As a result of exclusion, specific conceptions of virtue and the common good mirrored the interests and values of the white Protestant mainstream. In other words, while the republican democratic concepts of virtue and the common good remained nebulous in the abstract, they closely mirrored mainstream (and wealthy) white Protestant male values and inter-ests in concrete political (and judicial) contexts.

Second, the constitutional framers believed the state governments of the 1780s provided valuable experiences in the drafting of constitutions. Most important, the state constitutions had been based on extreme optimism, conceptualizing American citizens as predominantly virtuous. Virtue alone supposedly would sustain the republican state governments. Experience had deflated that optimism. During Shays' Rebellion, indebted landowners in Massachusetts sought government refuge for money owed. John Jay wrote to George Washington: "Private rage for property suppresses public consid-erations, and personal rather than national interests have become the great objects of attention. Representative bodies will ever be faithful copies of their originals, and generally exhibit a checkered assemblage of virtue and vice, of abilities and weakness."[12] All too often, it seemed, factional groups used the institutions of government to satisfy their own interests. Consequently, the framers believed that, in constructing a republican government, they needed to devote greater attention to protecting individual rights, especially property rights.[13] Before the Revolution, Americans understood the need to protect individual rights from the British monarchy. With the repudiation of the monarchy, however, the protection of rights from the government seemed less urgent. After all, in the American (state) republics, the people were the source of government, and the government represented the people. Could the people threaten their own rights? Surprisingly, the experiences of the 1780s had an-swered that question affirmatively. In The Federalist Papers—essays written pseudonymously (as Publius) by Madison, Alexander Hamilton, and John Jay in defense of constitutional ratification—Publius unequivocally declared that Lockean rights to liberty and property must be strongly protected. Even though liberty and property caused factionalism—Madison metaphorically explained that "[l]iberty is to faction what air is to fire"—protecting such individual rights should be, said Madison, "the first object of government."[14]

The framers' propensity for political exclusion and their concern for property rights invidiously combined in their protection of slavery as a legal institution. In 1787, slaves constituted approximately 20 percent of the Amer-ican population, though the percentage was much higher in the southern states. Of the fifty-five delegates who participated during at least part of the

Constitutional Convention, twenty-five owned slaves. In fact, the delegates from South Carolina, North Carolina, and Georgia threatened to abandon the proposed constitution if it did not sufficiently protect slavery.[15] The delegates first began substantive discussions on May 29, 1787, and the very next day they turned to an issue, legislative representation, that implicitly revolved around slavery. In debates that unfolded over several weeks, the delegates focused on two opposed methods of proportional representation: one based on wealth (quotas of contribution), and one based on population (number of free inhabitants). The Virginia Plan, the starting point for all discussions, had ambivalently proposed that "the rights of suffrage in the National Legislature ought to be proportioned to the Quotas of contribution, or to the number of free inhabitants, as the one or the other rule may seem best in different cases."[16] The delegates initially turned to this proposal on May 30, 1787, and it immediately provoked controversy, largely because southern delegates wanted increased representation due to their slave populations, though slaves would not vote. In the end, the delegates opted to base representation on population, but rather than equating population solely with the number of free inhabitants, they chose to count each slave as three-fifths of a person.[17]

During the convention, a few delegates condemned slavery as immoral. When discussing whether Congress should have power to regulate or prohibit the slave trade, Roger Sherman of Connecticut denounced it as "iniquitous." Luther Martin of Maryland stated that the slave trade "was inconsistent with the principles of the revolution and dishonorable to the American character." The Pennsylvanian Gouverneur Morris uttered perhaps the strongest condemnation of slavery: "It was a nefarious institution. It was the curse of heaven on the States where it prevailed. [If the northern states accepted it, they would] sacrifice of every principle of right, of every impulse of humanity."[18] Apparently, then, at least some of the delegates understood the moral ramifications of slavery, but the typical reaction to these moral denunciations was silence—or, at most, quick dismissal. The framers never engaged in an extended debate on the ethics of slavery. John Rutledge spoke for many delegates when he declared: "Religion and humanity had nothing to do with this question. Interest alone is the governing principle with nations." In other words, the framers' overwhelming sentiment was that slaves were property, and, in Charles Cotesworth Pinckney's words, "property in slaves should not be exposed to danger."[19]

The Constitution in the end included multiple provisions protecting slavery as a legal institution, though the framers avoided using the words "slave" and "slavery" in the constitutional text. The debate over legislative representation ended with a clause that apportioned not only congressional representation (in the lower house) but also direct taxes by counting slaves as three-fifths of a person. Another clause prohibited Congress from banning the slave trade before the year 1808. The Fugitive Slave Clause mandated that an escaped slave did not become free on entering a free state; to the contrary, the escaped slave was to be "delivered up on Claim" of the slave owner. The Article Five mechanism for officially amending the Constitution precluded before 1808 any amendments that would alter the provisions shielding the slave trade and tax proportionality (accounting slaves as three-fifths of a person).[20] Some protections of slavery were subtler but no less significant. For instance, when discussing the possible methods for choosing a chief executive (president), the delegates primarily considered the legislature (Congress), the people (in a direct vote), and a group of electors (an Electoral College). James Wilson favored election by the people and "perceived with pleasure that the idea was gaining ground." Madison immediately *agreed* about the merits of the people. "The people at large," Madison stated, "was in his opinion the fittest in itself [to choose the executive]." But Madison nonetheless did not support this method. "There was one difficulty however of a serious nature attending an immediate choice by the people," he explained. "The right of suffrage was much more diffusive in the Northern than the Southern States; and the latter could have no influence in the election on the score of the Negroes. The substitution of electors obviated this difficulty and seemed on the whole to be liable to fewest objections." In other words, because black slaves could not vote, southern states would not accept a direct vote by the people when choosing the executive. In a direct vote, northern (white) votes would typically outweigh southern (white) votes. But an Electoral College would allow southern states to receive electoral credit for their slaves (based on the three-fifths accounting) without allowing slaves themselves to vote.[21]

The southern delegates to the convention were more than satisfied with the constitutional protections for slavery. Pinckney reported back to the South Carolina legislature: "In short, considering all circumstances, we have made the best terms for the security of this species of property it was in our power to make. We would have made better if we could; but on the whole, I do not think them bad."[22] Early presidential elections underscored the long-term political ramifications of the slavery provisions. Slave states dominated because of their outsize power in the Electoral College. Of the first seven presidents, from George Washington to Andrew Jackson, from 1789 to 1836, five were slave owners. The two non–slave owners, John Adams and his son, John Quincy Adams, were the only single-term presidents during that time. And not insignificantly, slave-owning presidents were empowered to nominate federal judges who supported and protected slavery.[23]

Regardless, from the perspective of most framers, the constitutional protection of slavery remained consistent with a commitment to civic republican principles—namely, the virtuous pursuit of the common good. "The aim of every political constitution is, or ought to be," Madison declared, "first to obtain for rulers men who possess most wisdom to discern, and most virtue to pursue, the common good of the society; and in the next place, to take the most effectual precautions for keeping them virtuous whilst they continue to hold their public trust."[24] Given the framers' desire to protect property rights—including property rights in the ownership of slaves—how could a constitution respect such individual rights while simultaneously maintaining civic republican principles? The framers answered this question by conceptually distinguishing two separate spheres: that of civil society (the private sphere) and that of government (the public sphere). In the private sphere, individuals were expected to act as self-interested commercial and economic strivers. If people enjoyed liberty, then they would revel in their passions and interests. The strongest and most enduring interest was economic (property and wealth).[25] Moreover, the framers recognized that many, if not most, citizens would be motivated to pursue their own passions and interests not only in the commercial or private world but also in the public world. They understood that factions would inevitably form and seek to control government.

But still, the framers insisted that virtue and reason could overcome passion and interest in public affairs and that therefore government could be conducted in accord with civic republican ideals. The framers believed in the existence of a virtuous elite—including themselves—who would pursue the common good in the public sphere even while pursuing their own interests in the private sphere. In a properly structured constitutional system, the people would at least sometimes elect the virtuous elite to public offices. And in the event that an insufficiently virtuous individual was elected, the system would be structured to control the "effects" of self-interest and factionalism.[26] Mechanisms such as federalism, separation of powers, bicameralism, and checks and balances dispersed power among a multitude of government institutions, departments, and officials, each of which would have its own interests. "[T]he constant aim is to divide and arrange the several offices in such a manner as that each may be a check on the other—that the private interest of every individual may be a sentinel over the public rights."[27] In other words, the Constitution dispersed power among so many institutions, departments, and officials that the self-interested grasping of one would inevitably be met by the self-interested grasping of another. Ultimately, the framers intended the various structural mechanisms to promote the virtuous pursuit of the common good in the public sphere while also protecting individual rights and liberties in the private sphere.[28]

What, then, was the relationship between the government and individual rights, as understood by the framers? On the one hand, the framers feared that factions—especially factions constituted by the poor—would use government institutions to trample individual rights, particularly property rights. The various checks and mechanisms in the constitutional system were needed to temper the democratic potential of the government. On the other hand, and perhaps most important, the framers believed the government could diminish or infringe on individual rights and liberties *if the government acted in pursuit of the common good* (and otherwise acted consistently with the Constitution). In this sense, the public took priority over the private. Wilson, for instance, stated: "[A]s I have said before, no government, either single or confederated, can exist, unless private and individual rights are subservient to the public and general happiness of the nation." The Fifth Amendment in the Bill of Rights explicitly manifested this view: "nor shall private property be taken for public use without just compensation."[29] This provision protected private property, but only partially: The government could, in fact, take private property for public use—that is, to promote the common good—as long as the government paid just compensation. From the framers' perspective, the pursuit of the common good simultaneously empowered and limited the government. The government could do almost anything—even taking property—as long as it was for the common good, but the government could not perform an action unless it was for the common good. In this way, the framers aimed to achieve a balance between government power and the protection of property and other rights. Or, from another perspective, the Constitution successfully curbed the democratic energies of the people without disabling the government.[30]

Subsequent to the framing, individuals would sometimes challenge the legality of government actions. During the long-running republican democratic era, courts would frequently resolve such disputes by focusing on the distinction between, on the one hand, the common good and, on the other hand, partial or private interests—or, as it was sometimes phrased, the difference between reasonable and arbitrary action. The key to the judicial analysis was the categorization of the government purpose: Was it for the common good or not? If the legislature had acted for the common good, then the court would uphold the government's action. If the legislature had instead acted for the benefit of private or partial interests, then the court would invalidate the government's action. In the latter situation, the court might condemn the law as class legislation because it favored one particular class rather than all of the people.[31]

In the early decades of nationhood, courts frequently emphasized that the government could not indiscriminately take property from one citizen and give it to another. In typical language, Chief Justice Stephen Hosmer of Connecticut stated: "If the legislature should enact a law, without any assignable reason, taking from A. his estate, and giving it to B., the injustice would be flagrant, and the act would produce a sensation of universal insecurity." Even so, as Chancellor James Kent emphasized, "[P]rivate interest must be made subservient to the general interest of the community." Individual rights and liberties were of the utmost importance and protected from government interference, but such rights and liberties were always subordinate to the government's power to act for the common good. Even property rights could be diminished or sacrificed for the benefit of the community.[32]

This approach to judicial review continued through the nineteenth century. An 1845 case, *Commonwealth v. Rice*, illustrates the normal mid-nineteenth-century judicial treatment of an economic regulation. A Boston municipal bylaw required a seller to show "that all the said articles are the produce of his own farm, or of some farm not more than three miles distant from his own dwelling-house." An entrepreneur violated this marketplace regulation by selling in Boston poultry that he had acquired in New Hampshire. In defense, the entrepreneur contended that "the by-law is contrary to common right, in restraint of trade, against public policy, unreasonable and void." In an opinion by Lemuel Shaw, the court upheld the regulation, reasoning that the city had provided "accommodations" for sales by "actual producers." The city had "a right so to control them, as best to promote the welfare of all the citizens. And we think they are well calculated to promote the public and general benefit," notwithstanding the restrictions on the economic marketplace.[33]

In fact, state and local regulations of the marketplace were widespread during the early and mid-nineteenth century, being accepted as integral to the maintenance of a "well-ordered society." To be sure, the requirement that government act for the common good limited legislative actions. For example, laws granting special privileges or subsidies to individuals or private businesses were sometimes struck down. In an 1826 Vermont case, the legislature passed a law that authorized inhabitants of Mountholly to pass along a turnpike without paying the ordinary toll. The court concluded that this action was contrary "to correct and just legislation, and of course void."[34] Even so, marketplace regulations were so common at midcentury that Shaw was able to describe the government's extensive police power as "the power vested in the legislature by the constitution, to make, ordain and establish all manner of wholesome and reasonable laws, statutes and ordinances, . . . as they shall judge to be for the good and welfare of the commonwealth." Shaw elaborated:

> There are many cases in which such a power is exercised by all well ordered governments, and where its fitness is so obvious, that all well regulated minds will regard it as reasonable. Such are the laws to prohibit the use of warehouses for the storage of gunpowder near habitations or highways; to restrain the height to which wooden buildings may be erected in populous neighborhoods, and require them to be covered with slate or other incombustible material; to prohibit buildings from being used for hospitals for contagious diseases, or for the carrying on of noxious or offensive trades; to prohibit the raising of a dam, and causing stagnant water to spread over meadows, near inhabited villages, thereby raising noxious exhalations, injurious to health and dangerous to life.[35]

Other courts compiled analogous lists. Isaac Redfield of Vermont noted that courts had sustained laws imposing on property owners "[t]he expense of sidewalks and curbstones in cities and towns." Courts had also upheld laws "[prohibiting] the driving or riding [of] horses faster than a walk in certain streets; [prohibiting] bowling alleys, or the exhibition of stud horses or stallions in public places; [and] regulating the mode of driving upon the highway or upon bridges." Courts had even allowed "[t]he destruction of private property in cities and towns, to prevent the spread of conflagrations," which, according to Redfield, demonstrated "the subserviency of private rights to public security."[36]

Nevertheless, in response to cultural, social, and economic pressures, conceptions of virtue and the common good significantly changed through the course of the nineteenth century. While the framers largely believed virtue was concentrated in an elite segment of American society, a growing number of Americans began in the early nineteenth century to believe virtue was shared equally by all common people (particularly by white Protestant men).[37] Similarly, from the Revolution until the 1820s, political parties were deemed inconsistent with republican democratic government. Institutionalized political parties were viewed as factional interest groups that corruptly pursued private and partial interests rather than the common good. Yet in the 1820s and 1830s, political parties became accepted institutions in republican democracy; they were increasingly understood to encourage political participation by the average man.[38]

Perhaps most important for understanding FDR's court-packing plan—still decades in the future—the Supreme Court's interpretation of the common good in relation to the economic marketplace transformed in the late nineteenth and early twentieth centuries. After the Civil War, the nation changed from being predominantly agrarian and rural to being industrial and urban. In 1859, the value added from manufacturing (equaling the value of shipments minus the cost of materials and the like) for the entire nation totaled less than $8.6 million. By 1899, that total stood at approximately $4.6 billion. It leaped to more than $8 billion in 1909, and then to nearly $24 billion in 1919. The leading industrial states of New York and Pennsylvania alone jumped from having approximately 73,000 manufacturing establishments in 1870 to 130,000 in 1900. During this same time period, from 1870 to 1900, even the southern states of Virginia and North Carolina increased their manufacturing establishments to number more than 15,000, growth of more than 50 percent. In 1870, agricultural workers far outnumbered industrial workers (in manufacturing, construction, transportation, and related jobs)—approximately seven million to four million—but by 1900, the now nearly fourteen million industrial workers outnumbered agricultural workers by more than three million.[39]

The growth of industry corresponded with growth in urban populations, as a disproportionate number of factories were located in burgeoning northeastern and midwestern cities. In 1870, more than 28 million Americans lived in rural areas, while only 9.9 million lived in urban ones, but these numbers shifted over the next decades. By the 1890s, the superintendent of the 1890 Census could observe that the American frontier had finally been exhausted. The expanding population could no longer keep moving west in search of rural expanses. The rural and urban populations were almost equal by 1910. By 1920, more Americans lived in cities than in rural areas, 54.1 million compared with 51.5 million, and the trend toward urbanization would continue unabated over the next decades.[40]

As the nation transformed, an increasing number of Americans became enamored with the ideology of laissez-faire. Whereas antebellum Americans had frequently equated law and regulation with "the release of [creative and economic] energy"[41]—government, it seemed, promoted commercial prosperity—wealthier Americans after the Civil War increasingly viewed government regulation suspiciously, as a threat to economic development and wealth. Given that during the postbellum era more and more Supreme Court justices were culled from the ranks of corporate law firms, the Court became especially receptive to the legal arguments from industrialists and corporations. Responding to those arguments, the Court narrowed its interpretation of the common good in accord with laissez-faire ideology, shielding the economic marketplace from government control and restriction.

For instance, in *Allgeyer v. Louisiana*, decided in 1897, the Court held that a state's restriction on insurance contracts violated due process. The Court's reasoning solidified an alchemical (and laissez-faire) transformation of free labor ideology into "liberty to contract." The concept of free labor, which originated in the mid-nineteenth century in opposition to slave labor, had provided a rallying cry for Abraham Lincoln's Republican Party before, during, and after the Civil War. Justice Rufus Peckham's unanimous *Allgeyer* opinion acknowledged the "right of the state to enact . . . legislation in the legitimate exercise of its police or other powers as to it may seem proper." But such exercises of the police power, according to the Court, must be consistent with individual rights and liberties, including liberty of contract, protected by due process under a republican democratic form of government. Liberty, Peckham reasoned, includes "not only the right of the citizen to be free from the mere physical restraint of his person, as by incarceration, but [also] the right of the citizen to be free in the enjoyment of all his faculties; to be free to use them in all lawful ways; to live and work where he will; to earn his livelihood by any lawful calling; to pursue any livelihood or avocation; and for that purpose to enter into all contracts which may be proper, necessary, and essential to his carrying out to a successful conclusion the purposes above mentioned."[42]

Besides following laissez-faire ideology during this time period, which spanned the late nineteenth century and early twentieth century—known as the *Lochner* era—the Court also used formalist reasoning, which assumed the existence of preexisting objective categories such as the common good and interstate commerce. The justices claimed to discern the content and boundaries of these categories without inquiring into the context or empirical effects of disputed laws and activities. *Lochner v. New York* held unconstitutional a state law that proscribed bakery employees from working more than ten hours per day or sixty hours per week. Peckham again wrote the majority opinion, and, as in *Allgeyer*, he began by acknowledging that the state could exercise its police power to regulate for "the safety, health, morals, and general welfare of the public." He emphasized, though, that due process prescribed "a limit to the valid exercise of the police power by the state." The state cannot infringe on individual rights and liberties under the "mere pretext" of exercising its police powers for the common good.[43]

Peckham specifically considered whether the law could be upheld as a health regulation, promoting the common good, but he concluded that the job of a baker was not "unhealthy" to "the common understanding." In accord with formalism, Peckham refused to seriously consider empirical evidence that showed otherwise. In dissent, though, Justice John M. Harlan reviewed the evidence and concluded "there is room for debate and for an honest difference of opinion" about the health of bakery employees. On that basis, Harlan recommended deferring to the legislative judgment. "We are not to presume that the state of New York has acted in bad faith. Nor can we assume that its legislature acted without due deliberation, or that it did not determine this question upon the fullest attainable information and for the common good." Justice Oliver Wendell Holmes Jr. also dissented, arguing likewise that the Court should have deferred to the legislature because "[a] reasonable man might think [the disputed statute] a proper measure on the score of health." Holmes condemned the majority's formalist definition of the common good as shaped by laissez-faire or social Darwinist ideology. "[A] Constitution is not intended to embody a particular economic theory, whether of paternalism and the organic relation of the citizen to the state or of laissez faire."[44]

Whereas *Lochner* invalidated a state statute, the Court followed similar formalist reasoning to strike down numerous federal statutes, often concluding that Congress had exceeded the bounds of its commerce power. In *United States v. E. C. Knight Company*, decided in 1895, the Court held that Congress could not constitutionally regulate the manufacture of refined sugar. Manufacturing, the Court reasoned, is an inherently local rather than national activity, regardless of the product manufactured, the resources used, and the commercial or social effects of the manufacturing. As such, manufacturing is beyond the scope of the congressional power over interstate commerce. Commerce, the Court explained, might come after manufacture. But "[t]he fact that an article is manufactured for export to another state does not of itself make it an article of interstate commerce, and the intent of the manufacturer does not determine the time when the article or product passes from the control of the state and belongs to commerce."[45]

To be clear, the Court did not invalidate every economic regulation during the *Lochner* era. Sometimes the Court found that a legislature had acted in pursuit of the common good. In 1908, for instance, the Court in *Muller v. Oregon* upheld a state law that prescribed maximum hours for female employees. The Court concluded that the law was for the common good because working excessive hours endangered the health of women. Regardless, the *Lochner*-era Court struck down nearly two hundred state, as well as many federal, laws.[46]

Pluralist Democracy

During the late nineteenth and early twentieth centuries, industrialization and urbanization combined with immigration to stress the republican democratic regime of government. Industrialization in the growing northeastern and midwestern cities generated tensions between those geographic areas and more agrarian regions, produced wealth disparities previously unseen in the United States, and introduced dangerous and mind-numbing factory jobs, as well as bureaucratic corporate organizations. Meanwhile, the manufacturers encouraged immigration so they would have a surplus supply of inexpensive laborers, but then massive immigration engendered cultural tensions as millions of eastern and southern Europeans flooded into this country. These pressures generated mass political movements such as Populism and Progressivism, which challenged republican democracy but ultimately left intact the central republican concern for pursuing the common good.[47]

The republican democratic regime finally crumbled in the 1920s and 1930s. The foundations for republican democracy in America—agrarian economics, widespread landownership, and Protestant values—no longer fit the urban, industrial, and culturally diverse America that consolidated between the World Wars. To be sure, old-stock Americans continued to resist urban and immigrant intrusions. A surging nativist backlash (with widespread Progressive support) produced Prohibition, a religious and cultural strike against Catholics. Then in 1924, the nativists managed to severely restrict immigration. While these nativist successes might have slowed a coming paradigm shift in democratic government, they could not stop the forces of change. In the midst of 1920s prosperity, manufacturers realized that greater profits lay not in the oppression of workers but in the conversion of those workers into consumers. With the help of the burgeoning mass media—movies, radio, and print—a consumer culture took hold. Urban immigrants, just like other Americans, were welcomed to spend their money on mass-produced, mass-marketed products.[48]

Eventually, in the political realm, conceptions of the republican common good that had long reinforced traditional American Protestant values were called into question. Emblematic of this change, the Democrats nominated Al Smith, a Catholic New Yorker, as their presidential candidate in 1928.[49] Soon, the Great Depression accelerated the transition in democracy. Whereas republican democracy had assumed a distinct separation between a private sphere of economic pursuits and a public sphere of government activity—government intrusions into the private sphere were proscribed unless for the common good—demands for government intervention in the capitalist marketplace became commonplace in the 1930s. Franklin Roosevelt successfully built his New Deal coalition by responding to these calls for relief from economic deprivation. The coalition strengthened when unskilled immigrant workers, previously alienated from national politics, metamorphosed into voters, largely through the avenue of the labor movement. While labor unions had struggled before the 1930s, New Deal legislation helped them flourish. Unions added members by the millions and, in turn, mobilized workers as democratic participants, swelling support for the New Deal. Massive numbers of immigrants and their children became part of the American polity.[50]

The rise of totalitarian governments in Europe during the 1930s reinforced the transformation of democratic practices in the United States. In Europe, fascists and Nazis authoritatively dictated to their populaces; arbitrarily imposed punishments; and suppressed religious, racial, and other minorities. In opposition, Americans ostensibly stressed democracy; the rule of law, including constitutional rights; and the protection of minorities. These supposed components of American life and government separated *us* from *them*.[51] In *Martin v. City of Struthers*, decided during World War II, the Court struck down the conviction of a Jehovah's Witness under an ordinance proscribing door-to-door distribution of written materials. In reasoning that the application of this ordinance violated the First Amendment, Justice Hugo Black's majority opinion stressed that "[f]reedom to distribute information . . . is so clearly vital to the preservation of a free society that . . . it must be fully preserved." Justice Frank Murphy's concurrence, joined by Justices William O. Douglas and Wiley Rutledge, accentuated the difference between American and authoritarian governments. "Repression has no place in this country. It is our proud achievement to have demonstrated that unity and strength are best accomplished, not by enforced orthodoxy of views, but by diversity of opinion through the fullest possible measure of freedom of conscience and thought."[52]

B y the mid-1930s, intellectuals had planted the seeds for a new theory of democracy, and by the end of the decade, they were explaining and justifying the new democracy.[53] This pluralist democracy was, of course, still based on popular sovereignty—on the consent of the governed—but now citizens were to pursue their private interests. Politics was about building coalitions—interest groups—and jostling for advantages in the political arena, compromising when necessary to maximize the satisfaction of one's interests. Under republican democracy, the ultimate criterion of government legitimacy was the substantive pursuit of the common good. But under pluralist democracy, the ultimate criterion of government legitimacy was a fair and open process. Supposedly, all groups and individuals were to participate, to express their interests and values in the democratic marketplace. None were excluded merely because of their racial, religious, or ethnic status—or ostensible lack of civic virtue. Pluralist democracy accepted an ethical relativism. While totalitarian governments claimed knowledge of objective values and forcefully imposed those values and concomitant goals on their peoples, democratic governments allowed their citizens to express multiple values and goals. A pluralist democratic government should not dictate particular goals or visions of a good and proper life. Rather, the government should remain neutral, accommodating "our multigroup society" by providing a framework of processes (and rights) that would allow diverse individuals and interest groups to assert a plurality of visions.[54]

Theorists of pluralist democracy dwelled on the requisites of a fair process. The prominent post–World War II political scientist Robert A. Dahl reasoned that, in a democratic election, the weight of each individual's vote is "identical," a candidate or policy alternative "with the greatest number of votes is declared the winning choice," and "orders of elected officials [shall be] executed."[55] The crux of pluralist democracy, though, is "effective participation": Citizens must have "adequate" and "equal" opportunities "for expressing their preferences . . . for placing questions on the agenda and for expressing reasons for endorsing one outcome rather than another." From this perspective, a right to free expression is crucial; without it, Dahl insisted, "the democratic process does not exist."[56] Moreover, throughout his many writings, Dahl always maintained that a people must maintain a democratic culture if they are to sustain pluralist democracy. If citizens are not widely committed to the rules of the democratic game—negotiation, compromise, and coalition-building—then the political community will splinter into sharply polarized interest groups.[57]

The reality of pluralist democracy often did not match the theory. The theory might demand full and equal democratic participation, but the white Protestant mainstream nonetheless developed various mechanisms to maintain their own social and cultural dominance and to thwart outsider participation, at least to some extent. The long struggle, lasting into the 1960s, to overcome legally protected racial discrimination as embodied in Jim Crow laws provides the most noteworthy example. And those outsiders who managed to become full participants in the democratic system often did so at a price. In order to participate, an individual typically needed to relinquish any strong identification with or markings of their racial, ethnic, or religious backgrounds. For instance, during the 1930s, many Jews managed to land government jobs, but only if they did not appear to be distinctly Jewish according to dominant stereotypes.[58]

The transition to pluralist democracy had numerous implications for American society and government. To take one especially important example, under republican democracy, lobbying was deemed a corrupt pursuit of partial or private interests contrary to the common good. A legal encyclopedia neatly summarized the general attitude toward lobbying: "Public policy requires that all legislators should act solely . . . with an eye single to the public interest, and the courts universally hold illegal all contracts for services which involve . . . the exercise of sinister or personal influences upon the legislators to secure their votes in favor of a legislative act." Yet during the 1930s, with the onset of pluralist democracy, lobbying by special interest groups became an accepted means of political participation.[59]

One key institution that resisted the transition from republican to pluralist democracy was the Supreme Court. Through much of the 1930s, the majority of justices continued to exercise the Court's power of judicial review in accord with republican democratic principles: The Court adjudicated the constitutionality of government actions based on the justices' concept of the common good, upholding those actions in pursuit of the common good and invalidating actions for partial or private interests. Moreover, in deciding these cases, the justices continued following other aspects of its *Lochner*-era approach. The justices usually interpreted the common good in harmony with laissez-faire ideology while also following a formalist methodology, ostensibly discerning and enforcing the common good and other legal categories, such as interstate commerce, without inquiring into the contexts or consequences of the disputed statutes or regulated activities.[60]

Once FDR and the New Dealers took office in March 1933, with the nation deep in the throes of the Great Depression, they proceeded to enact "the most extraordinary series of reforms in the nation's history." During the first one hundred days of the administration, they passed fifteen "historic laws," trying to help the millions of unemployed survive, protect farm and home owners from foreclosure, regulate Wall Street, and otherwise use government to regulate and improve the economy.[61] New Dealers at both the federal and state levels were willing to experiment to shake the nation out of its doldrums. A confrontation with the Court and its laissez-faire inspired limits on government was all too predictable.

To be sure, the Court occasionally found New Deal legislation to be constitutional. In *Home Building and Loan Association v. Blaisdell*, decided in 1934, the Court upheld a state law imposing a partial moratorium on mortgage payments, favoring farmers and homeowners to the detriment of lenders.[62] The same year, *Nebbia v. New York* upheld state regulations of milk prices, reasoning that the "category of businesses affected with a public interest" was flexible and expandable.[63] Such decisions suggested possible judicial flexibility, though the justices continued to apply republican democratic principles. Even more promising for the constitutionality of New Deal laws, in an address at Harvard Law School in 1936, Justice Harlan F. Stone advocated for a type of "judicial lawmaking" that, while ambiguous, suggested an openness to pluralist democratic processes. Stone denounced "mechanical" reliance on precedents that reduced the law to "a dry and sterile formalism." Instead, a judge should recognize that sometimes "he performs essentially the function of the legislator, and in a real sense makes law." In doing so, the judge should appraise and compare "social values"—or, in other words, assess "relative weights of the social and economic advantages . . . of one rule rather than another." Thus, at a time when pluralist democracy was becoming entrenched in actual political practices, Stone was arguing not only that legislators should weigh competing interests and values, but that judges should do so as well.[64]

Whereas Stone and the other more progressive justices, Benjamin Cardozo and Louis D. Brandeis, were receptive to New Deal legislation, the Court as a whole remained hostile to laws regulating the economy. Both *Blaisdell* and *Nebbia* were five-to-four decisions, with the same four conservative dissenters, sometimes disparaged as the "Four Horsemen": Willis Van Devanter, George Sutherland, James C. McReynolds, and Pierce Butler.[65] More often than not, Justice Owen Roberts and, sometimes, Chief Justice Charles Evans Hughes joined the Four Horsemen to invalidate New Deal–type laws. Significantly, in 1935 and 1936, leading up to the 1936 presidential election, the Court struck down several key New Deal statutes along with multiple state social welfare enactments. *Railroad Retirement Board v. Alton Railroad Company* invalidated the Railroad Retirement Act of 1934 as being beyond Congress's commerce power. The Court denounced the statute as class legislation, favoring the class of employees over employers in contravention of the common good. In *A.L.A. Schechter Poultry Corporation v. United States*, the sick chicken case, the Court held the National Industrial Recovery Act as beyond congressional power. *United States v. Butler* struck down parts of the Agricultural Adjustment Act of 1933. Roberts's majority opinion quintessentially articulated the Court's mechanistic formalism: "When an act of Congress is appropriately challenged in the courts as not conforming to the constitutional mandate, the judicial branch of the government has only one duty; to lay the article of the Constitution which is invoked beside the statute which is challenged and to decide whether the latter squares with the former." *Morehead v. New York ex rel. Tipaldo* invalidated a state law setting a minimum wage for women. In *Carter v. Carter Coal Company*, the Court invalidated the Bituminous Coal Conservation Act as beyond congressional power. In formalist language reminiscent of *United States v. E. C. Knight Company*, decided in 1895, the *Carter Coal* Court reasoned that mining, like manufacturing, growing crops, and other types of production, was "a purely local activity" and therefore beyond the reach of congressional power.[66]

The Court's intransigence infuriated many commentators. Morris Cohen, a legal philosopher, and Robert Hale, a political scientist associated with a legal realist movement, published articles in the mid-1930s criticizing the Court's conceptualization of a laissez-faire-infused common good. As described by Cohen, the Court subscribed to a "cult of freedom." From the justices' perspective, a "desirable system of law" would recognize legal obligations as arising "only out of the will of the individual contracting freely." Any restraint on such freedom would necessarily be detrimental. From Cohen's and Hale's perspectives, this vision of the legal system blinked reality. One party to a contract typically lacks true freedom, especially in the employment context. While the Supreme Court rhapsodized about the public value of liberty to contract, most employees could not reasonably choose to reject an offer of employment. Because of wealth disparities, private employers, whether individuals or corporations, exerted coercive power over employees, who were frequently forced to accept inequitable contractual terms. Contrary to the Court's liberty of contract decisions, emblematic of the *Lochner* era, the absence of government regulation did not maximize individual liberty in an ostensible private sphere. In fact, as both Cohen and Hale argued, duties and obligations in the so-called private sphere existed because of government action. Contract and property rights arise and are enforceable only if the courts recognize and sanction them. Judges (and other government officials) carry "out the mandates of property owners," as Hale phrased it. Consequently, both Cohen and Hale recommended that the Court modify its approach to judicial review in accord with the realities of democracy—that is, in accord with the emergent pluralist democracy. Cohen, for instance, explained that Americans had never strictly followed the "cult of freedom." Even those who celebrated it in the 1930s still sought government assistance for their *own* businesses. The true question, Cohen declared, was not how to minimize government interference in some ostensibly private sphere of freedom; rather, it was what interests should be protected and who should control the government.[67]

Other legal realists criticized the Court's formalist methodology. The justices claimed to be rationally following the rule of law when they invoked formalist categories, such as the common good or interstate commerce. Deductive logic supposedly mandated the Court's decisions. But Felix Cohen (Morris's son) condemned formalist categories as "transcendental nonsense," concepts with no basis in social reality. "[G]eneral propositions are empty," Karl Llewellyn declared, "rules alone . . . are worthless." Cohen argued that judges should decide each case by closely attending to its factual details, weighing all specific interests relevant to the dispute rather than merely those embodied in a so-called common good.[68] The most radical realists argued that arbitrary stimuli, such as the hair color of a witness or the inflections of an attorney, produced idiosyncratic judicial decisions. Thurman Arnold explained that the legal system, like other human institutions, embodied "all sorts of contradictory ideals going in different directions." Judges and legal scholars constituted, in effect, "a priesthood devoted to the task of proving that which is necessarily false": that the legal system was rational and coherent and that judicial disputes were logically decided pursuant to legal rules. Judicial opinions and jurisprudential theories aimed "to make rational in appearance the operation of an institution which is actually mystical and dramatic."[69]

While the justices and their conservative supporters might have readily disregarded criticisms from intellectuals such as Morris and Felix Cohen or Karl Llewellyn, popular media also heaped ridicule on the Court. The *New York Times* reported that students at Iowa State had hung the conservative justices in effigy. A Kentucky newspaper denounced the justices as "nine old back-number owls (appointed by by-gone Presidents) who sit on the leafless, fruitless limb of an old dead tree." Such denunciations of the justices as too old and out of touch with the changing American society were typical. A bestselling book in 1936 reviled the justices as "Nine Old Men" who refused "to take cognizance of the speed of modern civilization in industrial and economic development, and [denied] posterity the right to express itself in regard to social and economic reform in its own way."[70] Among the Four Horsemen, Van Devanter had been born in 1859 and appointed in 1910; McReynolds, in 1862 (birth date) and 1914 (appointment); Sutherland, in 1862 (birth date) and 1922 (appointment); and Butler, in 1866 (birth date) and 1922 (appointment). The youngest, Butler, was seventy in 1936. In a letter written to FDR, an advertising agency executive in Chicago summarized the popular disgruntlement with the Court's decisions: "Are you aware that the people at large are getting damned tired of the United States Supreme Court, and that, if left to a popular vote, it would be kicked out?"[71]

FDR won the 1936 election by a landslide, receiving close to twenty-eight million popular votes, compared with Alf Landon's fewer than seventeen million. With the Court still blocking implementation of the demonstrably popular New Deal, FDR sought solutions. He and his advisers had begun discussing possibilities even before the election. No opportunities to nominate new justices had arisen during Roosevelt's first term, and FDR was disinclined to wait for one of the Four Horsemen to retire or die. From Roosevelt's perspective, with the Depression dragging on, too much was at stake. Advisers debated the merits of constitutional amendments changing the Court's structure, but Attorney General Homer S. Cummings recommended that a statute might be the best way to alter the makeup and politics of the Court. The administration could point to multiple precedents to suggest the appropriateness of changing the Court's size. Besides the seven pre-1870 statutory changes to the Court's makeup (as discussed in Chapter 2), Great Britain had gone through a type of court packing in 1911. As early as 1933, *The Nation* published an essay suggesting that court packing would be a suitable remedy if the Court were to obstruct the New Deal, while a book published in 1935 focused on the conflict between the Court and Congress and recommended "packing the bench."[72]

On February 5, 1937, Roosevelt sent a message to the Senate revealing his court-packing proposal.[73] Then, on March 9, 1937, in one of his radio Fireside Chats, Roosevelt publicly announced his plan to the American people. He described the nation as in "crisis—the need to meet the unanswered challenge of one-third of a Nation ill-nourished, ill-clad, ill-housed." Yet the Supreme Court, he continued, had cast "doubts on the ability of the elected Congress to protect us against [this] catastrophe by meeting squarely our modern social and economic conditions." FDR emphasized that "chance and the disinclination of individuals to leave the Supreme bench have now given us a Court in which five Justices will be over seventy-five years of age before next June and one over seventy." Moreover, in invalidating New Deal laws, the Court had been "acting not as a judicial body, but as a policy-making body." He insisted "new blood" was needed in the federal judiciary, especially on the Supreme Court, where the older justices were supposedly unable to carry the caseload. Ultimately, FDR maintained that the Court had to be changed to save the Constitution and democracy—and the Court itself. "We have . . . reached the point as a Nation where we must take action to save the Constitution from the Court and the Court from itself. We must find a way to take an appeal from the Supreme Court to the Constitution itself. We want a Supreme Court which will do justice under the Constitution—not over it. In our Courts we want a government of laws and not of men."[74]

Having defended the need for court packing, FDR laid out the details of his proposed legislation: "Whenever a Judge or Justice of any Federal Court has reached the age of seventy and does not avail himself of the opportunity to retire on a pension, a new member shall be appointed by the President then in office, with the approval, as required by the Constitution, of the Senate of the United States." Pursuant to this plan, the Court could have anywhere between a minimum of nine and a maximum of fifteen justices. Roosevelt claimed these changes would produce "speedier and therefore less costly" judicial decision making. Perhaps more important, if implemented, the plan would "bring to the decision of social and economic problems younger men who have had personal experience and contact with modern facts and circumstances."[75]

FDR's court-packing plan immediately provoked controversy. Even some of Roosevelt's New Deal supporters in Congress questioned the proposal. Critics feared the plan would skew the separation of powers among the coordinate federal branches, undermining the Court's independence and politicizing its decision making. Some of the justices themselves publicly opposed the plan, insisting they were fully capable of carrying the Court's caseload.[76] Yet Roosevelt also had many supporters of the plan. Numerous legal realists, including Karl Llewellyn and Thurman Arnold, gave their approval. After all, FDR's attitude toward judicial decision making and court packing resonated with the realist repudiation of legal formalism and advocacy for judicial decisions grounded in empirical reality.[77] More important from a political standpoint, New Dealers in the House of Representatives largely supported the plan. While the Senate was more divided, several key senators, including Democratic Senate Majority Leader Joe Robinson, Hugo Black of Alabama, and Robert M. La Follette of Wisconsin, pledged their support. Meanwhile, *The Nation* suggested that Roosevelt's plan did not go far enough: "It clearly does not meet the issue of the judicial power as an obstruction to democratic action." For a while, the number of supporters in both the Senate and the House seemed sufficient to pass the bill.[78]

However likely passage might have been, the Court soon changed the arithmetic. On March 29, 1937—less than one month after Roosevelt had publicly announced his plan—the Court handed down a five-to-four decision in *West Coast Hotel Company v. Parrish*.[79] An employer, challenging a state law setting minimum wages for women, argued that *Adkins v. Children's Hospital* was a controlling precedent. Decided in 1923, *Adkins* had held that a District of Columbia law setting minimum wages for women and children violated due process and liberty of contract. The *Adkins* Court had followed standard *Lochner*-era reasoning, concluding that the law was impermissible class legislation, promoting the partial or private interests of (women and children) employees rather than the common good.[80] In *West Coast Hotel Company*, Chief Justice Hughes rejected the employer's argument, overruled *Adkins*, and upheld the minimum wage law. Much of Hughes's opinion resonated with traditional principles of republican democratic judicial review.

He referred to the common good, reasoning that liberty can be restrained to promote "the health, safety, morals, and welfare of the people." But near the end of the opinion, Hughes seemed to accept the realists' critique of the Court's prior formalist and laissez-faire-infused conceptualization of the common good. "The exploitation of a class of workers who are in an unequal position with respect to bargaining power and are thus relatively defenseless against the denial of a living wage is not only detrimental to their health and well being, but casts a direct burden for their support upon the community," he wrote. "What these workers lose in wages the taxpayers are called upon to pay. The bare cost of living must be met. We may take judicial notice of the unparalleled demands for relief which arose during the recent period of depression and still continue to an alarming extent despite the degree of economic recovery which has been achieved. . . . The community is not bound to provide what is in effect a subsidy for unconscionable employers."[81]

In other words, contrary to laissez-faire ideology, the operation of an unregulated economic marketplace did not maximize employees' liberty. Instead, employers exploited workers by coercing them to work for unreasonable wages. If the government did not prevent such exploitation, then the government would, in effect, be subsidizing employers because it would no longer allow indigents to starve. In the end, the Court refused to invalidate the statute as impermissible class legislation, even though the statute distinguished between employers and employees and between women and men. Hughes emphasized that the legislature can choose the manner and degree to which it responds to social problems.[82] Of course, the dissenting Four Horsemen concluded otherwise, reasoning that the statute constituted "arbitrary" class legislation: "There is no longer any reason why [women] should be put in different classes in respect of their legal right to make contracts; nor should they be denied, in effect, the right to compete with men for work paying lower wages which men may be willing to accept."[83]

Only two weeks later, the Court issued its decision in *NLRB v. Jones and Laughlin Steel Corporation*, with the same five-to-four alignment and with Hughes again writing the majority opinion. Jones and Laughlin challenged a centerpiece of the New Deal—the National Labor Relations Act (NLRA)—which had engendered the growth of labor unions and politically empowered their members. Jones and Laughlin argued that Congress had exceeded its power by passing the NLRA: Because the statute favored employees (as union members) over employers, it amounted to class legislation under republican democratic principles. Besides, Jones and Laughlin argued, case precedents defined manufacturing as a form of production, beyond congressional control, rather than a type of interstate commerce.[84]

In rejecting these arguments, the Court repudiated its former reliance on formalist categories and laissez-faire ideology. "We are asked to shut our eyes to the plainest facts of our national life and to deal with the question of [the] effects [of manufacturing] in an intellectual vacuum." Instead of invoking formalist categories, the Court reasoned that it should understand interstate commerce as a "practical conception." Given this more pragmatic or realist approach, the justices concluded that they should defer to the congressional judgment. Let Congress decide whether a particular activity, such as manufacturing, bore a sufficiently "close and substantial relation to interstate commerce" as to justify legislative regulation. Consequently, the Court stopped pretending that corporations and other employers operated on an even footing with employees. Laissez-faire ideology had, in truth, allowed employers to exercise their market power to coerce employees into accepting inequitable wages and working conditions. The government could choose to balance the bargaining process in whatever manner Congress thought fruitful. "Employees have as clear a right to organize and select their representatives for lawful purposes as the [manufacturer-employer] has to organize its business and select its own officers and agents." A manufacturer should have a "right to conduct its business in an orderly manner," but employees should also have a "correlative right to organize for the purpose of securing the redress of grievances and to promote agreements with employers relating to rates of pay and conditions of work." Even if legislation were "one-sided," the Court emphasized, subjecting "the employer to supervision and restraint" while leaving "untouched the abuses for which employees may be responsible," the statute should still be constitutional. Congress could decide matters of policy, choosing which "evils" to remedy and in what manner to do so.[85]

These two decisions, *West Coast Hotel* and *Jones and Laughlin*, shredded the traditional structures of republican democratic judicial review. The Court accepted, at least implicitly, a fundamental component of pluralist democracy: Legislation is a product of competing interests, pressed by opposed groups. From this perspective, it no longer made sense for the Court to invalidate a statute as class legislation promoting partial or private interests rather than the common good. While the specific parameters of a new approach to judicial review, a pluralist democratic judicial review, were inchoate (as discussed in Chapter 4), the Court had unequivocally signaled a new willingness to uphold economic and social welfare statutes. In short order, the Court would decide cases reinforcing the right of workers to unionize and press their claims and upholding the constitutionality of the Social Security Act of 1935, providing for unemployment benefits.[86] Even in the rare subsequent case where the Court used language resonating with republican democracy, the words took on meanings different from in the past. Insofar as a common good or the general welfare existed under pluralist democracy, it was no more than an aggregation of private interests and values; these terms no longer signified the virtuous transcendence of self-interest. Congress had the discretion to legislate legitimately and openly in response to the entreaties of the most powerful or persuasive interest groups.[87]

The forces pushing the Court toward a change in direction, toward an acceptance of pluralist democracy, had been building for years, yet the Court's shift was conspicuous enough that contemporary observers immediately celebrated it. The *Washington Post* called *Jones and Laughlin* "a historic opinion which may well be a turning point in American political and economic life," and the *New York Times* "hailed [the] bench change."[88] The *Post* labeled the Court's transformation the "Roberts' Switch," and subsequent commentators agreed: Justice Owen Roberts is most often identified as being responsible for the so-called "switch in time that saved nine," abandoning the Four Horsemen and voting more consistently with the progressive justices.[89]

Historians have wondered whether Roberts and the Court changed direction because of political pressure—especially because of the threat of court packing. As some have noted, even though the Court issued its decision in *West Coast Hotel* after FDR publicly announced his court-packing plan, Roberts and the other justices had already met in conference to discuss the case, on December 19, 1936, and cast their votes, before the president's announcement. Regardless, to think the justices were oblivious to the political rumors that had been swirling around Washington for weeks stretches credulity. Almost three weeks before the case conference, the *Times* reported that the administration and Congress were considering possible legislative means for controlling the Court. According to the *Times* article, advocates for change realized that "Congress can enlarge the Supreme Court, increasing the number of justices from nine to twelve or fifteen."[90] The *Times* report was not anomalous. For a couple of years, dating back to early 1935, the press had been reporting similar rumors on a regular basis. Barely a week before the Court's December 19 conference, the *Post* reported an Institute of Public Opinion poll concluding that 41 percent of Americans favored "a constitutional amendment to curtail the power of the Supreme Court."[91] By the end of January 1937, Washington was buzzing with rumors about a pending announcement by Roosevelt concerning the Court. Significantly, a statistical study concluded that political pressure pushed Owen Roberts to shift temporarily leftward, but the pressure arose largely from FDR's landslide victory rather than the court-packing plan itself.[92]

In any event, the Court's decisions in *West Coast Hotel* and *Jones and Laughlin* diminished the likelihood that Congress would enact FDR's court-packing plan. Yet perhaps even more important than those decisions, one of the Four Horsemen, Justice Willis Van Devanter, announced on May 18, 1937, approximately one month after the *Jones and Laughlin* decision, that he planned to retire at the end of the term, on June 2.[93] FDR would finally have his first Supreme Court appointment. Then, on June 7, the Senate Judiciary Committee voted against the court-packing plan, though the vote was close: ten to eight (seven of the ten negative votes came from FDR's own Democratic Party). The committee report feared the expansion of "political control over the judicial department." By applying "force to the judiciary," the plan's "ultimate effect would [be to] undermine the independence of the courts." In short, the committee did not want to politicize the Court and its decision making. Even so, the court-packing plan still seemed to have a reasonable chance of passage—until July 14, 1937, when Senate Majority Leader Joe Robinson, a key supporter of the plan, unexpectedly died. On July 22, the full Senate voted to defeat the court-packing plan.[94]

In 1947, the Yale law professor Eugene V. Rostow would gush that the Court "died and was reborn in 1937."[95] Whether such hyperbole was apt, changes in its personnel would cement the Court's acceptance of pluralist democracy and the transformation of its approach to judicial review. In August 1937, after the congressional defeat of the court-packing plan, FDR nominated a staunch New Dealer, Senator Hugo Black of Alabama, to fill the empty Supreme Court seat. Another of the Four Horsemen, Justice George Sutherland, retired in 1938, leading to the nomination of Stanley F. Reed, who had been FDR's solicitor general. The following year, Felix Frankfurter (a Harvard law professor and Roosevelt confidant) and William O. Douglas (a legal realist and chair of the Securities and Exchange Commission) would be nominated and confirmed. By the end of 1943, Roosevelt had appointed eight justices to the Supreme Court, leading the political scientist C. Herman Pritchett to call it the "Roosevelt Court."[96]

The Roosevelt Court's stark repudiation of laissez-faire-tinged formalism and its endorsement of pluralist democracy was vividly displayed in *Wickard v. Filburn*, which challenged the constitutionality of the Agricultural Adjustment Act of 1938. The statute regulated the production of wheat, even if it was raised "wholly for consumption on [the grower's] farm." In upholding the congressional action under the Commerce Clause, a unanimous Court relied on realist rather than formalist methodology. Congressional power questions, the Court reasoned, "are not to be decided by reference to any formula which would give controlling force to nomenclature such as 'production' . . . and foreclose consideration of the actual effects of the activity in question upon interstate commerce." Moreover, the Court dismissed concerns that Congress might have favored one class or interest group over another because such class-based legislation typified pluralist democracy. "It is of the essence of regulation that it lays a restraining hand on the self-interest of the regulated and that advantages from the regulation commonly fall to others." Congress could decide between the values and claims of competing interest groups. The Court, in other words, exercised judicial restraint, allowing the democratic process to impose "effective restraints" on Congress's commerce power.[97]

From the mid-1930s through the early 1940s, the influence of politics on the Court—the intertwining of law and politics in the Court's decision making—was evident in multiple ways. First, the conservative Four Horsemen consistently interpreted the Constitution in accord with a laissez-faire ideology that supposedly protected the economic marketplace. Second, Owen Roberts and the Court shifted from republican to pluralist democracy in 1937 and rejected *Lochner*-style judicial review in response to political pressures arising from the court-packing plan, at least in part. And the post-1937 Court fully accepted and explored the parameters of pluralist democracy in response, again at least in part, to FDR's politically driven appointments to the Court. Yet when considering the court-packing plan in 1937, Congress had worried that its enactment would politicize the Court and undermine its (judicial) independence. The next three chapters explore whether such concerns were warranted.

4

THE HISTORY OF THE
LAW-POLITICS DICHOTOMY

The standard argument against changing the number of Supreme Court justices is that court packing will politicize the Court and its decision making. The Court will no longer stand as an independent judicial branch of the national government. In other words, the major criticism of court packing is that it will undermine a law-politics dichotomy: the sharp separation between law and politics. According to this outlook, Supreme Court adjudication must be based on the neutral application of the rule of law. If politics enters judicial decision making, it can only infect and corrupt the process. This chapter explains the historical development of the law-politics dichotomy and the concomitant legal-judicial commitment to formalism. Most significantly, the law-politics dichotomy is a historically contingent concept that developed for professional and political reasons.

In general, individuals trained in law—lawyers, judges, and law professors—have an interest in claiming that their specialized training is important (contributing some good to society), is too arcane for laypeople to understand, and is financially valuable in a marketplace economy. This professional stake in the law-politics dichotomy—often expressed in an endorsement of legal formalism—has played a significant role in the development of the legal profession during at least three key periods in American history.

The first period arose during the early national era. The framers cared about the separation of government powers, including the separation of judicial and legislative roles, as was evident in the organizational scheme of the

Constitution. Article I focused on legislative powers; article II, on executive powers; and article III, on judicial powers. Yet these three articles overlapped (thus, checks and balances) and left significant ambiguities; articles II and III were far less developed than article I. For instance, article III mentions "one Supreme Court, and . . . such inferior courts as the Congress may from time to time ordain and establish." The constitutional text leaves unclear the nature of the lower federal courts while simultaneously vesting power in Congress to specify that nature. Basically, to avoid hashing out disagreements, the framers sketched a broad framework for the federal judiciary while leaving the details to future haggling (in Congress). James Madison seemed so uninterested in the details of the judiciary that his notes from the Constitutional Convention pared down the relevant delegate debates and votes.[1]

The framers' articulation of the first three constitutional articles does not therefore signal a fully developed theory of separation of powers. In fact, the distinctiveness of judicial and legislative functions remained fuzzy during the early national years. In some states, legislatures performed functions, such as reviewing court decisions, now considered judicial. For instance, the Supreme Court case *Calder v. Bull* arose when the Connecticut state legislature overturned a state probate court decision. As Justice James Iredell observed, the legislature had been regularly exercising a "superintending power" over the state courts. Meanwhile, judges during this era sometimes overtly voiced their partisan political views from the bench, especially during grand jury charges.[2]

Overlapping legislative and judicial functions created potential conflicts between legislatures and courts. In the late 1790s and early 1800s, political rancor between the proto-parties of the Federalists and the Republicans (discussed in Chapter 2) brought these potential conflicts to the forefront. The courts developed the power of judicial review partly in response. By designating certain political issues as law, the courts solidified and strengthened judicial power over the designated (legal) issues. Simultaneously, the courts ostensibly limited that same judicial power by avoiding explicit partisan pronouncements, deemed appropriate for legislators. Chief Justice John Marshall played a key role in this development of judicial review, emphasizing formal law in opposition to politics, particularly with his opinion in *Marbury v. Madison.*[3]

Throughout his *Marbury* opinion, Marshall distinguished between law and politics. While the legislative and executive functions include the exercise of political discretion—for example, when the president nominates and Congress confirms a Supreme Court justice—the judicial function is to interpret and enforce the law. For instance, Marshall wrote: "The province of the court is, solely, to decide on the rights of individuals, not to enquire how the executive, or executive officers, perform duties in which they have a discretion. Questions, in their nature political . . . can never be made in this court." Likewise, he wrote that "[i]t is emphatically the province and duty of the judicial department to say what the law is." Marshall used this separation between the judicial function, on the one hand, and the legislative and executive functions, on the other—the distinction, that is, between law and politics—to justify the Supreme Court's power of judicial review, the power to rule on the constitutionality of legislative and executive actions. From Marshall's standpoint, the Court could enforce its interpretation of the law, including the law of the Constitution, against the legislative and executive branches.[4]

Marshall's reasoning had enormous ramifications for the allocation of power within American society. "When an issue is designated as law," Jennifer Nedelsky explains, "it is insulated not only from the clashes of politics, but from the attention of public debate." Going forward, the issue will be discussed in the technical terms of legal rules and rights—think of not only constitutional but also contract and property rights—while the political values and assumptions underlying the specific rights are often obscured. The political implications of the distinction between law and politics remain no less true and important today than they were in 1800.[5] For example, when the Supreme Court holds that corporations have a free-speech right to spend unlimited amounts of money on political campaigns, then Congress is precluded from restricting corporate campaigning. The political issue of campaign-spending restrictions is now a legal (constitutional) issue supposedly closed to further political debate and legislative control.[6]

The next key period in the development of the law-politics dichotomy and legal formalism was after the Civil War. During this time of industrialization, professions in general "came of age."[7] In particular, professionalization in law advanced rapidly. An elite corps of lawyers emerged to serve the burgeoning industries and large corporations, and these elite practitioners spurred the creation of state and local bar associations, as well as the national American Bar Association in 1878. While these organizations purportedly aimed to impose stricter bar admission standards and to reduce unprofessional behavior, they also enabled accredited members of the profession to gain social status and to monopolize a segment of the economic marketplace.[8]

Like other professions emerging during the postbellum decades, law benefited by forging ties with the new universities that themselves were developing in that era. Unlike antebellum colleges, these universities emphasized service and research. The universities and their faculty were generally expected to serve "in a utilitarian fashion" the rapidly evolving industrial society. Yet service often intertwined with research, "the pursuit of truth . . . for its own sake." And when doing research, many faculty cloaked themselves with the authoritativeness of science by claiming to discover objective truths through the use of formalist methods, focusing on axiomatic principles and logically ordered and coherent systems.[9]

Law legitimated itself as a profession by joining these new universities. The president of Harvard, Charles Eliot, personally selected Christopher Columbus Langdell for the law school faculty in 1869. One year later, Langdell became dean of the law school and began to implement Eliot's vision of a scientific university discipline.[10] "[I]f law be not a science," Langdell said, "a university will best consult its own dignity in declining to teach it. If it be not a science, it is a species of handicraft, and may best be learned by serving an apprenticeship to one who practices it."[11] The Langdellian conception of the science of law corresponded closely with the contemporary general view of science dominant within the universities. Langdellian legal scientists, in their research, sought to discover objective legal truths through the use of formalist methods. They focused on fundamental or axiomatic principles and a rationally organized system of law. Thus, to teach the science of law, as he understood it, Langdell introduced the case method: Instead of presenting legal principles and rules through lectures, as typified antebellum legal teaching, the case method required the professor to cover a series of judicial cases—or more specifically, a series of appellate opinions. By using a form of Socratic questioning, the professor was to lead the students through an analysis of the cases, helping them recognize the legal principles supposedly immanent or embodied in the cases. To Langdell, the case method was the best approach to teaching because the students learned how to handle the cases themselves, the "original sources" for legal science. The law professor was qualified to teach the students since, as a legal scientist, he (all the early professors were men) was experienced, not in the practice of law but, rather, in the learning of law—in the discovery of the principles from the cases.[12]

Because of the case method, an initial scholarly task for Langdellian law professors—a goal for their research—was to write the casebooks needed for teaching law as a science. These casebooks consisted of carefully selected and arranged cases, including many older English cases, that could be used to exemplify for the students the principles of law. In the preface to his first casebook on contracts, Langdell summarized his conception of legal science:

Law, considered as a science, consists of certain principles or doc-trines. . . . Each of these doctrines has arrived at its present state by slow degrees; in other words, it is a growth, extending in many cases through centuries. This growth is to be traced in the main through a series of cases. . . . But the cases which are useful and necessary for this purpose [of studying the law] at the present day bear an exceed-ingly small proportion to all that have been reported. The vast major-ity are useless, and worse than useless, for any purpose of systematic study. Moreover, the number of fundamental legal doctrines is much less than is commonly supposed; the many different guises in which the same doctrine is constantly making its appearance, and the great extent to which legal treatises are a repetition of each other, being the cause of much misapprehension. If these doctrines could be so classi-fied and arranged that each should be found in its proper place, and nowhere else, they would cease to be formidable from their number.[13]

This passage from Langdell's preface not only reveals why he was devoted to the case method of teaching—because the common law cases were "the ultimate sources of all legal knowledge." It also suggests the methodology for Langdellian scholarship, beyond the writing of casebooks. Langdellians would begin either by stating, in the abstract, a small number of axiomatic principles or by analyzing a series of cases to discover, through inductive reasoning, the necessary axiomatic principles. Those principles then could govern all possible disputes within the relevant field of law. More specific legal rules and the cor-rect resolutions of legal issues could be deduced from the principles through abstract logical reasoning. Ultimately, then, the common law could be logi-cally arranged into a formal and conceptually ordered system.[14]

What was the point of this research methodology? Most often, the Lang-dellian scholar aimed to discover and articulate high-level principles, to de-duce more specific legal rules, and to criticize those judicial decisions that had failed to follow this abstract doctrine. The very first article published in *Harvard Law Review*, in 1887, archetypically illustrates this scholarly ap-proach. Written by James Barr Ames, Langdell's protégé, the article, after a brief introduction, stated an abstract principle of property law: "A court of equity will not deprive a defendant of any right of property, whether legal or equitable, for which he has given value without notice of the plaintiff's equity, nor of any other common-law right acquired as an incident of his purchase." The remainder of the article largely elaborated, through deductive logic, the application of this principle in specific factual circumstances. Along the way,

Ames criticized the leading case on this issue, as well as other cases, which he, at one point, denounced as "hopelessly irreconcilable."[15]

Not all Langdellian scholarship conformed to this archetype, but most followed it to a large degree. For example, some articles focused on the historical development of an abstract principle in the case law, with the purpose of clarifying the precise nature of the principle.[16] Other articles were devoted more to the abstract rational classification and systematization of principles and rules, again for the purpose of clarification and precision.[17] Regardless of the exact focus of the scholarship, the premises of Langdellian legal science were clear: By carefully parsing cases, discovering axiomatic principles, and applying those principles with rigorous deductive logic, the scholar could discern specific legal rules, as well as the single correct result in any judicial dispute, whether hypothetical or real.

In terms of professionalization, for law professors as well as for lawyers and judges, the conception of law propagated by Langdellian legal science was exquisitely expedient. The Langdellians presented the common law as an arcane yet perfectly rational system of principles and rules. The implication was that only lawyers and judges trained at university-affiliated law schools could truly understand the law. "Brandishing their view of the 'scientific' nature of law as a justification for their power," writes the historian Gerard W. Gawalt, "lawyers became the new high priests of an increasingly legalistic, industrial society." And only Langdellian legal scholars, the professors at the university-affiliated law schools, were competent to train future lawyers and judges and to conduct the scientific research necessary for discovering the law. From this perspective, in the increasingly industrialized and complicated society of late nineteenth- and early twentieth-century America, university law professors, lawyers, and judges fulfilled necessary functions—and they were the only ones capable of performing those functions.[18]

One additional component of the Langdellian conception of law contributed heavily to the professionalization of law—namely, Langdellians viewed the legal system as autonomous from other aspects of society, so the science of law was necessarily purified of nonlegal considerations. Lawyers, judges, and legal scholars were supposedly never to consider the social consequences of a legal principle, legal rule, or judicial decision. Policy considerations, that is, were deemed outside the ambit of the law: Law and politics were dichotomous. To apply the law, one needed to discover the (legal) principles and apply them in a rigorous logical fashion. Because of the autonomy of the legal system, the Langdellians reasoned, the study of law required a highly specialized university department or discipline that was separate and independent from other disciplines, such as history, government, and so forth. And, of course, such a specialized university department of law required professional experts—lawyers—to constitute its faculty. When Ames succeeded Langdell as the dean at Harvard Law School, Ames unequivocally linked the Langdellian conception of law and the need to have lawyers as professors: "We are unanimously opposed to the teaching of anything but *pure law* in our department. . . . We think that no one but a lawyer, teaching law, should be a member of a Law Faculty."[19]

Langdell himself underscored the importance of this notion of pure law in a typical example of normative Langdellian scholarship. In one passage of his *Summary of the Law of Contracts*, Langdell explained why the mailbox rule—that a posted acceptance of an offer for a bilateral contract (the exchange of a promise for a promise) is effective on dispatch—is incorrect. According to Langdell, an acceptance of an offer for a bilateral contract contains an implicit counteroffer. By analytical definition, any counteroffer must be communicated, because "communication to the offeree is of the essence of every offer." Therefore, as a matter of deductive logic, an acceptance (as a counteroffer) that is mailed through the post cannot become effective until it is communicated or, in other words, received. Langdell recognized, however, that critics would argue his conclusion—that acceptance was effective on receipt rather than dispatch—might lead to unjust results. His response exemplified the focus on pure law. "The true answer to this argument," Langdell wrote, "is that it is irrelevant."[20]

This desire for a purified discipline, it is worth noting, was not (and is not) peculiar to law. Each academic department needs to legitimate its existence, and specialization in a unique discipline is a propitious means for doing so. If law schools were to teach and research subject matter already covered adequately in, for instance, economics, anthropology, or history departments, then why would we need law schools? The Langdellians were merely following suit, so to speak: They sought to show that the law school, as much as any other department, belonged in the new universities. Moreover, this academic differentiation and specialization needs to be reproduced with each new generation of professors or the discipline and department will be threatened. Indeed, academic disciplines often tend to become increasingly isolated, specialized, and parochial.[21]

The third key period in the development of the law-politics dichotomy and legal formalism was the 1930s and 1940s, when (as discussed in Chapter 3) the practices and theory of American democratic government dramatically transformed, going from republican to pluralist democracy. Under republican democracy, courts had typically reviewed government actions to confirm that they promoted the common good rather than partial or private interests. Pluralist democracy, though, no longer revolved around the common good, so what then became of the courts? What useful function could courts play in the new pluralist democratic regime? To be sure, with the acceptance of pluralist democracy and the New Deal, the Supreme Court regularly deferred to economic and social welfare laws, whether at the national or state level, but could the Court continue to play an active role in the American constitutional system?

The Court soon began to develop a role for itself, exercising judicial review in the new pluralist democracy, even while it continued to show restraint when reviewing New Deal and similar legislation. In 1938, *United States v. Carolene Products Company* upheld a federal statute, the Filled Milk Act, which restricted the interstate shipment of certain types of milk. Justice Harlan F. Stone wrote the majority opinion, deferring to the congressional regulation of the economy, but he added a footnote (number 4), initially drafted by one of his clerks, reasoning that such deference might sometimes be inappropriate. Footnote 4 suggested that a "presumption of constitutionality" would be improper if the democratic process itself had been illegitimate. Unlike the republican democratic era, however, democratic legitimacy no longer arose from the legislative pursuit of a particular substantive goal, the common good. Instead, under pluralist democracy, legitimacy depended on an open and fair legislative process allowing interest-group competition and compromise. If the pluralist democratic process were somehow defective or malfunctioning—if the government had restricted, in Stone's words, "those political processes which can ordinarily be expected to bring about repeal of undesirable legislation"—then the Court could and should question the legislative outcome, subjecting the law "to more exacting judicial scrutiny." For example, if the government prevented certain societal groups from voting or organizing politically, then the resulting legislation would not manifest a truly pluralist democratic process. More specifically, if the government intentionally discriminated against a "discrete and insular" minority, such as black Americans, then the democratic process was defective, and judicial deference would be inappropriate. Under pluralist democracy, all societal groups were supposed to be allowed to press their interests and values in a fair competition with other groups. If the government interfered, then "the operation of those political processes ordinarily to be relied upon" would be undermined.[22]

Whereas the post-1937 justices widely agreed that the Court should protect and nurture pluralist democratic processes, they often disagreed about how to achieve that judicial goal. One set of justices, including Stone, William O. Douglas, and Hugo Black, wanted the Court to vigilantly guard and defend pluralist democracy. From their perspective, pluralist democratic processes could deteriorate too readily if unprotected by the judiciary—with the end result being tyranny of some or all of the people. The other set of justices, led by Felix Frankfurter and Robert Jackson, believed pluralist democracy must be allowed to operate and correct its own problems. The Court should generally avoid interfering with democratic processes. *Colegrove v. Green*, decided in 1946, illustrates the degree to which the justices brooded about the Court's role in relation to democracy—that is, the relation between law and politics. *Colegrove* held that the drawing of congressional district lines in Illinois presented a nonjusticiable political question; it would be overruled in 1962 in *Baker v. Carr*, which led the Court to establish the crucial pluralist democratic doctrine of one person, one vote.[23] In *Colegrove*, Frankfurter wrote a plurality opinion, while Black wrote a dissent. They both agreed that a pluralist democratic system should promote widespread participation. But on the one side, Frankfurter reasoned that pluralist democracy was inherently partisan—the drawing of district lines reflected "party contests and party interests"—so the Court should not try to correct inequitable district lines. Instead, when a state legislature draws unfair district lines, the proper remedy lies in the partisan democratic process itself, "to secure State legislatures that will apportion properly, or to invoke the ample powers of Congress." On the other side, Black emphasized that the Illinois district lines, as then drawn, produced grossly disparate representation. Some districts had fewer than 200,000 people, while one district had more than 900,000, yet each district, regardless of population, could elect one representative. A vote in a high-population district was worth less than a vote in a low-population district. Representation was disproportionate because each vote was not accorded "equal weight." From Black's perspective, the Court could not trust the pluralist democratic process to self-correct exactly because the disproportionate representation prevented certain groups from fully participating, from having adequate opportunity to influence future legislative actions.[24]

The role of the Court in relation to other government institutions, such as Congress, became a central concern of a jurisprudential movement, "legal process," that emerged after World War II.[25] Legal process scholars, such as Henry M. Hart, Herbert Wechsler, and Albert Sacks, believed that the prewar legal realist attacks on formalism—central to both *Lochner*-era judicial reasoning and Langdellian legal science—had gone too far and undermined the rule of law (think of the radical realists, such as Thurman Arnold, discussed in Chapter 3). To a great degree, the legal process scholars sought to reinvigorate the study of pure law. The Langdellians had focused on the purity of the substantive law—the axiomatic principles and the logically deduced rules. Legal process, as the name suggests, instead sought purity through legal processes. Hart and Sacks sounded the clarion call of legal process: "[Government] decisions which are the duly arrived at result of duly established procedures . . . ought to be accepted as binding upon the whole society unless and until they are duly changed." As distinct institutions, courts and legislatures operated pursuant to processes unique to their respective goals and functions. While legislatures channeled the negotiating and compromising of political interest groups, courts decided cases by following the process of "reasoned elaboration," which required judges to articulate reasons for a decision, to explain those reasons in a detailed and coherent manner, and to relate the decision to a relevant rule of law applied in a manner logically consistent with precedent. In constitutional cases, reasoned elaboration translated into a requirement that judges decide pursuant to "neutral principles," which supposedly precluded judges (or justices) from using rules or principles that bore any political valence. If Supreme Court justices allowed their political preferences to influence a constitutional decision, that decision would be illegitimate.[26]

During the postwar era, constitutional scholars became obsessed with the so-called countermajoritarian difficulty. Under pluralist democracy, legislative decisions were legitimate because they emerged through the appropriate (democratic) processes. From this perspective, a properly enacted statute represented the majoritarian will of the people—or, at least, the will of the people's democratically elected representatives. Why, then, should Supreme Court justices (or other federal judges) ever articulate neutral principles and invalidate the substantive judgments of elected legislators? After all, in a pluralist democratic system, grounded on ethical relativism, the justices could not claim knowledge of or access to absolute truths or values. Moreover, the justices could not claim to represent the majoritarian will—certainly not to the extent that elected legislators did so. The justices were entrenched in their positions because of the article III constitutional protections of the federal judiciary: All federal judges enjoyed lifetime appointments, and their salaries could not be diminished. They were politically insulated and did not need to worry about running for reelection. Thus, whenever the Court invalidated legislation, especially congressional legislation, the justices seemingly contravened the majoritarian will as expressed by the people's elected representatives.[27]

Ironically, the post-1937 justices contributed fuel to this fear of the countermajoritarian difficulty, despite their propensity to defer to legislative regulations of the economy. Starting in the early 1940s, the justices began writing an increasing number of dissents and concurrences. In fact, the percentage of unanimous opinions plunged during the 1946–47 term to a then record low of 36 percent. The explanation for this development was unclear, but the political scientist C. Herman Pritchett suggested one possibility: The justices were using their opinions to assert their respective political interests and values. Pritchett, that is, viewed the Court through the prism of pluralist democratic interest group struggles. Under pluralist democracy, politics equaled partisanship; the pursuit of self-interest had become legitimate and normal. Consequently, a judge (or justice) who appeared to be political was necessarily partisan—there was no other type of politics. And even if the justices were not crassly pursuing their own political preferences, they seemed, at best, merely to referee among contesting interest groups. Indeed, led by Pritchett, postwar political scientists largely accepted the radical realist critique of the rule of law and argued that the Supreme Court was "a political institution performing a political function."[28] If true, if the Court functioned to adjudicate among competing interests and values—if the Court made law to gratify particular societal groups and disappoint others—then interest groups might be expected to begin pressing their claims to the Court. It was alarming, then, that the number of friend of the court (amicus curiae) briefs began to increase dramatically (though a Supreme Court rule change contributed to this increase). More than 10 percent of the cases had at least one amicus in 1953. That year, Fowler V. Harper and Edwin D. Etherington wrote that "[m]ore and more the Court was being treated as if it were a political-legislative body, amenable and responsive to mass pressures from any source." The number of amici continued to grow so that, by 1993, more than 90 percent of the cases had at least one.[29]

In light of the post–World War II fears of the countermajoritarian difficulty, when might the Court appropriately pronounce neutral principles and substitute its substantive judgment for that of Congress? Never. Or so answered John Hart Ely, a legal process scholar who eventually developed Justice Stone's footnote 4 approach into a full-fledged theory of judicial review: representation reinforcement. The Court, Ely argued, should generally presume the constitutionality of legislative decisions. Regardless of the outcome of the legislative process, the Court should not disapprove legislation as contravening some substantive criterion, such as a neutral principle or the common good, because no such criterion existed (or, at least, the justices could not reliably identify such a criterion). Legislative goals supposedly manifested no more than the interests and values of the democratic winners. As the Court explained in 1955, "[t]he day is gone when this Court [strikes down] laws, regulatory of business and industrial conditions, because they may be unwise, improvident, or out of harmony with a particular school of thought." Yet, Ely reasoned, the Court could review the *processes* that had led the legislature to take aim at one substantive goal rather than another. If those processes were fair and open, then the Court must defer to the legislative choice. But if the processes appeared skewed, then the Court should scrutinize the legislation more closely. Judicial invalidation of legislation that had arisen from a defective or malfunctioning democratic process would not be countermajoritarian. It would be the very opposite: It would foster fair and open pluralist democracy. From this perspective, the Court's exercise of judicial review would be purely process-based. In a relativistic (or pluralist) world, the Court should never pronounce and apply neutral principles or any other substantive principles or values. Properly understood, then, representation reinforcement theory dissolved the countermajoritarian difficulty because it promoted and bolstered rather than undermined democracy.[30]

Ultimately, the Court's judicial role under pluralist democracy appeared to invigorate the dichotomy between law and politics. Citizens and legislatures engaged in politics and chose societal goals and values. But the judiciary's only role was to "police" the democratic process, at least according to representation reinforcement theory.[31] Courts were to ensure that all individuals and groups were able to assert their respective political interests and values and fully participate in the democratic arena. Therefore, courts could articulate and uphold legal rights such as voting and free expression that constituted the procedural framework for the political battles and compromises that arose among competing interest groups and individuals, but courts were not to attempt to pronounce and enforce more substantive rights, especially rights not explicit in the constitutional text. According to this version of pluralist democratic theory, in other words, the judicial function is purely legal. Judges protect the legal framework for political debate and legislative lawmaking but do not themselves enunciate political interests, values, and goals.[32]

The historical development of the law-politics dichotomy underscores that political and professional forces engendered and sustain the dichotomy. The sharp separation of law and politics has a political and professional payoff. Lawyers, judges, and law professors trace, justify, and protect a realm of power—legal-judicial power—by distinguishing that realm from politics. Supposedly, within the legal-judicial realm, only lawyers and judges are trained and equipped with sufficient knowledge to understand and resolve *legal* issues and disputes. In other words, the lay public might be empowered to debate political issues, vote, and otherwise participate in democracy, but they are ill equipped to understand, discuss, and resolve legal issues.

The paradox, of course, is that lawyers, judges, and law professors justify and increase their political power by denying their political power. This is especially true for judges and courts—including the Supreme Court. The justices are empowered to decide cases in accord with their political views partly because they maintain that they are rigidly following the law. Given this, the justices (as well as other legal professionals) seemingly have strong incentives to present their positions as being apolitical or neutral—as being purely legal, based on formal law bereft of external considerations.

In light of the development and maintenance of the law-politics dichotomy, many commentators unsurprisingly view the possibility of court packing as anathema. From their perspective, court packing would destroy the foundation for the rule of law. Court packing would infect the Supreme Court with politics. The next chapter, however, demonstrates the mythical nature of the beast. Despite widespread belief in a law-politics dichotomy, it does not exist. And if the law-politics dichotomy does not exist, then the primary reason for opposing court packing dissolves: Court packing cannot undermine the legitimacy of the Court as a pristine legal-judicial institution free of politics because a politics-free Court has never existed.

5

THE MYTH OF THE
LAW-POLITICS DICHOTOMY

(Or, Understanding the Law-Politics Dynamic)

Through American history, legal professionals have developed and burnished the law-politics dichotomy and the concomitant concept of formal law. Lawyers, judges, and law professors trace, justify, and protect a realm of power—legal-judicial power—by distinguishing that realm from politics. And within that legal-judicial realm of power, Supreme Court justices stand the tallest. As judges on the highest and most esteemed court in the nation, the justices are ostensibly most qualified to resolve legal issues and decide cases pursuant to the neutral application of the rule of law.

Lawyers, judges, and law professors are not the only professionals driven to accentuate their own methods and knowledge. The same forces drive other professionals, including academicians—in particular, political scientists. Starting in the early to mid-twentieth century, political scientists sought to study political actions through the rigorous application of social science techniques. In the 1940s, they turned this method of study on Supreme Court decision making. To analyze the Court's decisions scientifically, political scientists believed they needed to reduce the decisions to concrete and empirically observable events. Consequently, they followed a behavioral approach, focusing on discrete judicial actions or, in other words, at the Supreme Court level, on how the justices vote vis-à-vis their political orientations. C. Herman Pritchett was an early leader of this movement, arguing that Supreme Court justices acted pursuant to their "individual predilections": The justices cast their votes to decide cases in accord with their political values. Like other political actors, the justices participated "in the power struggles of American politics," as understood from the pluralist democratic perspective.[1]

For much of the twentieth century, then, law professors and political scientists analyzed Supreme Court decision making, but they traveled different paths, usually ignoring their fellow travelers on the other path. On both paths, law professors and political scientists typically refused to mix law and politics. Law professors insisted that legal texts and doctrines controlled Supreme Court decision making, while political scientists maintained that political preferences dictated the justices' votes. On the law side, many scholars believed that political considerations corrupted the judicial process. On the political science side, many believed that judicial opinions disguised political preferences with no more than fancy window dressing.[2]

In recent years, an increasing number of scholars on both sides of the disciplinary divide have recognized a connection between law and politics, yet the traditional dichotomy persists. In the legal academy, for example, the persistent harping about activist judges arises from the assumption that law and politics are distinct.[3] Supposedly, activist judges (and justices) illegitimately pursue their political agendas rather than follow the rule of law. Supreme Court justices generally agree that law and politics must remain separate. "To expect judges to take account of political consequences," wrote Justice Antonin Scalia in 2004, "is to ask judges to do precisely what they should not do." Meanwhile, the political scientist Martin Shapiro declared: "Courts and judges always lie. Lying is the nature of the judicial activity." To prove the point, Jeffrey A. Segal and Harold J. Spaeth sought to test the "mythology of judging." They devised a "legal model," which hypothesized that "the decisions of the Court are based on the facts of the case in light of the plain meaning of statutes and the Constitution, the intent of the framers, precedent, and a balancing of societal interests." The legal model, as constructed by Segal and Spaeth, demanded that Supreme Court decisions be "objective, impartial, and dispassionate."[4] Segal and Spaeth then ran quantitative studies that revealed the failings of the legal model. The evidence demonstrated "that traditional legal factors, such as precedent, text, and intent, had virtually no impact" on Supreme Court decision making. Segal and Spaeth were unsurprised; they had maintained all along that political ideologies determine the justices' votes.[5]

Many scholars are subtler, avoiding extreme positions of pure law or pure politics, yet even these scholars can stumble into the abyss of the law-politics dichotomy. The renowned First Amendment legal scholar Robert Post published a sophisticated "sociological account of the relationship between law and politics that suggests how judicial statesmanship [read: politics] can further the essential social functions of both law and politics." Ju-dicial statesmanship, according to Post, should be combined with judicial craftsmanship "because law and politics should be mutually interdependent and sustaining." Yet Post implicitly suggested that law and politics belong ultimately to separate realms. True, he sought to mix them beneficially, but he nonetheless explained that "judicial craft may *at times* appropriately be supplemented by judicial statesmanship." If political considerations (judicial statesmanship) may "at times" supplement law (judicial craft), then appar-ently at other times law may be pristine, untouched by politics.[6]

This chapter proposes a path around the law-politics dichotomy. Schol-ars, such as Post, conceive of law and politics as distinct, even though they attempt to mix them together. In the end, for these scholars, law and politics inevitably settle apart, like oil and water. A handful of legal and political science scholars, however, have attempted to combine law and politics in a more permanent blend. Think of an emulsion, in which two liquids are joined together to form a stable substance, such as mayonnaise. But even these scholars have rarely attempted to explain the mechanism by which law and politics join. How, exactly, do law and politics emulsify? The answer lies in an understanding of legal interpretation. Most important, politics lies at the heart of the legal interpretive process. Politics is inescapably an integral part of legal interpretation and, therefore, an integral part of Supreme Court decision making. To be clear, in this chapter I describe Supreme Court deci-sion making as it actually occurs rather than prescribing how it ought to be. The description, however, necessarily limits the feasibility of normative pre-scriptions. If politics is integral to legal interpretation, then it would be futile to recommend the justices follow an interpretive method that ostensibly ban-ishes politics by, for example, divining an original constitutional meaning.[7]

While this chapter draws heavily on legal and political science schol-arship, the question of Supreme Court decision making is not merely an academic one. Far from it. Public commentators and politicians typically echo and advocate for the pure-law view of Supreme Court decision mak-ing: The justices should decide according to the rule of law and should not allow politics to influence their votes or decisions. For example, when he was a senator, Jeff Sessions said: "What our legal system demands, is a fair and unbiased umpire, one who calls the game according to the existing rules." In a *New York Times* op-ed, Ilya Shapiro wrote: "A judge's job is to apply the law to a given set of facts as best he or she can and let the political chips fall where they may." Commentators often express alarm when President Donald Trump, no great student of judicial decision making, accuses a judge of being political. When federal District Judge James L. Robart blocked Trump's initial executive order banning immigrants and travelers from seven predominantly Muslim countries, Trump publicly labeled Robart a "so-called judge" and denounced the ruling as "ridiculous."[8] With an appeal pending at the Ninth Circuit Court of Appeals, Trump castigated the "courts [for being] so political." Not only did many commentators fear that Trump's statements threatened the rule of law, but Neil Gorsuch, at the time a Trump Supreme Court nominee, called Trump's attacks "demoralizing" and "disheartening."[9]

Recent Senate confirmation hearings for Supreme Court nominees typically involve a bizarre intermingling of political hardball, on the one hand, and homages to the law-politics dichotomy, on the other. Justice Gorsuch epitomized this strange juxtaposition when he toured the State of Kentucky with Senate Majority Leader Mitch McConnell, the individual most responsible for refusing to give President Barack Obama's nominee, Merrick Garland, a Senate hearing (thus leaving the Court seat open for a subsequent appointee—namely, Gorsuch). While some critics termed the trip a political "victory lap" for the Republicans, Gorsuch stated during his speeches: "I don't think there are red judges, and I don't think there are blue judges. All judges wear black." Gorsuch apparently was not speaking ironically. In fact, nowadays, every Supreme Court nominee must avow fealty to the rule of law. John Roberts famously stated: "Judges and justices are servants of the law, not the other way around. Judges are like umpires. Umpires don't make the rules; they apply them. . . . [M]y job is to call balls and strikes and not to pitch or bat."[10] During his Senate hearings, Brett Kavanaugh, previously vetted by the conservative Federalist Society, proclaimed that politics would not influence his judicial positions. He reiterated this claim in a renowned post-hearings *Wall Street Journal* editorial. On the progressive side, Elena Kagan and Sonia Sotomayor also emphasized during their confirmation hearings that they would follow the rule of law, regardless of their political inclinations.[11]

This chapter begins by drawing on legal and political science scholarship to elaborate the traditional separation of law and politics. It next describes the oil-and-water approach to Supreme Court decision making. After that, the chapter analyzes the writings of scholars who combine law and politics more permanently, in an emulsion. It culminates with a fuller explanation of the nature of legal interpretation and Supreme Court decision making. This analysis pokes a gaping hole in the major criticism of court packing: If law and politics always intertwine in Supreme Court adjudication—in a law-politics dynamic—then court packing cannot destroy the Court's purity as a legal-judicial institution, bereft of politics. In the end, court packing cannot destroy something that never existed in the first place.

At the outset, it might help to elaborate certain terms as they relate to the distinction between law and politics. Most important, the ostensible law-politics dichotomy is more slippery than is often assumed. Some political scientists who study adjudication, particularly Supreme Court decision making, adopt a narrow definition of politics for purposes of their quantitative studies. They might maintain that a justice votes in accord with politics if he or she votes pursuant to his or her policy preferences or political attitudes. The political scientist might then derive the justice's preferences, attitudes, or ideology from newspaper characterizations (during the nomination and confirmation process) or the political party of the appointing president.[12] Even so, the key distinction in many analyses of adjudication is between proper and improper considerations. That is, does the judge (or justice) consider proper or improper factors when deciding a case? The identification of proper and improper factors is typically derived from an internal rather than external viewpoint. Arguably, within the practice of law and adjudication, judges are supposed to decide cases pursuant to legal rules, standards, or other doctrines derived from case precedents, statutes, and other legal texts. A decision grounded in legal doctrines and texts is proper, but a decision based on alternative factors is improper. What might those alternative factors be? Frequently, they are politics, narrowly defined, but they can be anything other than traditional legal doctrines and texts. For instance, a decision arising from the religious and cultural backgrounds of a judge would be improper. Such a decision is improper precisely because it is based on factors that are supposedly external to the legal-judicial process. Proper and improper considerations, in other words, can also be called, respectively, internal (inside or proper) or external (outside or improper). Indeed, from the internal standpoint, any external consideration can be called political, loosely defined. If a Protestant judge consistently holds against Muslim free-exercise complainants, that outlook can be deemed political, even if it is unrelated to the Republican or Democratic party. In this broad sense, law and politics are opposed, standing on their own sides of a crucial boundary. Meanwhile, scholarly analyses of judicial decision making can also be distinguished as internal or external. An internal analysis revolves around the texts and doctrines that are appropriate or proper considerations from the inside of legal and judicial practices. An external analysis focuses on factors that are deemed improper from the inside of legal and judicial practices. With regard to examinations of Supreme Court adjudication, a political scientist's study focusing on politics is an external analysis, while a law professor's study focusing on legal doctrines and texts is an internal analysis.[13]

THE PURISTS

Numerous scholars are purists. They advocate for a monocausal approach: Judicial decision making is either all law or all politics. Purist scholars in the legal academy typically maintain that the Court must decide cases pursuant to law by drawing on traditional legal materials such as case precedents, statutes, and constitutional text. Purist scholars in political science typically maintain that politics alone determines Supreme Court votes.[14]

On the law side, the pristine legal approach is historically rooted in the work of Christopher Columbus Langdell and his disciples, discussed in Chapter 4. Teaching at university-based law schools during the late nineteenth and early twentieth centuries, the Langdellians treated law as a closed system of rules and axiomatic principles that dictated judicial outcomes. The legal system was supposedly autonomous from societal influences. From the Langdellian perspective, judges were not to contemplate political interests or even conceptions of justice. Judges were to do one thing: logically apply the rules and principles in a mechanical fashion.[15]

To be sure, nobody today would claim to be Langdellian, yet the Langdellian goal of a pure or formal law continues to shape the practices of law professors. The still influential legal process scholars of the late twentieth century, also discussed in Chapter 4, emphasized the distinct processes of different government institutions. Courts and legislatures operate pursuant to processes unique to their respective goals and functions. Legislators engage in politics, negotiating and compromising, but courts need to neutrally apply the rule of law.[16] Today, an all-law approach is most clearly displayed by scholars and justices who ostensibly follow originalism in constitutional interpretation. Most originalists demand that judges discern the (supposedly) objective meaning of the constitutional text as it was understood at the time of its adoption. Constitutional meaning, from this perspective, is static, fixed at the time of its ratification, regardless of changing political and societal contexts:[17] "Words have original meanings that are fixed no matter what current majorities may say to the contrary." Theoretically, then, originalism has unequivocal implications for judging. As explained by Justice Neil Gorsuch, "[T]he Constitution's meaning was fixed at its ratification and the judge's job is to discern and apply that meaning to the people's cases and controversies." Furthermore, according to Scalia, originalism is the only interpretive method consistent with the rule of law rather than politics. The originalist method, Scalia wrote, is "the only one that can justify courts in denying force and effect to the unconstitutional enactments of duly elected legislatures. . . . To hold a governmental Act to be unconstitutional is not to announce that *we* forbid it, but that the *Constitution* forbids it." Justice Clarence Thomas, perhaps more than any other justice, comes closest to following original-ism consistently and thoroughly (to the extent that doing so is possible). For instance, in multiple Establishment Clause cases, Thomas has written concurrences suggesting that state and local governments can establish or support religious institutions. Based on his originalist understanding of the First Amendment, the Establishment Clause precludes the national govern-ment from creating a national church, but the clause does not similarly limit state and local governments.[18]

Multiple political scientists now provide quantitative research supporting some type of legal approach, despite Segal and Spaeth's rejection of the so-called legal model. Using law models different from Segal and Spaeth's, these other political scientists have concluded that legal texts and doctrines or "jur-isprudential regimes" influence judicial decisions. "The Supreme Court is not simply a small legislature," explain Mark J. Richards and Herbert M. Kritzer. "Law matters in Supreme Court decision making in ways that are specifically jurisprudential. [More precisely], jurisprudential regimes structure Supreme Court decision making by establishing which case factors are relevant for de-cision making and/or by setting the level of scrutiny the justices are to employ in assessing case factors." For instance, Richards and Kritzer's quantitative research shows that the application of a three-pronged doctrinal test from *Lemon v. Kurtzman* influences whether the justices decide that a government action violates the Establishment Clause. More broadly, other quantitative research demonstrates that attorneys' legal arguments sway the justices.[19]

Such quantitative support is important, but even if it were lacking, one should not dismiss the legal approach. To be sure, many social scientists focus on quantitative research and therefore seek to construct models amenable to quantitative testing. The studied phenomena must be reducible to numeric data. If a potential causal factor cannot adequately fit into a testable model, then these social scientists are apt to disregard that factor. The political scien-tist Tom S. Clark describes this approach to Supreme Court decision making: "A hallmark characteristic of this line of research is a concern with elements of judicial choice that are objectively observable, quantifiable, and lend them-selves to systematic analysis." Yet, as Clark underscores, not all political scien-tists are committed to this type of research. Many also engage in qualitative research, as is also true for many historians, as well as researchers in other social (or human) sciences. Like quantitative evidence, qualitative evidence is empirical, though unlike quantitative evidence, it cannot be reduced to numeric data. Qualitative research explores relationships, actions, and events that must be interpreted. It can include anecdotal evidence, but it also typically suggests commonalities (and differences) among distinct phenomena. Qualitative research is generally not falsifiable because testing conditions are not repeatable. A legal historian, for instance, cannot repeat the constitutional framing to test a hypothesis about its causes. Yet, qualitative research can still be empirically valid if the researcher provides an illuminating narrative of the phenomena that is persuasively grounded on the evidence.[20]

Qualitative evidence of the legal approach is boundless. Most lawyers, judges, and law professors would (and do) testify to the sincerity of their reliance on legal texts and doctrines. From their experiences, the invocation of legal materials is significant, not immaterial subterfuge. With specific regard to judicial decision making, Supreme Court justices (and other judges) are subject to professional norms that demand they identify and refer to relevant legal texts and doctrines when deciding a case. The justices not only discuss relevant precedents, statutes, and constitutional provisions in their judicial opinions—which admittedly might be for public consumption, to help legitimate their decisions—but also discuss such textual and doctrinal sources among themselves when behind closed doors, during post-oral argument conferences. Even more to the point, the justices sometimes bargain and negotiate among themselves about the contents of their majority opinions, as if the precise wording of a single paragraph or even a single sentence mattered. Furthermore, the justices claim that they never openly discuss or consider partisan politics in relation to pending cases.[21]

Whereas Segal and Spaeth's dismissal of the legal approach is unpersuasive, their argument that justices vote in accord with their personal policy preferences is powerful. Perhaps more so than any other political scientists, Segal and Spaeth represent the all-politics position. According to their so-called attitudinal model, "[T]he Supreme Court decides disputes in light of the facts of the case vis-à-vis the ideological attitudes and values of the justices." And a justice's personal policy preferences (or ideological attitudes) are formed exogenously to the legal system—that is, the justice's preferences do not form because of his or her institutional position within the federal judiciary. Segal and Spaeth gave this stark example: "Simply put, [William] Rehnquist votes the way he does because he is extremely conservative; [Thurgood] Marshall voted the way he did because he is extremely liberal." Most important, Segal and Spaeth support their conclusion—that Supreme Court decisions are "overwhelmingly explained by the attitudes and values of the justices"—with extensive quantitative evidence. For instance, in a study comparing the justices' ideologies with their votes in criminal cases, Segal and Spaeth concluded that "justices who are more liberal have substantially higher rates of support for accused criminals than do justices who are more conservative. Indeed, the fit of the model is extremely high." From Segal and Spaeth's perspective, the attitudinal model is far superior to the legal model as a method for predicting "judicial behavior" or, in other words, the justices' votes.[22]

While attitudinalists tend to stress the quantitative support for their approach, one should recognize that qualitative evidence also lends credence. An obvious example that demonstrates the power of politics in Supreme Court decision making is the five-to-four decision in *Bush v. Gore*, which resolved the 2000 presidential election. Numerous scholars, even those who believe that law ordinarily shapes the Court's decisions, argued that this case could not be explained in any way other than as a pure partisan power grab. The conservative majority claimed to apply equal protection reasoning, but it was novel and inconsistent with anything they did before or since. Based on this flimsy justification, the five conservative justices held for George W. Bush and effectively installed him as the next president (which allowed him to nominate conservative replacements for Chief Justice Rehnquist and Justice Sandra Day O'Connor). Michael Klarman underscored the Court's blatant partisanship by rhetorically asking: "Had all the other facts in the Florida election imbroglio remained the same, but the situation of the two presidential candidates been reversed, does anyone seriously believe that the conservative Justices would have reached the same result?"[23]

Despite such quantitative and qualitative support, the attitudinal model is not the only political science approach to emphasize politics in judicial decision making.[24] Rational choice theorists, such as Lee Epstein, maintain that the justices generally want to vote in accord with their personal policy preferences but that various institutional constraints might compel the justices to alter their behavior. As Epstein, Jack Knight, and Andrew D. Martin elaborate, in the rational choice or strategic model, "(1) judges make choices in order to achieve certain goals [usually policy preferences]; (2) judges act strategically in the sense that their choices depend on their expectations about the choices of other actors; and (3) these choices are structured by the institutional setting in which they are made." For example, while Justice Thomas believes the Establishment Clause does not apply to state and local governments, he might nonetheless vote with other conservatives who believe otherwise. By strategically modifying his behavior, Thomas enables the conservatives to form a majority and to interpret the Establishment Clause narrowly, permitting governments to propagate and bolster religion more than progressives would allow.[25]

Another approach emphasizing politics maintains that the justices vote in accord with the predominant political regime. Robert A. Dahl wrote the seminal article in this genre in 1957. Based on an empirical study of cases in which the Supreme Court had invalidated congressional statutes, Dahl observed that, despite popular assumptions, the Court did not protect minorities from majoritarian overreaching. As Dahl phrased it, "[I]t would appear to be somewhat naive to assume that the Supreme Court either would or could play the role of Galahad." To the contrary, the Court acted as an integral "part of the dominant national alliance." The Court therefore decided cases in harmony with the interests and values of that dominant political alliance or regime. "As an element in the political leadership of the dominant alliance," Dahl tersely stated, "the Court of course supports the major policies of the alliance." Terri Peretti has further explained this regime politics approach: "'Regimists' focus on the incentives and power of politicians to construct courts in particular ways that would benefit the ruling regime. By granting jurisdiction, encouraging certain types of litigation, and selecting specific justices with specific political and jurisprudential views, elected officials enlist the Court as a partner in their electoral and policy aims."[26] Occasionally, when one dominant political regime replaces another, the Court might be temporarily aligned with the former regime. During such times, conflict between the Court and, for instance, the Congress—if it is controlled by the new regime—might be intense. Yet before long, the Court is likely to be consolidated with the new regime, often because of new appointments. From the regime politics perspective, the justices rarely depart too far from the political mainstream.[27] An example is *Brown v. Board of Education*, which held unconstitutional de jure racial segregation in public schools. Regimists maintain that *Brown* did not show the Court boldly championing the rights of black Americans in the face of white majoritarian pressures. Instead, the Court in *Brown* followed the interests and values of a dominant national political coalition or regime that favored the eradication of Jim Crow. White southerners who supported legalized racial segregation had become national outliers; the Court forced them to acquiesce to more mainstream views, as understood from a national vantage.[28]

The regime politics approach, it should be recognized, can be understood as a specific type of rational choice theory. Regimists agree with rational choice theorists insofar as both groups maintain that institutional constraints prevent justices from arrantly voting pursuant to their personal policy preferences. The difference between regimists and other rational choice theorists is that regimists emphasize that the overriding institutional constraints on the justices arise from other political actors in the predominant regime, including members of the legislative and executive branches. The justices must behave (or vote) in ways that are likely to discourage retributive "attacks on their independence and overrides of their decisions." In fact, since rational choice theorists usually assume that justices would vote according to their personal policy preferences but for various institutional constraints, one might even view the regime politics approach as a stylized version of the attitudinal model.[29]

Nonetheless, many political scientists consider the regime politics approach and the attitudinal model to be opposed to each other in at least two ways. First, attitudinalists emphasize the justices' personal policy preferences but do not speak to the origins of those preferences, whereas regimists care deeply about such origins. Attitudinalists write as if policy preferences "arrive like orphans in the night at the Court's doorstep," while regimists analyze how preferences "are deliberately planted there by the dominant governing coalition." Second, the justices' personal policy preferences sometimes appear to diverge from the values of the predominant regime (e.g., when one dominant regime is replacing another). In such instances, attitudinalists insist that the justices follow their personal preferences, while regimists insist that the justices follow partisan (or regime) values. Basically, attitudinalists stress the freedom and independence of the justices: The "justices behave like any other political actor—only more so, since justices do not have electoral incentives to compromise their ideological preferences." Meanwhile, regimists stress that the justices are, in effect, constantly looking over their shoulders: The justices are constrained at least as much as other political actors, even if the justices need not worry about re-election, and thus the justices largely remain loyal to the predominant regime that brought them to office.[30]

A LITTLE BIT OF THIS, A LITTLE BIT OF THAT

Quantitative and qualitative evidence support *both* law *and* politics as being causal factors in Supreme Court decision making. Given that numerous law professors and political scientists are purists, subscribing to a monocausal approach, such evidence might be problematic: How can decision making be all law or all politics if evidence corroborates both approaches? An obvious solution to this problem is to posit that *both* law *and* politics influence the justices' votes. And indeed, while many law professors and political scientists remain purists, an increasing number of scholars in both disciplines now argue that some mix of law and politics is at play. But this solution engenders a further problem: How do law and politics combine or interrelate in the decision-making process? I discuss two possibilities: First, politics sometimes affects Supreme Court decision making, but politics and law nonetheless remain distinct; and second, politics and law are integrally entwined so that decision making is always partly political.

The most common method for mixing law and politics is to maintain that politics qua politics sometimes enters the judicial decision-making process even though law and politics remain independent and separate. Within the legal academy, the crux of this approach is the belief that traditional legal materials—texts and doctrines—control most cases, but occasionally, in the gaps or on the edges of the law, political (or policy) considerations become relevant. From this perspective, many disputes make easy cases: cases that are so obviously governed by uncontested rules that they are unlikely to reach even a trial court. For instance, a testator must have his or her will witnessed by two individuals; failure to do so results in an invalid will, not in a Supreme Court decision. Political considerations enter the judicial calculus only in those cases where a gap or area of doubt in the law exists, where "the law runs out."[31]

Advocates of this approach insist that law and politics exist in distinct realms. Law and politics can be stirred together, we might say, but they ultimately remain segregated, like oil and water.[32] Some legal process scholars, for example, maintained that a judge in appropriate situations should apply the law "in the way which best serves the principles and policies it expresses." Yet the judicial process of reasoned elaboration neatly and safely cabined such political concerns so that they would supposedly intrude into judicial deliberations only in certain narrowly defined circumstances. The law supposedly controlled most cases without politics playing any role. A Supreme Court tax decision illustrates this outlook. The eight-justice majority opinion recognized that its proposed interpretation of the relevant statutory provision would allow certain corporate shareholders to realize "a 'double windfall.'" Regardless, the Court deflected such political considerations as beyond its domain: "Because the Code's plain text permits the taxpayers here to receive these benefits, we need not address this policy concern."[33]

Even political scientists who are committed to the attitudinal model, such as Segal and Spaeth, acknowledge that law can feasibly govern cases, particularly in the lower courts. "[P]recedent certainly matters to lower court judges," write Segal, Spaeth, and Sara Benesh. "[N]o such judge worthy of the name is likely to uphold prohibitions on previability abortions, require the segregation of students on racial grounds, or allow public school officials to lead students in prayer service, regardless of the judge's [political] predilections." Of course, at the level of the Supreme Court, where hard cases are the norm, Segal and Spaeth insist that legal texts and doctrines control the justices' votes in only the rarest of instances, though they grudgingly admit that it sometimes appears to happen—obviously, however, not often enough to cause them to waver in their commitment to the attitudinal model.[34] Some rational choice theorists also assert that legal texts and doctrines are among the institutional constraints that can compel the justices to deviate from their personal policy preferences. Justices "are strategic actors who take into consideration the constraints they encounter as they attempt to introduce their policy preferences into the law," write a group of political science researchers, who then add that "these constraints often take the form of formal rules or informal norms that limit the [justices'] choices."[35]

In short, scholars on both the legal and political science sides recognize that quantitative and qualitative evidence suggests that some mix of law and politics goes into Supreme Court decision making. In fact, some scholars have attempted to demonstrate that neither an all-law nor an all-politics approach suffices to describe the complexity of the judicial process. Frank Cross, a law professor, and Blake Nelson, a political scientist, joined together to conduct a quantitative study of the Supreme Court directed toward this purpose. They rejected all the univocal descriptions of the Court's decision making: "An assumption that judges are naïvely legal or political or utterly strategic is too simple to come close to describing the reality of decisionmaking." Instead, Cross and Nelson found that "[j]ustices are driven by a complex mix of factors—legal, ideological, and strategic. Models are considerably simplified by an assumption of a single-peaked preference along one dimension." Even so, Cross and Nelson conceptualized law and politics as distinct. One could measure the effects of legal materials, standing alone, just as one could measure the effects of political ideology (or political preferences), standing alone.[36]

An Emulsion

The oil-and-water mix of law and politics represents an advance on the all-law and all-politics approaches because it accounts for the quantitative and qualitative evidence supporting both approaches. Even so, the oil-and-water approach retains a vestigial remnant of the purist approaches—namely, it retains the vision of law and politics as dichotomous, as sharply distinct. An alternative approach mixes law and politics together in a way that overcomes this dichotomy. As an advance over the oil-and-water approach, this alternative does not merely posit that law and politics are occasionally stirred together; rather, they are fully integrated into a permanent emulsion. An emulsion, like mayonnaise or milk, is stable; the components do not settle or separate out. With foreknowledge, one can identify the elements that went into the emulsion—law and politics—but the final product is a unified whole: a Supreme Court decision.

Some regimists, law professors as well as political scientists, fall into this emulsification category. In discussing Supreme Court decisions, they tend to emphasize the surrounding political contexts, accentuating how the justices largely follow the political mainstream. They also discuss, though, relevant legal texts and doctrines and the justices' reliance on these legal materials; law, from this perspective, does not merely mirror social and economic interests. For instance, the law professor L. A. Powe views the Court "as a part of a ruling regime doing its bit to implement the regime's policies." The Court "is staffed by men (and in recent years a few women) who for the most part are in tune with their times." Yet Powe also writes about legal developments from the inside, from the lawyer's or judge's perspective. In a book on the history of the Supreme Court, he explains: "I have written in the context of history with the insights of political science but remaining true to the ways the justices perceived their own work. Doctrine may be driven by events and the intellectual currents of the times, but nevertheless the justices, for the most part, take it seriously."[37] In an earlier book, on the Warren Court, Powe examined Supreme Court decisions dealing with legislative apportionment that required the Court to displace settled democratic practices and overrule earlier decisions. In 1946, before Earl Warren became chief justice, a plurality had held in *Colegrove v. Green* that a state legislative drawing of congressional district lines presented a nonjusticiable political question (discussed in Chapter 4). In 1962, however, the Warren Court rejected *Colegrove* and instead held, in *Baker v. Carr,* that an allegation of disproportional representation and concomitant vote dilution constituted a justiciable claim, whether for a state legislature, as in *Baker*, or for the House of Representatives, as in *Colegrove*. The *Baker* holding, that disputes over legislative apportionment were justiciable, engendered a series of cases challenging apportionment practices. Most famously, *Wesberry v. Sanders*, focusing on congressional districts, and *Reynolds v. Sims*, focusing on state legislative districts, established the doctrine of "one person, one vote." After extensively elaborating the doctrinal arguments debated in these cases, including dissenting and concurring, as well as majority, positions, Powe discussed how these decisions sparked political opposition, especially from those legislators who were likely to lose their seats because of the judicially forced redistricting. Thus, *Baker* and its progeny could certainly be understood, from a legal vantage, as breaking new doctrinal ground while boldly defending the right to participate in democratic processes. But Powe also argued that the Court's decisions "conformed to the values that enjoyed significant national support in the mid-1960s." Indeed, the same year the Court decided *Wesberry* and *Reynolds*, a national political coalition would produce the Civil Rights Act of 1964 and then, one year later, the Voting Rights Act of 1965.[38]

Clearly, for Powe, law matters, yet regime politics also influences the justices. A significant contingent of political scientists, categorized as "historical institutionalists," display a similar outlook. As the name implies, historical institutionalists, such as Howard Gillman and Mark Graber, are concerned primarily with the historical development of institutions, including legal and judicial institutions. Like regimists, historical institutionalists are interested in understanding the origins of the justices' political preferences. They aim "to explore the broader cultural and political contexts of judicial decision making [and explain] how judicial attitudes are themselves constituted and structured by the Court as an institution and by its relationship to other institutions in the political system at particular points in history." Historical institutionalists view law as a component of the judicial institution that constrains and directs decision making. Supreme Court justices talk about legal texts and doctrines because they truly believe these legal materials matter, not merely because they need to rationalize their political preferences or goals. And legal materials (as well as legal reasoning) do, in fact, matter because of an institutional imperative: the professional mission of justices sitting on the Supreme Court to interpret and apply the law.[39]

A subcategory of historical institutionalism is American political development (APD). In a definitive book, Karen Orren and Stephen Skowronek explain that APD "grapples with . . . the historical construction of politics, and with political arrangements of different origins in time operating together." APD is primarily concerned with using the histories of these political arrangements to explain political change or development (and resistance to change). When it comes to research on law and the courts, APD asserts that law and politics are, in effect, emulsified. The question whether Supreme Court decision making is a matter of law or politics, explain Ronald Kahn and Ken I. Kersch, should be "conceptualized as a debate over the respective influences of internal and external factors . . . , with law being an important potential internal influence, . . . and electoral politics being a significant potential [external] influence." This interplay between the internal and external—between law and politics—is "distinctive to courts as institutions." Crucially, the interplay gives courts "a certain autonomy from ordinary politics at certain times and in certain areas that leads them to ignore, resist, and even disregard robust political pressure." Gillman, for instance, described how the early twentieth-century Court—the *Lochner*-era Court—continued to apply nineteenth-century legal doctrine even though the surrounding political environment was radically changing and rendering the doctrine unworkable.[40]

One ambiguity lingers in much of the work of emulsification law professors and political scientists. They see law and politics as integrally entwined so that Supreme Court decision making is always partly political. But if the justices are institutionally and professionally obligated to interpret and apply the law, then how does politics enter the adjudicative process? Put in metaphorical terms, what is the recipe for creating the law-politics emulsion? When Powe touches on this question, he becomes uncharacteristically (for him) vague. "Law is not just politics," he writes, "but judges are aware of the political context of their decisions and are, like everyone else, influenced by the economic, social, and intellectual currents of American society." Barry Friedman, another historically minded and regime-oriented law professor, offers a fuller explanation, but he still does not delve into the details. One might say that Friedman deals with the mechanism for emulsifying law and politics at a macro rather than micro level. He discusses how political pressure is brought to bear on the justices and how presidents seek to appoint justices who will implement their political-constitutional visions, yet for the most part he does not explain how politics enters into the justices' deliberations of specific cases.[41]

So, at a micro level, how does politics enter the judicial calculus? Gillman is a historical institutionalist who nearly answers this question. Contrary to all-politics political scientists, Gillman does not dismiss law as irrelevant merely because justices do not apply legal texts and doctrines in a mechanical fashion. Instead, he argues that, within the institution of the Supreme Court, the justices feel a "formal responsibility to decide actual legal disputes based on their best understanding of the law." Judicial decisions, including at the Supreme Court, "are considered legally motivated if they represent a judge's sincere belief that their decision represents their best understanding of what the law requires." A justice, in other words, is ordinarily motivated to interpret the law accurately rather than to pursue explicitly and openly his or her political goals. When a justice interprets and applies the law, however, the justice often must exercise discretion. Here, Gillman follows the legal philosopher Ronald Dworkin by distinguishing strong from weak discretion. Strong discretion allows an individual, to a great extent, to do whatever he or she wishes within wide parameters—for example, "Go to the supermarket and buy some fruit." Weak discretion requires the individual to exercise judgment in following more specific directions or orders—"Go to the supermarket and buy the ripest pears." Justices (and other judges), according to Dworkin and Gillman, exercise weak rather than strong discretion, even in hard cases. Thus, "[L]egal norms can matter even if they cannot be mechanically applied—that is, . . . law can motivate and even shape a decision without determining the result." The justice, we might say, still must decide which pears are ripest. Moreover, the judicial exercise of weak discretion "often" coincides with the judge's "political ideology." Indeed, political attitudes sometimes can transform "to the point that they become internal to the practice [of judging]."⁴²

Gillman is an emulsification theorist: He maintains that politics is always part of legal interpretation. At one point, he even writes: "Meaning is extracted from [legal] sources by interpreters, and interpreters cannot help but be influenced by their particular cultural, social, and political context." Yet when he attempts to explain how politics enters the judicial calculus, he wavers and introduces ambiguities. Many of his explanatory statements include vague qualifiers, such as "often" and "to the extent." Gillman walks to the edge, but hesitates: "[S]o long as judges draw on beliefs about public values, because they believe the law recognizes this as an inevitable part of interpretation (*in some circumstances*), . . . then the influence of legality is at work." Why are public values or politics part of interpretation only "in some circumstances"? Gillman does not elaborate, but his wavering harks back to an oil-and-water approach to law and politics. In particular, when Gillman follows Dworkin, he implicitly suggests that politics enters the adjudicative process through the exercise of judicial discretion. A judge (or justice) might often exercise discretion but does not always do so. From this perspective, if the judge does not need to exercise discretion in a specific case, then politics apparently does not enter the calculus. Legal interpretation, it seems, might still sometimes be pure, unaffected by politics.⁴³

Why might an emulsification theorist such as Gillman settle for this unsatisfactory explanation? One possible answer is that he, like Friedman, works more on the macro than the micro level. As a historical institutionalist, Gillman seeks to describe how the Court as an institution changes (and resists change) in particular political environments. In describing institutional change, Gillman articulates an important position within political science by maintaining that justices and other judges sincerely interpret legal texts. He is able to explain the interplay of law and politics in the institutional context without delving into the details of the decision-making process for specific and concrete cases (though this question apparently intrigues him). Yet the secret to creating the fully integrated law-politics emulsion can be discovered only at the micro level. One must start with the presupposition that the justices sincerely interpret legal texts—that the law matters—but then ask: How? How do the justices interpret legal texts? Or, in other words, how do the justices emulsify politics and law?

UNDERSTANDING LEGAL INTERPRETATION: THE LAW-POLITICS DYNAMIC

To answer this question—the how?—one needs to focus on the heart of the adjudicative process: the interpretation of legal texts and doctrines. As Gillman recognizes, judges feel duty-bound to interpret and apply legal materials, such as case precedents, statutes, and constitutional provisions. And, as Gillman also recognizes, legal interpretation is not mechanical.[44] But what does it mean to say that interpretation is not mechanical? In short, no method (or mechanical process) enables one to access some preexisting and pristine textual meaning. Interpretation is not an arithmetic problem in which one adds the numbers and indubitably arrives at the correct answer. This is not to say, though, that there is no correct or right answer to interpretive disputes. Yet the only means for gleaning the correct meaning of a text is through interpretation itself. Quite simply, judges *must* interpret legal texts and doctrines (if they are to act like judges).[45]

So judges must interpret, and interpretation is never mechanical. How, then, does interpretation occur? Most important, an interpreter who turns to a text must always do so from within his or her horizon. Literally, the horizon is the distance that one can see from one's current position or place. The concept of the horizon, therefore, is both enabling and constraining: We can see as far as the end of the horizon, but we can see no farther. Metaphorically, the interpretive horizon is the range of possible understandings or interpretations that an individual brings to any text. We are empowered to understand texts, but we are also limited to understandings within our respective horizons.[46] Hence, we find politics at the heart of the interpretive process: How, after all, does one's horizon form?

The horizon is constituted by an uncertain amalgamation of one's interests, prejudices, expectations, and values, all of which are imbued in the individual by prior experiences of culture, religion, politics, and one's structural position in society. An individual's interpretive horizon, then, is not a private possession. It arises from the individual's experience and education within a community (or communities) and the community's cultural traditions.[47] Research in cognitive psychology elucidates. "All mental processing draws closely from one's background knowledge," writes Dan Simon. "A decision to cross a street, for example, is contingent on one's experience-born knowledge about vehicles, motion, and driver behavior. A choice to form a friendship is influenced by one's knowledge of cues for trustworthiness, love, selfishness, and the like." Given this formative process, the interpretive horizon is never static. An individual's horizon moves because of changing experiences of culture, religion, politics, and societal structures. As Simon puts it, one's "background belief system . . . is hardly fixed." Instead, new experiences can cause "background beliefs [to] shift."[48]

Whenever the Supreme Court justices decide a case, they must interpret legal texts, including the Constitution, statutes, and case precedents. In interpreting legal texts, including doctrines from precedents, the justices necessarily do so from the vantage of their respective horizons. A justice who was educated at an American law school, practiced law, and decided prior cases understands and generally abides by the internal practices of law and adjudication. Those internal practices—the know-how of the law—are part of the justice's horizon.[49] In most cases, therefore, the justice will attempt in good faith to interpret the relevant legal texts correctly. But the justices' horizons also encompass their political preferences or ideologies. Even well-meaning justices cannot possibly escape the influence of their background prejudices and emotions, according to neuroscience research. Consequently, in the vast majority of cases, when the justices sincerely interpret legal texts and doctrines, their horizons generate interpretations that coincide with their political preferences and allegiances.[50]

In sum, a full understanding of the interpretive process reveals precisely why politics matters in legal interpretation: Justices sincerely interpret legal texts, and politics (as part of the horizon) always shapes sincere interpretation. Politics is integral to legal interpretation—or, in other words, Supreme Court decision making always entails the operation of a law-politics dynamic. From this perspective, we can see that the lack of a mechanical process for resolving interpretive disputes does not mean that "anything goes" in legal interpretation. An interpreter, including a Supreme Court justice, is not free to impose any or no meaning at all on a text, as if guided by no more than personal whims. To the contrary, interpretation of case precedents, constitutional provisions, or any other text always is constrained because of communal traditions and the concomitant expectations, interests, and prejudices. Precisely because of the nature of the interpretive process, it is perfectly sensible to seek not only the meaning of a legal text but the best meaning of that text, even though there is no mechanical process for determining that best meaning.[51]

A distinction between politics writ small and politics writ large illuminates the law-politics dynamic. In judicial decision making, politics writ large occurs if a justice or judge purposefully or self-consciously pursues political goals qua political goals (either preferences or allegiances) when deciding a case. In other words, a judge pursuing politics writ large acts like a legislator. For example, as mentioned earlier in this chapter, many commentators have argued that the conservative justices decided *Bush v. Gore* because they wanted George W. Bush rather than Al Gore to be the next president. In the year 2000, after the election, the Florida Supreme Court had ordered manual recounts of the votes cast for president in several different counties. The U.S. Supreme Court reversed with a five-to-four decision and ordered the termination of the recounts. A politically conservative bloc of justices constituted the Court majority, while the progressives were in the minority. The key part of the Court's majority opinion held that the State of Florida had violated equal protection because different counties and different recount teams had used divergent standards to determine voters' intent, which state law established as the criterion for determining votes. This equal-protection reasoning was not only strikingly novel but also disregarded that the recounts were needed to correct for substantial discrepancies in the original counting of votes—discrepancies that arose because of the diverse and unequally effective procedures used in different counties. Some counties used punch-card ballots while other counties used more modern optical-scan systems, even though punch cards produced a far higher percentage of nonvotes (ballots that did not register votes in the machines). If the manual recount procedure violated equal protection, as the Court reasoned, then the best interpretation of equal protection would appear to suggest that the original vote counting was similarly unconstitutional. The conservative justices skirted this obvious inconsistency in their reasoning. Consequently, even those constitutional scholars who usually maintain that traditional legal reasoning closely controls Supreme Court decision making found *Bush v. Gore* to be problematic—that is, the justices seemed to follow their politics.[52]

Despite the significance of *Bush v. Gore* for post-2000 American political developments, such instances of Supreme Court politics writ large seem rare. Judicial decision making in accord with politics writ small, however, is common—in fact, it is unavoidable unless the judge opts for politics writ large.[53] When a judge sincerely interprets the relevant legal texts and decides a case (or votes to decide a case) accordingly—with the judge's horizon, including political ideology, naturally shaping her or his interpretation and decision— then the judge has decided pursuant to politics writ small. Politics writ small, that is, inheres in legal interpretation. Or to put it conversely, legal interpretation is politics writ small. The concept of politics writ small accentuates that a judge (or justice) always interprets legal texts from within his or her horizon, which encompasses political preferences or ideologies.[54]

All-politics and oil-and-water approaches are premised on politics writ large. Attitudinalists and all-politics regimists maintain that the justices purposefully pursue either their political preferences (attitudinalists) or the goals of the predominant political order (regimists). Oil-and-water approaches assume that politics writ large enters the judicial calculus whenever the law runs out. If a justice encounters a gap in the legal doctrine, for instance, then the justice justifiably pursues politics writ large. But contrary to these politics-writ-large approaches, the justices in most cases take seriously their duty to interpret and apply the relevant legal texts and doctrines the best they can. Moreover, since politics is integral to legal interpretation, the justices' sincere interpretations typically correspond with their political goals and ideologies. This correspondence between law and politics in interpretation and adjudication accords with the empirical evidence. Since quantitative and qualitative studies suggest that both law and politics influence judicial decision making, then maybe it is true: *Both* law *and* politics influence judicial decision making. In fact, Michael A. Bailey and Forrest Maltzman concluded a book-length quantitative study by finding support for a type of law-politics emulsion: "Our evidence suggests a nuanced portrait of the Supreme Court and the choices justices make, a portrait of policy-motivated but legally and institutionally constrained justices."[55]

The insight that the justices' sincere interpretations usually correspond with their political goals and ideologies should be underscored. Precisely because politics writ small is integral to legal interpretation, judges' (or justices') sincere interpretations of legal texts typically coincide with their political goals and allegiances. In most cases, especially at the Supreme Court level, justices do not experience a conflict between their sincere interpretations of the relevant texts and doctrines and their political preferences or allegiances. A justice rarely considers a case and reasons: "The best interpretation of the relevant texts and doctrines necessitates conclusion X, but my political preference is conclusion Y. What should I do?" Instead, the justice likely reasons: "The best interpretation of the relevant texts and doctrines necessitates conclusion Z (and fortuitously, conclusion Z corresponds with my political preference)." Of course, such correspondence between law and politics is not truly fortuitous; it is built into the interpretive process.

Once again, cognitive psychology strongly supports the natural correspondence between a justice's textual interpretation and the justice's politics (writ small). Research demonstrates that when individuals confront complex decisions, their cognitive systems will shift "toward a state of coherence with either one of the decision alternatives." Decision makers' motivations or goals, including legal and political goals, substantially affect "their mental processes" and contribute toward this shift to coherence. In other words, according to "coherence-based reasoning research," when a justice (or other judge) must decide a case, the justice's legal and political views will tend ultimately to coincide rather than conflict. Psychologists agree that this tendency to reach coherent conclusions is often unconscious. To take one example, "[A] judge who identifies as a liberal Democrat may know that she favors affirmative action," explains Eileen Braman, "but she may not be aware of whether (or how) that policy preference influences her interpretation of evidence and/or legal authority in cases involving that issue." Most important, an individual's coherence-based reasoning in accordance with his or her goals is perfectly natural. As Simon concludes, shifts toward coherent conclusions "do not represent conscious, strategic, or deceitful conduct on the part of a decision-maker; rather, they are the natural consequence of the normal mechanisms of cognitive processing."[56]

Not only will lawyers and judges (including justices) often find a happy coincidence between their own interpretive and political judgments, but also multiple lawyers and judges will often agree on the meaning of a particular text. In fact, some cases are easy cases because most lawyers and judges agree on the result. Such widespread consensus arises because of the communal quality of interpretation. An individual's horizon of expectations, interests, and prejudices is engendered by the community's traditions, cultures, societal structures, and so forth. Consequently, many lawyers and judges share overlapping horizons encompassing generally uncontested cultural values and societal practices. The purpose of law school, in part, is to acculturate a student—a would-be lawyer—to the traditions of the legal profession so that the student is imbued with the proper expectations, interests, and prejudices. The student will (or should) have learned the methods (or know-how) appropriate to discussing and resolving legal issues.[57] After a student finishes a course in constitutional law, for instance, she or he will know that constitutional issues can be legitimately resolved by reference to, among other things, constitutional text, framers' intentions, and government structures, but not by reference to the Sunday comics or the flip of a coin. A student who attends pharmacy school instead of law school, meanwhile, will not be equipped with the know-how appropriate to interpreting legal texts in accord with professional norms (though the pharmacy student will have the know-how to understand a doctor's instructions regarding pharmaceutical prescriptions). The pharmacy student might realize that reliance on the Sunday comics or the flip of a coin would be inappropriate but might not know that reference to the framers' intentions or government structures would be legitimate.[58]

Interpreters often agree about the meaning of a text, but, of course, interpreters also often disagree. And now we can appreciate why they disagree (when, after all, they are reading the same text). Suppose two Supreme Court justices—let's say, Justices Samuel Alito and Ruth Bader Ginsburg—confronted an Establishment Clause issue that required them to interpret the First Amendment. They both sincerely interpreted the constitutional text and relevant precedents, yet they ultimately disagreed about the correct interpretation. Such disagreement suggests neither that one of the justices was insincere—being disingenuous about the best interpretation—nor that a best answer does not exist. Rather, disagreement arose because the justices approached the constitutional text from significantly different, albeit overlapping, horizons. Their horizons overlapped because, in part, both justices had been trained and immersed in the culture of the American legal community, but their horizons diverged because, in part, they had different political commitments (not to mention religious backgrounds). Alito's conservative politics shapes his interpretive horizon, while Ginsburg's progressive politics shaped her horizon. The justices, in this situation, could attempt to persuade each other of the correct interpretation, and they might have done so. Yet because interpretation is not mechanical—no method can prove the correct answer—disagreement might have persisted. Such disagreement, it should be clear, is not due to a failure of the interpretive process; rather, it is part and parcel of the interpretive process. One can never escape the horizon-bound nature of interpretation.[59]

At the same time, Supreme Court adjudication does have an end point or conclusion—namely, when the justices vote and decide a case. The institutional or structural position of the Court in our government system—at the apex of our judiciaries—differentiates Supreme Court adjudication from many other interpretive enterprises.[60] When the justices vote and decide a case, they terminate their interpretive debates about the relevant legal materials, at least temporarily—even though the justices themselves have no more access than anybody else to a mechanical method for resolving interpretive disputes. Compare a Supreme Court case with a dispute between two literature professors over the interpretation of Franz Kafka's *Metamorphosis*. Like Alito and Ginsburg, the two literature professors can attempt to persuade each other about the superiority of their interpretations. "Gregor's transformation into a gigantic insect is merely symbolic," says the first professor. "No, Gregor really turns into a bug," says the second. They can offer reasons for their positions and attempt to refute the other's reasons. But ultimately, their dispute might never end because there is no institutional mechanism for reaching a conclusion. But when Supreme Court justices disagree about the best interpretation of the First Amendment or any other legal text, there is an institutional means for ending the *adjudicative* dispute. The justices vote, and the majority wins. Crucially, though, this institutional mechanism does not actually resolve the *interpretive* dispute. The justices might continue to disagree about the best interpretation of the text, as might lawyers, other judges, and law professors, but the adjudicative dispute is, for all intents and purposes, over.[61] The justices will move on to the next case on the docket. The existence of an institutional mechanism for culminating adjudicative disputes does not, however, change the nature of interpretation. There still is no mechanical process or method for resolving the interpretive disagreement.

To be sure, the litigants can continue to disagree with each other about the best interpretation of the legal text, and one or both of them can disagree with the Court's interpretation, but regardless, the litigants (and the lower court judges) must accept the Court's decision and act accordingly or risk suffering severe sanctions. Of course, if losing litigants have access to sufficient resources, then they can seek to overcome the Court's resolution in some other manner, such as attempting to convince members of Congress to initiate the process for a constitutional amendment. Indeed, members of Congress, other politicians, and other citizens must accept the Court's resolution of the adjudicative dispute to a degree, but they nonetheless can and often do resist the implications of the decision through a variety of formal and informal techniques (often far short of a constitutional amendment).[62] The efforts of southern school boards to thwart the racial desegregation required under *Brown v. Board of Education*—for instance, by closing all the schools in a district or by terrorizing black schoolchildren who attempted to attend a previously all-white school—are perhaps the best known but certainly not the only example of disregard (or disdain) for the Court's interpretations of the Constitution and other legal texts. Yet despite such occasional resistance, the Court's pronouncement in any particular case ends the adjudication between those litigants.[63]

The Second Amendment provides an illustration. For most of the nation's history, the Second Amendment—"[A] well regulated Militia, being necessary to the security of a free State, the right of the people to keep and bear Arms, shall not be infringed"—generated neither much litigation nor much academic interest. Over the past thirty years or so, however, academic interest has exploded, sparked initially by political debates over gun control and more recently by the never-ending spectacle of mass shootings. Politicians and commentators debate the wisdom and constitutionality of restrictions on gun possession, while books and symposia have collected essays written by historians and legal scholars about the meaning of the Second Amendment. Does the Second Amendment create an individual right to own a gun for personal use? Or does the Second Amendment create only a collective right to possess guns within a government militia? Or does the Second Amendment protect a right to possess guns for the purpose of insurrection against a tyrannical government? The controversy is, of course, interpretive: What does the constitutional text mean? This ultimate issue leads to additional interpretive questions. What did the Constitution's framers intend? Should the framers' intentions matter in the interpretation of the Second Amendment? Does the changing technology of firearms affect the understanding of the Second Amendment? These interpretive questions already have generated diverse viewpoints and much interesting scholarship and will, in all likelihood, continue to do so. Significantly, while politicians, commentators, and scholars (both legal and historical) can reasonably debate their various positions by marshaling evidence and constructing persuasive arguments, there is no mechanical process for definitively resolving the interpretive dispute. Although there very well might be a best answer to the ultimate question regarding the meaning of the Second Amendment, Americans could in theory debate the issue indefinitely.[64]

The Supreme Court avoided Second Amendment issues for decades, but it thrust itself into the interpretive debate in 2008 when it decided *District of Columbia v. Heller*. With a five-to-four decision, Justice Scalia wrote the majority opinion for the conservative bloc—an opinion that would be called his "judicial magnum opus." Scalia ostensibly followed an originalist approach and concluded that the original meaning of the Second Amendment was to protect an individual right to own and possess firearms. From his perspective, the current meaning could be no different. As interpreted, the Second Amendment necessarily took certain legislative or "policy choices off the table," including the District of Columbia's "absolute prohibition of handguns held and used for self-defense in the home."[65]

Heller did not, however, resolve the interpretive dispute over the meaning of the Second Amendment. In fact, Justice Stevens wrote a dissent, also in the style of originalism, and concluded that the Constitution protected a right to possess firearms only for members of a militia. According to his interpretation, the Second Amendment does not protect an individual right to own or possess guns. And, of course, politicians and commentators continue to debate precisely what government regulations of guns are constitutionally permissible. Nevertheless, the Court acted within its institutional domain and mechanically resolved the *Heller* dispute by voting five to four to interpret the Second Amendment as protecting an individual right. The Court's vote and Scalia's opinion ended the adjudication. Period. But no method or mechanical process can end the interpretive dispute. And so it continues.[66]

Consider the legal-judicial operation, in general, of stare decisis, the following of case precedents. Courts can interpret precedents just as they can interpret any legal texts. Lawyers, judges, and law professors can reasonably debate what interpretation of a particular precedent constitutes its best reading. Yet many legal professionals might misunderstand the doctrine of stare decisis. They might mistake the rigid finality of adjudication, which is resolved through a mechanical process, for a rigid finality in legal interpretation, which cannot be similarly determined. Interpretive constraints (from our horizons) enable us to deliberate reasonably about the best reading of case precedents, but they never produce a final, determinate resolution to an interpretive problem.

Take as an example the interpretation of *Heller*, as the key Second Amendment precedent. Does *Heller* allow, let's say, a state to prohibit the open carrying of handguns in public buildings? If a colleague and I disagree about the best interpretation of *Heller*, we can try to persuade each other. In such a situation, our interpretations of *Heller* are, of course, constrained: Neither of us is free to declare that the meaning of the case corresponds with our mere personal preference for no reason other than that it is our personal preference—at least, we cannot do so if we intend to make a reasonable argument that might persuade. Moreover, even if my colleague and I eventually agree on the meaning of *Heller* as a precedent, our interpretive dispute never reaches an unequivocal and determinate resolution.

But if my colleague and I were to present our arguments before the Supreme Court, then the situation changes. Regardless of the interpretive dispute at the heart of the case, regardless of the persuasiveness of our respective arguments, adjudication is partly a mechanical process that has a final, determinate resolution. Most important, a variety of factors, including political ideologies, can shape that final judicial resolution. Yet when the Court issues its opinion, it might invoke stare decisis, *as if* the case precedent of *Heller* mechanically determined the Court's conclusion. Regardless of the Court's issued opinion, though, the *votes* of the justices rather than the interpretation of *Heller* provided the final mechanical determination to the adjudicative dispute. Many legal professionals, in accepting the Court's decision, might then conflate the process of interpretation with the process of adjudication. True, interpretation is part of adjudication, but the final resolution of an adjudicative dispute is mechanical in a way that interpretation can never be.

L aw. Politics. Two words. The language, the terminology, suggests separate and independent concepts. Purists, in effect, conceive of law and politics as ideal types. Law is clear, logical, and ordered. Politics is flexible, expedient, and deliberative. As such, law and politics are opposites. Each is taboo to the other. Law destroys politics by enforcing rigidity, while politics corrupts law by injecting discretion and instrumentalism. As discussed in Chapter 4, political and professional forces drive individuals in law and political science to accentuate these pure ideal types, embodied in the law-politics dichotomy. But as this chapter shows, these ideal types do not represent the reality of Supreme Court decision making. In Supreme Court adjudication, law and politics are not opposites. They are not separate and independent. Rather, they naturally draw together into a stable interpretive emulsion.

If the law-politics dichotomy is a myth and Supreme Court decision making always entails a law-politics dynamic, then the primary criticism of court packing evaporates. If politics is always part of Supreme Court adjudication, then court packing cannot destroy the Court's purity as a legal-judicial institution because a politics-free Court has never existed. What other implications or consequences follow from the recognition of the law-politics dynamic? The next chapter explores this question.

6

IMPLICATIONS OF THE
LAW-POLITICS DYNAMIC

Supreme Court decision making is and always has been partly political. Simultaneously, Supreme Court decision making is and always has been partly legal. Contrary to the opposed purist-legal and -political science views, Supreme Court decision making arises from a law-politics *dynamic*. The law-politics *dichotomy* is a myth. Neither pure law nor pure politics determines Supreme Court votes and decisions. In most cases, the justices sincerely interpret legal texts and precedents, but their respective political horizons influence how they interpret the law. Consequently, Supreme Court decision making always entails politics writ small, if not politics writ large (in the rare case).

Most important, then, concerns that court packing will politicize the Court are ill-conceived. This chapter explores further implications of the law-politics dynamic for, first, Supreme Court justices; then politicians, commentators, and other citizens; and finally, legal and political science scholars (when studying Supreme Court decision making).

FOR SUPREME COURT JUSTICES

From the perspective of the justices themselves, the recognition and acceptance of the law-politics dynamic might be relatively insignificant to the practice of Supreme Court decision making. Oddly, Thomas Kuhn's historical study of the Copernican Revolution illuminates the relationship between the scholarly insight of the law-politics dynamic, on the one hand, and Supreme

Court practices, on the other. From the fourth century B.C.E. to the sixteenth century C.E.—that is, before Copernicus—the predominant cosmological outlook was the "two-sphere universe." As explained by Kuhn, "[T]he earth was a tiny sphere suspended stationary at the geometric center of a much larger rotating sphere which carried the stars." The sun moved within the space between the two spheres (i.e., between the earth and the stars). Nothing existed beyond the outer sphere of the stars. Copernicus revolutionized the science of cosmology by proposing that the sun, not the earth, was the center of a solar system with revolving planets, including the earth. Kuhn notes, however, that even in the twentieth century the simpler conception of the two-sphere universe remained functionally useful for many people, including navigators and surveyors. The post-Copernican scientific model of the universe proved too complex for such practical enterprises. "Most handbooks of navigation or surveying open with some sentence like this: 'For present purposes we shall assume that the earth is a small stationary sphere whose center coincides with that of a much larger rotating stellar sphere.'" In other words, the two-sphere model continues to work successfully for certain practices, though scientists no longer accept it as true or representative of reality.[1]

The practice of Supreme Court decision making can be understood similarly. *Scholars* might reject the simplicity of an all-law (or all-politics) approach. An increasing number might recognize the dynamic integration of law and politics in Supreme Court decision making. But the law-politics dynamic presents a far more complex depiction of Supreme Court adjudication than do purist and oil-and-water approaches, discussed in Chapter 5. Even some political scientists will undoubtedly reject the law-politics dynamic exactly because it is too complex to be readily reduced to quantifiable criteria. To be certain, we can recognize the law-politics dynamic (or emulsion) and measure some aspects of it in quantifiable terms—for example, by using the attitudinal model to measure the influence of political ideology—but ultimately, our acceptance of the dynamic must be based partly on qualitative evidence. Regardless, Kuhn's discussion of the Copernican Revolution suggests that Supreme Court justices (and other judges) can continue to function in accord with a simpler purist approach—specifically, an all-law approach.[2]

The justices can and will sincerely interpret legal texts and doctrines. They can and will avoid consciously considering their respective political views and overtly discussing political goals. They can and will, in other words, spurn politics writ large. John Roberts, Neil Gorsuch, and other justices can continue to declare that, in all honesty, they decide cases pursuant to the rule of law. Perhaps, some justices might admit that they occasionally consult policy factors in the limited manner permitted under an oil-and-water approach. Significantly, though, many justices throughout American history have in good faith followed the rule of law while not defining the rule of law in accord with solely formal legal rules or pure law, especially in constitutional cases. The practice of Supreme Court decision making, that is, frequently does not adhere to a narrow theory of judicial decision making, such as originalism. In practice, many justices follow a pluralist or eclectic approach to constitutional interpretation and adjudication.[3]

One can study Supreme Court opinions from the 1790s through the 1800s and up through today and find justices discussing a variety of factors in their search for constitutional meaning. What sorts of factors? The original public meaning of the constitutional text (which many originalists claim to be the be-all-and-end-all of constitutional interpretation); the intentions of the Constitution's framers (which other originalists claim to be the be-all-and-end-all of constitutional interpretation); the likely practical consequences of potential judicial decisions; the purposes of the Constitution as a whole; prior judicial interpretations of the disputed constitutional text; natural rights and natural law principles; social science evidence; the history of various social practices (such as abortion and homosexuality); and on and on. A single 1827 Supreme Court decision, *Ogden v. Saunders*, shows multiple justices using a wide variety of interpretive approaches when searching for constitutional meaning. The majority held that the congressional bankruptcy power, under article I, section 8, clause 4, was not exclusive and that a state bankruptcy statute did not violate the Contracts Clause so long as it applied to contracts entered subsequently to the legislative enactment. The justices issued five opinions—one each by the four majority justices, William Johnson, Robert Trimble, Smith Thompson, and Bushrod Washington, and one by the dissenting Chief Justice John Marshall, joined by Gabriel Duvall and Joseph Story.[4]

Justices Johnson and Trimble invoked public meaning, based on how the people actually understood the Constitution at the time of the framing. Johnson, for instance, emphasized "the sense put upon [the Constitution] by the people when it was adopted by them." Both justices believed that contemporary constructions of the document provided the best evidence of public meaning. Johnson gleaned such evidence from legislative actions taken after ratification, while Trimble quoted from the Federalist Papers to illustrate "the contemporary construction" given during the ratification process. Johnson explained that "the contemporaries of the constitution have claims to our deference on the question of right, because they had the best opportunities of informing themselves of the understanding of the framers of the constitution, and of the sense put upon it by the people when it was adopted by them." Consistent with a public meaning approach, two justices—Johnson and Thompson—suggested that some constitutional provisions had a plain meaning. Thompson, for example, wrote: "If this provision in the constitution was unambiguous, and its meaning entirely free from doubt, there would be no door left open for construction." He then referred to "the plain and natural interpretation" of the Contracts Clause. Reasoning inversely, so to speak, Johnson found it significant that "nothing . . . on the face of the Constitution" directly prohibited states from enacting bankruptcy laws. Justice Washington emphasized the textual arrangement of the words within particular provisions. Johnson and Trimble also thought that the fabric of the whole Constitution was relevant to interpretation. "The principle," Trimble wrote, "that the association of one clause with another of like kind, may aid in its construction, is deemed sound."[5]

Four justices—Washington, Johnson, Thompson, and Trimble—relied on the framers' intentions. Trimble referred to the framers as "sages," while Washington wrote: "I have examined both sides of this great question with the most sedulous care, and the most anxious desire to discover which of them, when adopted, would be most likely to fulfil the intentions of those who framed the constitution of the United States." Related to the framers' intentions, Washington and Johnson believed that the Constitution's overall purposes should inform its interpretation, while Thompson considered "the reason and policy" of particular provisions to be relevant.[6]

Three justices—Washington, Johnson, and Thompson—suggested that natural law principles should inform constitutional interpretation. Two justices—Johnson and Marshall (dissenting)—reasoned that the history of the political problems that provoked the Philadelphia (constitutional) convention was germane to constitutional interpretation. Marshall, for instance, emphasized that state government corruption in the 1780s produced unjust debtor-relief laws, which engendered the inclusion of the Contracts Clause in the Constitution. Two justices, Johnson and Thompson, considered the practical consequences of different possible constitutional interpretations. For instance, when considering what constituted an "obligation" under the Contracts Clause, Thompson contemplated whether a particular interpretation would "facilitate commercial intercourse." Finally, two justices—Johnson and Thompson—examined judicial precedents concerning disputed constitutional meanings.[7]

In sum, the five justices writing opinions in *Ogden* employed a dizzying array of interpretive strategies. No justice relied on only one, exclusive interpretive approach, whether public meaning or otherwise. Every justice used multiple approaches. These justices, significantly, did not view themselves as departing from the rule of law. Rather, they were applying the rule of law. Justice Washington even admitted that constitutional interpretation was not mechanical, and constitutional meaning was not objective and determinate. He explained his interpretive judgment: "I should be disingenuous were I to declare, from this place, that I embrace [a particular interpretation of the Contracts Clause] without hesitation, and without a doubt of its correctness. The most that candour will permit me to say upon the subject is, that I see, or think I see, my way more clear on the side which my judgment leads me to adopt, than on the other, and it must remain for others to decide whether the guide I have chosen has been a safe one or not."[8]

Justice Joseph Story, one of the few justices not to write an opinion in *Ogden*, elsewhere explained the capaciousness of the rule of law in constitutional cases. For the first century of the nation's existence, Story's *Commentaries on the Constitution of the United States*, published in 1833, was unquestionably the preeminent treatise on constitutional law. Story acknowledged that commentators and judges had strongly disagreed about the proper approach to constitutional interpretation. He proposed to clarify: "Let us, then, endeavour to ascertain, what are the true rules of interpretation applicable to the constitution; so that we may have some fixed standard." With unwitting irony, he then *reduced* constitutional interpretation to *nineteen* rules. Consider rule 1: "The first and fundamental rule in the interpretation of all instruments is, to construe them according to the sense of the terms, and the intention of the parties." This statement suggested an emphasis on public meaning ("the sense of the terms") and original intent, but Story followed with a large qualification. "[The English judge and scholar] Blackstone has remarked that the intention of a law is to be gathered from the words, the context, the subject-matter, the effects and consequence, or the reason and spirit of the law." Story went on to repudiate "all notions of subjecting [the Constitution] to a strict interpretation" and instead advocated for a pluralist or eclectic approach open to all "reasonable" constitutional readings.[9]

Given this history, one would be hard pressed to criticize more recent examples of pluralist or eclectic constitutional interpretation as contravening the rule of law. Justice Harry Blackmun did not depart from the rule of law in *Roe v. Wade*, establishing a woman's right to choose whether to abort a pregnancy, when he discussed the history of laws restricting abortion going back to ancient Greece and Rome. Likewise, in partly reaffirming a woman's right to choose, the joint opinion in *Planned Parenthood v. Casey* remained consistent with the rule of law when it contemplated the potential (practical) consequences of overruling *Roe*. Justice Anthony Kennedy did not contravene the rule of law when, in *Lawrence v. Texas*, which constitutionally protected homosexual conduct, he discussed the history of laws prohibiting homosexuality. In the affirmative action decision *Adarand Constructors v. Pena*, Justice Ruth Bader Ginsburg's dissent appropriately discussed "the persistence of racial inequality" in American society. Citing empirical studies, she wrote:

> Job applicants with identical resumés, qualifications, and interview styles still experience different receptions, depending on their race. White and African American consumers still encounter different deals. People of color looking for housing still face discriminatory treatment by landlords, real estate agents, and mortgage lenders. Minority entrepreneurs sometimes fail to gain contracts though they are the low bidders, and they are sometimes refused work even after winning contracts. Bias both conscious and unconscious, reflecting traditional and unexamined habits of thought, keeps up barriers that must come down if equal opportunity and nondiscrimination are ever genuinely to become this country's law and practice.[10]

To be sure, not all justices understand the rule of law so capaciously. An originalist such as Justice Gorsuch insists that, in constitutional cases, the Court should consider the constitutional text and its original public meaning. And that's it. To Gorsuch, this approach allows the justices "to study dictionary definitions, rules of grammar, and the historical context, all to determine what the [particular constitutional provision] meant to the people when their representatives adopted it." All in all, though, the practical enterprise of Supreme Court decision making has worked successfully in the past by following a legal approach—understood in different ways by different justices—and can continue to do so in the future, without any conscious consideration of the law-politics dynamic or other fancy law-politics theory. Of course, politics will nonetheless continue to work below the surface, as politics writ small, as part of the law-politics dynamic or emulsion embodied in legal interpretation. In fact, the practice of Supreme Court adjudication functions so successfully partly because of politics writ small. The law-politics dynamic and politics writ small ensure that justices ordinarily experience a correspondence between their interpretive and political views. Justices rarely confront the angst that would arise if their interpretive and political views diverged: Should I follow the rule of law or my political ideology? Professional and political forces would press in opposite directions. If such cases arose frequently, they would strain the practical enterprise of adjudication. Justices would constantly be questioning professional norms and the usefulness of fidelity to those norms. Fortunately, cases creating a law-politics angst are extraordinary—exactly because politics writ small is integral to legal interpretation. Roberts and the other justices, therefore, can go on their merry ways, remaining oblivious to the law-politics dynamic.[11]

The law-politics dynamic and the concomitant politics writ small, however, do not demand heedless ignorance. A justice can be aware of a correspondence between his or her interpretive and political views. To some justices, such correspondence might seem serendipitous, even though it is not; the correspondence arises because of the nature of the interpretive process. In fact, some justices might recognize the operation of the law-politics dynamic, might recognize how politics is integral to legal interpretation. Still, though, such a justice would likely continue to follow professional norms and duties. The justice would continue to vote and decide in accord with his or her best interpretation of the relevant legal materials. For the most part, the practice of Supreme Court decision making would continue as before. Only naïveté would be lost. Our insightful justice would merely be aware that political ideology always informed legal interpretation. Most important, then, such awareness would not be liberating. The justice would not be freed from his or her interpretive horizon and suddenly able to interpret and apply pure law in a mechanical fashion, free of political influence. Likewise, the justice would not be freed to follow his or her politics indiscriminately. The professional norms of judicial decision making would still compel the justice to interpret legal texts and doctrines the best he or she can. Escape to either a pure law or a pure politics is impossible.

FOR POLITICIANS, COMMENTATORS, AND CITIZENS

Critics of the Supreme Court need to recognize that the lack of a (mechanical) method for settling interpretive disputes insulates the Supreme Court justices from ever being *proved* wrong, by others or themselves. While we can disagree with the justices over their interpretation of case precedents and constitutional provisions, and in doing so we can offer persuasive arguments, we nonetheless cannot draw on any mechanical process to demonstrate that the justices were determinatively wrong—because there is no such process. To be sure, the *justices* use an institutionalized mechanical process, majority voting, to resolve adjudicative disputes, but they, like everybody else, do not mechanically interpret legal texts. Obviously, too, the Court's critics cannot appropriate the justices' adjudicative process of majority voting to condemn the Court methodically or demonstrably because, quite simply, the critics are not institutionally or structurally empowered to do so. Only the appointed justices are institutionally empowered to resolve adjudicative disputes as *the*

Supreme Court. Therefore, while the justices are not protected from criticism, they are insulated from being proved categorically wrong. Moreover, the conjunction of, first, the lack of an interpretive method, and second, the existence of an institutionalized adjudicative method further minimizes the justices' cognitive dissonance: They readily understand their interpretive views as conforming (rather than clashing) with their political preferences. The inherent indefiniteness of the interpretive process, the lack of a determinative method, frees the justices from confronting proof that they have themselves politicized adjudication—though, of course, because of the nature of legal interpretation, the justices cannot avoid politicizing adjudication.[12]

Should commentators (including critics, scholars, and scholarly critics) advocate for the justices to accept the law-politics dynamic and therefore become more self-aware—to become more conscious of the political aspect of their case votes and decisions? For more than a century, at least some legal scholars have made similar arguments. For instance, writing early in the twentieth century, sociological jurisprudents such as Roscoe Pound and Benjamin Cardozo argued that judges should apply legal rules and principles with the goal of administering justice: From their perspective, the rule of law is not rigidly formal. Such advocacy does no harm, but commentators should remember that Supreme Court decision making is never solely about jurisprudential theory. In other words, a theoretical argument for better decision making does not magically transform the Court's decision-making process. Politics is always part of the process. Material, cultural, and professional forces always shape legal and judicial practices, including a commitment to the law-politics dichotomy and legal formalism. Theory (which we might think of as cultural) might influence the justices, but it never controls their judicial votes and decisions.[13]

Unquestionably, though, politicians (especially members of Congress), commentators, and other citizens should dismiss the claims of justices and would-be justices (Supreme Court nominees) to be apolitical and neutral in applying the rule of law. The justices might sincerely interpret (and apply) the law, but legal interpretation is always partly political. We can expect, of course, Supreme Court *nominees* to continue declaring their allegiance to the neutral rule of law, just as we can expect the justices themselves to insist that they are apolitical. Antonin Scalia provided a prototypical example in *Planned Parenthood v. Casey*, which in 1992 partly reaffirmed *Roe v. Wade* and a woman's right to choose abortion. Concurring and dissenting, Scalia complained that the majority, in refusing to overrule *Roe*, had decided pursuant to the justices' "value judgments" rather than the "objective" rule of law. He insisted that "political pressure" had targeted the Court, as if the justices "were engaged not in ascertaining an objective law but in determining some kind of social consensus."[14]

Paradoxically, however, the Court justifies and increases its political power by denying its political power, as discussed in Chapter 4. The justices are empowered to decide cases in accord with their political views partly because they maintain that they are rigidly following the law. Given this, they naturally have strong incentives to present their positions as being apolitical or neutral. In constitutional jurisprudence, originalists have gained the political upper hand by insisting that originalism is the only apolitical method of constitutional interpretation.[15] Scalia, one of the most conservative justices since World War II, persistently decided cases in accord with his political views. Yet he persuaded numerous scholars, judges, and much of the general public to believe that his ostensible commitment to originalism rendered his judicial decisions apolitical (though his judicial opinions often disregarded originalist sources). Likewise, Justice Gorsuch, Scalia's replacement, insists that originalism is not politically conservative: Originalism, he writes, "offers neutral (non-political, non-personal) principles for judges to follow to ascertain [the Constitution's] meaning."[16]

For example, in cases deciding the scope of congressional power, Scalia consistently reached conservative outcomes—imposing limits on government power—regardless of originalist sources and arguments. The issue in *Printz v. United States* was whether the Tenth Amendment barred Congress from commanding state and local executive officers (police) to follow congressional directives. The Tenth Amendment states: "The powers not delegated to the United States by the Constitution, nor prohibited by it to the states, are reserved to the states respectively, or to the people." The challenged federal statute required state and local executive officers to perform background checks on prospective buyers of handguns. Scalia, writing the majority opinion, began with a strange statement coming from an originalist: "Because there is no constitutional text speaking to this precise question, the answer . . . must be sought in historical understanding and practice, in the structure of the Constitution, and in the jurisprudence of this Court." If Scalia had followed his originalist methodology, then presumably he should have deferred to the legislature. As he would explain elsewhere, "The principle that a matter not covered is not covered is so obvious that it seems absurd to recite it." When the constitutional text is silent, the legislature should be free to decide policy—to make a political decision. Of course, deference to the legislature in this case would have led the Court to uphold the disputed (progressive) gun-control statute. Unwilling to accept that result, Scalia disregarded the implications of the silent text and instead inquired into historical understandings and practices. He ostensibly uncovered "the original understanding of the Constitution" by examining the actions of the first Congresses and statements of the framers. Based on this reasoning, Scalia reached the conservative conclusion, invalidating the statute.[17] But as other critics have noted, contrary to Scalia's assertions, *Printz* and similar decisions prohibiting Congress from commandeering state and local governments are "not based on the text or history of our Constitution."[18]

Politicians, commentators, and citizens should recognize that, like Scalia in *Printz*, the conservative justices consistently reach conservative case conclusions because they are conservative rather than because of their chosen interpretive methodologies or jurisprudential theories. To be sure, in most cases, these justices sincerely interpret the legal texts, but the law-politics dynamic and politics writ small ensure that their sincere interpretations correspond with their conservative political ideologies. Moreover, while their interpretive methodologies and jurisprudential theories do not determine case outcomes, they facilitate reaching conservative conclusions. Consider originalism, which supposedly requires the justices to interpret the Constitution in accord with the original public meaning of the text. Originalists claim that their method uncovers an objective constitutional meaning fixed at the time of the framing. Politics is ostensibly cleansed from the interpretive process. As Scalia explained, an originalist approach is "the only one that can justify courts in denying force and effect to the unconstitutional enactments of duly elected legislatures. . . . To hold a governmental Act to be unconstitutional is not to announce that *we* forbid it, but that the *Constitution* forbids it."[19]

All of these originalist claims are false: Originalism is not apolitical—the law-politics dynamic is always part of interpretation—and therefore it cannot uncover objective and fixed constitutional meaning. But originalism facilitates constitutional inquiries focused on American society at the time of the framing: a society that largely excluded the poor, women, and racial and religious minorities from participating in government processes. In fact, voting rights were denied to the vast majority of people. The framing-era society was unequivocally misogynist and racist, fully accepting and building on the legal institutions of coverture and slavery; one-fifth of the population was enslaved. Originalists, in other words, claim to find definitive constitutional meanings in a society in which wealthy, white, Protestant men were empowered pursuant to law to dominate all others. When armed with such an interpretive approach, conservative justices unerringly find conservative constitutional meanings and reach conservative case outcomes.[20]

Originalism, in truth, is merely one manifestation of legal formalist reasoning. Formalists insist that they must apolitically apply legal rules, regardless of societal context or consequences. As Scalia said, the rule of law must be "the law of rules." Formalists therefore emphasize the law-politics *dichotomy* while denying the law-politics *dynamic*. To take one example, formal equality allows conservative justices to claim neutrality while impeding government attempts to attain substantive equality. Formal equality supposedly requires the government to treat all people the same under the law, regardless of disparities of wealth; regardless of histories of subjugation; regardless of social contexts that, in reality, influence the degree of power people can exercise in the private and public spheres. From the perspective of the conservative justices, formal equality mandates that, under equal protection, race-based affirmative action programs are constitutionally indistinguishable from Jim Crow laws. Laws assisting historically disadvantaged racial groups are deemed equivalent to laws propagating a racial caste system. In short, formalism contains an inherent political tilt favoring those who already wield power in the private sphere. Usually, the "haves" come out ahead while societal outsiders lose. Formalism favors the wealthy over the poor, whites over people of color, men over women, Christians over non-Christians, straights over LGBTQ. Conservative justices invoke formalist legal rules while insisting the government must efface, deny, or ignore the structures of power embedded in the private sphere, including racism, sexism, anti-Semitism, and homophobia.[21]

To be clear, formalism does not automatically produce conservative case outcomes, partly because interpretation of formal legal rules is not mechanical. Supreme Court decision making is always at least politics writ small (and occasionally politics writ large). Moreover, the Court could in theory invoke formal rules to protect members of peripheral groups and other outsiders lacking power. But history shows that the Court generally does not do so, as the political science regimist literature underscores; the justices rarely depart too far from the political mainstream—or, in other words, the haves typically win while the have-nots lose. In those instances when outsiders win—think of *Brown v. Board of Education*—their interests and values usually converge with the mainstream interests and values of the dominant national alliance, as discussed in Chapter 5. A victory for the outsiders is also a victory for the insiders. Regardless, in the typical case in which the Court invokes a formal rule, the conservative justices claim to legitimate a conservative conclusion: The justices ostensibly justify their decisions as being purely legal—politically neutral.[22]

Given the extent to which politics always influences Supreme Court decision making—regardless of the justices' claims to neutrality—it is unsurprising that throughout American history presidents have chosen and Senates have confirmed Supreme Court nominees based partly on political considerations. Nevertheless, conservatives often blame Democrats for politicizing the confirmation process. In particular, conservatives claim that the Democrats' refusal to confirm Robert Bork to the Supreme Court in 1987 transformed the previously collegial and apolitical confirmation process into a wild and vicious gantlet of partisan attacks. In one typical statement, uttered about the 2018 confirmation battle over Brett Kavanaugh, the conservative Leonard Leo, an adviser to the Trump White House on Supreme Court nominations, said, "It's really just been a continuation and sometimes an escalation of what we saw in 1987."[23]

In 1987, when President Ronald Reagan nominated Bork to the Court, Bork already had long been an unmitigated defender of originalism. And while his views of originalist methodology had shifted over the years, he never wavered from insisting that originalism (however he defined it) was the only acceptable approach to constitutional interpretation. From Bork's perspective, originalism was the only interpretive approach that could uncover politically neutral conclusions. When the Court interpreted the Constitution, Bork maintained, "[a]ll that counts is how the words used in the Constitution would have been understood at the time [of their adoption]."[24] Partly because of his staunch commitment to originalism, Bork had articulated multiple controversial legal-political positions. "He opposed the Civil Rights Act of 1964. . . . He defended the poll tax, which had been used in the South to hinder African Americans from voting during the Jim Crow era, saying 'It was a very small tax, it was not discriminatory, and I doubt that it had much impact on the welfare of the nation one way or the other.' He argued that *Roe v. Wade* had no basis in law and that the 14th amendment could not be used to protect women's reproductive rights."[25]

In short, Bork's jurisprudential theories and conclusions, as articulated in his scholarly publications and testimony before the Judiciary Committee, reasonably worried progressives and moderates. Yet Bork himself strongly contributed to the Republican-conservative myth that the Democrats radically politicized the confirmation process when they rejected his Supreme Court nomination. In his opening statement before the Judiciary Committee, Bork asserted his political neutrality: "My philosophy of judging . . . is neither liberal nor conservative." Then in a book subsequently published, in 1990, Bork insisted that the Senate had previously limited confirmation inquiries to the professional qualifications of the nominees. In his case, though, Democratic senators had "politicized [the confirmation process] more than ever before in American history." He quoted a Republican senator who claimed that the reason for controversy surrounding Bork's nomination could be "found in one word, which is tragic in this judicial context, and that word is 'politics.'"[26]

In fact, Bork's historical assertion about the confirmation process was flat wrong: Politics had always infused the nomination and confirmation processes. After all, as discussed in Chapters 2 and 3, Congress and the president had repeatedly fought and negotiated over the number of justices on the Court. Why wouldn't they do the same during the nomination and confirmation processes? To be sure, the political issues animating nominations and confirmations have changed over time, but politics has always been in the mix. In 1795, the Senate even rejected President George Washington's nominee for chief justice, John Rutledge, because Rutledge had opposed ratification of the Jay Treaty, negotiated by John Jay with Britain in 1794 and ratified by the Senate in 1795. Rutledge was swept up (and out) in the growing tensions between the Hamilton-led Federalists and the Madison-led Republicans, discussed in Chapters 2 and 4. The Republicans, including Rutledge, hated the treaty because it favored Britain over France.[27]

Over the years, the Senate has changed its confirmation process. Initially, the Senate did not hold hearings on nominees. A Senate Judiciary Committee did not exist until 1816, and even after its creation, it often did not hold hearings. Moreover, from 1816 to 1867, only approximately one-third of the nominees were referred to the committee. The committee held its first hearing on a nominee in 1873, when it investigated corruption charges against George Williams, nominated for chief justice by President Ulysses S. Grant. The hearings consisted of the examination of documents, as well as the taking of testimony by outside witnesses; the nominee himself did not participate. The committee eventually approved Williams, but the full Senate refused, leading Grant to withdraw the nomination. The Senate had already voted down a previous Grant nominee, Ebenezer R. Hoar, and Grant would soon need to withdraw yet another nominee, Caleb Cushing, because of his chameleon-like political loyalties (he had apparently corresponded with Jefferson Davis).[28]

The committee did not hold hearings again until 1916, when considering Louis Brandeis, nominated as an associate justice by President Woodrow Wilson. Brandeis would be one of the most strongly opposed nominees in history. Like Williams before him, Brandeis did not testify during the committee hearings—the first hearings open to the public. An enormously successful attorney in private practice in Boston, Brandeis had become known as "The People's Lawyer" because of his commitment to progressive politics and public interest causes. Significantly, if confirmed, he would be the first Jewish justice on the Court. Opposition was fierce because of Brandeis's politics, as well as rampant anti-Semitism. Former President and future Chief

Justice William Howard Taft wrote: "It is one of the deepest wounds that I have ever had as an American and a lover of the Constitution and a believer in progressive conservatism, that such a man as Brandeis could be put in the Court, as I believe he is likely to be. He is a muckraker, an emotionalist for his own purposes, a socialist, prompted by jealousy, a hypocrite, a man who has certain high ideals in his imagination . . . who is utterly unscrupulous." The president of Harvard University, Abbott Lawrence Lowell, an overt anti-Semite, circulated a petition opposing Brandeis and collected fifty-five signatures from prominent Bostonians. Seven former presidents of the American Bar Association signed and sent a letter to the committee "declaring Brandeis unfit to serve on the high court." In the end, the committee approved Brandeis on a straight party-line vote, and the Senate confirmed him four months after his nomination, still the longest time between nomination and confirmation.[29]

Harlan Fiske Stone, nominated by President Calvin Coolidge in 1925, would be the first nominee to testify before the Judiciary Committee. Stone answered questions focused on his involvement with the Teapot Dome scandal during his time as attorney general. In 1939, a Franklin Roosevelt nominee, Felix Frankfurter, would become the first to take "virtually unrestricted questions" during open and public committee hearings. Frankfurter was a Jewish immigrant, a longtime Harvard law professor, and a confidant to FDR. Opposition was not only overtly political, with accusations that Frankfurter was a communist, but also in part explicitly anti-Semitic. Pressed by a senator, a witness named Allen A. Zoll explained his opposition to Frankfurter: "There are two reasons why I opposed [Frankfurter's] appointment. . . . One is because I believe his record proves him unfitted for the position, irrespective of his race, and the other is because of his race." While there are many "fine Jews," Zoll continued, Frankfurter was one of those Jews "fostering movements that are subversive to the Government." The Senate, in control of New Dealers, nonetheless confirmed Frankfurter.[30]

Nominee testimony became customary only in 1955, with President Dwight Eisenhower's nomination of John Marshall Harlan II. Again, political outlooks shaped the inquiry, though it was more the Court than Harlan himself that provoked the committee questioning. The Warren Court had recently decided *Brown v. Board of Education* (*Brown I*), which held that separate-but-equal public schools violated the Fourteenth Amendment and equal protection. *Brown I*, though, had not specified a remedy for the constitutional violation, and furious southern Democratic senators sought to delay and resist the implications of the decision. The Court would eventually decide *Brown v. Board of Education* (*Brown II*) and order legally segregated school districts to desegregate with all deliberate speed, but the Harlan hearings occurred prior to that decision. Mississippi Senator James Eastland repeatedly asked Harlan questions that underscored his belief that the Court had acted politically and had failed to follow the rule of law. Eastland asked Harlan, for instance, whether he agreed that the Court "should change established interpretations of the Constitution to accord with the economic, political, or sociological views of those who from time to time constitute the membership of the Court." The Senate would confirm Harlan, but the wideranging jurisprudential questions would set a precedent for future Judiciary Committee hearings.[31]

The four-year period from 1967 to 1970 produced seven nominations, four of which failed. The first nomination was of Thurgood Marshall, by President Lyndon B. Johnson. Marshall not only was the first black Supreme Court nominee; he also had been the lead attorney for the National Association for the Advancement of Colored People's Legal Defense Fund in the *Brown* cases. Given this, his confirmation process cannot be understood without accounting for the changing racial politics of the 1960s. After the Court decided *Brown II* in 1955, ordering desegregation with all deliberate speed, many white southerners hostilely resisted social change, thwarting civil rights protesters with force, intimidation, and legal sanctions. By the late 1950s and early 1960s, many Americans were witnessing these atrocities on television, which by then had become the primary source of news. Every night, white and black Americans recoiled in horror as they watched southern government officials assail black (and white) protesters with billy clubs, fire hoses, and attack dogs. By the mid-1960s, unprecedented national support for legal and social changes existed. Led by President Johnson, a national political coalition pushed for civil rights reforms, producing significant constitutional and legislative changes. The Twenty-third Amendment, ratified in 1961, extended a right to vote in presidential elections to citizens in the heavily black District of Columbia, and the Twenty-fourth Amendment, ratified in 1964, proscribed poll taxes in federal elections. The Civil Rights Act of 1964, in part, prohibited discrimination "on the ground of race, color, religion, or national origin" in employment and in places of public accommodation, such as hotels and restaurants. The Voting Rights Act of 1965 (VRA) and other parts of the Civil Rights Act eradicated literacy, educational, and character tests that had been used to deny or discourage people of color from voting. The VRA was soon changing American government. The number of black Americans elected to state legislatures and Congress more than doubled between 1966 and 1973. Even in a Deep South state such as Mississippi, the percentage of black Americans registered to vote jumped from 6.7 percent in 1964 to 66.5 percent in 1969.[32]

When Johnson nominated Marshall in the summer of 1967, the nation was in the midst of these revolutionary racial and political changes. While much of the nation supported the transition, many white southerners still resisted. Southern senators were quick to use the Marshall hearings to express their lingering hostility toward him and the Court's *Brown* decision for undermining the racial caste system codified in the Jim Crow laws. The first blow against Marshall came even before the hearings began, from a Louisiana representative speaking on the House floor. After complaining about race riots and increased crime, John Rarick proclaimed that "the American people are now forced to tolerate more salt in their despairing wounds by suffering one of the originators and activists of the problem that now plagues America . . . [who] upset 180 years of law and order in the nonlegal decision known as *Brown against the Board of Education*, by the use of intentionally misrepresented facts and suppressed truths." South Carolina Senator Strom Thurmond was one of the most belligerent opponents of Marshall. Thurmond had left the Democratic Party and become a Republican in 1964 because of his opposition to civil rights. He would later publish a book attacking the Warren Court and the *Brown* decision. "The most devastating and relentless assault on the Constitution is coming from the Supreme Court itself," he would write.[33] During Marshall's confirmation hearings, Thurmond bombarded the nominee with more than sixty questions about the historical details of the Reconstruction amendments (the Thirteenth, Fourteenth, and Fifteenth Amendments). For instance, "Turning to the provision of the Thirteenth Amendment forbidding involuntary servitude, are you familiar with any pre-1860 cases which interpreted this language?" And "[W]hat committee reported out the Fourteenth Amendment and who were its members?" And "Why do you think the Equal Protection Clause of the original draft of the first section of the Fourteenth Amendment required equal protection in the rights of life, liberty and property only?" Marshall repeatedly responded by admitting that he could not answer these questions. In the end, Thurmond pronounced: "I think it is a fair observation to say that the nominee displayed a surprising, for him, lack of knowledge of the area in which he is almost daily depicted as the outstanding scholar." Other senators reiterated the assertion that *Brown* had violated the law-politics dichotomy; that the Court had ignored the Constitution and decades of precedents in repudiating the separate-but-equal doctrine. North Carolina Senator Sam Ervin asked Marshall whether the Court had "failed in recent years to confine itself to its allotted constitutional sphere, that of interpreting the Constitution rightly?"[34]

Despite this truculent southern opposition to Marshall, the strong national coalition favoring civil rights led to Marshall's Senate confirmation. Johnson's next nominee, Abe Fortas—nominated to move from an associate's to the chief justice's chair—would not fare as well. In March 1968, Johnson announced he would not seek a second term, largely because of the swirling controversy of the Vietnam War. On June 13, 1968, Chief Justice Warren notified Johnson that he planned to retire, "effective at your leisure." Johnson chose his close friend, Justice Fortas, to become the chief justice and simultaneously nominated "old crony" Homer Thornberry to fill Fortas's associate position. Republican senators were anticipating a presidential election victory by Richard Nixon and wanted him to nominate a chief justice.

Regardless, Johnson was a renowned political master with deep knowledge of Senate procedures, so he anticipated having both Fortas and Thornberry soon confirmed. Johnson, though, made numerous political miscalculations, with several senators mounting unexpected opposition. In his lame-duck position, Johnson was unable to manipulate and control senators and congressmen as he had previously done. And as with Marshall's confirmation, Thurmond and other southern senators on both sides of the aisle used the Fortas hearings as an opportunity to condemn the Warren Court. The hatred of the Warren Court extended well beyond *Brown* to decisions protecting voting rights (one person, one vote), free speech, and the rights of criminal defendants. Fortas had been part of the Warren Court only since 1965, but he was questioned and criticized for many decisions issued prior to that year. Some senators were angry because Fortas had continued advising Johnson after becoming an associate justice, though many prior justices had performed similar political functions both publicly and privately—behind closed doors, so to speak. Other senators became alarmed when they learned Fortas had accepted $15,000 for delivering a series of university lectures. The committee eventually approved Fortas, but a filibuster stopped him on the Senate floor. When a cloture vote failed to end the filibuster, Fortas and Johnson withdrew the nomination. With that, the Thornberry nomination was terminated. Several months later, *Life* magazine reported that Fortas had received a $20,000 fee from a financier who would be convicted of securities fraud. Fortas soon resigned.[35]

Ironically (or tragically), Fortas's travails led first Warren and then Chief Justice Warren Burger to seek resolutions requiring justices to file annual financial disclosures. Justices nowadays regularly reap substantial income from speaking engagements, adjunct teaching, writing, and gifts. In 2016, when Scalia passed away at a Texas resort, he was staying for free in a $700 per night room.[36]

President Nixon had successfully filled the chief justiceship with Burger, but he needed three tries to fill Fortas's seat. Nixon first nominated Clement Haynsworth, a conservative southerner. Senate questioning focused on his business dealings and controversial positions on civil rights. Nixon complained about the "'brutal' and 'vicious' politics," but to no avail. The Senate voted against confirmation. Nixon next nominated Harrold Carswell, another southerner. Soon after he was nominated, it was learned that he had explicitly approved white supremacy several years earlier. Given the broad acceptance of *Brown* and civil rights, he, too, went down to Senate defeat. Nixon finally nominated Harry Blackmun, and the Senate confirmed.[37]

This brief historical review of the nomination and confirmation processes underscores that political ideologies always infuse the makeup of the Court. If anything, then, the most bizarre aspect of the Bork rejection was not the political aspect of his hearings but, rather, his accusation that Democrats had somehow warped the process—and the willingness of conservative Republicans to continue this trope ever since. If Supreme Court decision making were truly apolitical, in accord with the law-politics dichotomy, then the political jockeying over the appointments of justices throughout American history would be nonsensical. As it turns out, from "1789 to 2017, Presidents have made 162 nominations to the Court. [The] Senate confirmed 125 of these nominations, or roughly three-fourths." In other words, the Senate did not confirm almost one-quarter of the presidential choices: thirty-seven nominees. The assertion that confirmation hearings have only recently become political is patently false. In fact, the rejection rate was slightly higher during the nineteenth century than during the twentieth and twenty-first centuries. Yet, as previously mentioned, the politics surrounding each nomination and confirmation varies in accord with the contemporary political issues that seem most pressing. Are senators brooding about the Jay Treaty, the nominee's religion, the nominee's race, *Brown* and racial segregation, or *Roe* and abortion? Over the past thirty years or so, since the rejection of Bork, crucial changes in the nomination and confirmation processes have revolved around the changing nature of American politics. In particular, the nation has become increasingly polarized, and that polarization has affected the appointment of new justices, as well as the Court's decision making.[38]

FOR SCHOLARS

The law-politics dynamic presents a potential problem for law professors, political scientists, and other scholars interested in studying Supreme Court adjudication. Many scholars display "irrational exuberance" in their efforts to describe and study adjudication as either pure law or pure politics. They seek to deny one part of the law-politics dynamic and to focus exclusively on the other. One reason for such exuberance is the drive for discipline. When a student is educated in an academic or professional discipline, the student is simultaneously empowered and constrained. The tools or methods of the discipline—for instance, political science—enable the student to study events or phenomena in a new and often enlightening way. Novel insights into the events or phenomena become possible. At the same time, the student is trained to use the particular disciplinary tools rather than other tools or methods. If the disciplinary methods cannot be brought to bear on a question, then the question cannot be pursued. Indeed, a scholar who does not use the proper methods is likely to be, in a literal sense, disciplined. Colleagues in the field will not respect the rogue scholar's work. If the rogue seeks to publish a paper in a peer-reviewed journal, colleagues will reject the manuscript. For this reason, academic and professional disciplines naturally tend to become increasingly specialized, isolated, and parochial.[39]

In short, disciplinary methods channel scholars to understand phenomena, such as judicial decision making, in particular ways. The tools we possess direct or influence our outlook and behavior. If I have a hammer, then I am looking for a nail. If I have a screwdriver, then I am looking for a screw. If I have a hammer but find only a screw, I will probably try hammering it anyway. The distinct disciplinary methods of law and political science inevitably push law professors and political scientists to perceive and study adjudication differently. Put in different words, education and training in their distinct disciplines engender different interpretive horizons for law professors and political scientists. Indeed, their respective disciplinary methods can push law professors and political scientists to seek purity in adjudication. Law professors have been educated to focus on the rule of law. They were trained to parse cases, decipher complex statutes, and carefully read the Constitution and other texts. Law professors were educated to denounce politics as fouling the adjudicative process. Politics, from this perspective, is foreign to judicial decision making. Meanwhile, political scientists have been educated to study politics, especially as manifested in government institutions. When political scientists study the government institution of the courts, including the Supreme Court, they are inclined to see politics at play. And some political scientists are likely to be skeptical of judicial declarations concerning legal principles and doctrines.[40]

These disciplinary urges lead to efforts to police the law-politics dichotomy—or, that is, to deny the law-politics dynamic at the heart of adjudication. The nature of legal interpretation inextricably links law and politics in judicial decision making. Yet many law professors and political scientists have sought their own purities for decades, and some inevitably will continue to do so in the future. For those inclined toward the extremes, their disciplinary drives pressure them to focus on either the rule of law or the rule of politics. On the political science side, Jeffrey A. Segal and Harold J. Spaeth most notably maintain not only that Supreme Court justices vote their political preferences, but that "traditional legal factors, such as precedent, text, and intent, [have] virtually no impact" on Supreme Court decision making.[41] On the law side, constitutional originalists are merely the latest legal scholars to claim they can purify legal interpretation of political influence. Most originalists insist that they can discern a fixed and objective constitutional meaning. Randy Barnett, a leading originalist, explicitly argued that the "appeal of originalism rests on the proposition that the original public meaning is an objective fact." Politics, then, is supposedly banished from legal interpretation (including, in particular, constitutional interpretation).[42]

To be sure, law professors and political scientists can continue to separate law and politics in their studies of Supreme Court decision making. They can be purists, relying respectively on all-law or all-politics approaches, or they can be oil-and-water scholars, mixing law and politics but ultimately deeming them independent and separable. And realistically, we should expect many legal scholars and political scientists to continue along these well-worn paths partly because it is easier to do so than to strike out in different directions. Political scientists refer to this phenomenon as path dependence. Institutional arrangements develop because individuals naturally follow behavioral patterns they have previously followed. The past facilitates the present and the future. In light of path dependence, one should expect many legal scholars and political scientists to follow the paths of their respective disciplines. This disciplinary loyalty is not necessarily bad. A hammer works well if one finds a nail. Disciplines provide tools that can generate knowledge. To take one example, political scientists' methods of quantification have led to valuable insights about the persistent influence of politics on Supreme Court adjudication. Thus, following their disciplinary paths, purists and oil-and-water scholars can continue to make important contributions to our knowledge of judicial decision making.[43]

Yet these scholars will nonetheless be omitting a large part of the Court's decision making. Disciplines provide methods for gaining knowledge but simultaneously constrain the outlooks (or horizons) of practitioners. A political scientist committed to quantification methods will limit his or her research to events or causes that can be reduced to numeric data (read: quantified).[44] Quite obviously, a purist, rejecting interdisciplinary approaches, will leave much of the Supreme Court puzzle scattered and unexamined. All-law scholars will be blind to political influences on Supreme Court adjudication, while all-politics scholars will continue to dismiss legal reasoning in judicial opinions as either subterfuge or delusional nonsense. Oil-and-water scholars at least will account for both law and politics, but they nonetheless will disregard the emulsification of the two within the adjudicative process.[45]

Law and politics *together* course through Supreme Court decisions and opinions. And only a scholar who recognizes the fully integrated emulsion will be able to explore the richness of the law-politics dynamic. How might such a scholar account for the law-politics dynamic when studying or teaching a constitutional law decision? Consider the landmark *Marbury v. Madison*. A law professor could study or teach *Marbury* by focusing on the legal doctrine of judicial review, explaining the Court's power to review government actions and invalidate those it deems unconstitutional. This law approach would emphasize Chief Justice John Marshall's multiple arguments for judicial review based on the language of the constitutional text. Or a political scientist could study or teach *Marbury* by emphasizing the political conflict that had developed during the 1790s between the Federalists, led by Alexander Hamilton and John Adams, and the Republicans, led by Thomas Jefferson and James Madison (discussed in Chapters 2 and 4). From this perspective, *Marbury* pitted a Federalist chief justice, Marshall, against the Republican president, Jefferson, and secretary of state, Madison. But either of these approaches to teaching *Marbury* would miss a large part of the story—namely, the law-politics dynamic. Marshall interpreted the constitutional text, particularly article III on judicial power, but he did not discover some fixed and objective meaning. The text did not explicitly grant the Court the power of judicial review over either the executive branch or Congress. Yet Marshall's reading of the Constitution was reasonable and in accord with a developing contemporary understanding of the judiciary's role in American government. Simultaneously, Marshall's conclusions that the Court had the power of judicial review over the executive branch and Congress corresponded with his Federalist political orientation. Might Marshall have repudiated judicial review if he had been a Republican? We cannot know for certain, but we can recognize that Marshall walked a legal tightrope over a political minefield of Republican opposition. While reasonably interpreting the constitutional text to reach doctrinal conclusions consistent with his political ideology, he ultimately gave Jefferson and Madison their desired result.

He held that the Court lacked jurisdiction to grant the requested relief to a Federalist appointee, William Marbury, who hoped to secure a position as a justice of the peace in Washington, DC.[46]

A second example is *United States v. Lopez*, a landmark commerce power case. *Lopez* held that Congress had exceeded its commerce power when it enacted the Gun-Free School Zones Act (GFSZA), a generally applicable law proscribing the possession of firearms at school. A political scientist could describe *Lopez* as a bald political decision. When the Court decided this case, in 1995, political conservatives were in the midst of an attack against so-called big government. They constantly criticized Congress, in particular, for its attempts at progressive social engineering. They traced expansive congressional power to the New Deal and denounced the Court's 1937 acceptance of such power (and pluralist democracy). One can, therefore, readily analyze *Lopez* from this political perspective. The five conservative justices (Scalia, Kennedy, Clarence Thomas, Sandra Day O'Connor, and William Rehnquist, who wrote the majority opinion) outvoted the four progressive justices (John Paul Stevens, David Souter, Stephen Breyer, and Ginsburg) and reached the conservative conclusion. They invalidated progressive legislation and constrained congressional power, and in so doing chipped away at big government.[47]

But this political analysis does not explain the landmark status of *Lopez*, which revolves around legal doctrine. Rehnquist's majority opinion began by presenting the Commerce Clause text and asserting that the Court would apply it in accord with a rational basis test, the doctrine the Court had consistently applied in commerce power cases since 1937. Unlike in many of those post-1937 cases, however, Rehnquist did not apply the rational basis test as a mechanism of judicial deference to congressional judgment and the democratic process. With only two exceptions—and the Court had quickly overruled one of the two—the post-1937 Court had upheld every congressional action taken pursuant to the commerce power. If the people did not like congressional action, the Court had consistently reasoned, then the people could vote for new legislators. But in *Lopez*, Rehnquist reformulated the rational basis test rather than deferring to Congress and the democratic process. In so doing, Rehnquist added formalist distinctions that resonated with pre-1937 (*Lochner*-era) Supreme Court commerce power decisions—distinctions that the post-1937 Court had repudiated. For instance, Rehnquist relied on an ostensible dichotomy separating economic from noneconomic activities; he reasoned that gun possession at schools (the subject matter of the GFSZA) is a noneconomic enterprise unrelated to commerce. To Rehnquist, "economic" and "noneconomic" were a priori categories, and gun possession could readily be placed in one (noneconomic) rather than the other (economic). Breyer's (progressive) dissent argued contrariwise, rejecting the majority's formalist approach. Breyer emphasized that, from a practical standpoint, the effects of educational activities closely and realistically intertwine with economic (commercial) development. "Schools that teach reading, writing, mathematics, and related basic skills serve *both* social and commercial purposes, and one cannot easily separate the one from the other." Disregarding this criticism, Rehnquist used similar pre-1937 formalism when he reasoned that gun possession at schools is a local rather than a national matter and thus falls outside Congress's commerce power. His distinction between "what is truly national and what is truly local" echoed language from the Court's 1918 decision in *Hammer v. Dagenhart*, which held that Congress had exceeded its commerce power by regulating child labor. Indeed, Rehnquist cited numerous pre- and post-1937 commerce power decisions to support his reformulation of the rational basis test into a type of formalist doctrine.[48]

The most interesting aspect of *Lopez* was neither the doctrine, standing alone, nor the political orientation, standing alone. Rather, it was the law-politics dynamic—the interrelationship of the law and the politics. Rehnquist and the other conservative justices started with a rational basis doctrine that had exemplified judicial restraint and deference to democracy and manifested progressive political acceptance of government. They transformed it into a doctrine implementing aggressive judicial oversight of and limitations on congressional power and embodying politically conservative distrust of government. Rehnquist's choice of relevant precedents—both pre- and post-1937—manifested the justices' concern for the legal doctrine, including the precise reformulation of the rational basis test as encompassing formalist distinctions. Moreover, the law-politics dynamic underscores that *Lopez* had potentially significant legal *and* political consequences for the future. In particular, the *Lopez*-reformulated rational basis doctrine has guided courts in subsequent cases to invalidate congressional actions. To be sure, the doctrine does not render these conservative conclusions inevitable, but they became more likely after than before *Lopez*.[49]

The concepts of the law-politics dynamic and politics writ small suggest an additional insight about the interaction of politics and law over time. When the justices interpret the law and decide a case in accord with politics writ small, their political orientations tend to be shaped by current political disputes. For example, from the late 1960s to the early 1980s, conservatives railed against the supposed activism of the Warren Court and early Burger Court. This attack on activism led conservative jurists and legal scholars to advocate for judicial restraint: The justices should defer to legislative judgments rather than impose their own political preferences. For example, in commercial speech cases of the late 1970s and early 1980s, Rehnquist argued that the Court ought to defer to legislatively imposed restrictions on commercial advertising. But political outlooks frequently change more rapidly and readily than do legal doctrines, which are solidified pursuant to the doctrine of stare decisis. Consequently, doctrine that appears to have a conservative (or progressive) slant today might appear differently tomorrow, as the surrounding political environment changes.[50]

Gonzales v. Raich, a commerce power case decided after *Lopez*, demonstrates how doctrinal frameworks can slide in unexpected political directions because of changing contexts. *Raich* presented conservatives (and progressives) with a paradox because the challengers argued that Congress had exceeded its power by enacting a law that proscribed the possession of marijuana. The conservative justices generally would lean toward restricting congressional power, as they had in *Lopez*, but some of those same conservative justices might also wish to allow the government to impose moral values (law and order) by restricting the use of drugs. In the end, the moderately conservative Kennedy flipped his vote and joined the progressive justices to uphold the statute. Justice Stevens wrote a majority opinion that retained the *Lopez* doctrinal framework but reasoned that marijuana possession substantially affected interstate commerce. Even Scalia voted to uphold this congressional statute, though he refused to join Stevens's opinion. Instead, Scalia's concurrence (in the judgment only) emphasized that the case raised a factually unique situation in which the Necessary and Proper Clause empowered Congress to regulate drug possession. Scalia refused to interpret the *Lopez* doctrine, the reformulated rational basis test, to allow expansive congressional power under the Commerce Clause. From Scalia's perspective, the case had almost no precedential value. And notwithstanding *Raich*, the Rehnquist and Roberts Courts have displayed an aggressive conservative righteousness in congressional power cases that contrasts sharply and ironically with the conservative calls for judicial restraint during the Warren and Burger Court years.[51]

These examples—*Marbury*, *Lopez*, and *Raich*—suggest that scholars (and teachers) should devote less energy to reinforcing or policing the law-politics dichotomy and more to exploring the law-politics dynamic. When scholars deflect or deny the law-politics dynamic, they are likely to miss crucial aspects of legal developments—namely, the distinct ways in which law and politics interact in Supreme Court decision making. When law professors, in particular, propagate a pure-law account of Supreme Court decisions, we implicitly encourage disregard of the social, economic, and political contexts and ramifications of the cases. If we study and teach constitutional law and other subjects solely by parsing precedents and analyzing legal doctrines, we present a partial and misleading depiction of the Court's adjudicative process.[52]

The recognition of the law-politics dynamic has one final and important ramification that still needs to be explored: The very conservative Roberts Court has handed down a large number of significantly conservative judicial decisions. Given the political nature of Supreme Court decision making (politics writ small), the arrant conservatism of the Roberts Court demands a political (progressive) response by Democrats. The Roberts Court's conservatism is the subject of the next chapter.

THE ROBERTS COURT'S
CONSERVATISM

Politics has always pervaded the Court's makeup, as well as the Court's decision-making process. As shown in this book's historical chapters (Chapters 2–4) and analytical chapters (Chapters 5 and 6), the law-politics dichotomy is a myth; for that reason, the primary criticism of court packing falls. Court packing cannot destroy the purity of the Court as a legal-judicial institution because the Court has never been pure—that is, free of politics. Court packing, then, is justifiable as a general matter. But is court packing justified today, in our current political circumstances? In other words, should the Democrats pack the Court when they have the opportunity? This chapter answers that question by surveying numerous Roberts Court decisions. This survey demonstrates that the Roberts Court's conservatism is so deep and wide that Democratic court packing is justified.

Most important, the Roberts Court has decided cases that protect an undemocratic society in which wealthy white Christian men consistently emerge victorious. This chapter emphasizes constitutional decisions, though it mentions several others. The chapter specifically discusses the following: the Court's denigration of democratic government; the Court's protection of wealth and the economic marketplace; the Court's failure to protect women; the Court's protection of whites and disregard for people of color; and the Court's protection of Christianity but not non-Christian religions. A final section of the chapter examines counterexamples: Roberts Court decisions that might be deemed liberal or progressive. As will be explained, even these decisions often harbor significant conservative elements. All in all, the conservative justices of the Roberts Court have regularly delivered conservative judicial decisions and constructed conservative constitutional doctrines that, if left untouched, can lead to conservative results in the Supreme Court and the lower courts for decades.

JUDICIAL DENIGRATION OF DEMOCRATIC GOVERNMENT

Many of the Roberts Court's decisions resonate with a decades-long conservative commitment to neoliberal ideology. Neoliberalism is laissez-faire on steroids. Like laissez-faire, neoliberalism celebrates the wonders of the economic marketplace. Neoliberals agree with the laissez-faire concept of the invisible hand operating through the free market to naturally generate individual satisfaction and societal good. In 1976, the economist Milton Friedman offered this prototypical tribute to the invisible hand and free market: "The market, with each individual going his own way, with no central authority setting social priorities, avoiding duplication, and coordinating activities, looks like chaos to the naked eye. Yet through [Adam] Smith's eyes we see that it is a finely ordered and delicately tuned system . . . which enables the dispersed knowledge and skill of millions of people to be coordinated for a common purpose."[1]

Yet neoliberals do not stop with such encomiums to the economic marketplace. They continue by demonizing democratic government. Friedrich Hayek denounced government regulation and control as hubris. "Human reason can neither predict nor deliberately shape its own future," he wrote in 1960. "Progress by its very nature cannot be planned." The real world is too complex for government to predict and direct. Even seemingly rational designs go awry.

Friedman goes as far as to describe an inverse (and perverse) invisible hand operating through democratic processes. This "invisible hand in politics . . . is as potent a force for harm as the invisible hand in economics is for good." Even if government actors have the best of intentions, he argues, they inevitably pursue harmful goals. Elected government officials "become the front-men for special interests they would never knowingly serve." Government attempts to plan rationally for progress necessarily end in disaster.[2]

In short, neoliberals are market fundamentalists. They insist that the best society is one that leaves the maximum degree of decision making to the marketplace and the minimum to politics and government. The marketplace is rational and efficient. Because of hard work and merit, each individual earns his or her successes—and failures. Democracy, meanwhile, is necessarily corrupt and inefficient. According to Arthur Brooks, former president of the American Enterprise Institute, "The best government philosophy is one that starts every day with the question, 'What can we do today to get out of Americans' way?'"[3]

Given the ostensible functionality of the marketplace and dysfunctionality of democratic government, the Supreme Court has been restricting, denigrating, and disregarding democratic processes and government for more than twenty-five years, first under Chief Justice William Rehnquist and now under Chief Justice John Roberts. Judicial conservatism has not always frowned on democracy in this way. Starting in the 1960s, conservatives consistently attacked the Warren Court and the early Burger Court for supposedly being liberal activist courts—for ignoring the rule of law while implementing a liberal legal and social agenda. From this conservative standpoint, the Court was generally to exercise judicial restraint, deferring to the democratic process. Let the people's elected representatives decide societal values and goals. But under Rehnquist, the Court in the 1990s implicitly repudiated this form of judicial conservatism. As discussed in Chapter 1, ever since the conservative Clarence Thomas replaced the progressive Thurgood Marshall in 1991, conservative blocs of justices have controlled the Court. And with that control, the conservatives shifted from judicial restraint to a judicial outlook manifesting the neoliberal hostility toward democratic government—what might be called "abusive judicial review," issuing decisions that denigrate and weaken rather than protect and strengthen democracy.[4]

Under Rehnquist, in cases such as *United States v. Lopez*, discussed in Chapter 6, the Court interpreted the Commerce Clause so as to restrict congressional power. In cases such as *Printz v. United States*, also discussed in Chapter 6, the Court interpreted the Tenth Amendment as barring Congress from commandeering state and local officials to follow congressional directives. In other cases, the Court narrowed congressional power to enforce the equal-protection and due-process guarantees of the Fourteenth Amendment.[5] Systematically limiting Congress's reach, the Rehnquist Court resurrected judicial methods that the conservative *Lochner*-era Court had used to invalidate government actions. First, the Court began to define and enforce formalist legal categories rather than examining the empirical effects or consequences of the congressionally regulated activities (such as bringing a gun to school). Formalism contains an inherent political tilt favoring those who already wield power in the private sphere (again, as discussed in Chapter 6). Wealthy, white, mainstream Christian, straight men consistently win, while the conservative justices ostensibly legitimate their conclusions pursuant to formal legal rules.[6]

Second, the Rehnquist Court in the 1990s began questioning Congress's competence to deliberate and find facts in support of its legislative actions.[7] Conservative political commentators had long been criticizing Congress for its attempts at social engineering, especially for progressive objectives. As discussed in Chapter 6, most conservatives traced expansive congressional power to the New Deal and denounced the Court's 1937 acceptance of such power. Conservative scholars called for the Court to reverse "the mistakes of 1937." From the conservative vantage, Congress repeatedly got things wrong, not only by pursuing the wrong goals, but by passing laws that produced unforeseen detrimental consequences. For instance, progressives intended race-based affirmative action programs to increase equality, but conservatives charged that such programs (whether congressionally or otherwise imposed) produced instead both a culture of victimhood among its beneficiaries and a sense of resentment among whites.[8]

The Roberts Court has pushed both of these conservative judicial methods even further in invalidating progressive congressional actions. In *National Federation of Independent Business v. Sebelius*, the Roberts Court dealt with the constitutionality of the Patient Protection and Affordable Care Act (ACA), a flagship accomplishment of President Barack Obama's administration. Congress enacted the ACA to increase the number of Americans covered by health insurance and to decrease the cost of health care. Two key provisions in the statute were an individual mandate and a Medicaid expansion. The individual mandate required most Americans to maintain "minimum essential" health insurance coverage. If an individual was not exempt from the mandate, he or she could satisfy it by purchasing insurance from a private company. Starting in 2014, individuals who did not comply with the mandate were required to pay a "penalty" to the Internal Revenue Service along with their taxes. The Medicaid program, in general, offered federal funding to states primarily to assist the poor in obtaining medical care. The ACA expanded the scope of the Medicaid program by increasing the number of covered individuals. As described by Roberts, "[T]he Act requires state programs to provide Medicaid coverage to adults with incomes up to 133 percent of the federal poverty level, whereas many States now cover adults with children only if their income is considerably lower, and do not cover childless adults at all."[9]

Focusing first on the individual mandate and Congress's commerce power, Roberts's opinion extended the Rehnquist Court's formalist reasoning to constrain Congress. *Lopez* had reformulated the post-1937 rational basis test to incorporate formalist dichotomies, sharply distinguishing economic from noneconomic activities and national from local activities.

Ironically, although the conservative justices of the Rehnquist Court had crafted the *Lopez*-reformulated rational basis doctrine as a means to diminish congressional commerce power, the *Lopez* doctrine loomed as an obstacle for the conservative *Sebelius* justices. One could strongly argue that, pursuant to *Lopez*, the ACA's individual mandate was a constitutional exercise of the commerce power. Indeed, Justice Ginsburg articulated this precise argument in her opinion, concurring in part and dissenting in part. Under *Lopez*, any economic activity that is national in scope and has substantial effects on interstate commerce falls within Congress's power. Ginsburg wrote: "Straightforward application of these principles would require the Court to hold that the minimum coverage [individual mandate] provision is proper Commerce Clause legislation." The health-care market is clearly economic and national. Moreover, those individuals who choose to go uninsured but inevitably, at some point, avail themselves of medical services substantially affect commerce in the health-care market. Health-care providers raise their prices and insurance companies increase their premiums so that insured individuals pay extra to cover costs for the uninsured. "Congress found that the cost-shifting . . . 'increases family [insurance] premiums by on average over $1,000 a year.'" Quite reasonably, then, Ginsburg maintained that "Congress had a rational basis for concluding that the uninsured, as a class, substantially affect interstate commerce."[10]

In other words, conservative justices had honed the *Lopez* doctrine to constrain Congress's commerce power, but in *Sebelius* the application of the reformulated rational basis test suggested that Congress had acted constitutionally. Yet by extending the *Lopez* formalist reasoning, Roberts (and the other four conservative justices) ultimately concluded that Congress had exceeded its commerce power. More specifically, in *Sebelius* Roberts invoked two formalist distinctions that the *Lopez* Court had not mentioned. First, Roberts distinguished action from inaction. He reasoned that Congress has always been limited to regulating *activity* under its commerce power; Congress cannot regulate *inactivity*. But the ACA's individual mandate would force inactive individuals to enter or become active in the health insurance market. People who had not bought and did not want to buy health insurance would be forced to do so. The other conservative justices (the joint dissenters) completely agreed with Roberts on this point, even though they did not join his opinion.[11] Meanwhile, Ginsburg argued otherwise. She pointed out that Congress, on multiple occasions in the past, had in fact ordered individuals to act, even when the individuals might prefer not to do so. She offered several examples, including the 1792 Militia Act, which required individuals "to purchase firearms and gear in anticipation of service in the Militia." Roberts responded by reasoning that in none of these instances, including the Militia Act, had Congress acted pursuant to its commerce power. In other words, from Roberts's perspective, Congress could in general force individuals to take action but could not do so when invoking its commerce power.[12]

Roberts also relied on a formalist distinction between regulation and creation. The Constitution grants Congress the power to "regulate commerce," Roberts reasoned, but not to create it. Under the ACA, he continued, Congress was attempting to create commercial activity where none previously existed. And again, the other conservative justices completely agreed with Roberts on this point. "To be sure," wrote the joint dissenters, "purchasing insurance is 'Commerce'; but one does not regulate commerce that does not exist by compelling its existence."[13]

In sum, with regard to the Commerce Clause, *Sebelius* marks a doctrinal turn that can restrain congressional power even more than *Lopez* did. First, the justices (or other judges) might invoke the specific *Sebelius* distinctions or categories in future cases as a means to limit Congress. Second, the justices have demonstrated their willingness to use formalist-style reasoning to generate additional categories that can further constrain congressional power. In a future case, one should not be surprised if the justices invalidate a congressional action by invoking a formalist distinction or category that appears in neither *Lopez* nor *Sebelius*.[14]

Congress invoked its spending power to justify its enactment of the ACA Medicaid expansion. Before 1937, the Court had held that Congress had broad power to spend, but also that the Tenth Amendment protection of state sovereignty limited such power. In *United States v. Butler*, decided in 1936, the Court held unconstitutional the Agricultural Adjustment Act of 1933, which provided subsidies to farmers in order to stabilize agricultural production. In the first part of the opinion, the *Butler* Court reasoned that Congress's spending did not have to be directly linked to or in furtherance of Congress's other expressly enumerated powers. Instead, Congress could spend for the general welfare. Nonetheless, the Court continued by applying the Tenth Amendment protection of state sovereignty in a formalist fashion. Specifically, the Court reasoned that all forms of "production," including agricultural production, were inherently a matter of "state concern" and thus beyond congressional control.[15]

Starting in 1937, the Court continued to recognize broad spending power in Congress while repudiating its formalist interpretation of the Tenth Amendment. As with the commerce power, post-1937, limitations on the spending power arose from the democratic process rather than by judicial imposition. All congressional spending for the general welfare would be judicially upheld as long as the congressional act did not violate another constitutional provision, such as the First Amendment.[16] Moreover, pursuant to its broad spending power, Congress could attach conditions to grants or subsidies that it offered to state and local governments. In such instances, Congress had to express the condition "unambiguously." Furthermore, the condition had to be related to the purpose of the spending program, broadly construed. For instance, Congress could condition funding to state governments for highways by requiring the states to set certain speed limits, but Congress could not condition highway funds on a state's expressed stance on abortion. In one case, the Court upheld a condition on highway funds that required states to set a drinking age of twenty-one because, the Court reasoned, drinking was related to highway safety.[17]

Despite Congress's expansive spending power, Roberts (and the joint dissenters) held in *Sebelius* that Congress had exceeded its power by enacting the Medicaid expansion. How did Roberts reach this result? He began by acknowledging that, since 1937, the Court had not invalidated exercises of Congress's spending power, but he also emphasized that the spending power was not beyond judicial limits. The limits, Roberts explained, arise from the Tenth Amendment concern with protecting "the status of the States as independent sovereigns in our federal system." Roberts here returned to a pre-1937 concern, as he had done when discussing the commerce power. Moreover, in interpreting the specific limits that the Tenth Amendment imposes on Congress's spending power, Roberts continued along this pre-1937 path by once again invoking a formalist distinction. He distinguished congressional "pressure" from congressional "compulsion"—or, as he phrased it elsewhere in his opinion, "encouragement" versus "coercion." Congress can provide financial incentives that pressure or encourage states to take certain actions, but Congress cannot compel or coerce state government actions. At some point, Roberts reasoned, congressional (financial) incentives cross the line from encouragement to compulsion.[18]

In this case, Congress claimed that the ACA merely amended or modified the Medicaid program. The act encouraged states to expand the scope of Medicaid by providing additional funds. But Roberts reasoned that the ACA imposed such severe costs on noncomplying states that the act's Medicaid expansion should be deemed a completely separate program (rather than a modification of the existing Medicaid program). Any state that did not comply with the Medicaid expansion would not merely lose the funding that Congress had offered for the expansion; the state would also lose all of its current Medicaid funding. According to Roberts, the potential loss in federal funding for the states was so severe as to preclude any real choice. As Roberts put it, the Medicaid expansion was "a gun to the head." Imagine that you are walking down the street when a thief jumps out of the shadows, points a gun at you, and says, "Give me your wallet." In a sense, you can choose whether or not to give the thief your wallet. Yet this predicament does not present a true choice because you do not have a reasonable alternative to relinquishing your wallet. Roberts concluded that, with the ACA Medicaid expansion, Congress had crossed the line from encouragement to coercion. And again, the joint dissenters agreed with Roberts on this point while also admitting that this conclusion was novel in the post-1937 legal world. Unquestionably, though, as with the commerce power, the *Sebelius* Court constrained Congress's spending power by articulating (or resurrecting) formalist limits that hark back to the pre-1937 era.[19]

Congress invoked not only its commerce power but also its taxing power in enacting the ACA's individual mandate. Given that article I, section 8, clause 1 refers jointly to Congress's powers to tax and to spend, the two powers are typically lumped together: Congress's taxing and spending power. Consequently, much of the discussion of the history of the spending power is similarly true of the taxing power. After 1937, the Court interpreted congressional taxing power broadly. Congress has the power to tax for the general welfare as long as the congressional act does not violate another constitutional provision, such as the First Amendment. Congress is not limited to taxing in furtherance of the other enumerated powers. Article I, section 9, though, expressly imposes a limitation on the taxing power: Any capitation or direct tax, such as one on real property, must be allocated proportionally among the states based on population. Even so, case law has undermined any distinction between direct and indirect taxes. Thus, for the most part limitations on the taxing power have arisen from the democratic process rather than from judicial decisions. If citizens do not like federal taxes, their recourse is to vote for different government officials.[20]

Significantly, in *Sebelius* Roberts and the Court—the four progressive justices joined Roberts—did not diminish Congress's taxing power. Instead, Roberts explained that the individual mandate was within the scope of the taxing power. Much of Roberts's opinion on this issue revolved around statutory construction and the question of whether the individual mandate should be categorized as a tax. In fact, this question of statutory construction was the crux of the disagreement between Roberts and the other conservative justices: It is why the other conservatives refused to join Roberts's opinion and instead jointly dissented. Unlike Roberts, the joint dissenters did not interpret the individual mandate to be a tax. They reasoned that it must be either a tax or a penalty; it could not be both. Since, from their perspective, it was clearly a penalty, it logically could not be a tax. Consequently, they did not even consider whether the mandate was within Congress's taxing power. Meanwhile, once Roberts deemed the mandate to be a tax, he emphasized that Congress could tax inactivity even though, by his reasoning, it could not reach such inactivity pursuant to its commerce power.[21]

In *Sebelius*, Chief Justice Roberts articulated conservative constitutional doctrines regarding Congress's commerce and spending powers. The unequivocal political slant of Roberts's opinion was antigovernment: He emphasized the judicial definition and enforcement of formalist constraints on congressional power. In some ways, Roberts's doctrinal statements went beyond any judicial limits previously imposed on Congress since the 1937 turn. And Roberts's doctrines are likely to generate conservative judicial outcomes for years to come. Yet simultaneously, Roberts repeatedly proclaimed that the Court was obligated to decide *Sebelius* without regard for politics. In three instances, Roberts explicitly stated that the justices should not consider the political wisdom of the ACA. From his perspective—at least as he professed it—political decisions are left to Congress and the people. The Court's determination of the constitutional scope of congressional power was purely a legal issue, divorced from other considerations.[22]

In other words, Roberts reiterated the law-politics *dichotomy* while denying the law-politics *dynamic*. His opinion in *Sebelius* was so politically deft that numerous conservative commentators criticized him for betraying Republicans and voting with the progressives to uphold the constitutionality of the ACA's individual mandate. Most of these critics, of course, missed the operation of the law-politics dynamic within the case. Roberts managed to reinforce the myth of the law-politics dichotomy despite the strong conservative thrust of his opinion. Remarkably, Roberts's political and legal feints and dodges continued even beyond his articulation of conservative legal doctrine for Congress's commerce and spending powers. The precise legal ground that Roberts chose to stand on when upholding the individual mandate was itself politically salient. He categorized the mandate as a *tax*. In other words, he neatly placed the ACA in one of the most unacceptable of contemporary political boxes. "Aha," conservatives did not hesitate to declare when they saw Roberts's opinion. "Obama and the Democrats raised taxes!"[23]

The Roberts Court has manifested its hostility toward democratic government not only in other decisions invalidating congressional enactments but also by allowing antidemocratic actions. In 2008, *Crawford v. Marion County Election Board* held that states could constitutionally require individuals to show photo identification before voting.[24] The importance of the Court's constitutional approval of that voting restriction grew exponentially in 2013, when the Court decided *Shelby County v. Holder*. The Court there invalidated a provision of the Voting Rights Act (VRA), passed pursuant to Congress's power under the Fifteenth Amendment, a Reconstruction-era amendment that prohibits the state and federal governments from denying or abridging the right to vote "on account of race, color, or previous condition of servitude." The coverage provision of the VRA specified which jurisdictions needed special government approval or preclearance before they could change their voting laws (to prevent the enactment of state laws undermining suffrage). Enacted in 1965, the VRA largely functioned as planned, as mentioned in Chapter 6. It effectively invigorated black voting, especially in former Jim Crow states such as Mississippi and Alabama. In Alabama, for instance, black voter registration increased by more than 40 percent by 1969. In 1966, no American city had a black mayor, but many cities, large and small, had black mayors by the end of the 1970s. In the late 1980s, only three black Americans represented southern states in the House of Representatives, even though nearly one-half of the black population still resided in the South. But the 1990 census, combined with earlier (1982) amendments to the VRA, led to the creation of new minority-majority districts—congressional districts where people of color constituted a voting majority—which facilitated the election of more black Americans. With thirteen black Americans being elected from new southern districts, the total number of African American representatives increased from twenty-five (before the 1990 census) to forty-one (after the redistricting).[25]

Nevertheless, the Court in *Shelby County*, a five-to-four decision, doubted Congress's competence and invalidated the coverage provision of the VRA because of a lack of adequate congressional findings. In an opinion by Roberts, the Court acknowledged that the coverage provision was sensible in 1965, when Congress first enacted the statute. Congress, though, had reauthorized the act several times over the years, and the Court concluded that the coverage provision did not fit the nation's current circumstances. "Coverage today is based on decades-old data and eradicated practices." Robert's opinion suggested that Congress left the Court with no choice but to invalidate the statutory provision. The Court, as Roberts explained, had sidestepped a similar constitutional challenge to the VRA several years earlier and had encouraged Congress to update the coverage formula. "Its failure to act leaves us today with no choice but to declare [the provision] unconstitutional. The formula in that section can no longer be used as a basis for subjecting jurisdictions to preclearance."[26]

When one reads Ginsburg's *Shelby County* dissent, however, the case appears remarkably different. Ginsburg pointed to extensive and detailed congressional findings: "Congress determined, based on a voluminous record, that the scourge of [voting] discrimination was not yet extirpated. . . . With overwhelming support in both Houses, Congress concluded that, for two prime reasons, [the VRA] should continue in force, unabated. First, continuance would facilitate completion of the impressive gains thus far made; and second, continuance would guard against backsliding. Those assessments were well within Congress' province to make and should elicit this Court's unstinting approbation."[27]

Ginsburg's dissent highlighted the conservative majority's disdain for Congress and its democratic processes.[28] The Court did not merely ask Congress to make more specific findings. Rather, the Court demanded that Congress make different findings. In reality, the conservative justices might not have been satisfied by any congressional findings, given that the justices apparently did not approve of the substance of Congress's action. And as Ginsburg feared, the Court's invalidation of the preclearance provision prompted an outburst of discriminatory attacks on the democratic process. Voter-identification laws, approved in *Crawford*, became prevalent.[29] More than thirty-one states enacted laws restricting suffrage in various ways, discriminating especially against individuals who lack money, leisure time, and bureaucratic know-how. A new Texas law allowed individuals with concealed-gun permits to vote but did not similarly allow individuals with student photo identification cards. North Carolina enacted a multipronged antisuffrage law: It required voters to present government-issued photo identification at the polls, shortened the previously allowed early voting period, ended preregistration for sixteen- and seventeen-year-olds, and eliminated same-day voter registration. In fact, shortly before the Court decided *Shelby County*, a Pew Center study concluded that "at least 51 million eligible U.S. citizens are unregistered, or more than 24 percent of the eligible population," while in Canada, as a comparison, more than 93 percent of eligible voters are registered. Between 2014 and 2016—in the years immediately after the *Shelby County* decision, states purged 33 percent more voters than between 2006 and 2008. And disfranchisement can change election results: A study of the 2014 midterm elections concluded that voter suppression laws potentially swung several gubernatorial and senate races.[30]

The Court again shielded antidemocratic action in a 2019 decision, *Rucho v. Common Cause*, yet another five-to-four decision (resolving two consolidated lower court cases). With Roberts writing for the conservative bloc, the Court refused to invalidate congressional district lines in two states, North Carolina and Maryland, despite extreme partisan gerrymandering. The challengers had raised numerous constitutional issues, including free-expression, equal-protection, and other claims. In fact, the district courts held for the challengers in both the North Carolina and Maryland cases based partly on the free-expression claims. The gist of these claims was that the state legislature, in the control of one political party, penalized voters who had expressed support for the other party.[31]

The Court resolved *Rucho* by ostensibly applying a formal rule: the political question doctrine (mentioned in Chapters 4 and 5). The premise of the political question doctrine is none other than the law-politics dichotomy: The Court supposedly should resolve cases based solely on the neutral application of legal rules and should not decide political (or nonjusticiable) questions. As the *Rucho* Court explained, a constitutional issue is nonjusticiable unless the Constitution provides "limited and precise standards that are clear, manageable, and politically neutral." In this case (and any other partisan gerrymandering case), the Court concluded that it could not find any such rule or standard to determine the constitutionality of partisan gerrymanders. For instance, with regard to the free-expression claims, the Court reasoned that the First Amendment provided "no 'clear' and 'manageable' way of distinguishing permissible from impermissible partisan motivation [in gerrymandering]." From this vantage, if the Court had attempted to resolve these gerrymandering disputes in accord with the First Amendment or other constitutional provisions, it "would risk assuming political, not legal, responsibility."[32]

Consequently, the Court concluded that the rule of the political question doctrine defeated the free-expression and other constitutional challenges to gerrymandering, regardless of the consequences. In fact, the Court did not deny that extreme gerrymandering contravenes constitutional principles.[33] In dissent, Justice Elena Kagan declared: "For the first time ever, this Court refuses to remedy a constitutional violation because it thinks the task beyond judicial capabilities." Most important, the Court disregarded that partisan gerrymandering potentially endangers democratic government: Partisan gerrymandering exacerbates political polarization, undermines "free and fair elections," and allows government officials to entrench their own power by choosing their voters, rather than vice versa (letting the voters choose the officials). In the words of Kagan, "[T]he partisan gerrymanders here debased and dishonored our democracy, turning upside-down the core American idea that all governmental power derives from the people."[34]

The *Rucho* Court's invocation of the political question doctrine as a categorical or formal bar to the First Amendment and other constitutional challenges was deeply (albeit unwittingly) ironic. The ostensible reason for relying on the political question doctrine was that neither the First Amendment nor the other relevant constitutional provisions provided sufficiently clear and precise legal rules or standards for judicial decision. Yet the political question doctrine is itself notoriously malleable: The doctrine does not provide a clear and precise rule or standard for its own application.[35] Put in other words, the justices in *Rucho* relied on a patently manipulable rule—the political question doctrine—to reject the free-speech and other constitutional claims as being too politically manipulable for courts to resolve.

If anything, the Court can invoke the political question rule when it produces a result that harmonizes with the political preferences of a majority of the justices. And the result in *Rucho* resonated strongly with the politics of the conservative bloc. Given their neoliberal bent, the conservative justices are not overly concerned about the operation of the democratic process: It is inevitably inefficient and corrupt, so why worry about a little partisan gerrymandering?

Moreover, while both Republicans and Democrats engage in gerrymandering, Republicans have done so more egregiously and frequently.[36] At this point in time, gerrymandering benefits Republicans far more than Democrats. Even in the *Rucho* case, the two instances of gerrymandering—Republicans in North Carolina and Democrats in Maryland—were hardly equivalent. In North Carolina in 2012, after the implementation of a gerrymandered districting plan, "Republican candidates won 9 of the State's 13 seats in the U.S. House of Representatives, although they received only 49% of the statewide vote." After a district court invalidated that districting plan, the Republican-controlled state legislature asked Thomas Hofeller, a Republican districting specialist, to help craft an equally effective gerrymandering scheme (effective in protecting Republican power). When the Republican cochair of the State Assembly's redistricting committee presented the newly proposed plan, he "explained that the map was drawn with the aim of electing ten Republicans and three Democrats because he did 'not believe it [would be] possible to draw a map with 11 Republicans and 2 Democrats.'" Meanwhile, in Democratic-controlled Maryland, the legislature also purposefully gerrymandered, but the result was to flip one congressional district from the Republican to the Democratic side.[37]

The truth is, of course, that Supreme Court decision making is always partly political, as I have emphasized. The failure of the political question doctrine to provide a formal rule that the Court can apply neutrally and apolitically is not unique to the political question doctrine. Despite the claims of formalism, law and politics always intertwine in legal interpretation. The law-politics dynamic and politics writ small are integral to Supreme Court decision making. The political question doctrine, however, provides an example of a legal rule or doctrine that patently interweaves with political ideology when interpreted and applied. Regardless, the flimsiness of the political question doctrine as a formal rule did not stop the conservative bloc in *Rucho* from invoking it to categorically bar all constitutional challenges to partisan gerrymandering.

The Roberts Court conservatives are at best indifferent, and often are hostile, to democratic government.[38] Their dismissive attitude toward democracy is manifested in multiple ways, including numerous cases in which the Court has invalidated congressional actions. Contrary to the prior conservative endorsement of judicial restraint (running from the 1960s to the 1980s), the Rehnquist and Roberts Courts have engaged in one of the "most notable binges of congressional-law striking in history." The Rehnquist Court invalidated more congressional acts than had any previous Court. From 1995 to 2001 alone, the Court struck down thirty federal laws, more than the Warren Court invalidated from 1953 to 1969. Statistically, compared with the Rehnquist Court, the Roberts Court has slowed the pace, invalidating fewer laws proportionally. Yet the current conservative justices have consistently and aggressively reached to strike progressive laws inconsistent with the contemporary conservative political agenda, particularly laws regulating the economic marketplace, as discussed in the next section.[39]

In the summer of 2020, the Court decided *Seila Law L.L.C. v. Consumer Financial Protection Bureau*, a case that straddles the conservative hostility toward democracy and the conservative protection of the marketplace.[40]

After the 2008 financial crisis, Congress created the Consumer Financial Protection Bureau (CFPB) as an independent agency focused on protecting consumers in the financial marketplace. Leading the agency would be a director appointed by the president with the advice and consent of the Senate and removable by the president "only for 'inefficiency, neglect of duty, or malfeasance in office.'"[41] The issue was whether the limitation on the president's power to remove the director violated separation of powers. The case revolved around the theory of a unitary executive, which asserts that the president holds "unitary authority over the execution of federal law." It follows, under this theory, that the president must have the "power to remove subordinate policy-making officials at will, the . . . power to direct the manner in which subordinate officials exercise discretionary executive power, and the power to veto or nullify such officials' exercises of discretionary executive power."[42] The conservative justices and other neoliberals have long favored the unitary executive theory, typically preferring strong executive power over the supposed irrationality of congressional decision making.[43]

Significantly, while Congress and Democratic President Obama had joined together in creating the CFPB, President Trump and his administration declined to defend the law and urged its invalidation.[44] The Court decided on the merits five to four, in a typical conservative-progressive split, holding that "the CFPB's leadership by a single individual removable only [for cause] violates the separation of powers." Roberts, writing the majority opinion, invoked article II of the Constitution: "Under our Constitution, the 'executive Power'—*all of it*—is 'vested in a President,' who must 'take Care that the Laws be faithfully executed.'"[45] The conservative bloc of justices, in other words, cast their support for the unitary executive: "The entire 'executive Power,'" wrote Roberts, "belongs to the President alone."[46] From this perspective, the president must be empowered to remove the CFPB director at will—for cause or for no cause at all. In dissent, Kagan emphasized that the Court was "second-guessing" or repudiating a democratic decision of "the political branches." She explained: "Congress and the President [Obama] came together to create an agency with an important mission. It would protect consumers from the reckless financial practices that had caused the then-ongoing economic collapse." To allow the CFPB to properly monitor and regulate the marketplace, Congress and the president had believed the agency needed to be politically independent—hence, the legislative restriction on the president's power to remove the director. And as Kagan stressed, the constitutional text, including article II, contains no express limits on the removal power.[47]

Many of the Roberts Court cases that protect wealth and the marketplace also undermine the democratic process, so this section and the next overlap. Before moving on, however, it is worth noting that some conservatives might defend the Court by claiming that it has sought to protect state sovereignty from federal overreaching. From this perspective, the conservative justices are concerned with the values of federalism: Rather than being hostile to democratic government in general, the justices are hostile to national power specifically. For this reason, the Court has invalidated numerous congressional actions. This defense of the Court, though, cannot be squared with the broad negative ramifications for democracy of cases such as *Shelby County* and *Rucho*. Plus, this argument clashes with the numerous cases in which the Roberts Court has invalidated state and local government actions.[48]

JUDICIAL PROTECTION OF WEALTH AND THE ECONOMIC MARKETPLACE

During the Rehnquist Court years, the Court vacillated over the degree to which the government could regulate corporate spending on political campaigns, but the Roberts Court's landmark 2010 decision, *Citizens United v. Federal Election Commission*, ended the uncertainty. With a five-to-four vote, the conservative bloc of justices invalidated provisions of the Bipartisan Campaign Reform Act of 2002 that imposed limits on corporate (and union) spending for political campaign advertisements. The majority opinion began by articulating two First Amendment premises. First, the Court reiterated the maxim, initially stated in *Buckley v. Valeo* in 1976, that spending on political campaigns constitutes speech. Second, the Court emphasized that, as stated in *First National Bank of Boston v. Bellotti* in 1978, free-speech protections extend to corporations. With these premises in hand, the Court focused on the crux of its reasoning: the self-governance rationale for free expression. "Speech is an essential mechanism of democracy," Justice Anthony Kennedy wrote. "The right of citizens to inquire, to hear, to speak, and to use information to reach consensus is a precondition to enlightened self-government and a necessary means to protect it." Under the First Amendment, in other words, free expression must be a constitutional lodestar because democracy cannot exist without it. Moreover, corporate expenditures on political campaigns, from the Court's perspective, go to the core of the First Amendment. Restrictions on such political speech and writing destroy "'liberty'" and are unconstitutional unless the government can satisfy strict scrutiny, showing that the regulation is necessary to achieve a compelling purpose.[49]

The Court acknowledged that the prevention of corruption constituted a compelling government purpose. In fact, the dissenting Justice John Paul Stevens emphasized that Congress had relied on "evidence of corruption" when enacting the campaign restrictions.[50] Social science research shows that excessive expenditures, corporate and otherwise, skew the democratic process. First, wealth can shape the outcomes of elections. For instance, because running for office requires massive funding, wealthy contributors can "determine the pools of potential officeholders." More broadly, social and cognitive psychology research demonstrates that wealth can be used to fund campaign strategies that purposefully manipulate the electorate and "induce sub-optimal vote decisions." Second, after the elections, wealth can influence the behavior of elected officials. In exchange for their money, wealthy contributors get "privileged access" to government officials, including congressional committee members concerned with the contributors' business interests. Basically, wealthy contributors to campaigns buy future political influence. Predictably, then, government officials generally ignore the interests of low-income citizens.[51]

The Court nonetheless rendered the evidence of corruption irrelevant by severely narrowing the definition of corruption. According to the *Citizens United* majority, only a direct contribution to a candidate or officeholder can constitute corruption or its appearance. An independent expenditure, even on behalf of a specific candidate or officeholder, cannot do so. Anything short of a bribe or the appearance of a bribe is permissible. Given this narrow view of corruption, the Court concluded that the government did not satisfy strict scrutiny. The Court reinforced its conclusion by invoking the search-for-truth rationale, another traditional philosophical reason for protecting expression. Restrictions on corporate campaign expenditures, the Court reasoned, interfere "with the 'open marketplace' of ideas protected by the First Amendment."[52]

The *Citizens United* majority added an originalist flourish. Quoting from James Madison and The Federalist No. 10, Kennedy concluded: "There is simply no support for the view that the First Amendment, as originally understood, would permit the suppression of political speech by media corporations." Stevens, concurring in part and dissenting in part, criticized this historical reasoning on two grounds. The Court misunderstood, first, the nature of free expression at the time of the framing, and second, the role of corporations during the early national years. Antonin Scalia wrote a concurrence specifically criticizing Stevens's opinion, especially his originalist analysis. The crux of Scalia's argument was that the original meaning of the First Amendment could not be construed to deny corporations full constitutional rights to express political viewpoints. In effect, Scalia elaborated the majority's brief invocation of originalism.[53]

Scalia's (as well as the majority's) history was shockingly wrong in two ways. First, he mistakenly equated conceptions of free expression from the mid- to late twentieth century with conceptions from the framing era. He wrote in his concurrence: "[I]f speech can be prohibited because, in the view of the Government, it leads to 'moral decay' or does not serve 'public ends,' then there is no limit to the Government's censorship power." But from the framing through the early twentieth century, governments could punish expression that was likely to produce bad tendencies or harmful consequences. The government, in other words, could limit expression exactly because it might undermine morals or, more broadly, because it contravened the common good. The Supreme Court itself upheld numerous government punishments of expression pursuant to this approach. The Court abandoned this narrow interpretation of free expression only when it shifted from republican to pluralist democracy in the 1930s. This transformation of democracy gave birth to the self-governance rationale for free speech. As the post-1937 Court shifted its focus to the process of pluralist democracy, discussed in Chapter 3, it reconceptualized free expression as crucial to that process. Pluralist democracy required free and open citizen participation, so citizens must be able to express their interests and values. While the Court had not even arguably upheld any free-expression claims until 1931, the post-1937 Court upheld one free-speech claim after another.[54]

Second, Scalia mistakenly asserted that the framers' generation would not have differentiated corporations from individual citizens for purposes of free expression. Scalia seemingly read the history through the lens of twenty-first-century neoliberal market fundamentalism, but the framers were not even full-fledged capitalists, much less laissez-faire ideologues. The constitutional protection of slavery as a legal institution underscores that the framing generation was not committed to a capitalist free-market economy. Capitalism is based on the drive for profit in a competitive free market. Slavery is the antithesis of a free market; it is coerced labor. Without doubt, slavery enabled slave owners to accumulate capital in a commercial market economy and thus facilitated the eventual emergence of capitalism.

Regardless, throughout the pre–Civil War decades, slavery skewed the natural movement of capital among various productive and profitable market activities. Slavery, consistent with a premodern mercantilist economy, constrained the marketplace, as well as human freedom. Given this, the framers' generation unsurprisingly did not conceptualize corporations in a way that would even resemble the profit-driven multinational behemoths that dominate the twenty-first-century marketplace. During the early decades of nationhood, corporations could be formed only when legislatures specially chartered them—general incorporation laws did not exist—and legislatures rarely granted such special state charters. Legislatures almost never granted corporate charters to businesses that focused solely on profit making. Instead, in another manifestation of the lingering mercantilist outlook, states would charter corporations that promoted the common good by performing a function useful to the public. For example, corporate charters were typically granted for the building of infrastructure, including roads, bridges, and canals, as well as for the operation of ferries, banks, and insurance companies. In the end, Scalia's (and the majority's) suggestion in *Citizens United* that the framing generation would have viewed corporations as indistinguishable from individual citizens for purposes of free expression is so ahistorical as to be nonsensical.[55]

In short, the conservative justices in the *Citizens United* majority, bolstered by Scalia's concurrence, made several dubious moves in interpreting the First Amendment. Their understanding of free speech and corporate history was questionable. And despite their invocation of the self-governance rationale—based on the operation of pluralist democracy—the justices disregarded the dangers that corporate (and other excessive) wealth bring to the democratic process. Yet the *Citizens United* decision is exactly what one might expect from a Court imbued with neoliberal ideology. The Court protected great wealth while simultaneously showing disdain for democratic government. In fact, the Roberts Court conservatives often seem to conceive of the American citizen as homo economicus, an economic self that seeks only to maximize the satisfaction of its own (economic) interests. This "economic man," first developed by neoclassical economists, fits perfectly with the Roberts Court's preferred formalist approach. He "has neither a childhood nor a context. He grows out of the ground like a mushroom."[56] All too predictably, then, when the *Citizens United* Court invoked the marketplace-of-ideas free-speech rationale, the justices confounded that marketplace (of ideas) with the economic marketplace.

The marketplace-of-ideas or search-for-truth rationale has historical roots going back to John Milton in the seventeenth century (during the English Civil War) and John Stuart Mill in the nineteenth century. "Let [truth] and falsehood grapple," Milton wrote, "[and] who ever knew truth put to the worse, in a free and open encounter?"[57] The crux of the search-for-truth rationale is that truth is a societal good and that the free exchange of ideas is the best means for society to identify truth and falsity. In 1919, Justice Oliver Wendell Holmes Jr., dissenting in *Abrams v. United States*, recast this rationale: "[W]hen men have realized that time has upset many fighting faiths, they may come to believe even more than they believe the very foundations of their own conduct that the ultimate good desired is better reached by free trade in ideas—that the best test of truth is the power of the thought to get itself accepted in the competition of the market, and that truth is the only ground upon which their wishes safely can be carried out."[58]

Whereas Holmes analogized the search for truth to a marketplace of ideas—this was during an era dominated by laissez-faire ideology, after all— he never suggested that wealth or the economic marketplace itself produced truth. Yet the *Citizens United* majority stated: "The censorship we now confront is vast in its reach. The Government has 'muffle[d] the voices that best represent the most significant segments of the economy.'" Speech, from the Court's perspective, does not emanate from people, from citizens, but from "segments of the economy." But a business corporation pursues profits, not truth. In the words of Peter Drucker, an influential theorist of business management, the only valid purpose for a business is "to create a customer." Consider commercial advertisements. Whether the advertisement is an unsophisticated and direct urge to buy a product or a complex and subtle association of a product with an attractive lifestyle, the business corporation that pays for the advertisement always has the same goal. The corporation does not care whether the individual viewer or society as a whole is moving toward truth. The corporation cares only whether the advertisement successfully induces the viewer to become a purchaser or other source of corporate revenue. Pursuant to *Citizens United*, the economic marketplace and private sphere subsume government and the public sphere.[59]

Citizens United is not an anomaly. Empirical studies show that the Roberts Court is the most pro-business Supreme Court since World War II. As of 2013, the five conservative justices ranked among the top ten justices most favorable to business, with Samuel Alito and Roberts being first and second on the list. The evidence also suggests that the pro-business justices shape the Court's docket in accord with their interests. A study focusing on the period from May 19, 2009, to August 15, 2012, concluded that the U.S. Chamber of Commerce, representing business, not only filed more certiorari-stage amicus briefs than any other organization but also enjoyed the second highest success rate. Finally, as the political scientist Thomas Keck has explained, campaign finance restrictions historically have "clear partisan implications." The imposition of statutory regulations represents "a longstanding Democratic legislative effort," whereas "business interests and the Republican Party" have generally opposed restrictions.[60]

Since *Citizens United* in effect created a formal First Amendment rule prohibiting campaign finance restrictions, the decision generated a dramatic increase in campaign spending. Yet the Court continued in subsequent cases to press its formalist neoliberal interpretation of the First Amendment. *American Tradition Partnership, Inc. v. Bullock* held unconstitutional a Montana statute providing that a "corporation may not make . . . an expenditure in connection with a candidate or a political committee that supports or opposes a candidate or a political party." The Montana Supreme Court had upheld this statute in the face of a First Amendment challenge because of a specific history of corporate-engineered corruption in the Montana democratic process. Once again, with another five-to-four vote, the U.S. Supreme Court's conservative bloc found a free-speech violation. Reasoning that "[t]here can be no serious doubt" *Citizens United* controlled, the Court prevented the state from even attempting to demonstrate that its factual situation uniquely needed regulation. *Citizens United*, it seemed, had created an iron-clad rule prohibiting campaign finance restrictions, regardless of context or effects.[61]

In another case, *Arizona Free Enterprise Club's Freedom Club PAC v. Bennett*, Arizona created a campaign-finance "matching funds scheme": A candidate for state office who accepted public financing would receive additional funds if a privately financed opponent spent more than the publicly financed candidate's initial allocation. As Justice Kagan emphasized in dissent, this public financing system would roughly equalize the amounts available for publicly and privately financed candidates. It did not limit or restrict political expression. If anything, she wrote, it "subsidizes and so produces *more* political speech." Nevertheless, in another five-to-four decision, the conservative bloc applied its formal First Amendment rule prohibiting campaign finance restrictions. Asserting that the public financing scheme imposed a "penalty" on privately financed candidates, the Court reasoned: "[E]ven if the matching funds provision did result in more speech by publicly financed candidates and more speech in general, it would do so at the expense of impermissibly burdening (and thus reducing) the speech of privately financed candidates and independent expenditure groups."[62] And in another case, *McCutcheon v. Federal Election Commission*, Roberts's plurality opinion emphasized the narrow definition of corruption articulated in *Citizens United*: "'The hallmark of corruption is the financial quid pro quo: dollars for political favors.'" Government restrictions on contributions must therefore be "closely drawn" or "narrowly tailored" to prevent "'quid pro quo' corruption or its appearance." From Roberts's vantage, contributing large sums of money to political campaigns amounts to "'robustly exercis[ing]' [one's] First Amendment rights." This view suggests that the more money people spend, the more vigorous their exercise of free expression. Of course, this viewpoint makes perfect sense if one conceptualizes the citizen as homo economicus: The economic self acts, politically or otherwise, by spending (or making) money. Ultimately, in *Citizens United* and its progeny, the Roberts Court proclaimed that corporations and other wealthy entities and individuals can spend unlimited sums in their efforts to control elections and government policies.[63]

In contexts other than campaign finance, the Roberts Court has protected business and the wealthy in the economic marketplace but has not been so kind to employees. *Citizens United*, in theory, applied equally to corporations and unions. But *Knox v. Service Employees International Union* considered whether a public employee union imposing a special assessment fee to support political advocacy had satisfied free-speech requirements when it failed to allow nonmembers to opt out of the fee. The conservative bloc held that even if the union had provided an opt-out for the nonmembers, it would have been insufficient to satisfy the First Amendment. After this case, then, unions' efforts to raise money for political campaigns would face obstacles far beyond those faced by corporations. To compound problems facing employees and unions, *Janus v. American Federation of State, County, and Municipal Employees, Council 31* held that public-sector workers cannot be forced to pay union fees related solely to collective bargaining representation, even though the workers benefit from the representation. As Justice Kagan emphasized in dissent, the Court's decision would weaken unions by encouraging free riders—employees who benefit from without financially supporting the union. She accused the conservative bloc of "weaponizing the First Amendment" to protect the wealthy and undermine democratic decision making.[64]

Such weaponizing of the First Amendment was on full display in *Sorrell v. IMS Health Inc.* The case involved a crucial issue for our digital age: data mining—specifically, the gathering and business use of medical data, a widespread and highly profitable enterprise.

Pharmacies routinely record information about prescriptions, such as the doctor, the patient, and the dosage. Data-mining businesses, such as IMS Health Inc., buy this information, analyze it, and sell or lease their reports to pharmaceutical corporations. Using this information, the pharmaceutical corporations can market their drugs more effectively to doctors. Vermont passed a statute to stop pharmacies from selling the prescription information to protect the privacy of patients and doctors and improve public health. Doctors, after all, should prescribe medicine based on their patients' needs rather than on corporate marketing. IMS Health Inc. challenged this state law as violating the First Amendment. Justice Stephen Breyer's dissent characterized the statute as a police power regulation of the economic marketplace that did not even trigger free-speech concerns. The Court's conservative majority disagreed. It viewed the statute as raising an unusual commercial speech issue, although the statute, as the Court admitted, did not restrict advertising per se—the usual subject matter of commercial speech cases. The Court proceeded to invoke the First Amendment and apply "heightened judicial scrutiny," a standard more rigorous than the one typically used for commercial speech. In the end, the Court invalidated the statute and, in so doing, blocked the regulation of marketplace activities only tenuously connected to expression.[65]

To be clear, the Roberts Court is not firmly committed to protecting free expression. In numerous cases, the Court has found expression to be outside of First Amendment guarantees. Despite the Court's use of the First Amendment to protect wealth and the economic marketplace, it has a "dismal record" overall in free-speech cases. Whether the Court ostensibly decides pursuant to a formal rule or not, the haves consistently come out ahead. Which parties have lost free-speech cases during the Roberts Court era? Public employee unions (as mentioned above), prisoners, high school students, government employees, and those seeking an equal voice in democracy (discussed in the previous section). In every instance, the party wielding greater power has won the case.[66]

The Roberts Court, it should be emphasized, does not rely solely on the First Amendment to protect the wealthy and the marketplace. The Court can invoke other constitutional provisions to achieve similar results, sometimes directly and sometimes indirectly. Judicial restrictions on the scope of congressional and other government power can shield wealth and corporate power. Similarly, the Court's protection of an individual right to own and possess firearms under the Second Amendment can benefit gun manufacturers. Moreover, the Court has repeatedly interpreted statutes and the Federal Rules of Civil Procedure (FRCP) to protect corporate businesses from lawsuits and liability. For example, the Court has interpreted the FRCP to impede class-action lawsuits brought by employees and consumers against corporations such as Walmart and Comcast. In a similar vein, the Court has interpreted the Federal Arbitration Act to protect customer-contract provisions requiring individuals to submit to arbitration (rather than suing) while prohibiting class-wide arbitration. The Court has also interpreted Title VII to make proof of discrimination more difficult for plaintiff-employees.[67]

The Roberts Court's protections of the wealthy and the marketplace often simultaneously deny legal protections to women and people of color, the subjects of the next two sections.

LACK OF JUDICIAL PROTECTION FOR WOMEN

In *Ledbetter v. Goodyear Tire & Rubber Company*, the Roberts Court protected a business corporation while refusing to protect a female employee. Lilly Ledbetter alleged that Goodyear had discriminated sexually by paying her less than it paid male employees for much of her nineteen years of employment. In fact, Goodyear paid Ledbetter $3,727 per month while paying male area managers between $4,286 and $5,236 per month. Moreover, Ledbetter learned of the pay disparities only shortly before she filed for early retirement. The district court awarded Ledbetter $360,000 in damages. In a five-to-four decision, with a majority opinion by Alito, the Court held in favor of the corporation and against Ledbetter, reasoning that her claim was time-barred under the antidiscrimination provisions of Title VII. Based on the Court's interpretation of the statute, Ledbetter would have needed to sue before she knew about the discrimination, even though Goodyear purposefully tried to keep its pay scales confidential. In the end, Goodyear did not have to pay a penny of compensation to Ledbetter, even though it had unlawfully discriminated against her for years.[68]

When it comes to the Constitution and abortion, *Roe v. Wade* held that the Due Process Clause of the Fourteenth Amendment includes a constitutionally protected right of privacy encompassing a woman's interest in choosing abortion. Regulations (or restrictions) on abortion, *Roe* reasoned, should be reviewed pursuant to strict scrutiny: The government would need to show that its regulations were necessary to achieve a compelling state purpose. Based on that requirement, *Roe* developed a trimester framework, emphasizing viability as a key line of demarcation. During the first trimester of a pregnancy, the state is prohibited from regulating abortions in any manner. During the second trimester, the state's interest in protecting the health of pregnant women justifies state regulations of abortions but solely for the purpose of protecting pregnant women. Finally, after viability and during the third trimester, the state's "interest in protecting the potentiality of human life" is so strong as to justify state prohibitions of abortions, unless "necessary to preserve the life or health" of the pregnant woman.[69]

Planned Parenthood v. Casey reaffirmed the "central holding" of *Roe v. Wade*—that prior to viability, women have a constitutionally protected right to choose abortion—but *Casey* nonetheless severely diminished that right.

Casey repudiated two key aspects of *Roe*. First, *Casey* rejected the trimester framework because it supposedly undervalued the government's interest in protecting potential human life. After *Casey*, then, a state might be able to regulate abortion during the second trimester to protect the potential human life; a state's second trimester regulation no longer needed to be for the protection of pregnant women. Second, *Casey* rejected the strict scrutiny test. Instead, *Casey* articulated the less rigorous "undue burden" test to evaluate government regulations of abortion: "An undue burden exists, and therefore a provision of law is invalid, if its purpose or effect is to place a substantial obstacle in the path of a woman seeking an abortion before the fetus attains viability." Under this new test, the Court overruled earlier decisions and upheld multiple state regulations. For instance, the Court upheld a regulation requiring a woman, after receiving certain information about abortions, to wait twenty-four hours before having the procedure.[70]

The Roberts Court continued hollowing out the right to choose, particularly in a case involving late-term abortions. The Rehnquist Court, in 2000, had already invalidated a state statute restricting late-term abortions—the statute referred to the procedures as "partial birth abortions." That 2000 decision, *Stenberg v. Carhart*, reaffirmed three key points about abortion. First, women have a right to choose before viability. Second, the appropriate standard of judicial scrutiny for a regulation is the undue burden test. Third, even after viability, state regulations or prohibitions of abortion must allow abortion "where it is necessary, in appropriate medical judgment, for the preservation of the life or health of the mother." The Court had expressly articulated this health exception in *Roe* and had reaffirmed it in *Casey*.[71]

Not long after *Stenberg*, though, the ultraconservative Justice Alito replaced the moderately conservative Justice Sandra Day O'Connor. With this crucial personnel change on the Court, the justices took up the late-term abortion issue again in 2007. The Roberts Court's five-to-four decision in *Gonzales v. Carhart* upheld a federal statute restricting late-term abortions, even though the law did not contain a health exception. Moreover, the statute applied to "both previability and postviability" abortions. Writing for the conservative bloc, Justice Kennedy worried about women's frail psychology: "Respect for human life finds an ultimate expression in the bond of love the mother has for her child. . . . Whether to have an abortion requires a difficult and painful moral decision. While we find no reliable data to measure the phenomenon, it seems unexceptionable to conclude some women come to regret their choice to abort the infant life they once created and sustained. Severe depression and loss of esteem can follow." Justice Ginsburg denounced this passage for its paternalism and lack of empirical support: "[T]he Court invokes an antiabortion shibboleth for which it concededly has no reliable evidence. . . . Because of women's fragile emotional state . . . the Court deprives women of the right to make an autonomous choice, even at the expense of their safety. This way of thinking reflects ancient notions about women's place in the family and under the Constitution—ideas that have long since been discredited."[72]

Disregarding Ginsburg's objections, Kennedy justified the decision by ostensibly distinguishing the federal statute upheld in *Gonzales* from the state statute invalidated in *Stenberg*. But as critics of the decision pointed out, Kennedy's opinion appeared to describe a fetus as "a morally consequential entity of the highest degree," as equivalent to a baby. Having made this controversial moral judgment—"this magnificently undecided (and potentially undecidable) presupposition" that is the crux of all abortion disputes—the Court's conclusion when applying the undue burden standard was nearly predetermined. As a practical matter, most, if not all, restrictions on abortion would necessarily be upheld.[73]

Even so, in *Whole Woman's Health v. Hellerstedt*, the Court in 2016 surprisingly invalidated two Texas state restrictions on abortion—the key statutory requirement forced doctors who performed abortions to have admitting privileges at a nearby hospital. In an opinion written by Justice Breyer, the Court reasoned that the undue burden test required the weighing of a women's interest in choice against the state's interest in regulating abortion. In other words, the Court clarified what had previously seemed implicit: the undue burden standard was a stylized balancing test, where the judicial determination of whether a regulation imposed an *undue* burden (or a *substantial* obstacle) necessitated a balancing or weighing of interests.[74] Then, in applying the undue burden standard, the Court emphasized that the effect of the restrictions would be to reduce the number of licensed abortion facilities in Texas from forty to seven or eight, all of which would be located in the largest urban centers. The Court did not accept the state's assertion that those remaining facilities would be able to meet the demand of women wanting abortions. Moreover, because of the locations of the remaining facilities, the restrictions would "erect a particularly high barrier for poor, rural, or disadvantaged women."[75] The vitality of this decision, however, is highly questionable. The Court decided the case after Justice Scalia's death and before Justice Neil Gorsuch's appointment (i.e., during the time that Mitch McConnell and the Republican-controlled Senate refused to consider Merrick Garland and therefore de facto reduced the size of the Court to eight). Kennedy, despite his *Gonzales* opinion, voted with the four progressive justices to strike down the statute five to three.

With the retirement of Kennedy and the appointments of Gorsuch and Brett Kavanaugh, the Court will likely either minimize or eliminate a woman's right to choose. Kavanaugh, who replaced the retired Kennedy, will almost certainly join the other conservative justices in their opposition to *Roe*. Before his Supreme Court appointment, Kavanaugh was a judge on the District of Columbia Court of Appeals. In a 2017 en banc decision, that court stopped the Trump administration from preventing an undocumented minor, a seventeen-year-old, from getting an abortion. (She was in the custody of Immigration and Customs Enforcement.) Kavanaugh dissented: He would have, in effect, forced the teenager to carry the pregnancy to term unless a sponsor was found to accept custody of the teen. After Kavanaugh's appointment to the Supreme Court, he participated in the Court's decision regarding a Louisiana statute mandating admitting privileges for doctors performing abortions, similar to the statute invalidated in *Whole Woman's Health*. (Like the Texas statute, the Louisiana statute would force the closing of abortion clinics.) The plaintiff in *June Medical Services, L.L.C. v. Gee* petitioned the Court for a stay to prevent the implementation of the statute during litigation. In a brief order not discussing the merits of the claim, the Court granted the stay, temporarily maintaining the status quo. Kavanaugh, Gorsuch, Thomas, and Alito all voted to deny the stay, and Kavanaugh wrote a dissent. Kavanaugh, in short, is clearly hostile to a woman's right to choose. Gorsuch's position is not as clear, but given his vote in *June Medical Services*, his avowed commitment to originalism, and his wide-ranging conservatism, he, too, is likely to support the minimization or elimination of the right. In fact, Gorsuch has celebrated the ultraconservative Scalia, a longtime opponent of abortion rights, as a "lion of the law."[76]

When the Court subsequently decided *June Medical Services* on the merits, during the summer of 2020, the precariousness of the right to choose crystallized more clearly. Roberts joined the progressives in a five-to-four decision invalidating the Louisiana statute—thus temporarily preserving the right to choose—but significantly, Roberts refused to join Breyer's plurality opinion. Breyer followed *Whole Woman's Health*, applying the undue burden standard as a balancing test and concluding that the statutory admitting privileges requirement contravened the constitutional right to choose.[77] Roberts concurred in the judgment because, in his view, the doctrine of stare decisis required the Court to follow the outcome of *Whole Woman's Health*: The Louisiana statute (challenged in *June Medical Services*) was "nearly identical" to the Texas statute (invalidated in *Whole Woman's Health*).[78] But Roberts expressly rejected Breyer's interpretation of the undue burden standard as a balancing test; in fact, Roberts emphasized that he dissented in *Whole Woman's*

Health. Roberts denigrated balancing tests in general—where "unweighted factors mysteriously are weighed"—and condemned balancing in abortion cases more specifically as requiring the weighing of "imponderable values."[79]

For a variety of reasons, the other conservative justices—Thomas, Alito, Gorsuch, and Kavanaugh—argued that stare decisis and *Whole Woman's Health* did not mandate the invalidation of the Louisiana statute. Perhaps more important for the future of the right to choose, all four justices agreed with Roberts's interpretation of the undue burden standard: It is not a balancing test. Like Roberts, these justices generally dislike balancing tests and specifically repudiate balancing in abortion cases. "The benefits and burdens [to be weighed] are incommensurable," wrote Gorsuch, "and they do not teach such things in law school."[80] How can a court determine if a burden is "undue" or an obstacle is "substantial" if not through a weighing or balancing of interests? The conservative justices do not fully explain, though their sentiments are apparent. They want a more formal rule that will facilitate greater state regulation of abortion (while disregarding women's interests in choosing abortion), or they want to eliminate the right to choose altogether.[81] As to the newest justices, Gorsuch and Kavanaugh erased any doubts: They are hostile to a woman's right to choose.[82]

JUDICIAL PROTECTION FOR WHITES, NOT PEOPLE OF COLOR

The Roberts Court's judicial protection of the wealthy has a disparate or discriminatory effect against people of color. In the United States, wealth and income inequalities have been egregious for decades and continue to worsen—across all races. For instance, in 2016 the share of wealth held by the top 20 percent was 77 percent of total household wealth. Before 2010, the middle class owned more wealth than the top 1 percent, but that distribution has changed (with the middle class being the middle 60 percent). By 2016, the top 1 percent owned 29 percent of household wealth, far more than the entire middle class. Income inequality is just as dispiriting. Adjusting for inflation, "the average post-tax incomes of the lower half of society grew by just 39% from 1968 to 2014, as incomes for the richest one percent almost tripled." Significantly, wealth and income are not evenly distributed among racial groups. Far from it. Black Americans and Hispanics lag far behind whites. The differences in wealth and income for white and black families are staggering. As of 2016, "[T]he median black worker earned 75 percent of what the median white worker earned in an hour; the median black household earned 61 percent of the income the median white household earned in a year; and the value of net worth for the median black family was just 10 percent of the value for the median white family." The median net worth of white families was $171,000 but only $17,600 for black families.[83]

Meanwhile, in constitutional cases explicitly involving race, the Roberts Court acts as if the United States either does not have a history of slavery, Jim Crow, and racism or has successfully eradicated all vestiges of that historical past. *Shelby County v. Holder*, discussed earlier in this chapter, invalidated the crucial preclearance coverage provision in the VRA. Roberts's opinion concluded that the nation had moved past racial discrimination in voting and no longer needed the VRA protections. From his perspective, the evidence suggested that Congress might have correctly enacted the law in 1965, but times had changed. Of course, after the Court decided *Shelby County* and invalidated the preclearance provision, we discovered just how much times had not changed. More than half the states soon passed new restrictions on voting that disproportionately disfranchised black voters.[84]

The Court's disregard for the nation's legacy of racism is nowhere clearer than in its Fourteenth Amendment equal-protection decisions. In *Adarand Constructors, Inc. v. Peña*, decided in 1995, the Rehnquist Court held that all affirmative action programs are subject to strict scrutiny: The government could justify an affirmative action program only if it could prove the program was narrowly tailored to achieve a compelling government purpose. Justice O'Connor's majority opinion acknowledged, though, that the government might in some circumstances satisfy this rigorous judicial standard. Government affirmative action programs might occasionally be constitutional. In separate concurrences, however, Scalia and Thomas both argued for a formalist concept of equal protection that would preclude the government from ever justifying affirmative action. From their perspective, the Constitution mandated that the government be color-blind. Scalia wrote: "[U]nder our Constitution there can be no such thing as either a creditor or a debtor race." Thomas was more vehement: "So-called 'benign' discrimination teaches many that because of chronic and apparently immutable handicaps, minorities cannot compete with them without their patronizing indulgence. . . . These [affirmative action] programs stamp minorities with a badge of inferiority and may cause them to develop dependencies or to adopt an attitude that they are 'entitled' to preferences. . . . In my mind, government-sponsored racial discrimination based on benign prejudice is just as noxious as discrimination inspired by malicious prejudice. In each instance, it is racial discrimination, plain and simple."[85]

In 2007, the Roberts Court decided *Parents Involved in Community Schools v. Seattle School District No. 1*, which involved public school affirmative action programs (in Seattle and Louisville). Under the challenged programs, school officials maintained racially integrated public schools by considering race when assigning students to elementary and high schools. Roberts, writing for a five-justice majority (joined by Scalia, Thomas, Alito, and Kennedy), applied strict scrutiny and invalidated the programs. In a plurality section of his opinion (which Justice Kennedy did not join), Roberts emphasized that equal protection required the government to be color-blind. According to Roberts, affirmative action programs and Jim Crow laws are constitutionally indistinguishable. The principle of equality embodied in *Brown v. Board of Education*, Roberts explained, mandated the invalidation of the *Parents Involved* affirmative action programs. "The way to stop discrimination on the basis of race is to stop discriminating on the basis of race." Thomas wrote a concurrence emphasizing the importance of color-blindness and criticizing the dissenters. "Disfavoring a color-blind interpretation of the Constitution," Thomas wrote, "[the dissenters] would give school boards a free hand to make decisions on the basis of race—an approach reminiscent of that advocated by the segregationists in *Brown v. Board of Education*. This approach is just as wrong today as it was a half-century ago."[86]

After *Parents Involved*, the Court decided two cases involving affirmative action and the University of Texas. In *Fisher v. University of Texas at Austin* (*Fisher I*), the Court emphasized that the university's race-based affirmative program for admissions must be judicially evaluated pursuant to strict scrutiny. The Court was reacting to a 2003 Rehnquist Court decision, *Grutter v. Bollinger*, which had concluded that the University of Michigan School of Law satisfied strict scrutiny in defending its affirmative action admissions program. In *Fisher I*, the Court stressed that, despite the result in *Grutter*, strict scrutiny should not be enfeebled or diminished in its rigor. The Court remanded the case to the lower court so it could apply the appropriate rigorous level of scrutiny. Once again, Scalia and Thomas wrote concurrences stressing the need for government color-blindness. "The Equal Protection Clause strips States of all authority to use race as a factor in providing education," wrote Thomas. "All applicants must be treated equally under the law, and no benefit in the eye of the beholder can justify racial discrimination."[87]

The case returned to the Supreme Court in *Fisher II*, decided in 2016. In a four-to-three decision, the Court surprisingly upheld the university's race-based affirmative action program. Kennedy's majority opinion reiterated the *Fisher I* holding, but he was willing to show some deference to the university in setting a goal of student body diversity. In dissent, Alito emphasized that deference was inappropriate under strict scrutiny, and Thomas once again argued for color-blindness.[88] In any event, as with the 2016 abortion decision in *Whole Woman's Health v. Hellerstedt*, the vitality of *Fisher II* is highly questionable. This was the first and only time that Kennedy voted to uphold an affirmative action program. More important, the Court decided *Fisher II* shorthanded, after Scalia's death, when the Court had only eight justices. (Also, Kagan recused herself on both *Fisher* cases.) Since the new conservative justices, Gorsuch (filling Scalia's seat) and Kavanaugh (filling Kennedy's seat), are likely to join the three *Fisher II* dissenters—Alito, Thomas, and Roberts—the Court seems poised to proclaim affirmative action unconstitutional under all circumstances.

In fact, in 2018 and 2019 the Court decided cases suggesting its likely direction with regard to race. In 2018, the recently appointed Gorsuch and Kennedy, in his final year on the bench, joined Thomas, Roberts, and Alito in a five-to-four decision, *Abbott v. Perez*, in which race and democracy intersected. A three-judge federal district court had held that the Texas legislature violated equal protection and the VRA by intentionally discriminating on the basis of race when it adopted a districting plan for Congress and the Texas (legislative) House. The Supreme Court reversed the lower court and upheld the districting plan, except for one Texas House district. Justice Alito's majority opinion emphasized that, in an equal-protection case, if the challenged law is facially neutral—in other words, the law does not overtly classify on the basis of race—then the challenger bears the burden of proving that the government intentionally discriminated on the basis of race. Proof of racially disparate or discriminatory effects, standing alone, is insufficient to establish discriminatory intent. Alito concluded that the lower court "committed a fundamental legal error" by shifting the burden of proof onto the government. Moreover, from Alito's standpoint, evidence of the Texas legislature's history of racial discrimination in congressional districting was insufficient to prove that the legislature had intentionally discriminated in adopting its new districting plan.[89]

Justice Sonia Sotomayor dissented. She emphasized that the lower court had not shifted the burden of proof. To the contrary, the lower court had applied a multifactor test, spelled out previously in *Arlington Heights v. Metropolitan Housing Development Corporation*, in determining that the legislature had intentionally discriminated on the basis of race. A "substantial amount of evidence," including the legislature's history of discrimination, supported this conclusion. Sotomayor emphasized the degree to which the Court majority was shielding inequality in the democratic process. The Court's decision "comes at serious costs to our democracy. It means that . . . minority voters in Texas—despite constituting a majority of the population within the State— will continue to be underrepresented in the political process." Whereas "all voters in our country, regardless of race, [should securely enjoy] the right to equal participation in our political processes," Sotomayor wrote, the Court was facilitating "[s]tates' efforts to undermine the ability of minority voters to meaningfully exercise that right."[90]

To underscore a crucial point, one should not miss the significant interplay between *Parents Involved*, involving affirmative action, and *Abbott*, involving proof of racial discrimination. If a white plaintiff challenges a race-based affirmative action program as violating equal protection, the Court automatically reviews the law pursuant to strict scrutiny, the most rigorous level of judicial scrutiny, even if the law, as is most often the case, is intended to benefit historically subordinated societal groups—namely, black Americans and other people of color. But if a black plaintiff challenges a facially neutral law that has disparate or discriminatory racial effects—such as the legislative districting law in *Abbott*—then the Court will not apply strict scrutiny unless the plaintiff proves that the government intentionally discriminated on the basis of race. And as *Abbott* shows, proving intentional racial discrimination in court is extremely difficult. The Court's doctrinal framework is racially skewed: Whites challenging affirmative action will almost always win, while people of color challenging laws with even grossly discriminatory effects will usually lose.[91]

The Court's interpretation of equal protection, in other words, perversely reinforces the racial status quo, with historically produced and entrenched structural racism privileging whites at the expense of people of color. Suppose a city has racially discriminated for years in the awarding of construction contracts. Let's say that black Americans constitute 50 percent of the city's population, but the city awarded fewer than 1 percent of all construction contracts to black-owned businesses. If a black contractor sued the city for violating equal protection, the contractor would likely lose. The Court would require the contractor to prove the city had intentionally discriminated on the basis of race, but the statistical evidence comparing the population demographics with the awarding of construction contracts would be insufficient to prove such intent. Now suppose the City Council recognized the injustice of the city's historical discrimination in the awarding of construction contracts. In an effort to rectify that injustice, the city voluntarily adopted an affirmative action program requiring at least 10 percent of all construction contracts be awarded to businesses owned by people of color. If a white contractor sued the city, the Court would apply strict scrutiny and invalidate the affirmative action program. Quite simply, the Court's approach to racial discrimination and injustice, especially the conservative justices' commitment to color-blindness, "ignores the lived reality of people of color" and propagates white privilege.[92]

In 2019, Gorsuch and the newly appointed Kavanaugh joined Alito, Thomas, and Roberts in a five-to-four decision, *Manhattan Community Access Corporation v. Halleck*, that involved free speech and race. Kavanaugh wrote the majority opinion for the conservative bloc. Two producers of public access programming, DeeDee Halleck and Jesus Papoleto Melendez, made a film protesting public access TV's alleged neglect of East Harlem, a predominantly Hispanic and black neighborhood in New York City. The city had contracted with the Manhattan Community Access Corporation (operating as the Manhattan Neighborhood Network, or MNN) to run its public access television channels, and MNN aired Halleck and Melendez's film. When some viewers complained, however, MNN suspended the two producers from further access to its TV facilities. Halleck and Melendez sued, claiming that MNN had violated their free-speech rights by denying them access based on the content of their expression. The Court applied an ostensible formal rule, the state action doctrine, and held that MNN was not subject to First Amendment limitations because it was a private rather than a government actor. In accord with the conservative approval of neoliberal ideology, Kavanaugh's opinion emphasized the importance of the public-private dichotomy, particularly as it relates to the protection of private property rights and "a robust sphere of individual liberty." The consequences of MNN's actions and the Court's decision for people of color and race relations in the city were irrelevant under Kavanaugh's analysis.[93]

JUDICIAL PROTECTION OF CHRISTIANITY

The Roberts Court has adamantly protected Christianity while showing hostility toward other religions. The Court has pushed its pro-Christian agenda pursuant to both First Amendment religion clauses: the Establishment Clause and the Free Exercise Clause. The First Amendment language is as follows: "Congress shall make no law respecting an establishment of religion, or prohibiting the free exercise thereof." Since the 1940s, the Court has applied both clauses not only against Congress and the national government but also against state and local governments.[94] During the Roberts Court years, the conservative justices have tended toward a narrow interpretation of the Establishment Clause, allowing greater government involvement with Christianity, and a broader interpretation of the Free Exercise Clause, granting greater protection to Christian practices. These tendencies reverse, however, when a minority religion is involved.

On the Establishment Clause side, a five-to-four decision in 2014, *Town of Greece v. Galloway*, upheld the opening of Town Board meetings with overtly sectarian Christian prayers. Here is one example: "Lord, God of all creation, we give you thanks and praise for your presence and action in the world. We look with anticipation to the celebration of Holy Week and Easter. It is in the solemn events of next week that we find the very heart and center of our Christian faith. We acknowledge the saving sacrifice of Jesus Christ on the cross. We draw strength, vitality, and confidence from his resurrection at Easter." The conservative bloc found that such prayers did not violate the Establishment Clause because they were integral to American traditions, though this particular town did not begin the practice until 1999.[95]

The opinion underscored three important points, all of which were in tension with earlier Establishment Clause decisions. First, when delivering prayers, the government does not need even to pretend to aim for ostensibly nonsectarian prayers. Second, the Court is moving away from enforcing the Establishment Clause pursuant to the so-called *Lemon* test, first fully articulated in the 1971 decision *Lemon v. Kurtzman*: "First, the statute must have a secular legislative purpose; second, its principal or primary effect must be one that neither advances nor inhibits religion; finally, the statute must not foster 'an excessive government entanglement with religion.'" Applying *Lemon*, the Court had previously interpreted the Establishment Clause to prohibit nonsectarian prayers in public schools, moments of silence in the public schools, and the posting of the Ten Commandments in county buildings. Given these decisions, conservatives have long criticized the three-pronged *Lemon* standard as manifesting a wall of separation between church and state and, as such, being too hostile toward religion. Significantly, the *Town of Greece* Court did not even mention the *Lemon* test. Third, the Court emphasized that it was appropriate to interpret the Establishment Clause in accord with tradition—especially Christian tradition. That is, tradition did not create an exception from the best interpretation of the Establishment Clause; rather, tradition informed the best interpretation from the outset.[96]

In another Establishment Clause decision, *American Legion v. American Humanist Association*, decided in 2019, the Court upheld the constitutionality of a thirty-two-foot Christian cross displayed on public land, a traffic island in a busy intersection of Bladensburg, Maryland. The "Bladensburg Peace Cross" had been erected in 1925 "as a tribute to 49 area soldiers who gave their lives in the First World War." Alito wrote the opinion for the Court, though parts of his opinion were only plurality, joined by three other justices. In a plurality section of his opinion, Alito explicitly criticized the *Lemon* test, running through a litany of its "shortcomings." Instead of applying *Lemon*, Alito emphasized the importance of tradition, urging "a presumption of constitutionality for longstanding monuments, symbols, and practices." Follow-

ing this approach, Alito reasoned that, although the cross is generally considered "a symbol of Christianity," it can also take "on a secular meaning,"
depending on the context and length of time of its display. And from Alito's
perspective, whatever the original purpose of the Bladensburg Cross might
have been, its decades-long display had made it part of the "community's
landscape and identity." For that reason, the display of the Bladensburg Cross
was now secular and did not violate the Establishment Clause. In fact, Alito
suggested that a finding of unconstitutionality would have been "aggressively
hostile to religion." Ginsburg dissented. She acknowledged that memorial-
izing the service and sacrifice of American soldiers is secular, but the display
of a Christian cross is not. The Bladensburg Cross, she emphasized, did not
honor those soldiers who observed other religions or no religion at all.[97]

On the Free Exercise Clause side, the Court in 2018 decided *Masterpiece
Cakeshop, Ltd. v. Colorado Civil Rights Commission*, holding that the First
Amendment invalidated government sanctioning of a baker, Jack Phillips,
who had discriminated against a same-sex couple. Phillips had refused to
bake a cake for the couple's wedding reception because he opposed same-
sex marriage on religious grounds. The Colorado Civil Rights Commission
concluded that Phillips had violated the Colorado Anti-Discrimination Act
(CADA), a statute expressly prohibiting discrimination based on sexual orientation. As one commissioner emphasized, religious beliefs could not justify
statutorily prohibited discrimination. The Supreme Court overturned the
commission's decision. Justice Kennedy, writing for the majority, reasoned
that the commission had failed to treat Phillips's religious beliefs with "neutral and respectful consideration." According to Kennedy, the commission
had purposefully discriminated against Phillips when adjudicating the discrimination claim against him.[98]

The Court supported its finding of purposeful discrimination by primarily focusing on a commissioner's statement about religion and discrimination. "Freedom of religion and religion has been used to justify all kinds
of discrimination throughout history," the commissioner stated, "whether it
be slavery, whether it be the [H]olocaust, whether it be—I mean, we—we
can list hundreds of situations where freedom of religion has been used to
justify discrimination. And to me it is one of the most despicable pieces of
rhetoric that people can use to—to use their religion to hurt others." According to the Court, this statement undermined the state's argument that
the commission had been fair, impartial, and neutral. More specifically, the
Court appeared to condemn the commissioner's statement for two reasons:
the commissioner's historical connection of religion and discrimination and
the commissioner's normative judgment about religious discrimination.[99]

Breaking down the commissioner's statement, he asserted a historical fact: "Freedom of religion and religion has been used to justify all kinds of discrimination throughout history."[100] But despite the Court's unhappiness with this assertion, it was unequivocally correct. History is littered with attempts to justify discrimination and persecution based on religious beliefs. The most obvious example involves Christian anti-Semitism and persecution of Jews. The Christian Bible (or New Testament) explicitly blames Jews for killing Jesus Christ and for stubbornly refusing to accept him as the son of God. The Jews, from this perspective, therefore deserve to suffer and to be endlessly persecuted. Indeed, the condemnation of Jews and Judaism became an integral "aspect of Christian self-identity." For centuries, New Testament discourse ostensibly justified anti-Semitism and persecution. Christian rulers forced Jews to wear badges or other signs of identification, isolated Jews in ghettos, and exiled Jews from entire countries. Christians repeatedly accused, condemned, and punished Jews for supposedly sacrificing Christian children for religious purposes as part of Jewish rituals.[101]

Nineteenth-century Americans frequently invoked Christianity and the Bible as justifying slavery. For instance, in the introduction to *Cotton Is King*, an anthology published in 1860, E. N. Elliott wrote: "We understand the nature of the negro race; and in the relation in which the providence of God has placed them to us, they are happy and useful members of society." In one of the *Cotton Is King* essays, a Baptist pastor, Thornton Stringfellow, explained: "Under the gospel, it has brought within the range of gospel influence, millions of [slaves] among ourselves, who but for this institution, would have sunk down to eternal ruin; knowing not God, and strangers to the gospel. In their bondage here on earth, they have been much better provided for, and great multitudes of them have been made the freemen of the Lord Jesus Christ, and left this world rejoicing in hope of the glory of God." In another essay in the same volume, Albert Taylor Bledsoe, an American Episcopal minister and a professor at the University of Virginia, maintained that "the institution of slavery, as it exists among us at the South, is founded in political justice, is in accordance with the will of God and the designs of his providence, and is conducive to the highest, purest, best interests of mankind."[102]

Through the twentieth century, segregationists continued to use religion to justify their racist policies and laws. The Baptist Reverend James F. Burks argued in favor of segregation in 1954: "The Word of God is the surest and only infallible source of our facts of Ethnology, and when man sets aside the plain teachings of this Blessed Book and disregards the boundary lines God Himself has drawn, man assumes a prerogative that belongs to God alone." Mississippi Senator Theodore G. Bilbo maintained that "miscegenation and amalgamation are sins of man in direct defiance with the will of God." In a case that ended in the Supreme Court, *Loving v. Virginia*, the trial judge explained why antimiscegenation laws were ostensibly necessary: "Almighty God created the races white, black, yellow, malay and red, and he placed them on separate continents. And but for the interference with his arrangement there would be no cause for such marriages. The fact that he separated the races shows that he did not intend for the races to mix."[103]

The *Masterpiece Cakeshop* Court also denounced the commissioner's normative judgment about religious discrimination. "And to me," the commissioner stated, "it is one of the most despicable pieces of rhetoric that people can use to—to use their religion to hurt others." But contrary to the Court's conclusion, this normative statement did not reveal hostility toward religion when understood in the context of the dispute. Remember, Phillips had invoked his religion to justify discrimination against the same-sex couple. Phillips would not bake a wedding cake for their marriage. The commission was adjudicating whether Phillips had violated CADA, the state antidiscrimination statute, which prohibits discrimination based on sexual orientation (among other things). The prohibited discrimination could not be allowed, regardless of Phillips's justification. Like others before him, Phillips might alternatively have invoked freedom of contract, federalism concerns for state sovereignty, a fear of government tyranny, or any ostensible reason to insulate his conduct from government regulation. Phillips's asserted justification was irrelevant to the commission's determination of whether he had engaged in prohibited discriminatory conduct. The commissioner's normative statement was therefore unnecessary—because it did not address the fact of the prohibited discriminatory conduct—but in this context, the statement was eminently reasonable. If anything, the commissioner appeared to suggest that religion should have a higher calling. It can promote social justice, social harmony, personal redemption, and the like. A person acts despicably, according to the commissioner, when he or she twists religious tenets (as well as the constitutional principle of free exercise) to justify discrimination, persecution, or subordination of others. As Justice Kagan explained in a concurrence, "[A] vendor [such as Phillips] cannot escape a public accommodations law because his religion disapproves selling a product to a group of customers, whether defined by sexual orientation, race, sex, or other protected trait."[104]

During the summer of 2020, the Court decided five to four, with a conservative-progressive split, another free-exercise case by stretching to find purposeful state discrimination against religion. *Espinoza v. Montana Department of Revenue* arose after the Montana state legislature created a tax credit for those donating money to student scholarship organizations.[105] Under the program, scholarship money could be used at any private school, including religious schools. The state constitution, though, contained a provision that precluded the public funding of religious schools. Consequently, the Montana Department of Revenue promulgated a rule prohibiting families from using the scholarship money at religious schools. Three parents of children attending the Stillwater Christian School challenged the rule preventing them from using scholarship money under the tax credit program. The parents explicitly chose Stillwater, which covered prekindergarten through twelfth grade, "because it 'teaches the same Christian values that [they] teach at home.'"[106] In response to this challenge, the Montana Supreme Court struck down the entire tax credit program: Therefore, no private schools, whether religious or otherwise, could continue to receive scholarship money.

Nevertheless, the conservative bloc of justices, with Roberts writing the opinion, concluded that the state court decision amounted to purposeful discrimination against religion, which violated the Free Exercise Clause. As Ginsburg reasoned in dissent, the parent-challengers to the tax credit program argued "that the Free Exercise Clause requires a State to treat institutions and people neutrally when doling out a benefit—and neutrally is how Montana treats them in the wake of the state court's decision."[107] In effect, the Roberts Court's decision would force the state to financially support religious schools and their overtly religious practices.[108] Given this, it is worth underscoring that "most of private schools that would benefit from the [scholarship] program were 'religiously affiliated' and 'controlled by churches,'" as even Chief Justice Roberts acknowledged.[109] More specifically, "94 percent of the scholarships [in 2018] went to students attending religious schools," with religious schools constituting 70 percent of the private schools in the state—the vast majority of the religious schools being associated with some form of Christianity.[110]

Another case focused on religion, *Burwell v. Hobby Lobby Stores, Inc.*, dealt with a statute, the Religious Freedom Restoration Act (RFRA), rather than the First Amendment. While the *Masterpiece Cakeshop* Court interpreted the Free Exercise Clause to allow religiously motivated discrimination against a same-sex couple, despite the Court's currently protecting a constitutional (due process) right to same-sex marriage, the *Hobby Lobby* Court interpreted the RFRA to allow religiously motivated discrimination against women using contraceptives, despite a currently protected constitutional (due process) right to use contraceptives. In fact, in *Hobby Lobby*, decided in 2014, the conservative bloc managed to protect simultaneously both corporate power and Christianity. Regulations under the Affordable Care Act required corporations to provide health insurance coverage to employees for various types of contraceptives. Closely held and for-profit corporations nonetheless argued that complicity in supplying certain types of contraceptives—which the corporations claimed were abortifacients—violated their rights to religious freedom as protected under the RFRA. The government replied, in part, that corporations do not exercise religion and consequently do not have rights under the RFRA. The Court disagreed and held in favor of the corporations. Alito wrote for the majority: "Protecting the free-exercise rights of corporations like Hobby Lobby," controlled by conservative Christians, "protects the religious liberty of the humans who own and control those companies." In dissent, Justice Ginsburg castigated the majority's "expansive notion of corporate personhood."[111]

In sum, the conservative bloc interprets the Establishment Clause, the Free Exercise Clause, and statutes to protect Christian practices and beliefs, even when those practices and beliefs detrimentally affect others.[112] The conservative bloc is not nearly as sympathetic to or protective of non-Christian religions. In *Masterpiece Cakeshop*, the Court dug deeply into the Colorado Civil Rights Commission's proceedings to uncover ostensible animus against Christianity. But the Court in *Trump v. Hawaii* upheld a presidentially imposed travel ban infected with anti-Muslim animus. The travel ban, ostensibly instituted to protect national security, went through several versions and legal challenges before reaching the Court for final adjudication. In the end, the ban imposed restrictions (on entry into the United States) on nationals from eight nations—"Chad, Iran, Iraq, Libya, North Korea, Syria, Venezuela, and Yemen"—six of which were predominantly Muslim. Throughout the processes of revision and litigation, President Trump vehemently and persistently denounced Islam, as Justice Sotomayor emphasized in dissent:

> Taking all the relevant evidence together, a reasonable observer would conclude that the Proclamation was driven primarily by anti-Muslim animus, rather than by the Government's asserted national-security justifications. Even before being sworn into office, then-candidate Trump stated that "Islam hates us," warned that "[w]e're having problems with the Muslims, and we're having problems with Muslims coming into the country," promised to enact a "total and complete shutdown of Muslims entering the United States," and instructed one of his advisers to find a "lega[l]" way to enact a Muslim ban. The President continued to make similar statements well after his inauguration. . . . Moreover, despite several opportunities to do so, President Trump has never disavowed any of his prior statements about Islam. Instead, he has continued to make remarks that a reasonable observer

would view as an unrelenting attack on the Muslim religion and its followers.

In fact, the administration appeared to include the non-Muslim countries of North Korea and Venezuela on the final list of targeted nations to disguise the travel ban's "otherwise clear targeting of Muslims."[113]

In a five-to-four decision, the conservative bloc held that the travel ban did not violate the Establishment Clause. The Court dismissed the president's overtly anti-Muslim statements as irrelevant because the ban was facially neutral—it listed the eight countries without expressly mentioning Islam or Muslims. Moreover, the Court stressed that it should defer to presidential judgments regarding immigration and national security. As Sotomayor suggested, though, the conservative justices' casual disregard for explicit anti-Muslim animus could not be harmonized with their worried search for anti-Christian animus in *Masterpiece Cakeshop*.[114]

The Court displayed a similar inhospitable attitude toward another non-Christian religion in a free-speech case, *Pleasant Grove City v. Summum*, decided in 2009. The city of Pleasant Grove displayed in a public park several privately donated monuments, including one showing the Ten Commandments, contributed years earlier by the Fraternal Order of Eagles. Summum, a minority religious group, offered to donate a monument showing its Seven Aphorisms, also called the Seven Principles of Creation. The city refused to accept the monument. The case resembled several Rehnquist Court decisions that had held public school properties to be public forums open for Christian organizations. For example, in *Rosenberger v. Rectors and Visitors of the University of Virginia*, the Court held that the First Amendment required a public university to fund an overtly religious student newspaper. Likewise, in *Good News Club v. Milford Central School*, the Court held that the First Amendment required a public elementary school to allow a private Christian organization to hold club meetings on school property. Such public forum decisions seemed to mandate that Pleasant Grove display the Summum monument in its public park, a traditional public forum. But the Court disagreed, instead invoking a formal rule that completely excused the government from First Amendment strictures: "[T]he placement of a permanent monument in a public park is best viewed as a form of government speech and is therefore not subject to scrutiny under the Free Speech Clause." In other words, under the Court's "recently minted" government speech doctrine, the display of the Summum monument "is not a form of expression to which [public] forum analysis applies."[115]

COUNTEREXAMPLES: HOW CONSERVATIVE IS THE ROBERTS COURT?

Not every Roberts Court decision is conservative.[116] Some cases are not politically salient—neither conservatives nor progressives are likely to care politically about the outcome.[117] More important, a handful of the Court's prominent and politically salient decisions might be deemed liberal or progressive. These are the counterexamples; the cases that an opponent of court packing might emphasize while declaring that the Roberts Court is not conservative enough to justify Democratic court packing, even if court packing might sometimes be justifiable.[118]

There are two responses to these counterexamples. The first (and briefer) response is to recall the political science empirical studies explained in Chapter 1. Through various measures, political scientists have consistently rated the Roberts Court justices as highly conservative, even if they occasionally issue decisions that offend conservative observers. They are conservative according to general measures of political ideology, and they are conservative specifically in that they favor business in a variety of contexts and conservative speakers in First Amendment cases, and they shape the docket to favor conservative causes.[119]

The second (and lengthier) response requires an examination of the counterexample cases. Typically, these ostensibly liberal decisions contain significant conservative elements. The key to analyzing these cases is the law-politics dynamic: The justices—conservatives and progressives alike—care about more than the politics of the case result. They also care about legal doctrine and its implications for the future. Politics *and* law both matter. Thus, conservative justices want not only to reach conservative case results but also to articulate conservative legal doctrine: doctrine that is likely to lead to conservative results in future cases, whether at the Supreme Court or in the lower courts. For example, in a congressional power case, conservative constitutional doctrine would facilitate limiting the scope of congressional power. In an affirmative action case, conservative doctrine would facilitate invalidating race-based affirmative action.[120]

A concern with the creation of conservative doctrine was never more evident than in Chief Justice Roberts's opinion in *Sebelius*, the Affordable Care Act case. With regard to the constitutionality of the individual mandate, recall that Roberts considered whether Congress could enact the mandate under either its commerce or taxing power. First, he reasoned pursuant to formalist categories that Congress had exceeded its Commerce Clause power.

Second, he concluded that the individual mandate was nonetheless constitutional, being within Congress's taxing power. Given Roberts's conclusion on the taxing power, Ginsburg expressed puzzlement: Why had Roberts needed to discuss the commerce power at all? If he believed the individual mandate was constitutional under the taxing power—as he did—he could have avoided discussion of the commerce power. That discussion was not relevant to the final judicial conclusion; it could even be dismissed as dicta. "Why should the Chief Justice," Ginsburg asked, "strive so mightily to hem in Congress' capacity to meet the new problems arising constantly in our ever-developing modern economy?"[121]

Of course, Ginsburg's question was rhetorical. The answer was obvious: Roberts reached to discuss Congress's commerce power, when it was unnecessary to do so, precisely because he wanted to articulate doctrine that would, going forward, "hem in Congress' capacity" to regulate the economy. In other words, he wanted to establish conservative doctrine that resonated with neoliberal ideology, doubting congressional capability to enact rational regulations for the economic marketplace. And in that, Roberts was extraordinarily successful: As discussed previously in this chapter, he articulated formalist doctrines that are likely to constrain congressional actions for years to come. Yet while doing so, he simultaneously shielded the Court from Democratic attacks by upholding the constitutionality of the individual mandate (as a tax)—the Court issued this decision on June 28, 2012, less than six months before a presidential election (Barack Obama versus Mitt Romney).

In most cases, the conservative justices can articulate and apply conservative legal doctrine to reach the conservative result. But in the rare case, a conservative justice must choose between articulating and following conservative legal doctrine, on the one hand, and reaching the conservative result, on the other. *Bostock v. Clayton County, Georgia*, decided during the summer of 2020, illustrates this type of dilemma. *Bostock* was not a constitutional case; it required the Court to interpret a statute, Title VII, which prohibits employment discrimination on the basis of "sex" (among other things). The issue was whether the prohibition of sex discrimination protects LGBTQ individuals.[122]

Since the mid-1980s, Justice Scalia had been advocating for a conservative approach to statutory interpretation: textualism. According to textualism (similar to originalism in constitutional interpretation), the justices (and other judges) should interpret statutes based solely on the text—"the most probable meaning of the words of the enactment." Textualism is conservative because it is likely to narrow the reach or scope of legislative enactments. Even when statutory language seems ambiguous, the justices are not to consider legislative history, the underlying purpose of the statute, or the possible consequences of different potential interpretations.[123] In fact, textualism is grounded on the conservative neoliberal assumption that legislatures, Congress included, do not have discernible coherent purposes behind their enactments. Courts should not pretend otherwise when interpreting statutes.[124]

Justice Gorsuch has fully subscribed to and defended textualism. "A judge faithful to textualism seeks to enforce a statute's ordinary meaning at the time of its enactment," he wrote in his book, *A Republic, If You Can Keep It.* The judge, then, should not start digging into legislative history or evaluating the likely consequences of alternative interpretations. The advantage of textualism, according to Gorsuch, is that it preserves the law-politics dichotomy— that is, the purity of law: "[T]extualism offers a known and knowable methodology for judges to determine impartially and fix what the law is, not simply declare what it ought to be—a method to discern the written law's content without extraneous value judgments about persons or policies."[125] In *Bostock*, then, Gorsuch had a vested interest in interpreting Title VII from a textualist perspective. The problem for Gorsuch was that textualism would likely lead to the liberal (progressive) result, extending statutory protections against discrimination to LGBTQ individuals. Gorsuch chose to follow his conservative textualist methodology rather than reaching the conservative outcome, which the dissenters, Alito, Thomas, and Kavanaugh, preferred (Roberts and the four progressive justices joined Gorsuch's opinion).[126]

Gorsuch began by emphasizing the judicial commitment to textualism: "This Court normally interprets a statute in accord with the ordinary public meaning of its terms at the time of its enactment." For Gorsuch, whether the statutory prohibition of *sex* discrimination applied to LGBTQ individuals was solely about the meaning of the word "sex." He concluded that employment discrimination against LGBTQ individuals was necessarily sex discrimination.

Suppose an employer has two employees, one man and one woman, and both employees "are attracted to men"; otherwise the two employees are identical (e.g., with regard to job performance). If the employer fires the gay man but not the straight woman, the employer has discriminated on the basis of sex. The man would not have been fired if he had been a woman. The only difference between the two employees—one now fired, the other still employed—is their sex. That's the end of the matter for Gorsuch: He cared about neither the immorality of LGBTQ discrimination nor the purposes of the congressional drafters of the statute. The fact that the drafters "might not have anticipated their work would lead" to the protection of LGBTQ individuals was irrelevant.[127]

One cannot evaluate the political significance of the *Bostock* decision by attending solely to the outcome, the statutory protection of LGBTQ individuals against employment discrimination. To be sure, that result is important. But so is the Court's adherence to the conservative interpretive doctrine of textualism. And in the long run, the following of textualism in the Supreme Court and the lower courts is likely to facilitate many conservative outcomes. In effect, Gorsuch confronted a traditional trolley dilemma. A trolley is speeding along the tracks. If it continues straight, it will kill five people before it can stop. But you are standing at a switch in the tracks. If you throw the switch, the trolley will veer on to a different track, where it will kill one person. What do you do? Gorsuch did not hesitate. He threw the switch, sacrificing the one case (accepting the liberal result) to save the many cases (likely to reach conservative results pursuant to textualism).[128]

To be clear, textualist statutory interpretation is not mechanical. It will not automatically produce conservative results in future cases. Most important, its application will always be a matter of politics writ small. Textualism does not magically transport us to a land where the law-politics *dichotomy* is real. Even when applying textualism, the Court will decide pursuant to the law-politics *dynamic*. Hence, one should be unsurprised to find that Alito, dissenting in *Bostock*, insisted that he was the true textualist; that Gorsuch was an imposter. Scalia, Alito insisted, would have "excoriated" Gorsuch's statutory analysis. As Alito put it, Gorsuch's conclusion that the statutory prohibition of sex discrimination protects LGBTQ individuals was "preposterous." He explained: "Even as understood today, the concept of discrimination because of 'sex' is different from discrimination because of 'sexual orientation' or 'gender identity.' And in any event, our duty is to interpret statutory terms to 'mean what they conveyed to reasonable people at the time they were written.'"[129] Regardless, even though Gorsuch and Alito disagree about how to apply textualism in this case, legal doctrine matters. And just as originalism facilitates reaching conservative outcomes in constitutional cases, textualism facilitates reaching conservative results in cases of statutory interpretation.

Other Roberts Court counterexample decisions can be understood similarly. The Court reached the liberal or progressive result—usually because one or two of the conservative justices voted with the progressive justices—but the opinion articulated either overtly conservative doctrine (as in Roberts's commerce power discussion in *Sebelius*) or doctrine resonant with conservative ideology.[130] Consider two recent cases decided pursuant to administrative law doctrine. *Department of Homeland Security v. Regents of the University of California*, like *Bostock* decided during the summer of 2020, involved the

Deferred Action for Childhood Arrivals (DACA) program, which allows un-documented immigrants who were brought to the United States as children to remain legally in the country, at least temporarily. The Trump administra-tion, in accord with its anti-immigration stance, rescinded DACA. The issue in *Department of Homeland Security* was whether the administration's rescis-sion was consistent with procedural requirements imposed by the Adminis-trative Procedure Act (APA). In a five-to-four decision, Roberts voted with the progressive justices and wrote the Court's opinion holding the rescission to be arbitrary and capricious and therefore a violation of the APA.[131] Roberts made a similar move in *Department of Commerce v. New York*, decided a year earlier. *Department of Commerce* involved a challenge to the Trump adminis-tration's addition of a citizenship question to the 2020 census. Roberts, again writing for the Court, concluded that the administration's justification for adding the citizenship question was "contrived" and therefore did not satisfy the APA requirement for "reasoned decisionmaking."[132]

In both decisions—the DACA case and the census case—the Court reached the progressive result contravening the Trump administration. Yet in both cases, the Court reasoned that an administrative agency had failed to follow proper procedures. The conservative gist of the Court's doctrinal approach was distrust of the government. To be sure, in these cases, distrust of the administration seemed wholly justified on the facts, but nonetheless the Court's reasoning harmonized with the neoliberal hostility toward gov-ernment action, including agency action.[133] In fact, in both cases Roberts noted that the Court was not invalidating the administration's decision on the merits. The administration could reimplement its conservative policies, whether rescinding DACA or adding a citizenship question; the administra-tion merely needed to follow the proper procedures when doing so.[134]

Finally, one might view any seemingly liberal decisions issued during the summer of 2020—for example, *Bostock* (LGBTQ discrimination) and *De-partment of Homeland Security* (DACA)—with a healthy dose of cynicism. The Court handed down these decisions mere months before a presidential election. As with *Sebelius* in 2012, these decisions can provide political cover for the Court—Roberts, in particular, feints left, appearing moderate (the fury unleashed by conservative commentators helps), and tries to remove the Court from the forefront of election-year debates.[135] Unquestionably, one can understand in this vein the Court's summer 2020 abortion decision, *June Medical Services, L.L.C. v. Russo*, discussed earlier in this chapter. Roberts feinted left, joining the progressive justices in a five-to-four decision temporar-ily preserving a woman's right to choose, but Roberts refused to join Breyer's plurality opinion and instead invalidated the Louisiana antiabortion statute on the narrowest ground possible. He reasoned that the Louisiana statute, which required doctors performing abortions to have hospital admitting privileges nearby, was practically identical to the Texas statute invalidated in *Whole Woman's Health v. Hellerstedt*, also discussed earlier. According to Roberts, then, stare decisis mandated invalidating the Louisiana statute. Simultaneously, though, he weakened the doctrinal protection of the right to choose. He rejected Breyer's reasoning in both *Whole Women's Health* and *June Medical*, which sensibly interpreted the *Casey* undue burden standard as a balancing test, weighing a women's interest in choice against the state's interest in regulating abortion. In conjunction with the other conservatives, all dissenting in *June Medical*, Roberts pointed the Court toward, at best, a formal rule facilitating greater state regulation of abortion, ignoring women's interests in choice, or quite possibly, the complete repudiation of the right to choose.

Roberts largely succeeded in shielding the Court from intense political scrutiny in 2012, but he might not be as successful this time around. His gentle nods to the left might be too little and too late to pacify the Democrats. First, Democratic views of the Court have shifted since 2012, given the Merrick Garland debacle, the Gorsuch and (especially contentious) Kavanaugh confirmations, and the rushed nomination and confirmation of Barrett just before the 2020 election. Second, while Roberts might occasionally shift left in a high-profile case, he reveals his persistently strong conservatism in low-profile decisions, when few people pay attention—decisions that belong to the Court's so-called "shadow docket." The Supreme Court has traditionally granted emergency stays of lower court orders against the government in only extraordinary cases, when it determines that the government will suffer irreparable harm. Given such a high bar, the government has rarely sought such relief. During the sixteen years of the George W. Bush and Barack Obama administrations, the government asked the Court for such relief only eight times, with the government request granted half the time. But the Trump administration has sought such relief twenty-nine times, and the Court has granted the requests in whole or part seventeen times. Roberts's receptiveness to the administration's stay applications has been key, while the progressive justices have frequently opposed the granting of relief.[136]

One should not forget that, before his retirement, it was Justice Kennedy rather than Roberts who was rightly considered the swing vote on the Court. Roberts, in fact, was unlikely to vote with the progressives in close and politically salient cases.[137] For instance, Kennedy joined the progressive justices and wrote the Court's opinion in *Obergefell v. Hodges*, the five-to-four decision concluding that same-sex couples enjoy a constitutional right to marry. Roberts wrote a dissent complaining that Kennedy and the majority felt "compelled to sully those on the other side of the debate," piling "assaults on the character of fairminded people" who believe marriage must be only between a man and a woman.[138] In *Whole Woman's Health*, Kennedy again joined the progressives in invalidating the Texas antiabortion restrictions, while Roberts dissented. Likewise, in *Fisher II*, discussed earlier, the Court upheld, four to three, a university's race-based affirmative action program. Once again, Kennedy provided the decisive vote (and wrote the majority opinion), while Roberts dissented.[139] And now, all of these liberal decisions are of questionable vitality given Kennedy's departure and the appointments of Justices Gorsuch, Kavanaugh, and Barrett.

In short, Chief Justice Roberts's occasional feints to the left should not mislead Democrats. He might be the closest thing to a swing vote on this conservative Court, but he should not be confused with a political moderate who might vote progressive in any salient case. First of all, when Roberts joins the progressives to create a majority, Court rules provide that he, as Chief Justice, can assign the opinion to any justice in the majority; by assigning the opinion to himself, he is enabled to write the narrowest (or most conservative) opinion possible.[140] More important, he has demonstrated little concern for preserving democratic processes. To the contrary, he has authored crucial decisions undermining democracy. He wrote the majority opinion in the catastrophic *Shelby County* decision, invalidating as beyond congressional power a key provision of the Voting Rights Act and thus ushering in a rash of state voter suppression laws. He also wrote the majority opinion in *Rucho v. Common Cause*, holding that the political question doctrine protects even extreme partisan gerrymandering from judicial review.[141] And he has been instrumental in the Court's issuance of preliminary orders undermining the democratic process (decisions that typically attract little or only fleeting public attention). For instance, in *Merrill v. People First of Alabama*, the conservative bloc (with the four progressive justices dissenting) issued an order, with an unsigned opinion, that stayed a district court preliminary injunction. The injunction would have facilitated voting by absentee ballot during the COVID-19 (novel coronavirus) pandemic.[142] Prior to that, in another five-to-four decision, *Republican National Committee v. Democratic National Committee*, the Court again stayed a lower court's preliminary injunction. In that case, the Court granted the Republican Party's request to block the lower court from requiring Wisconsin to extend the time for receiving and counting absentee ballots. As Ginsburg emphasized in dissent, the lower court had acted to safeguard voting rights during the pandemic.[143] If Democrats believe they can rely on Roberts to temper the political inclinations of the conservative bloc of justices, they are likely to be sorely disappointed.

The Roberts Court has always been controlled by at least five conservative justices. And as this chapter demonstrates, the Roberts Court has consistently reached conservative conclusions. Yet I do not intend to suggest that the conservative justices ordinarily ignore the law, whether constitutional or otherwise, and merely follow their political preferences or ideologies. In most cases, the justices sincerely interpret the relevant legal texts, but legal interpretation is never mechanical. Politics is always part of legal interpretation. The law-politics *dichotomy* is a myth, while the law-politics *dynamic* describes the reality of Supreme Court decision making. In most cases, then, the justices decide pursuant to politics writ small. Politics informs their interpretations of the legal texts and doctrines. To be sure, in some cases, the justices might instead follow politics writ large. They might invoke legal materials as mere subterfuge or window dressing for overt and self-conscious political power grabs. In fact, the increasing political polarization between Republicans and Democrats, including Supreme Court justices, might provoke at least some justices to press for their preferred political outcomes, regardless of legal texts or doctrines.[144] In many cases, moreover, one might be hard-pressed to discern whether the justices followed politics writ small or large. Nevertheless, as discussed in Chapter 5, normal Supreme Court decision making generally follows the law-politics dynamic and politics writ small.

After all, Supreme Court justices would gain little advantage by pursuing politics writ large. In almost all instances, the justices can reach the same outcome by following professional norms, sincerely interpreting legal texts and doctrines, and allowing politics writ small to lead them to their politically favored results. Because sincere legal interpretation corresponds with politics writ small, politics writ large is beside the point—and politics writ small goes unacknowledged. Unsurprisingly, then, the conservative Roberts Court justices have insistently proclaimed their commitment to apolitical adjudication. Congress and other legislative bodies can make political decisions (well, maybe sometimes, if the Court allows them), but the Court must neutrally follow the rule of law. In *Sebelius*, Roberts wrote: "We do not consider whether the [Affordable Care] Act embodies sound policies. That judgment is entrusted to the Nation's elected leaders. We ask only whether Congress has the power under the Constitution to enact the challenged provisions."[145] In *Masterpiece Cakeshop*, the baker's refusal to bake a wedding cake for a same-sex couple appeared to present the Court with a conflict between religious-freedom rights and LGBTQ rights. Neutrality appeared impossible, yet Kennedy's majority opinion insisted that "these disputes must be resolved with tolerance, without undue disrespect to sincere religious beliefs, and without subjecting gay persons to indignities when they seek goods and services in an open market."[146] And, of course, Scalia repeatedly emphasized that originalism is the only acceptable method of constitutional interpretation because all other interpretive methods force judges to inject their political preferences into adjudication. If the rule of law must be "the law of rules," as Scalia maintained, then constitutional "words must be given the meaning they had when the text was adopted." Any approach other than originalism requires judges to determine societal needs and values. Likewise, Gorsuch proclaims that originalism "offers neutral (non-political, non-personal) principles" for judicial decision making.[147]

Despite such pronouncements of judicial neutrality and apolitical decision making, politics is always part of Supreme Court interpretation and adjudication. Most important, then, as a general matter, court packing is justifiable: It cannot destroy the purity of the Court as a legal-judicial institution because the Court has never been pure—bereft of politics. As this chapter shows, court packing is specifically justified in our current political circumstances. The Democrats should pack the Court when they have the opportunity. The Roberts Court's decisions demonstrate that the Court's conservatism has been deep and wide: The justices have protected an undemocratic society in which wealthy white Christian men consistently emerge victorious. Of course, the Court's slew of conservative decisions were entirely predictable, since a conservative bloc of justices has always controlled the Roberts Court. The Democrats' best response to the Court, therefore, would be to add as many justices as necessary to create a progressive majority—a progressive majority that would predictably reach progressive decisions.

8

_____

CONCLUSION

Court Packing and Supreme Court Legitimacy

The law is one thing, politics is another, and never the twain shall meet. Or so goes the story of the law-politics *dichotomy.* But law and politics do meet in Supreme Court decision making. History shows that the Supreme Court has been (and will continue to be) permeated with politics. Politics has invariably been part of the nomination process, the confirmation process, and, perhaps most important at this time in American history, the process of setting the number of justices on the Court. Moreover, an analytic understanding of legal interpretation underscores that a law-politics *dynamic* always animates Supreme Court decision making. Supreme Court decision making, in other words, is politics writ small (and occasionally politics writ large). To pretend otherwise—to pretend that politics infects and corrupts the judicial process, to pretend that Supreme Court adjudication is somehow neutral or apolitical—is to blink reality.

And to be sure, the conservative bloc of justices on the Roberts Court has consistently delivered conservative judicial decisions, as discussed in Chapter 7. The Roberts Court has denigrated democratic government while shielding wealth and the economic marketplace. The Court has protected whites and Christians while disregarding the interests of women, people of color, and non-Christians. If the Democrats were to gain control of both houses of Congress and the presidency in 2021 or later and began enacting and implementing a progressive agenda, the Roberts Court, as currently constituted, would likely block many of these actions. The Court might invalidate laws creating universal health care, strengthening environmental protections and fighting climate change, combatting structural and unconscious racism, protecting public health from pandemics (such as the novel coronavirus), restricting gun ownership, restoring and fortifying voting rights, and protecting documented and undocumented immigrants.[1]

While the precise contours of any specific progressive enactments are unpredictable, consider one possibility. Suppose that in response to structural and systemic racism Congress realizes that funding for public schools (kindergarten through high school) needs to be equalized. Consequently, Congress enacts the Equal Education Act (EEA), which mandates that (§1) each state will equalize the allocation of educational funding per student, with exceptions for at-risk students; (§2) the federal government will provide additional funds to states that cannot reach a minimal level of acceptable funding per student; and (§3) the federal government will provide additional funding, above the per capita minimum, for at-risk students.[2] In support of the EEA, Congress held hearings and made extensive findings that underscored a link between disparate school funding and race. Predominantly white school districts, it found, received substantially more money than did districts predominantly serving people of color. The overall difference amounted to approximately $23 billion per year, with the average white student receiving $2,226 more in funding than the average student of color.[3]

Now consider the multiple ways that the conservative justices could declare section 1 of the EEA unconstitutional. If Congress invoked its commerce power to enact the EEA, the Court would apply the *Lopez*-reformulated rational basis doctrine, which the Rehnquist Court designed to constrain congressional power (discussed in Chapters 6–7). Under this conservative doctrine, the Court would likely emphasize that public school funding is traditionally a local and state matter and therefore beyond Congress's reach. Or the Court could reason that education is not economic in nature and therefore not substantially related to interstate commerce. Or the Court could question the adequacy of the congressional findings.[4] Or the Court could reason that Congress has contravened the Tenth Amendment protection of state sovereignty by commandeering state and local governments to implement a congressional plan.[5] If Congress also invokes its power under section 5 of the Fourteenth Amendment—empowering Congress to enforce the constitutional guarantees of equal protection and due process—then the Court is likely to emphasize that it has previously held that equal protection does not require states to provide equal funding for students in different school districts. Given this Supreme Court precedent, Congress could be precluded from trying to redefine the meaning or substance of equal protection.[6] And as with the analysis under the commerce power, the Court's doctrinal approach to the Fourteenth Amendment, section 5, power encourages a judicial questioning of the congressional findings.[7] Focusing on section 3 of the EEA, the Court might even reason that the provision of additional funding for at-risk students violates equal protection, though this result seems unlikely under current doctrine. Remember, however, that the conservative justices have previously modified seemingly conservative doctrine to avoid reaching a progressive result.[8]

The point is that, over the past 20–30 years, conservative justices of the Rehnquist and Roberts Courts have articulated and interpreted numerous conservative constitutional doctrines that will present potential obstacles to progressive enactments. With a conservative majority of justices interpreting and applying those doctrines, a statute such as the hypothetical EEA or any other progressive law would be constitutionally infirm. But with control of both houses of Congress and the presidency, the Democrats could also enact a statute adding justices to the Supreme Court. And even the Roberts Court might find it difficult to find such a court-packing law unconstitutional, given the long history of congressional adjustments to the Court's size.[9] Then, with a progressive majority controlling the Court, the justices might repudiate some or all of the conservative doctrines or, at least, interpret and apply them in a less formalist and restrictive fashion.

Ultimately, the politics of the Roberts Court demands a political response by Democrats. To stop the Roberts Court from handing down one conservative decision after another, to ensure effectively and directly that the Roberts Court does not thwart a progressive legislative agenda, the best Democratic approach is to change the makeup of the Court. As Chapter 1 discusses, Democrats could contemplate alternative political responses to the Court— for instance, court-curbing measures that limit the Court's jurisdictional reach, an imposition of term limits for the justices, or a stylized expansion of the Court (different from the straightforward court packing recommended here). But these alternatives have serious weaknesses, including being of questionable constitutionality. To be sure, besides court packing, Democrats could attempt to change the makeup of the Court through one other clearly constitutional approach: impeachment. The Constitution allows Congress to impeach and remove Supreme Court justices and other federal judges. But as discussed in Chapter 2, the only Supreme Court justice the House of Representatives has ever impeached was the Federalist Samuel Chase in 1804, and the Republican-controlled Senate could not muster the required two-thirds supermajority to convict him. Yet as the Constitution permits, Congress has changed the size of the Court multiple times through U.S. history. If the Democrats gain control of both houses of Congress and the presidency at some point in time, they should add at least four justices to the Court, increasing its size to thirteen. With the four additional justices—assuming they are progressives—the Roberts Court will be controlled by a progressive bloc. And a progressive Roberts Court (sounds like an oxymoron, doesn't it?) would predictably hand down mostly progressive decisions upholding new Democratic statutes and other government actions.

Some commentators, it should be acknowledged, argue that the final congressional rejection of Franklin D. Roosevelt's court-packing plan established a negative precedent or norm against court packing.[10] According to this interpretation of history, FDR's failure precludes Congress forevermore from changing the size of the Court from nine justices. This book, however, underscores the flimsiness of this anti-court-packing position. First, even if such a norm existed, Mitch McConnell and the Senate Republicans already shattered it in 2016 and 2017, when they refused to open confirmation hearings for Democratic President Barack Obama's nominee, Merrick Garland. McConnell and the Republicans de facto reduced the Court to eight justices for more than a year. When given a chance to confirm a conservative Republican, Neil Gorsuch, they returned the Court to its nine-justice size. The Republicans' rushed confirmation of Barrett just before the 2020 election only underscored their disregard for whatever norms might have existed. Second, this anti-court-packing position ignores much of American history, during which congressional enactments explicitly changed the size of the Court seven times, often for political reasons. This disregard for history and bloated emphasis on the legislative defeat of FDR's court-packing plan seems especially tenuous when one remembers that leading legal scholars and key members of Congress supported FDR's plan, as discussed in Chapter 3. Legal realists such as Karl Llewellyn, who had been questioning the Court's legal formalism for years, approved of FDR's approach to the Court. More important from a political standpoint, FDR's plan had enough congressional support to give it a reasonable chance of passage, until the sudden death of its primary supporter, Senate Majority Leader Joe Robinson. Finally, if a norm against court packing were to exist, it would be based on a fallacy: that the Supreme Court should be a pristine legal institution, free of politics. But political considerations pervade the makeup of the Court and its decision-making process. If anything, we should understand the threat of court packing as an important aspect of the separation of powers, part of the Constitution's checks and balances. The possibility of court packing gives the people a political check on the Court for when it departs too far from the dominant national political alliance.[11]

Rather than interpreting history, whether the failure to enact FDR's plan or other events, as establishing a norm against court packing, we should recognize that history shows the Court engaged in a type of dialogue with Congress, the president, and the public about the scope of judicial power.[12] The justices generally stick to their standard line—we are apolitical and neutrally apply the rule of law—but certain political crises have forced at least a few justices to self-consciously consider their political contexts and to adjust their judicial positions to preserve and protect the Court's power. When the Court decided *Marbury v. Madison* and *Stuart v. Laird* in the early 1800s, Chief Justice John Marshall and the other Federalist justices avoided directly challenging Republican President Thomas Jefferson and the Republican-controlled Congress, discussed in Chapter 2. The people (or, at least, the eligible voters) had chosen the Republicans and ousted the Federalists in the monumental 1800 election, and Marshall and his colleagues apparently realized the Court would lose in any direct confrontation. Likewise, during the Civil War the Court wisely avoided confronting President Abraham Lincoln when deciding the *Prize Cases*. The 1857 proslavery decision *Dred Scott v. Sandford* had undermined the Court's legitimacy, so one of the northern Democrats, Justice Robert Grier, who had signed on to Chief Justice Roger Taney's *Dred Scott* opinion, flipped his vote in the *Prize Cases*, also discussed in Chapter 2. Grier's vote and the Court's decision protected Lincoln's power to wage war against the Confederate states while simultaneously protecting the Court. In 1937, FDR's landslide reelection emboldened him to introduce his court-packing plan. Soon after, Justice Owen Roberts shifted his vote in two crucial cases, *West Coast Hotel Company v. Parrish* and *NLRB v. Jones and Laughlin Steel Corporation*, which marked the Court's acceptance of the nation's transition to pluralist democracy and protected FDR's wildly popular New Deal program, as discussed in Chapter 3. In fact, from this vantage, even though Congress never enacted FDR's plan, it might still be deemed a success rather than a failure because the Court ultimately changed direction.[13]

In cases such as *Marbury*, the *Prize Cases*, and *Jones and Laughlin*, decided during times of crisis, the justices generally do not acknowledge that they are departing from the usual practices of adjudication. The justices do not usually admit that politics might pressure them to shift judicial positions: To the contrary, they continue to justify their decisions pursuant to legal texts and doctrines. They continue to decide as if the law-politics dichotomy truly exists. The Roberts Court could similarly shift to protect its power and legitimacy if the Democrats were to sweep the elections in 2020 or some subsequent year, thus gaining control of Congress and the presidency. But the current political crisis is produced in part by the transformation of the political parties, as they have become increasingly polarized, separated by an ever-growing chasm. For many years, the Republicans in particular have refused to treat the Democrats as a legitimate opposition party.[14] In such circumstances, would any of the current conservative justices willingly shift his or her vote and join the progressive justices in upholding legislation likely to flow from a Democratic-controlled Congress and a Democratic president? In fact, after Barrett's confirmation, at least two conservative justices would need to vote with the progressives to uphold Democratic legislation. The most likely candidate to shift is Chief Justice John Roberts, as he has expressed concern with protecting the institutional independence of the Supreme Court. Yet, as discussed in the final section of Chapter 7, his nods to institutional legitimacy so far have been minimal: He consistently votes with the other conservative justices and writes conservative opinions. In the end, he might be too conservative to shift enough to save the Court from Democratic court packing.[15]

In rare instances, the Court has overtly contemplated its own power and legitimacy. *Planned Parenthood v. Casey*, decided in 1992, reexamined the issue of whether the Constitution protects a woman's right to choose abortion. *Roe v. Wade*, of course, had held in 1973 that a constitutional right of privacy encompasses this choice: States therefore could not prohibit abortions until viability, during the last trimester of a pregnancy. Before viability, states needed to justify abortion regulations by satisfying the judicially rigorous strict scrutiny test, showing that the regulation was narrowly tailored to achieve a compelling government purpose. Justice Harry Blackmun began the majority opinion in *Roe* by reasoning that, despite "the sensitive and emotional nature of the abortion controversy," the Court's decision would be legitimate because of its objectivity. As Blackmun phrased it, the Court would "earnestly" resolve the case "by constitutional measurement, free of emotion and of predilection."[16]

In *Casey*, the joint opinion authored by Justices Sandra Day O'Connor, Anthony Kennedy, and David Souter extensively discussed the doctrine of stare decisis—the judicial requirement to follow case precedents—and the possibility of overruling *Roe*. In light of this discussion, the *Casey* Court reaffirmed *Roe* in part, holding that there remained a constitutional right to choose abortion before viability. *Casey*, though, hollowed out many of the *Roe* protections for women, as discussed in Chapter 7. For example, *Casey* repudiated the strict scrutiny test for abortion regulations and instead adopted a less rigorous undue burden test, which has allowed states to impose far more extensive restrictions on abortion. In the course of discussing stare decisis and *Roe*, the joint opinion self-reflexively pondered how overruling *Roe* might undermine the Court's own legitimacy. Unlike in *Roe*, the *Casey* Court did not proclaim that its legitimacy arose from its objectivity. Instead, the *Casey* Court suggested its legitimacy arose from public perceptions of the Court and its decisions: For the Court to retain its power, the American people must believe that the Court's decisions are based on constitutional principles. If the Court were to overrule *Roe*, the joint opinion worried, the *Casey* decision would seem too political, injudicious, and unprincipled. The Court speculated that it could not even *"pretend"* to overrule *Roe* on a principled basis. A decision to overrule, the joint opinion concluded, would seriously undermine the Court's power and legitimacy.[17]

Whether the Court overtly contemplates its own legitimacy and power (as in *Casey*) or implicitly does so (as in *Marbury*, *Stuart v. Laird*, and similar cases), it must maintain its "sociological legitimacy": sufficiently widespread public approval and acceptance of its authority and decisions.[18] The people must, as a matter of fact, respect and obey the Court's decisions or the Court will no longer be able to fulfill its function within the American constitutional system. This emphasis on the Court's sociological legitimacy resonates with the political science regime politics perspective of the Court, which emphasizes that the justices rarely depart too far from the political mainstream, as discussed in Chapter 5. To maintain its own legitimacy and power, the Court must generally decide cases in harmony with the interests and values of the dominant political alliance or regime. The Court's ongoing dialogue with Congress, the president, and the public about the scope of judicial power revolves around the Court's sociological legitimacy, the consonance between the Court and the dominant political regime. And as in any dialogue, the justices occasionally need to adjust their statements and views to avoid conflict with others.[19]

The importance of the Court's sociological legitimacy suggests a final potential objection to Democratic court packing. Suppose this book's entire argument is valid: Solid historical, analytical, and political arguments support Democratic court packing. Should the Democrats nonetheless hesitate because court packing might threaten the Court's sociological legitimacy? In other words, even if the law-politics *dichotomy* is a myth, even if the Court always decides pursuant to a law-politics *dynamic*, what if Democratic court packing might cause many people to lose faith in the Court's authority? The question here is not how the Court actually decides cases but, rather, how the public perceives the Court. If the people believe in the myth of the law-politics dichotomy, then court packing might lead them to believe the Democrats were politicizing the Court, undermining the purity of law and corrupting judicial decision making.

Steven Levitsky and Daniel Ziblatt's important book *How Democracies Die* bolsters this criticism of court packing. Similar to Robert A. Dahl and other post–World War II pluralist democratic theorists discussed in Chapter 3, they argue that democracy depends on the preservation of certain cultural (democratic) norms, including "norms of forbearance" that preclude "constitutional hardball."[20] From their perspective, court packing would contravene such norms of forbearance and lead to "democratic breakdown." For that reason, autocrats such as Recep Tayyip Erdoğan in Turkey and Viktor Orbán in Hungary sought to pack and weaponize the courts, using the law to protect themselves while attacking opponents. In such situations, the people typically lose faith in the courts, as well as in other democratic institutions. Court packing, in short, is likely to contribute to the degradation and eventual destruction of democracy and its institutions. In our contemporary United States, then, court packing could undermine the Court's institutional (or sociological) legitimacy.[21]

Four reasons undermine this objection to court packing. First, we should be wary about attaching too much significance to public opinion about the Supreme Court. Polls leave much ambiguity regarding public perceptions in that area. Some polls show that Americans hold wildly diverse opinions about the Court, though the poll questions rarely distinguish between public perceptions of the Court as an institution and perceptions of specific and recent Court decisions.[22] To be certain, many polls suggest that most Americans know and care little about the Court. A 2018 C-SPAN survey showed that fewer than one-half of likely American voters could name at least one Supreme Court justice; the same was true in a 2009 survey. One 2016 poll revealed that almost 10 percent of college graduates believed that television's Judge Judy sat on the Court; the percentage rose to 13.1 when the poll expanded beyond college graduates. A 2015 poll found that 32 percent of Americans could not identify the Supreme Court as a branch of the U.S. government, while 28 percent believed five-to-four Court rulings were "sent back either to Congress for reconsideration or to the lower courts for a decision."[23]

My own (anecdotal) experience suggests the need for skepticism when evaluating public perceptions of the Court. Shortly after Justice Antonin Scalia's death, I happened to go to my dentist, an articulate man in his mid-thirties and obviously a graduate of college and dental school. Knowing I am a law professor, he disclosed that he believed Scalia had been a "great" justice. By coincidence, I had recently published an article on the history of originalism, so with trepidation I asked whether he would be interested in reading my article. My dentist's response? He had never heard of originalism. At that point, I decided not to ask him why he admired Scalia. Quite possibly my dentist had responded to "partisan source cues."[24] Being familiar with his family of origin, I suspect that he was politically conservative, and conservative commentators and political leaders had long heaped praise on Scalia's jurisprudence.[25] Such source cues can apparently engender concern, as well as support, for the Court. Exit polls from the 2016 presidential election revealed that 21 percent of voters named Supreme Court appointments as the most important factor in determining their votes, a greater percentage than in the 2008 election. Even so, prior to the 2016 election, surveys suggested that Supreme Court appointments were only the ninth most important issue.[26]

In any event, recent political science studies suggest caution when evaluating public knowledge about the Court. Evidence suggests that many people have general knowledge about the Court—for instance, that justices are appointed rather than elected—while those same people know few specific details, except when the details directly affect them.[27] My dentist illustrates this phenomenon: He knew something about the Court—in fact, he knew that Scalia had been a justice—but he did not know the details of Scalia's originalist jurisprudence. Most important, perhaps, this widespread general knowledge of the Court entails strong diffuse support for the Court as an institution rather than specific support for particular case decisions. This diffuse support or loyalty to the Court is grounded on, in the words of James L. Gibson and Gregory A. Caldeira, "broader commitments to democratic institutions and processes, and more generally in knowledge of the role of the judiciary in the American democratic system."[28]

The importance of this diffuse support for the Court leads to a second reason not to be overly worried about public perceptions of court packing. Regardless of how much people know and care about the Court, we should not condescend to those who do know and care. The crux of the objection to court packing—that it would cause the public to lose faith in the Court—is grounded on an assumption that the public (or that segment of the public with reasonable knowledge of the Court) could not handle the truth about judicial decision making: that the justices' political views matter in the Court's decisions. But if the law-politics dichotomy is a myth, if the Court instead decides pursuant to a law-politics dynamic, then must we still propagate the myth for fear the people need its comfort? If God is dead—or never existed—must we nonetheless encourage the people to keep praying? If so, then we might as well as renounce democracy. Tell the people the truth, as we understand it, and let the people decide. Sociological legitimacy might even increase if people understood the truth: that Supreme Court decision making is politics writ small.[29]

In fact, political science studies suggest that the public's diffuse support for the Court is resilient, sustained by "a reservoir of favorable attitudes or good will."[30] A "positivity bias" helps the Court maintain this goodwill and institutional legitimacy. According to positivity (bias) theory, "[A]nything that causes people to pay attention to courts—even controversies—winds up reinforcing institutional legitimacy through exposure to the legitimizing symbols associated with law and courts."[31] Even when the Court issues a decision contrary to an individual's personal views, that individual is unlikely to lose faith in the Court. If anything, when news of Court activities draws an individual's attention, then that attention (to the Court) will likely reinforce the individual's positive views of the institution. In a sense, the more one knows about the Court, the more one is likely to find its decisions legitimate (the opposite is true for Congress).[32]

To be sure, the Court's legitimacy is not bulletproof: It depends on a perception that the Court is not merely another political institution. For instance, a confirmation battle in the Senate is unlikely to damage the Court's legitimacy, but if widely viewed advertisements (related to the confirmation battle) attack the Court as purely political, then diffuse support for the Court is likely to diminish.[33] Thus, while a politically salient Supreme Court decision might offend some Americans based on political ideology,[34] a lack of specific support for that decision does not translate into a meaningful reduction of diffuse support. Only those Americans who already reject the Court as an institution—those individuals who have not developed a favorable attitude and goodwill toward the Court—are likely to denigrate it because of a small number of specific decisions. For the most part, the Court is able to maintain its institutional legitimacy despite "the ideological and partisan cross-currents that so wrack contemporary American politics."[35] Even so, sustained disappointment with the Court's decisions over the long term, especially in politically salient cases, can weaken diffuse support for the Court. To take one example, diffuse support for the Court diminished among black Americans during the post–Warren Court years (consider the Burger, Rehnquist, and Roberts Courts' consistent hostility toward race-based affirmative action).[36]

Most important, then, the people's diffuse support for and loyalty to the Court does not depend on the myth of pure law—that is, the myth of the law-politics dichotomy. To the contrary, many Americans seem to understand that Supreme Court decision making entails a combination of law and politics—the law-politics dynamic. As Gibson and Caldeira conclude: "[T]he American people seem to accept that judicial decisionmaking can be discretionary and grounded in ideologies, but also principled and sincere. Judges differ from ordinary politicians in acting sincerely."[37] This insight into the Court's institutional legitimacy has enormous implications for Democratic court packing. Although a court-packing controversy would undoubtedly entail debates over the Court's politically charged decisions, the Court's overall diffuse support would probably remain relatively stable. Most likely, in these hyperpolarized times, individuals' political ideologies—leaning Republican or Democratic—would influence reactions to a Democratic court-packing plan. Republicans, of course, would oppose it, but many Democrats would likely support it, especially if Democratic politicians emphasized that they sought to return the Court to sincere and principled decision making.[38] To the extent that individual views of the Court's legitimacy might change in response to a court-packing plan, partisan shifts would likely cancel each other out. In the end, despite divergent views of the court-packing plan, the overall legitimacy of the Court itself would likely be sustained (or even grow), whether because of a positivity bias favoring the Court or a widespread Democratic (policy) opposition to the Roberts Court's conservatism (as well as Democratic abhorrence toward recent Senate Republicans' maneuvers related to the Court, including the rushed confirmation of Barrett, which resulted in an ironclad six-justice conservative bloc).[39]

Hence, a third reason not to worry about the effect of court packing on the Court's legitimacy: Our views of court packing should be based on the political turn necessary for court packing to be considered in the first place. For example, if the Republicans retain control of the Senate in the 2020 election (still an uncertainty as of November, 7, 2020, because of runoffs for both Georgia Senate seats), then the Democrats will be unable to try court packing in 2021. Only if and when the Democrats sweep, gaining control of the presidency plus both houses of Congress, can they even attempt to pack the Court. Whenever a Democratic sweep occurs, whether in 2020 or subsequently, the thrust of public opinion might have shifted sufficiently in a progressive direction to make court packing publicly palatable.

To be clear, I have not attempted to delineate a specific set of criteria that must be satisfied to justify court packing. To the contrary, the determination must and will be made politically. The Court itself, of course, plays a significant role in this political determination. Have the justices been deciding cases that politically depart from a national political alliance? Most likely, abusive judicial review—issuing decisions denigrating and weakening rather than protecting and strengthening democracy—would provoke public concern.[40] Yet even abusive judicial review would not be a prerequisite to court packing; rather, in a still functioning democracy, the totality of political circumstances would be determinative. In the end, as positivity theory suggests, sustained disappointment with the Court's decisions, especially in politically salient cases, would weaken diffuse (political) support for the Court.[41] Consequently, if and when the Democrats sweep, Democratic voters would likely have soured on the conservative Roberts Court—which, after all, followed the conservative Rehnquist Court. In fact, although the Democrats have won the popular vote in six out of the last seven presidential elections, a conservative bloc of justices has controlled the Court for nearly thirty years.[42] A Democratic sweep, quite possibly, would manifest in part public support to "rein in" the conservative justices of the Roberts Court.[43] Historical evidence shows that in the 1930s, New Deal voters generally supported FDR's court-packing plan. More recently, during the decade of the 2010s, at least ten states attempted court packing in their state judiciaries, with two states being successful. If the people vote for a Democratic Congress and president, they very well might support a move to pack the Court.[44]

Without question, in the political atmosphere after a Democratic sweep, a Democratic court-packing plan would contribute to the ongoing dialogue over Supreme Court power and decision making. As a matter of political strategy, congressional Democrats would not need to falsely celebrate the law-politics dichotomy—the myth of pure law—but they would likely benefit by emphasizing that the current Court has departed from principled decision making, as Senator Sheldon Whitehouse argued in his friend of the court brief in *New York State Rifle & Pistol Association, Inc. v. City of New York, New York*, the gun-rights case discussed in Chapter 1.[45] The result of a Democratic court-packing plan would likely be an increase in the size of the Court, but another possible result would be the shifting of one or more justices to a more progressive outlook, as suggested above. Either way, the Court would be forced to bend to the political realities: If and when the Democrats electorally sweep Congress and the presidency, the Court will need to bend to Democratic political power. That necessity, that reality, is baked into the checks and balances of our tripartite national government. And history amply illustrates the operation of those constitutional grants of power to Congress and the president in the nomination and confirmation processes, as well as in setting the size of the Court.[46]

The final reason not to reject court packing for fear of public reaction paradoxically rests on a concern for the public. If we are truly concerned with public opinion, we should be worried about the integrity of our democratic process, through which public opinion is most clearly expressed and manifested. Yet the conservative justices on the Roberts Court have consistently denigrated democratic government while protecting wealth and the economic marketplace, as discussed in Chapter 7. Whether in relation to voting rights, gerrymandering, respect for Congress's representation of the people, or economic equality in political campaigns, the Roberts Court has refused to bolster democracy. If we must choose between protecting the Court (from court packing) and protecting democratic government (from the Roberts Court's conservative decision making), the choice is clear. We must preserve and enhance democracy. If the Court demonstrates hostility toward democratic government, then it is the Court that must be sacrificed.[47]

But in reality, the Court need not be sacrificed. Court packing will not suddenly politicize the Court and destroy its institutional legitimacy. The Court has always been, and will always be, political. Under the Constitution, the nomination and confirmation processes and the size of the Court are partly political. And the Court's decision-making process is always politics writ small (if not politics writ large). Democratic court packing will not change any of this. But what of Levitsky and Ziblatt's argument that court packing is a tool of autocrats that will undermine our democratic norms? To be sure, court packing can be useful for an autocrat, but it alone does not transform a duly elected president into an autocrat. When Democratic President-elect Joe Biden takes office, if he participates in Democratic court packing, he would not instantly become an autocrat. It would depend on the functioning of the Court, as well as Biden's other actions. And as discussed in Chapter 6, regardless of court packing, the Court should continue to decide cases as it has always done, in accord with a law-politics dynamic. A thirteen-justice Court would be, in this regard, no different from a nine-justice Court. The justices should continue to sincerely interpret the relevant legal texts (with politics writ small working in the background). In the end, Levitsky and Ziblatt fail to account for situations in which a high court, such as the U.S. Supreme Court, itself threatens democratic government. The relationship between court packing and democracy necessarily turns on the specific factual circumstances surrounding the court packing and the subsequent actions of the reconstituted court. For instance, when political pressure, whether from Roosevelt's court-packing plan or otherwise, induced the Court to shift its jurisprudential position in 1937, FDR and the New Dealers did not seek to undermine democratic government. To the contrary, they sought to have the Court accept pluralist democracy and the legislative outcomes of the democratic process.[48]

In fact, in our current political context, acknowledgment of the law-politics dynamic in Supreme Court interpretation and adjudication might have benefits that go beyond the justification of court packing. The quest for a formal or pristine law, purified of politics, can be harmful. Advocates for Supreme Court decision making based on pure law resemble neoliberal advocates for a pure or free economic marketplace. Neoliberals (and other libertarians) pressure us into seemingly endless arguments over the scope of government regulation and interference with the free market. Government interference is inevitably blamed for market failures. According to neoliberals, the market works best, or even perfectly, when government—that is, politics—is banished. But as many have long emphasized, the free market is a myth. Economic transactions do not occur unless the government designs and enforces the rules of the marketplace. Instead of wasting time worrying about government interference with a mythically pure market, we should examine and discuss the effectiveness and fairness of the current rules and possible government improvements of the marketplace.[49]

Likewise, advocates for pure law, for formalism, pressure us to dwell on the degree to which politics is contaminating judicial processes. We devote substantial energy to debates over originalism versus non-originalism (or living constitutionalism) and to arcane distinctions among various manifestations of originalism. Should we be old originalists, focusing on the framers' intentions, or new originalists, focusing on the original public meaning of constitutional text? Which originalist approach will take us to the most refined, the purest, level of constitutional meaning, bereft of political infestation?[50] But Supreme Court adjudication can never be pristine: It is always politics writ small (if not writ large). And when we waste time seeking the impossible—the preservation of a pure law and the maintenance of the mythical law-politics dichotomy—then we are likely to obscure or miss the political, social, and economic crises confronting the nation today and the potential implications of those crises for judicial decision making.

The Roberts Court finds itself in a situation similar to that of the Court toward the end of the *Lochner* era. During the 1930s, as discussed in Chapter 3, the nation confronted mass industrialization, urbanization, dramatic shifts in population demographics, a massive and long economic depression, a transformation in democratic processes, the rise of totalitarian and fascist governments abroad, and eventually a World War. Yet the conservative justices ignored these swirling events while supposedly applying formal legal rules—until 1937, when political and other forces finally impelled judicial change. Like the Court in the 1930s, the Roberts Court faces a nation and world in critical flux. The nation and world today are characterized by climate change and extreme weather, growing recognition of systemic and structural racism, disease and death from a novel coronavirus, deteriorating international agreements, the rise of new authoritarian demagogues, the Internet and digital technology, gross income and wealth inequality in the

United States and the world, mass incarceration in America, unprecedented political polarization in America, multinational corporations, globalization, mass surveillance, and terrorism around the world. Yet the Roberts Court decides constitutional cases by invoking formal legal rules and originalist arguments about the framing of the Constitution. The Court decides cases such as *Citizens United v. Federal Election Commission*, upholding (or creating) a right for corporations to spend unlimited sums on political campaigns, and then the justices claim that their conclusion is neutral and apolitical.[51]

But, of course, the Court's decisions, including *Citizens United*, are never neutral and apolitical. The law-politics dynamic always animates legal interpretation. The justices cannot escape politics writ small. Political commentators, legal scholars, and citizens in general should stop encouraging Supreme Court justices to pretend they can decide cases based on formal legal rules, on a law purified of politics. Formalism, after all, contains an inherent political tilt favoring those who already wield power in the private sphere: The "haves" consistently come out ahead while societal outsiders lose, as discussed in Chapter 6.[52] We should want and urge the justices to consider the social, economic, and political ramifications of decisions. When the Court decides a case such as *Citizens United*, the justices should not ignore empirical evidence demonstrating the extent to which excessive wealth skews democratic government. When the Court decides an affirmative action case, the justices should not ignore empirical evidence showing that structural and unconscious racism continue to infect American society. Such evidence should be central to the Court's decision-making process.

When all is said and done, the persistent failure of the Roberts Court's conservative justices to account for the realities of American society and democracy necessitates Democratic court packing. Some less serious political threat to the Court, such as a court-curbing statute, discussed in Chapter 1, is unlikely to produce the broad changes in the Court's jurisprudence that are needed today. The nation needs not merely to tamp down or check the Court's conservative inclinations but to repudiate its deep and wide commitment to neoliberal-conservative ideology—an ideology that animates most of its politically salient decisions. We can no longer have a Court that protects wealth and the marketplace, white privilege, Christian domination, and other manifestations of power rather than promoting real substantive equity and freedom. We need new justices who will develop a jurisprudence that recognizes the needs of the people to escape from the systemic and structural oppressions that have characterized American society from its outset. We need, in short, to pack the Court.

NOTES

On the Format of the Notes: The source of each quotation is identified in an endnote. If a series of quotations is from the same source, then one note is placed at the end of the final quotation (or at the next advantageous position). In many instances, though, I append one note for an entire paragraph—usually at the end of the paragraph—rather than using multiple notes within individual paragraphs. If a paragraph contains multiple quotations (but only one note), I cite the source of the first quotation first, the source of the second quotation next, and so on—plus, I link each quotation with its respective source by including the first words of the quotation in a parenthetical attached to the citation. If a subsequent quotation in the paragraph is derived from a source previously cited in the same note, then I add the page number to the earlier citation of that source (without repeating the entire citation). After citing the sources for all quotations, I sometimes cite additional materials, whether primary or secondary, that provide supplemental support and information.

CHAPTER 1

1. Larry Diamond, *Don't Mess with the Supreme Court*, THE HILL (May 20, 2020); Mondaire Jones, *To Save Our Democracy, We Must Expand the Supreme Court*, SALON .COM (Apr. 26, 2020); Jonathan Bernstein, *Don't Pack the Supreme Court. Fix It.*, BLOOMBERG OPINION (Sept. 18, 2019); Kevin D. Williamson, *The Partisan Majoritarianism of Jamelle Bouie's Court-Packing Argument*, NATIONAL REVIEW (Sept. 17, 2019); Jamelle Bouie, *Mad about Kavanaugh and Gorsuch? The Best Way to Get Even Is to Pack the Court*, N.Y. TIMES (Sept. 17, 2019); Ian Millhiser, *Five Democratic Senators Just Declared All-Out War on the Supreme Court*, THINKPROGRESS (Aug. 15, 2019). Even before the Supreme Court case, court packing had been in the news: Matt Ford, *The Weak Case for Packing the Supreme Court*, NEW REPUBLIC (Mar. 12, 2019); Alex Thompson, *Progressive Activists Push 2020 Dems to Pack Supreme Court*, POLITICO (Feb. 25, 2019); Harold Meyerson, *How Democrats Should Fight the Battle for the Court*,

AMERICAN PROSPECT (June 28, 2018); Scott Lemieux, *Democrats: Prepare to Pack the Supreme Court*, NEW REPUBLIC (May 10, 2018). Ultimately, the Court vacated and remanded the Second Amendment case: New York State Rifle & Pistol Association, Inc. v. City of New York, New York, 590 U.S. _ (No. 18-280) (Apr. 27, 2020).

2. New York State Rifle & Pistol Association, Inc. v. City of New York, New York, 139 S.Ct. 939 (Mem) (Jan. 22, 2019).

3. McDonald v. City of Chicago, 561 U.S. 742 (2010) (protection from state and local laws); District of Columbia v. Heller, 554 U.S. 570 (2008) (protection from federal law).

4. Suggestion of Mootness, Brief for Respondents, at 1, New York State Rifle & Pistol Association, Inc. v. City of New York, New York, 2019 WL 3451573 (U.S.) (No. 18-280) (July 22, 2019).

5. Response to Respondents' Suggestion of Mootness, Brief for Petitioners, New York State Rifle & Pistol Association, Inc. v. City of New York, 2019 WL 3545853 (U.S.) (No. 18-280) (Aug. 1, 2019).

6. Brief of Senators Sheldon Whitehouse, Mazie Hirono, Richard Blumenthal, Richard Durbin, and Kirsten Gillibrand as Amici Curiae in Support of Respondents, New York State Rifle & Pistol Association, Inc. v. City of New York, New York, 2019 WL 3814388 (U.S.) (No. 18-280) (Aug. 12, 2019).

7. *Id*. at 2, 12, 18.

8. Michael Klarman, *Why Democrats Should Pack the Supreme Court*, TAKE CARE (Oct. 15, 2018), https://takecareblog.com/blog/why-democrats-should-pack-the-su preme-court. There is more than one way to define court packing: David Kosař & Katarína Šipulová, *How to Fight Court-Packing?*, 6 CONSTITUTIONAL STUDIES 133, 135 (2020). As I explain in the text, I am limiting my definition to straightforward court packing—that is, simply adding justices to shift the partisan balance on the Court.

9. Letter from Senator Mitch McConnell to Scott S. Harris, Clerk, Supreme Court of the United States (Aug. 29, 2019), regarding *New York State Rifle & Pistol Association, Inc. v. City of New York* (No. 18-280). McConnell's letter resonated with what is sometimes denigrated as telephone justice: "Telephone justice describes a system in which an elected official may call a judge on the telephone and direct that judge to decide a particular case in a particular way." TOM S. CLARK, THE LIMITS OF JUDICIAL INDEPENDENCE 7 (2010).

10. The significance of the court-packing issue did not diminish when the Court vacated and remanded the Second Amendment case without reaching the merits. Three of the conservative justices (Alito, Gorsuch, and Thomas) dissented from the remand—wanting to reach the merits—while Kavanaugh agreed with them that the Court should strengthen gun rights. *New York State Rifle & Pistol Association*, 590 U.S.

11. Russell Wheeler, *Pack the Court? Putting a Popular Imprint on the Federal Judiciary*, BROOKINGS (Apr. 3, 2019) (quoting Holder); Michael Scherer, *"Court Packing" Ideas Get Attention from Democrats*, WASH. POST (Mar. 11, 2019) (discussing Holder). Senator Whitehouse had previously criticized the Roberts Court for politicizing adjudication. Sheldon Whitehouse, *Conservative Judicial Activism: The Politicization of the Supreme Court under Chief Justice Roberts*, 9 HARV. L. & POL'Y REV. 195 (2015).

12. Julian Castro was another Democratic candidate who opposed court packing. Ian Millhiser, *Bernie Sanders's Radical Plan to Fix the Supreme Court*, VOX.COM (Feb.

11, 2020); Kevin Uhrmacher et al., *Would You Support Adding Justices to "Pack" the Supreme Court?*, Wash. Post (Aug. 15, 2019); Adam Shaw, *Biden Bucks Dem 2020 Field on Court Packing, Decriminalizing Border Crossings*, Fox News (July 6, 2019); Rashaan Ayesh, *Court Packing: Where the 2020 Candidates Stand*, Axios (Apr. 13, 2019) (depoliticize). For a progressive commentator worrying about court packing: Matt Ford, *A Better Way to Fix the Supreme Court*, New Republic (June 4, 2019). For a list of additional articles discussing court packing, *see supra* note 1.

13. Ariane de Vogue, *John Roberts Says Supreme Court Doesn't Work in a "Political Manner,"* CNN Politics (Sept. 24, 2019); Richard Wolf, *His Supreme Court Divided like the Country, Chief Justice John Roberts Prepares for Outsized Role as Umpire*, USA Today (Sept. 25, 2019).

14. Something other than politics must govern legal interpretation and adjudication, and that "something else is law." William Baude & Stephen E. Sachs, *The Law of Interpretation*, 130 Harv. L. Rev. 1079, 1093 (2017). Paradoxically, as demonstrated by the Democratic senators' brief, the political corruption of Supreme Court decision making can also be used to justify court packing: Senator Whitehouse argues that the conservative justices have politicized Supreme Court adjudication and are therefore forcing Democrats to consider court packing.

15. For commentators worrying about escalating tit-for-tat responses, *see* Daniel Epps & Ganesh Sitaraman, *How to Save the Supreme Court*, 129 Yale L.J. 148, 172 (2019); David E. Pozen, *Hardball and/as Anti-Hardball*, 21 N.Y.U. J. Legis. & Pub. Pol'y 949, 950 (2019); *see* Mark Tushnet, *The Pirate's Code: Constitutional Conventions in U.S. Constitutional Law*, 45 Pepp. L. Rev. 481, 499–502 (2018) (questioning the tit-for-tat reasoning). Joe Biden has opposed court packing partly because of a concern that Republicans will respond in kind: Jordain Carney, *Democrats Warn Biden against Releasing SCOTUS List*, TheHill.com (June 12, 2020). Bernie Sanders worried about the Republicans responding to Democratic court packing tit-for-tat and delegitimizing the Court: Millhiser, *supra* note 12.

16. Hans-Georg Gadamer, Truth and Method 295, 309, 365 (Joel Weinsheimer & Donald Marshall trans., 2d rev. ed. 1989); Ronald Dworkin, *How Law Is like Literature, in* A Matter of Principle 146, 160 (1985).

17. Ron Elving, *What Happened with Merrick Garland in 2016 and Why It Matters Now*, National Public Radio (June 29, 2018).

18. Horne v. Department of Agriculture, 135 S.Ct. 2419 (2015) (holding that government restriction on the sale of raisins, based on a 1937 statute, was a taking and required just compensation); Comcast Corp. v. Behrend, 133 S.Ct. 1426 (2013) (interpreting Federal Rules of Civil Procedure to limit class actions against corporation); Sorrell v. IMS Health Inc., 131 S.Ct. 2653 (2011) (invalidating state law restricting corporate sale of medical data); Citizens United v. FEC, 558 U.S. 310 (2010) (invalidating restriction on corporate campaign expenditures); Exxon Shipping Co. v. Baker, 554 U.S. 471 (2008) (limiting punitive damage awards against corporations); Ledbetter v. Goodyear Tire & Rubber Co., 550 U.S. 618 (2007) (imposing restrictive time bar for employment discrimination lawsuits against corporations).

19. Janus v. American Federation of State, City, & Municipal Employees, Council 31, 138 S.Ct. 2448 (2018) (holding that workers cannot be forced to pay union fees related solely to collective bargaining representation even though the workers benefit

from the representation); Knox v. Service Employees International Union, 132 S.Ct. 2277 (2012) (holding that public employee union could not impose a special assessment fee to support political advocacy even if union members could opt out); Borough of Duryea v. Guarnieri, 131 S.Ct. 2488 (2011) (limiting government employee's First Amendment right to petition the government); Garcetti v. Ceballos, 547 U.S. 410 (2006) (limiting free-speech rights of government employees by distinguishing between speech as a citizen and speech as an employee).

20. Parents Involved in Community Schools v. Seattle School District No. 1, 551 U.S. 701 (2007) (invalidating race-based affirmative action programs).

21. June Medical Services, L.L.C. v. Gee, 139 S.Ct. 663 (2019) (Kavanaugh, Gorsuch, Thomas, and Alito voted to deny a stay of an admitting-privileges statute that would force the closure of abortion facilities); *Ledbetter*, 550 U.S. 618 (holding that a woman's sex discrimination claim under Title VII was time barred).

22. American Legion v. American Humanist Association, 139 S.Ct. 2067 (2019) (public display of thirty-two-foot Christian cross is constitutional); Trump v. Hawaii, 138 S.Ct. 2392 (2018) (upholding travel ban primarily targeting Muslims); Masterpiece Cakeshop, Ltd. v. Colorado Civil Rights Commission, 138 S.Ct. 1719 (2018) (protecting Christian baker from antidiscrimination statute after he refused to bake a cake for a same-sex couple); Pleasant Grove City v. Summum, 555 U.S. 460 (2009) (allowing city to refuse to display minority-religion monument when already displaying Ten Commandments).

23. Rucho v. Common Cause, 139 S.Ct. 2484 (2019) (refusing to invalidate extreme partisan gerrymandering); Abbott v. Perez, 138 S.Ct. 2305 (2018) (upholding Texas voting restrictions).

24. *McDonald*, 561 U.S. 742 (applying Second Amendment protections against state and local governments); *Heller*, 554 U.S. 570 (holding that the Second Amendment protects an individual right to own firearms).

25. For rankings of Supreme Court justices based on political ideology: Lee Epstein et al., The Behavior of Federal Judges 106–16 (2013), which includes comparisons with the Martin-Quinn scores (accounting for changes over time), http://mqscores.wustl.edu/index.php, and the Segal-Cover scores (quantifying Court nominees' perceived political ideologies at the time of appointment), http://www.sunysb.edu/polsci/jsegal/qualtable.pdf (data drawn from Jeffrey Segal & Albert Cover, *Ideological Values and the Votes of Supreme Court Justices*, 83 Am. Pol. Sci. Rev. 557–65 [1989]; updated in Lee Epstein & Jeffrey A. Segal, Advice and Consent: The Politics of Judicial Appointments [2005]).

26. *See, e.g.*, United States v. Morrison, 529 U.S. 598 (2000) (invalidating the Violence against Women Act); City of Boerne v. Flores, 521 U.S. 527 (1997) (invalidating Religious Freedom Restoration Act of 1993); United States v. Lopez, 514 U.S. 549 (1995) (invalidating the Gun-Free School Zones Act); New York v. United States, 505 U.S. 144 (1992) (focusing on the Tenth Amendment).

27. *See, e.g.*, Shelby County v. Holder, 133 S.Ct. 2612 (2013) (invalidating a section of the Voting Rights Act); National Federation of Independent Business v. Sebelius, 132 S.Ct. 2566 (2012) (invalidating parts of the Affordable Care Act).

28. J. Mitchell Pickerill & Cornell W. Clayton, *The Roberts Court and Economic Issues in an Era of Polarization*, 67 Case W. Res. L. Rev. 693 (2017); Lee Epstein et al.,

How Business Fares in the Supreme Court, 97 MINN. L. REV. 1431, 1449–51, 1472–73 (2013); J. Mitchell Pickerill, *Is the Roberts Court Business Friendly? Is the Pope Catholic?, in* BUSINESS AND THE ROBERTS COURT 35 (Jonathan H. Adler ed., 2016) (empirical study concluding that the Roberts Court is business-friendly, though it continues a trend starting years ago with Nixon's appointees); Corey Ciocchetti, *The Constitution, the Roberts Court, and Business,* 4 WM. & MARY BUS. L. REV. 385 (2013). For claims that the Roberts Court is not conservative enough, *see* Ramesh Ponnuru, *Supreme Court Isn't Pro-Business, but Should Be,* BLOOMBERG (July 5, 2011); Jonathan Adler, *Business, the Environment, and the Roberts Court: A Preliminary Assessment,* 49 SANTA CLARA L. REV. 943 (2009); Eric Posner, *Is the Supreme Court Biased in Favor of Business?,* SLATE (Mar. 17, 2008). But according to Mark Tushnet, the "Roberts Court's overall balance sheet in business cases fits the 'pro-business' view of the Court reasonably well": MARK TUSHNET, IN THE BALANCE: LAW AND POLITICS ON THE ROBERTS COURT 213 (2013); *id.* at 187–214 (discussing evidence). The political scientist Michael Bailey surveyed competing measures of the Court's political leanings and concluded that, as of 2012, the Court was moderately conservative: Michael Bailey, *Just How Liberal (or Conservative) Is the Supreme Court?,* VOX.COM (Feb. 22, 2016). The newest justices, Kavanaugh and Barrett, will only move the Court further rightward.

29. Lee Epstein et al., *Do Justices Defend the Speech They Hate? An Analysis of In-Group Bias on the US Supreme Court,* 6 J. OF LAW & COURTS 237 (2018).

30. Adam D. Chandler, *Cert.-stage Amicus "All Stars": Where Are They Now?,* SCOTUSBLOG (Apr. 4, 2013); Adam D. Chandler, *Cert.-stage Amicus Briefs: Who Files Them and to What Effect?,* SCOTUSBLOG (Sept. 27, 2007) (earlier study); *see* Benjamin Johnson, *The Supreme Court's Political Docket: How Ideology and the Chief Justice Control the Court's Agenda and Shape Law,* 50 CONN. L. REV. 581 (2018) (empirical study underscoring how politics influences the granting of cert petitions).

31. The Democrats might need to eliminate the Senate cloture (or filibuster) rule to facilitate enactment of progressive legislation: Molly E. Reynolds, *What Is the Senate Filibuster, and What Would It Take to Eliminate It?,* BROOKINGS POLICY 2020 (Oct. 15, 2019), https://www.brookings.edu/policy2020/votervital/what-is-the-senate-filibuster-and-what-would-it-take-to-eliminate-it.

32. Rich Lowry, *Elizabeth Warren's Threat to the Constitution,* NATIONAL REVIEW (Oct. 11, 2019). In a recent decision, Justice Alito expressed a desire to resurrect the non-delegation doctrine as a means of limiting congressional power, even though the Court had not invoked the doctrine since 1935. Gundy v. United States, 139 S.Ct. 2116, 2130–31 (2019) (Alito, J., concurring in the judgment). For progressives worrying about the Roberts Court: Klarman, *Why Democrats Should Pack the Supreme Court,* TAKE CARE (Oct. 15, 2018), https://takecareblog.com/blog/why-democrats-should-pack-the-supreme-court; Samuel Moyn & Aaron Belkin, *The Roberts Court Would Likely Strike Down Climate Change Legislation* (Sept. 2019) (report from the group Take Back the Court).

33. To be clear, I am not advocating for relativism, suggesting that anything goes, or claiming that words have no meaning. Stephen M. Feldman, *The Problem of Critique: Triangulating Habermas, Derrida, and Gadamer within Metamodernism,* 4 CONTEMP. POL. THEORY 296 (2005); Stephen M. Feldman, *Made for Each Other: The Interdependence of Deconstruction and Philosophical Hermeneutics,* 26 PHIL. & SOC. CRITICISM 51

(2000); Stephen M. Feldman, *An Arrow to the Heart: The Love and Death of Postmodern Legal Scholarship*, 54 VAND. L. REV. 2351 (2001).

34. Neal Devins & Lawrence Baum, *Split Definitive: How Party Polarization Turned the Supreme Court into a Partisan Court*, 2016 SUP. CT. REV. 301 (2016) (emphasizing how polarization has changed the Court). For cases suggesting that Roberts is the most likely conservative justice to shift leftward, *see* Department of Homeland Security v. Regents of the University of California, _ S.Ct. _ (2020) (Roberts opinion holding Trump administration rescission of Deferred Action for Childhood Arrivals [DACA] violated Administrative Procedure Act [APA] procedural requirements); Department of Commerce v. New York, 139 S.Ct. 2551 (2019) (Roberts opinion holding Trump administration addition of citizenship question to census violated APA procedural requirements).

35. JAMES L. GIBSON & GREGORY A. CALDEIRA, CITIZENS, COURTS, AND CONFIRMATIONS: POSITIVITY THEORY AND THE JUDGMENTS OF THE AMERICAN PEOPLE (2009). An alternative view suggests that a Democratic sweep would augur support for court packing based on political ideology: BRANDON L. BARTELS & CHRISTOPHER D. JOHNSTON, CURBING THE COURT (2020).

36. Stephen E. Sachs suggests some limit on the Court to this effect when he writes, "[W]e should precommit to limiting the Court's freedom of action, binding it to some discrete set of preexisting rules until there is a very broad consensus for changing them": Stephen E. Sachs, *Supreme Court as Superweapon: A Response to Epps & Sitaraman*, 129 YALE L.J. FORUM 93, 107 (2019).

37. CLARK, *supra* note 9, at 36–42 (types of court curbing); STEPHEN M. FELDMAN, FREE EXPRESSION AND DEMOCRACY IN AMERICA: A HISTORY 448–49 (2008) (jurisdiction-stripping bills focused on national security during the Red Scare); Stuart S. Nagel, *Court-Curbing Periods in American History*, 18 VAND. L. REV. 925 (1965); Shelden D. Elliott, *Court-Curbing Proposals in Congress*, 33 NOTRE DAME LAWYER 597 (1958).

38. MARK TUSHNET, TAKING THE CONSTITUTION AWAY FROM THE COURTS (1999).

39. Epps & Sitaraman, *supra* note 15, at 151–52.

40. Roger C. Cramton & Paul D. Carrington, *The Supreme Court Renewal Act: A Return to Basic Principles, in* REFORMING THE COURT: TERM LIMITS FOR SUPREME COURT JUSTICES 467 (Roger C. Cramton & Paul D. Carrington eds., 2006); Pozen, *supra* note 15, at 951–52; Roger C. Cramton, *Reforming the Supreme Court*, 95 CALIF. L. REV. 1313, 1323–24 (2007); Steven G. Calabresi & James Lindgren, *Term Limits for the Supreme Court: Life Tenure Reconsidered*, 29 HARV. J.L. & PUB. POL'Y 769 (2006).

41. Tracey E. George & Chris Guthrie, *Remaking the United States Supreme Court in the Courts' of Appeals Image*, 58 DUKE L.J. 1439, 1457–58, 1465–66 (2009); *see* Jonathan Turley, *Unpacking the Court: The Case for the Expansion of the United States Supreme Court in the Twenty-First Century*, 33 PERSP. ON POL. SCI. 155, 155–56 (2004) (recommending Court expansion).

42. Epps & Sitaraman, *supra* note 15, at 181. They add another requirement: "[O]nly a 6–3 supermajority of the Court, rather than a simple majority, could hold a federal statute (and possibly state statutes, depending on how one weighs federalism values) unconstitutional." *Id.* at 182.

43. *Id.* at 193. Among the Democrats campaigning for president in 2019, Pete Buttigieg and Beto O'Rourke seemed to support the Balanced Bench approach. David A.

Graham, *The Democrats Discover the Supreme Court*, THE ATLANTIC (June 4, 2019). One article suggested Bernie Sanders might consider something like the Supreme Court Lottery. Millhiser, *supra* note 12.

44. ERWIN CHEMERINSKY, CONSTITUTIONAL LAW: PRINCIPLES AND POLICIES 162–81 (6th ed. 2019); DAVID O'BRIEN, STORM CENTER 357–65 (12th ed. 2020); *see* Boumediene v. Bush, 553 U.S. 723 (2008) (invalidating congressional act stripping habeas corpus jurisdiction from the federal courts for enemy combatants). Epps and Sitaraman admit that their own proposals—the Supreme Court Lottery and the Balanced Bench—might be unconstitutional. Epps & Sitaraman, *supra* note 15, at 185–92, 200–05.

45. Nagel, *supra* note 37, at 926, 943.

46. O'Brien, *supra* note 44, at 363; *see* CLARK, *supra* note 9, at 256–58 (many court-curbing bills are introduced as mere political posturing).

47. Devins & Baum, *supra* note 34, at 305–06 (on the Court's shift rightward); *see* Osita Nwanevu, *We're Not Polarized Enough*, NEW REPUBLIC (May 19, 2020) (arguing to accept polarization, working from there, rather than trying to counter polarization). Joshua Braver is a legal scholar who supports court curbing rather than court packing. He argues that prior congressional changes to the Court's size were insufficiently political to support any historical argument in favor of court packing. Joshua Braver, *Court-Packing: An American Tradition*, 61 B.U. L. REV. 2747 (2020). One problem with his analysis is a failure to account for the influence of extreme polarization in today's political climate as opposed to the past. Tom S. Clark & Jonathan P. Kastellec, *Source Cues and Public Support for the Supreme Court*, 43 AM. POLITICS RESEARCH 504 (2015) (polarization is likely to influence public opinion of the Court's legitimacy); Devins & Baum, *supra* note 34 (emphasizing that polarization has changed the Court); *see* CLARK, *supra* note 9, at 25–61 (on the politics of numerous court-curbing episodes). One commentator has suggested reducing the Court to eight justices to avoid partisan decisions: Eric J. Segall, *Eight Justices Are Enough: A Proposal to Improve the United States Supreme Court*, 45 PEPP. L. REV. 547 (2018). Of course, in this situation, the Court might be unable to actually decide politically salient cases.

48. Depending on how one defines court curbing, it is possible to categorize court packing as a type of court curbing. CLARK, *supra* note 9, at 28, 37–39, 52–54.

49. Michael C. Dorf, *How the Written Constitution Crowds Out the Extraconstitutional Rule of Recognition*, *in* THE RULE OF RECOGNITION AND THE U.S. CONSTITUTION 69, 74–75, 79 (Matthew D. Adler & Kenneth Einar Himma eds., 2009) (acknowledging that text and history support the constitutionality of court packing).

50. New York State Rifle & Pistol Association, Inc. v. City of New York, 590 U.S. _ (No. 18–280) (April 27, 2020) (Alito, J., dissenting) (arguing that the Court should clarify Second Amendment protections).

51. Many progressives would argue that the Republicans, playing constitutional hardball, have packed the Court twice in the past twenty years. First, in the 2000 presidential election, Republicans fought the Florida vote recount that could have led to an Al Gore (Democratic) rather than a George W. Bush (Republican) victory, and that fight culminated with the Supreme Court's five-to-four decision terminating the recount: Bush v. Gore, 531 U.S. 98 (2000). Invoking a novel equal-protection argument, the conservative justices effectively declared Bush the winner. The decision em-

powered Bush, as the president, to fill the next Court openings and led to the eventual appointments of Roberts and Alito. Second, McConnell's and the Republicans' refusal to open hearings on Merrick Garland led to the appointment of Gorsuch. From this vantage, some progressives argue that they should pack the Court to offset these recent Republican actions. Scherer, *supra* note 11. While I discuss both of these events in the course of the book, my argument does not turn on categorizing either event as court packing per se. I discuss *Bush v. Gore* in Chapter 5 to illustrate politics writ large in opposition to the more typical politics writ small. *Bush* shows that the justices sometimes appear to disregard the law and instead blatantly pursue a political goal. I discuss the Garland fiasco in Chapter 2 to show that as recently as 2016 and 2017, Congress has changed the number of justices sitting on the Court for political reasons. Whether one categorizes either of these events as court packing per se is irrelevant to these arguments (it neither helps nor hurts my arguments).

CHAPTER 2

1. Mark Tushnet wrote: "Most of the changes in the Court's size were done for good-government reasons, with a soupçon of politics." MARK TUSHNET, TAKING BACK THE CONSTITUTION 214 (2020). He then modified this view by acknowledging that multiple changes "were purely political." *Id.*

2. In the words of Richard Fallon, the justices adjust their legal positions in order to maintain "sociological legitimacy." RICHARD H. FALLON JR., LAW AND LEGITIMACY IN THE SUPREME COURT 21–24 (2018); *see* TOM S. CLARK, THE LIMITS OF JUDICIAL INDEPENDENCE 4–6, 16–18 (2010) (emphasizing that the Court's legitimacy and independence depends on public support); DAVID SAVAGE, 2 GUIDE TO THE U.S. SUPREME COURT 901 (5th ed. 2010) (discussing political motivations for changing the Court's size); Elli Menounou et al., *Packing the Courts: Ideological Proximity and Expansions to the Federal Judiciary from 1937 to 2012*, J. LAW & COURTS 81 (2019) (discussing congressional political ideology as determining changing sizes of lower federal courts). For a general history of the manipulation of the Supreme Court for political purposes: JAMES MACGREGOR BURNS, PACKING THE COURT (2009). Note that Burns defines court packing as "the deliberate effort by the party in power—sometimes across several administrations and over decades—to use the presidential prerogative of appointing justices to ensure domination of the Supreme Court by its own partisans." *Id.* at 3. In other words, to Burns, the normal appointment of justices ideologically aligned with the president can constitute court packing. For a history of American democracy: STEPHEN M. FELDMAN, FREE EXPRESSION AND DEMOCRACY IN AMERICA: A HISTORY (2008) [hereinafter FELDMAN, FREE EXPRESSION]; STEPHEN M. FELDMAN, THE NEW ROBERTS COURT, DONALD TRUMP, AND OUR FAILING CONSTITUTION (2017) [hereinafter FELDMAN, FAILING CONSTITUTION]. For a general history of the Supreme Court: BERNARD SCHWARTZ, A HISTORY OF THE SUPREME COURT (1993). For general information on the Court: THE OXFORD COMPANION TO THE SUPREME COURT (Kermit L. Hall ed., 1992) [hereinafter OXFORD].

3. U.S. Const. art. III, § 1. Article I, section 8, also specifies Congress's power to "constitute tribunals inferior to the Supreme Court." U.S. Const. art. I, § 8, cl. 9; *see* U.S. Const. art. III, § 2 (articulating parameters of federal court jurisdiction).

4. RICHARD BEEMAN, PLAIN, HONEST MEN 236 (2009). For the most complete record of the Constitutional Convention: THE RECORDS OF THE FEDERAL CONVENTION OF 1787 (Max Farrand ed., 1966 reprint of 1937 rev. ed.) [hereinafter Farrand]. Significantly, though, James Madison's notes on the Constitutional Convention, central to Farrand, *supra*, should be understood as "both text and artifact." MARY SARAH BILDER, MADISON'S HAND: REVISING THE CONSTITUTIONAL CONVENTION 6 (2015). Madison edited his own notes subsequent to the convention, so the notes do not always reflect the precise thoughts and words of the convention delegates. *Id.* at 1–5, 202.

5. 1 Farrand, *supra* note 4 (June 4, 1787); *see id.* at 104–05 (Madison's notes on the vote for the national judiciary stating that motion passed nem. con., meaning unanimously).

6. The Federalist No. 81 (Alexander Hamilton), at 481 (Clinton Rossiter ed., 1961). *E.g.*, 2 Farrand, *supra* note 4, at 41 (July 18, 1787) (debating the appointment of federal judges); *see* BEEMAN, *supra* note 4, at 236–38 (describing discussions about the appointment of federal judges); RICHARD H. FALLON JR. ET AL., HART AND WECHSLER'S THE FEDERAL COURTS AND THE FEDERAL SYSTEM 7–8 (4th ed. 1996) (describing the framers' discussions about the federal courts). The federal judiciary was discussed at some of the state ratifying conventions. *See, e.g.*, PAULINE MAIER, RATIFICATION 286–91 (2010) (discussing Virginia ratifying convention).

7. The Judiciary Act of 1789, Act of Sept. 24, 1789, 1 Stat. 73, *reprinted in* 1 DOCUMENTS OF AMERICAN HISTORY 153, 153 (Henry Steele Commager ed., 9th ed. 1973) [hereinafter Commager]; *see* FALLON ET AL., *supra* note 6, at 28.

8. SCHWARTZ, *supra* note 2, at 18–19; 1 Commager, *supra* note 7, at 153–54; *see* FERGUS M. BORDEWICH, THE FIRST CONGRESS 108 (2016) (summarizing jurisdictional coverage of the district and circuit courts).

9. The Federalist No. 10 (James Madison), at 81–83 (Clinton Rossiter ed., 1961); The Federalist No. 51 (James Madison), at 323–25 (Clinton Rossiter ed., 1961); GORDON S. WOOD, THE CREATION OF THE AMERICAN REPUBLIC, 1776–1787, at 58–60 (1969).

10. JAMES ROGER SHARP, AMERICAN POLITICS IN THE EARLY REPUBLIC 8, 40–41 (1993); *see* FELDMAN, FREE EXPRESSION, *supra* note 2, at 70–100 (discussing the disputes of the 1790s and the ensuing Sedition Act crisis).

11. For an extensive discussion of the political disputes of the 1790s: STANLEY ELKINS & ERIC MCKITRICK, THE AGE OF FEDERALISM (1993).

12. SCHWARTZ, *supra* note 2, at 30–35; KATHLEEN SULLIVAN & NOAH FELDMAN, CONSTITUTIONAL LAW 9 (18th ed. 2013); BURNS, *supra* note 2, at 20–21 (discussing Federalist missteps).

13. SCHWARTZ, *supra* note 2, at 18 (quoting Iredell); *id.* at 19 (quoting Jay); Judiciary Act of 1801, 2 Stat. 89; Kathryn Turner, *Federalist Policy and the Judiciary Act of 1801*, 22 WM. & MARY Q. 3 (1965); Kathryn Turner, *The Midnight Judges*, 109 U. PA. L. REV. 494 (1961).

14. GORDON S. WOOD, EMPIRE OF LIBERTY: A HISTORY OF THE EARLY REPUBLIC, 1789–1815, at 419 (2009) (quoting Boston's COLUMBIAN CENTINEL [Jan. 14, 1801]); *see* Tara Leigh Grove, *The Origins (and Fragility) of Judicial Independence*, 71 VAND. L. REV. 465, 477 (2018) (discussing Federalist desire to fill new judgeships with Federalists).

15. SAVAGE, *supra* note 2, at 901; OXFORD, *supra* note 2, at 213–14.

16. Marbury v. Madison, 5 U.S. (1 Cranch) 137 (1803); An Act Concerning the District of Columbia, 2 Stat. 103 (Feb. 27, 1801); *see* BRUCE ACKERMAN, THE FAILURE OF THE FOUNDING FATHERS 148–49 (2005) (Jefferson and Madison spurning the Court). For additional discussions of *Marbury* and the surrounding political dispute: MICHAEL A. BAILEY & FORREST MALTZMAN, THE CONSTRAINED COURT: LAW, POLITICS, AND THE DECISIONS JUSTICES MAKE 95 (2011); James M. O'Fallon, *Marbury*, 44 STAN. L. REV. 219 (1992); William W. Van Alstyne, *A Critical Guide to* Marbury v. Madison, 1969 DUKE L.J. 1.

17. MITCHEL A. SOLLENBERGER, JUDICIAL APPOINTMENTS AND DEMOCRATIC CONTROLS 17 (2011) (quoting Jefferson).

18. U.S. Const. art. III, § 1; ACKERMAN, *supra* note 16, at 149–50 (Jefferson's views).

19. Repeal Act of 1802, 2 Stat. 132 (Mar. 8, 1802); SOLLENBERGER, *supra* note 17, at 17–19; Grove, *supra* note 14, at 477–80. For a fuller discussion of the debates: ACKERMAN, *supra* note 16, at 149–57.

20. *Marbury*, 5 U.S. at 299, 309; Judiciary Act of 1802, 2 Stat. 156 (Apr. 29, 1802); ACKERMAN, *supra* note 16, at 157–72; SULLIVAN & FELDMAN, *supra* note 12, at 10.

21. *Marbury*, 5 U.S. at 173–80; ACKERMAN, *supra* note 16, at 9, 163–98; Stephen M. Feldman, *Chief Justice Roberts's* Marbury *Moment: The Affordable Care Act Case (*NFIB v. Sebelius*)*, 13 WYO. L. REV. 335, 335–37 (2013) (briefly summarizing the politics of *Marbury*).

22. U.S. Const. art. II, § 4; *see* WOOD, *supra* note 14, at 422 (discussing Pickering's impeachment and conviction); Lynn W. Turner, *The Impeachment of John Pickering*, 54 AMERICAN HISTORICAL REV. 485 (1949) (same).

23. MELVIN I. UROFSKY & PAUL FINKELMAN, 1 A MARCH OF LIBERTY 199 (2d ed. 2002) (mobocracy); Senate Journal, Mar. 1, 1805, at 524–27; ERIK W. AUSTIN, POLITICAL FACTS OF THE UNITED STATES SINCE 1789, at 50 (1986) (Table 1.20, Partisan Composition of the United States Senate); ELKINS & MCKITRICK, *supra* note 11, at 699 (on Chase); James Haw, *Chase, Samuel, in* THE YALE BIOGRAPHICAL DICTIONARY OF AMERICAN LAW 103 (2009); *see* FELDMAN, FREE EXPRESSION, *supra* note 2, at 70–100 (explaining the Sedition Act controversy); 1 UROFSKY & FINKELMAN, *supra*, at 199–201 (discussing Chase's impeachment); WOOD, *supra* note 14, at 422–25 (same).

24. Act of Feb. 24, 1807, 2 Stat. 420; Act of March 3, 1837, 5 Stat. 176; HENRY J. ABRAHAM, JUSTICES, PRESIDENTS, AND SENATORS: A HISTORY OF U.S. SUPREME COURT APPOINTMENTS FROM WASHINGTON TO BUSH II, at 82–83 (5th ed. 2008); BURNS, *supra* note 2, at 59; SAVAGE, *supra* note 2, at 901.

25. 60 U.S. (19 How.) 393 (1857); AUSTIN, *supra* note 23, at 50–56 (Table 1.20, Partisan Composition of the United States Senate; Table 1.21, Partisan Composition of the United States House of Representatives).

26. BURNS, *supra* note 2, at 66–68.

27. Ex parte Merryman, 17 Fed. Cas. 144 (1861); 1 UROFSKY & FINKELMAN, *supra* note 23, at 414–15; BURNS, *supra* note 2, at 65–66 (Lincoln ignoring order); *see* JAMES M. MCPHERSON, BATTLE CRY OF FREEDOM: THE CIVIL WAR ERA 284–89 (1988) (discussing Maryland and the *Merryman* case).

28. Judicial Reorganization Act of 1862, 12 Stat. 576 (July 15, 1862); Act of March

3, 1863, 12 Stat. 794 (adding tenth justice); Act of March 2, 1855, 10 Stat. 631 (adding tenth circuit); SAVAGE, *supra* note 2, at 901; Timothy Huebner, *The First Court-Packing Plan*, SCOTUSBLOG (July 3, 2013), https://www.scotusblog.com/2013/07/the-first-court-packing-plan.

29. Prize Cases, 67 U.S. (2 Black) 635, 668–70 (1863); *id.* at 694–95 (Nelson, J., dissenting) (personal war); Act of March 3, 1863, 12 Stat. 794; BURNS, *supra* note 2, at 70–77; ROBERT G. McCLOSKEY, THE AMERICAN SUPREME COURT 98–100 (1960); McPHERSON, *supra* note 27, at 312–14, 378–82; SAVAGE, *supra* note 2, at 901; SCHWARTZ, *supra* note 2, at 131.

30. Act of July 23, 1866, 14 Stat. 209; ERIC FONER, RECONSTRUCTION, 1863–1877, at 176–280 (1988); SAVAGE, *supra* note 2, at 901; OXFORD, *supra* note 2, at 475.

31. The Legal Tender Cases, 79 U.S. 457 (1871) (*overruling* Hepburn v. Griswold, 75 U.S. 603 [1870]); McCLOSKEY, *supra* note 29, at 112–15; Act of April 10, 1869, 16 Stat. 44; BURNS, *supra* note 2, at 94–95; SAVAGE, *supra* note 2, at 901; OXFORD, *supra* note 2, at 920–21.

32. William W. Van Alstyne, *A Critical Guide to* Ex Parte McCardle, 15 ARIZ. L. REV. 229, 236 n.42 (1973) (quoting the *Vicksburg Times*, Nov. 6, 1867).

33. Ex Parte McCardle, 74 U.S. (7 Wall.) 506 (1869); An Act to Amend "An Act to Establish the Judicial Courts of the United States" (Feb. 5, 1867), § 1, 14 Stat. 385, 386; An Act to Amend an Act Entitled "An Act to Amend the Judiciary Act" (Mar. 27, 1868), § 2, 15 Stat. 44.

34. Ron Elving, *What Happened with Merrick Garland in 2016 and Why It Matters Now*, NATIONAL PUBLIC RADIO (June 29, 2018); *see* FELDMAN, FAILING CONSTITUTION, *supra* note 2, at 243–44 (discussing Gorsuch's conservatism).

35. SAVAGE, *supra* note 2, at 901–02; Grove, *supra* note 14, at 505–06; *see* FELDMAN, FREE EXPRESSION, *supra* note 2, at 445–50 (discussing congressional desire to limit the Court's jurisdiction in the 1950s).

CHAPTER 3

1. For sources on the transition in democracy and the New Deal: ANTHONY J. BADGER, THE NEW DEAL: THE DEPRESSION YEARS, 1933–1940 (1989); LIZABETH COHEN, MAKING A NEW DEAL (1990); HOWARD GILLMAN, THE CONSTITUTION BESIEGED: THE RISE AND DEMISE OF LOCHNER ERA POLICE POWERS JURISPRUDENCE (1993); DAVID M. KENNEDY, FREEDOM FROM FEAR: THE AMERICAN PEOPLE IN DEPRESSION AND WAR, 1929–1945 (1999); WILLIAM E. LEUCHTENBURG, FRANKLIN D. ROOSEVELT AND THE NEW DEAL (1963); ROBERT S. McELVAINE, THE GREAT DEPRESSION (1984).

2. Constitution of North Carolina (1776), *reprinted in* 2 THE FEDERAL AND STATE CONSTITUTIONS, COLONIAL CHARTERS, AND OTHER ORGANIC LAWS OF THE UNITED STATES 1409, 1409 (Ben Perley Poore ed., 2d ed. 1878) [hereinafter Poore]; Constitution of Pennsylvania (1776), *reprinted in* 2 Poore, *supra*, at 1540; Virginia Bill of Rights (1776), *reprinted in* 2 Poore, *supra*, at 1908, 1908–09; GORDON S. WOOD, THE CREATION OF THE AMERICAN REPUBLIC, 1776–1787, at 59 (1969) [hereinafter WOOD, CREATION].

3. The Federalist No. 10 (James Madison) (*note:* all citations in this chapter are to the Project Gutenberg e-text of The Federalist Papers); *see* JAMES MADISON, IN VIR-

GINIA CONVENTION, JUNE 5, 1788, *reprinted in* THE COMPLETE MADISON: HIS BASIC WRITINGS 46, 46 (Saul K. Padover ed., 1953) (arguing that majority factions have produced unjust laws) [hereinafter COMPLETE].

4. The Federalist No. 37 (James Madison) (partial); The Federalist No. 6 (Alexander Hamilton) (private).

5. Letter from Thomas Jefferson to James Madison (Dec. 20, 1787), *reprinted in* 2 GREAT ISSUES IN AMERICAN HISTORY 112, 115 (Richard Hofstadter ed., 1982); WOOD, CREATION, *supra* note 2, at 100.

6. ST. GEORGE TUCKER, BLACKSTONE'S COMMENTARIES: WITH NOTES OF REFERENCE TO THE CONSTITUTION AND LAWS, OF THE FEDERAL GOVERNMENT OF THE UNITED STATES; AND OF THE COMMONWEALTH OF VIRGINIA 31 (1803).

7. THOMAS J. CURRY, THE FIRST FREEDOMS: CHURCH AND STATE IN AMERICA TO THE PASSAGE OF THE FIRST AMENDMENT 219 (1986); STEPHEN M. FELDMAN, PLEASE DON'T WISH ME A MERRY CHRISTMAS: A CRITICAL HISTORY OF THE SEPARATION OF CHURCH AND STATE 161–68 (1997) [hereinafter FELDMAN, CRITICAL HISTORY]; *see* The Federalist No. 2 (John Jay) (emphasizing the homogeneity of the American people).

8. Helpful sources on the framing include: THE RECORDS OF THE FEDERAL CONVENTION OF 1787 (Max Farrand ed., 1966 reprint of 1937 rev. ed.) [hereinafter Farrand]; RICHARD BEEMAN, PLAIN, HONEST MEN (2009); MICHAEL J. KLARMAN, THE FRAMERS' COUP: THE MAKING OF THE UNITED STATES CONSTITUTION (2016); PAULINE MAIER, RATIFICATION (2010); FORREST McDONALD, NOVUS ORDO SECLORUM (1985); J. G. A. POCOCK, THE MACHIAVELLIAN MOMENT (1975); WOOD, CREATION, *supra* note 2. On the reliability and unreliability of James Madison's notes on the Constitutional Convention: MARY SARAH BILDER, MADISON'S HAND: REVISING THE CONSTITUTIONAL CONVENTION (2015).

9. ALEXANDER KEYSSAR, THE RIGHT TO VOTE: THE CONTESTED HISTORY OF DEMOCRACY IN THE UNITED STATES 54–60 (2000); ROGERS M. SMITH, CIVIC IDEALS 170–73 (1997); GORDON S. WOOD, THE RADICALISM OF THE AMERICAN REVOLUTION 294 (1991) [hereinafter WOOD, RADICALISM]. Keyssar writes: "By 1790, according to most estimates, roughly 60 to 70 percent of adult white men (and very few others) could vote." KEYSSAR, *supra*, at 24. Gordon Wood notes, however, that at least some Americans started arguing for universal suffrage during the Revolutionary era. WOOD, CREATION, *supra* note 2, at 182–83. By 1825, all but three states—Rhode Island, Virginia, and Louisiana—had eliminated property and wealth restrictions. WOOD, RADICALISM, *supra*, at 294. Keyssar reports that during the early nineteenth century, an increasing number of states barred free black Americans from voting. KEYSSAR, *supra*, at 55–57.

10. JOHN HIGHAM, STRANGERS IN THE LAND: PATTERNS OF AMERICAN NATIVISM, 1860–1925, at 6 (1992 ed.).

11. SMITH, *supra* note 9, at 209 (quoting Samuel Morse in the 1830s); PHILIP HAMBURGER, SEPARATION OF CHURCH AND STATE 234–40 (2002) (on the relation between politics and religion).

12. Letter from John Jay to George Washington (June 27, 1786), *reprinted in* 2 GREAT ISSUES IN AMERICAN HISTORY 80, 81 (Richard Hofstadter ed., 1982); *see* WOOD, CREATION, *supra* note 2, at 410–13.

13. The Federalist No. 6 (Alexander Hamilton) (discussing republican problems arising from human nature); James Wilson, *In the Pennsylvania Convention* (Nov. 24, 1787), *in* 3 Farrand, *supra* note 8, at 138, 141–42, appendix A (lamenting licentiousness of citizens and government problems).

14. The Federalist No. 10 (James Madison).

15. 2 Farrand, *supra* note 8, at 364 (Aug. 21, 1787) (Charles Pinckney stating "South Carolina can never receive the plan if it prohibits the slave trade"); BEEMAN, *supra* note 8, at 309–11.

16. 1 Farrand, *supra* note 8, at 20 (May 29, 1787).

17. U.S. Const. art. I, § 2, cl. 3; 1 Farrand, *supra* note 8, at 36 (May 30, 1787) (Rufus King, Massachusetts, on the problem of quotas of contribution); BEEMAN, *supra* note 8, at 152–53 (discussing interests of southern delegates).

18. 2 Farrand, *supra* note 8, at 220 (Aug. 8, 1787) (Sherman); *id.* at 364 (Aug. 21, 1787) (Martin); *id.* at 221–22 (Aug. 8, 1787) (Morris).

19. 2 Farrand, *supra* note 8, at 364 (Aug. 21, 1787) (Rutledge); 1 Farrand, *supra* note 8, at 594 (July 12, 1787) (Pinckney); BEEMAN, *supra* note 8, at 334; PAUL FINKELMAN, SLAVERY AND THE FOUNDERS 3–36 (3d ed. 2014); Staughton Lynd, *Slavery and the Founding Fathers, in* BLACK HISTORY: A REAPPRAISAL 115, 130–31 (Melvin Drimmer ed., 1968).

20. U.S. Const. art. I, § 2, cl. 3 (three-fifths); U.S. Const. art. I, § 9, cl. 1 (slave trade); U.S. Const. art. 4, § 2, cl. 3 (fugitive slave); U.S. Const. art. V (amendments). Another related clause prohibited any "Capitation, or other direct, Tax unless in Proportion to" the three-fifths counting of slaves. U.S. Const. art. I, § 9, cl. 4. For discussions of these constitutional provisions: BEEMAN, *supra* note 8, at 335–36; DERRICK BELL, RACE, RACISM, AND AMERICAN LAW 22–23 (2d ed. 1980); FINKELMAN, *supra* note 19, at 6–9.

21. 2 Farrand, *supra* note 8, at 56 (July 19, 1787) (Wilson); *id.* at 56–57 (Madison); Akhil Reed Amar, *The Troubling Reason the Electoral College Exists*, TIME (Nov. 8, 2016).

22. FINKELMAN, *supra* note 19, at 103 (quoting Pinckney); *id.* at 9–10 (southern attitudes toward protection of slavery); KLARMAN, *supra* note 8, at 297–303 (same). During ratification debates in the northern states, the proposed constitutional protections of slavery generated contentious debate. FINKELMAN, *supra* note 19, at 35–36; MAIER, *supra* note 8, at 175–76, 351–52.

23. ERIK W. AUSTIN, POLITICAL FACTS OF THE UNITED STATES SINCE 1789, at 94–95 (1986) (Table 3.1, National Electoral and Popular Vote Cast for President, 1789–1984).

24. The Federalist No. 57 (James Madison).

25. On property: The Federalist No. 10 (James Madison); JENNIFER NEDELSKY, PRIVATE PROPERTY AND THE LIMITS OF AMERICAN CONSTITUTIONALISM (1990) (emphasizing the importance of property to the framers). On the separation of the private and public: The Federalist No. 10 (James Madison) (distinguishing between "public and private faith," as well as "public and personal liberty"); The Federalist No. 14 (James Madison) (emphasizing that government would be "in favor of private rights and public happiness").

26. The Federalist No. 10 (James Madison); McDONALD, *supra* note 8, at 189–209; POCOCK, *supra* note 8, at 513–26; WOOD, CREATION, *supra* note 2, at 391–468.

27. The Federalist No. 51 (James Madison).

28. "To secure the public good and private rights against the danger of such a faction, and at the same time to preserve the spirit and the form of popular government, is then the great object to which our inquiries are directed." The Federalist No. 10 (James Madison). "The founders of the United States did indeed define and construct their new nation in accord with Enlightenment doctrines of individual liberties and republican self-governance more than any regime before and most since." SMITH, *supra* note 9, at 470–71.

29. U.S. Const. amend. V; James Wilson, *supra* note 13, at 141, appendix A.

30. "Madison's political thought was characterized by an often agonized effort to find a working balance between the rights of property and republican principles." NEDELSKY, *supra* note 25, at 12. Madison argued that the government could assist a particular business enterprise if doing so would further the common good. James Madison, *In First Congress* (April 9, 1789), *reprinted in* COMPLETE, *supra* note 3, at 276, 276; James Madison, *In First Congress* (1789), *reprinted in* COMPLETE, *supra* note 3, at 272, 272; James Madison, *Letter to Clarkson Crolius* (Dec. 1819), *reprinted in* COMPLETE, *supra* note 3, at 270, 270; James Madison, *Letter to D. Lynch, Jr. (June 27, 1817), reprinted in* COMPLETE, *supra* note 3, at 271, 271.

31. *E.g.*, Lawton v. Steele, 152 U.S. 133, 137 (1894).

32. Goshen v. Stonington, 4 Conn. 209, 221 (1822) (Hosmer); JAMES KENT, 2 COMMENTARIES ON AMERICAN LAW 276 (1827; Legal Classics Library Reprint). For additional examples: State Bank v. Cooper, 10 Tenn. 599 (1831) (Green, J.); Eakin v. Raub, 12 Serg. & Rawle 330 (Pa. 1825); Calder v. Bull, 3 U.S. (3 Dall.) 386, 388 (1798) (Chase, J.); VanHorne's Lessee v. Dorrance, 28 F. Cas. 1012 (C.C. Pa. 1795); *see* WILLIAM J. NOVAK, THE PEOPLE'S WELFARE (1996) (focusing on the antebellum nineteenth century and how the distinction between the common good and partial and private interests limited government power).

33. Commonwealth v. Rice, 9 Metcalf 253, 50 Mass. 253, 256–59 (1845); *see, e.g.*, Vandine's Case, 23 Mass. 187, 191–93 (1828) (upholding restriction on the removal of offal).

34. NOVAK, *supra* note 32, at 2 (well-ordered); Pingrey v. Washburn, 1 Aik. 264, 15 Am. Dec. 676 (1826); *see, e.g.*, State Bank v. Cooper, 10 Tenn. 599 (1831) (Green, J.) (invalidating a law as partial).

35. Commonwealth v. Alger, 61 Mass. 53, 7 Cush. 53, 85–86 (1851). John Marshall was the first judge to use the term "police power" in a constitutional context. Brown v. Maryland, 12 U.S. (Wheat.) 419 (1827); NOVAK, *supra* note 32, at 53–54.

36. Thorpe v. Rutland & Burlington Railroad Company, 27 Vt. 140, 156 n.a1 (1855); Howard Gillman, *Preferred Freedoms: The Progressive Expansion of State Power and the Rise of Modern Civil Liberties Jurisprudence*, 47 POL. RES. Q. 623, 631–32 (1994) (types of cases where government was held to extend beyond its legislative power).

37. TUNIS WORTMAN, A TREATISE CONCERNING POLITICAL ENQUIRY, AND THE LIBERTY OF THE PRESS 49 (1800; 1970 reprint ed.) ("judgment is a faculty possessed in common by mankind"); *see* RICHARD HOFSTADTER, ANTI-INTELLECTUALISM IN AMERICAN LIFE (1962) (discussing the development of an anti-elitism in American society); SMITH, *supra* note 9, at 201 (discussing "anti-elitist rhetoric" of Jacksonian years).

38. EDWARD PESSEN, JACKSONIAN AMERICA 197–232 (rev. ed. 1985); HARRY L. WATSON, LIBERTY AND POWER 171–74 (1990).

39. THE STATISTICAL HISTORY OF THE UNITED STATES FROM COLONIAL TIMES TO THE PRESENT 409 (1965) (Table: Manufactures Summary: 1849 to 1954) [hereinafter STATISTICAL HISTORY]; THE STATISTICS OF THE WEALTH AND INDUSTRY OF THE UNITED STATES; COMPILED FROM THE ORIGINAL RETURNS OF THE NINTH CENSUS 392 (1872); Compiled from the 1900 Census, http://fisher.lib.virginia.edu/collections /stats/histcensus/php/state.php; RICHARD F. BENSEL, THE POLITICAL ECONOMY OF AMERICAN INDUSTRIALIZATION, 1877–1900, at 19–100 (2000); STATISTICAL HISTORY, *supra*, at 74 (Table: Industrial Distribution of Gainful Workers: 1820–1940).

40. STATISTICAL HISTORY, *supra* note 39, at 14 (Table: Population in Urban and Rural Territory); Frederick Jackson Turner, *The Significance of the Frontier in American History* (read at the American Historical Association in Chicago, July 12, 1893), http:// xroads.virginia.edu/~HYPER/TURNER/chapter1.html#text1 (on the closing of the frontier).

41. JAMES WILLARD HURST, LAW AND THE CONDITIONS OF FREEDOM IN THE NINETEENTH-CENTURY UNITED STATES 21 (1956).

42. 165 U.S. 578, 589, 591 (1897). For an explanation of free-labor ideology and its transformation into liberty of contract: STEPHEN M. FELDMAN, FREE EXPRESSION AND DEMOCRACY IN AMERICA: A HISTORY 45, 154–57, 200–05 (2008).

43. Lochner v. New York, 198 U.S. 45, 53, 56 (1905). On the nature of formalism: Thomas C. Grey, *Langdell's Orthodoxy*, 45 U. PITT. L. REV. 1, 8, 11 (1983).

44. *Lochner*, 198 U.S. at 59; *id.* at 72–73 (Harlan, J., dissenting); *id.* at 75–76 (Holmes, J., dissenting). Peckham also rejected the state justification of the law as a regulation of labor relations. *Id.* at 57. Holmes added: "The Fourteenth Amendment does not enact Mr. Herbert Spencer's Social Statics." *Id.* at 75 (Holmes, J., dissenting).

45. United States v. E. C. Knight Co., 156 U.S. 1, 11–15 (1895).

46. Muller v. Oregon, 208 U.S. 412 (1908); ERWIN CHEMERINSKY, CONSTITU-TIONAL LAW: PRINCIPLES AND POLICIES 668–69 (6th ed. 2019) (discussing number of laws invalidated during *Lochner* era); KAREN ORREN, BELATED FEUDALISM 111–17 (1991) (same).

47. JOSEPH R. GUSFIELD, SYMBOLIC CRUSADE: STATUS POLITICS AND THE AMERI-CAN TEMPERANCE MOVEMENT 23 (1963); RICHARD HOFSTADTER, THE AGE OF RE-FORM 223, 231–33, 259–61 (1955); ARTHUR S. LINK & RICHARD L. McCORMICK, PROGRESSIVISM 54 (1983); WILLIAM M. WIECEK, THE LOST WORLD OF CLASSICAL LEGAL THOUGHT: LAW AND IDEOLOGY IN AMERICA, 1886–1937, at 82–83 (1998); Wil-liam E. Forbath, *The Shaping of the American Labor Movement*, 102 HARV. L. REV. 1109, 1218–19 (1989).

48. BADGER, *supra* note 1, at 58 (explaining divisions within American society); GARY CROSS, AN ALL-CONSUMING CENTURY: WHY COMMERCIALISM WON IN MOD-ERN AMERICA 20–41 (2000); LYNN DUMENIL, THE MODERN TEMPER 56–97 (1995); E. P. HUTCHINSON, LEGISLATIVE HISTORY OF AMERICAN IMMIGRATION POLICY, 1798– 1965, at 187–92 (1981); LEUCHTENBURG, *supra* note 1, at 332 (emphasizing the par-ticipation of former political outsiders in the New Deal coalition); McELVAINE, *supra* note 1, at 197–98 (discussing changing values in America). 2 WHO BUILT AMERICA? WORKING PEOPLE AND THE NATION'S ECONOMY, POLITICS, CULTURE AND SOCIETY

270–87 (Stephen Brier, supervising ed., 1992). Prohibition represented a cultural victory for "the old middle class in American society." GUSFIELD, *supra* note 47, at 122. During the 1920s, "considerable headway was made—through advertising, installment purchase plans, a rising living standard, and a new emphasis on consumerism—toward weaning workers from their traditional values and remolding them into acquisitive, amoral individualists." McELVAINE, *supra* note 1, at 202.

49. SAMUEL LUBELL, THE FUTURE OF AMERICAN POLITICS 48–55 (3d ed., rev., 1965). For an extensive statistical study of the 1928 election: ALLAN J. LICHTMAN, PREJUDICE AND THE OLD POLITICS: THE PRESIDENTIAL ELECTION OF 1928 (1979).

50. BADGER, *supra* note 1, at 248–50; LEUCHTENBURG, *supra* note 1, at 147–51, 184, 188–89, 239–41, 331–35. "By 1934, the pattern of the early New Deal was beginning to emerge. Its distinguishing characteristic was the attempt to redress the imbalances of the old order by creating a new equilibrium in which a variety of groups and classes would be represented." LEUCHTENBURG, *supra* note 1, at 84; *see* BRUCE ACKERMAN, WE THE PEOPLE: FOUNDATIONS 116–19 (1991) (emphasizing the development of a more activist national government during New Deal). Helpful sources on the labor movement during the New Deal include JEROLD S. AUERBACH, LABOR AND LIBERTY (1966); MELVYN DUBOFSKY, THE STATE AND LABOR IN MODERN AMERICA (1994); WILLIAM E. FORBATH, LAW AND THE SHAPING OF THE AMERICAN LABOR MOVEMENT (1991); ORREN, *supra* note 46.

51. For a contemporary emphasis on the differences between American and totalitarian governments: Clarence Dykstra, *The Quest for Responsibility*, 33 AM. POL. SCI. REV. 1 (1939). In 1940, Roosevelt said: "The surge of events abroad has made some few doubters among us ask: Is this the end of a story that has been told? Is the book of democracy now to be closed and placed away upon the dusty shelves of time?" LEUCHTENBURG, *supra* note 1, at 348 (quoting FDR).

52. Martin v. City of Struthers, 319 U.S. 141, 146–47 (1943); *id.* at 150 (Murphy, J., concurring); *see* West Virginia State Board of Education v. Barnette, 319 U.S. 624, 641 (1943) (contrasting United States with its "present totalitarian enemies").

53. For early theoretical supports of pluralist democracy: JOHN DEWEY & JAMES H. TUFTS, ETHICS (1932 ed.), *reprinted in* JOHN DEWEY, 7 THE LATER WORKS, 1925–1953, at 1, 359 (Jo Ann Boydston ed., 1985); WALTER LIPPMANN, THE GOOD SOCIETY (1937); CHARLES E. MERRIAM, THE NEW DEMOCRACY AND THE NEW DESPOTISM (1939); CHARLES E. MERRIAM, POLITICAL POWER (1934). For discussions of the transition in democratic theory: JOHN G. GUNNELL, THE DESCENT OF POLITICAL THEORY 105, 122–23, 127–45 (1993); EDWARD A. PURCELL JR., THE CRISIS OF DEMOCRATIC THEORY 112–14, 138 (1973).

54. WILFRED E. BINKLEY & MALCOLM C. MOOS, A GRAMMAR OF AMERICAN POLITICS 9 (1949). For contemporary accounts of (pluralist) democracy: V. O. KEY, POLITICS, PARTIES, AND PRESSURE GROUPS (4th ed. 1958) (first published in 1942) (emphasizing politics as the exercise of power, and discussing the role played by pressure groups in that exercise of power); DAVID B. TRUMAN, THE GOVERNMENTAL PROCESS (1951) (extensive study of the functioning and influence of political interest groups). For subsequent elaborations of pluralist democratic theory, *see* JOHN RAWLS, POLITICAL LIBERALISM xvi–xvii, xxvii, 10, 29–35 (1996 ed.) (articulating the philosophy of politi-

cal liberalism); MICHAEL J. SANDEL, DEMOCRACY'S DISCONTENT 3–24, 28, 250–73 (1996) (explaining procedural republic).

55. ROBERT A. DAHL, A PREFACE TO DEMOCRATIC THEORY 67, 71 (1956) [hereinafter PREFACE]; *see* ROBERT A. DAHL, DEMOCRACY AND ITS CRITICS (1989) [hereinafter DEMOCRACY].

56. DEMOCRACY, *supra* note 55, at 30, 106, 109, 170; *see id.* at 169–75 (discussing free speech and other rights integral to the democratic process).

57. ROBERT A. DAHL, A PREFACE TO ECONOMIC DEMOCRACY 48–49 (1985); DEMOCRACY, *supra* note 55, at 172; PREFACE, *supra* note 55, at 4, 143; *see* DANIEL J. BOORSTIN, THE GENIUS OF AMERICAN POLITICS 1, 162 (1953) (emphasizing a "genuine community of our values"); DAVID B. TRUMAN, THE GOVERNMENTAL PROCESS 129, 138, 512–13 (2d ed. 1971; 1st ed. 1951) (emphasizing the rules of the game for democracy).

58. JEROLD S. AUERBACH, UNEQUAL JUSTICE: LAWYERS AND SOCIAL CHANGE IN MODERN AMERICA 224–32 (1976); FELDMAN, CRITICAL HISTORY, *supra* note 7, at 213–14; *see* ROBERT A. BURT, TWO JEWISH JUSTICES: OUTCASTS IN THE PROMISED LAND 39 (1988) (Felix Frankfurter minimized his Jewish background to facilitate professional success). For discussions of the Civil Rights Movement: DAVID J. GARROW, BEARING THE CROSS: MARTIN LUTHER KING JR. AND THE SOUTHERN CHRISTIAN LEADERSHIP CONFERENCE (1986); ROBERT WEISBROT, FREEDOM BOUND: A HISTORY OF AMERICA'S CIVIL RIGHTS MOVEMENT (1990).

59. XV THE AMERICAN AND ENGLISH ENCYCLOPAEDIA OF LAW 969 (David S. Garland & Lucius P. McGehee eds., 2d ed. 1900); *see* DUMENIL, *supra* note 48, at 49–51 (on the acceptance of lobbying); STEPHEN M. FELDMAN, AMERICAN LEGAL THOUGHT FROM PREMODERNISM TO POSTMODERNISM: AN INTELLECTUAL VOYAGE 115–28 (2000) (explaining the development of legal process thinking after World War II).

60. Helpful sources discussing the Court during the period between the two World Wars include BRUCE ACKERMAN, WE THE PEOPLE: TRANSFORMATIONS (1998); BARRY CUSHMAN, RETHINKING THE NEW DEAL COURT: THE STRUCTURE OF A CONSTITUTIONAL REVOLUTION (1998); GILLMAN, *supra* note 1; KEN I. KERSCH, CONSTRUCTING CIVIL LIBERTIES: DISCONTINUITIES IN THE DEVELOPMENT OF AMERICAN CONSTITUTIONAL LAW (2004); WILLIAM E. LEUCHTENBURG, THE SUPREME COURT REBORN (1995) [hereinafter LEUCHTENBURG, REBORN]; KEVIN J. MCMAHON, RECONSIDERING ROOSEVELT ON RACE (2004); JEFF SHESOL, SUPREME POWER: FRANKLIN ROOSEVELT VERSUS THE SUPREME COURT (2010); G. EDWARD WHITE, THE CONSTITUTION AND THE NEW DEAL (2000); T. Alexander Aleinikoff, *Constitutional Law in the Age of Balancing*, 96 YALE L.J. 943 (1987); David E. Bernstein, *Lochner Era Revisionism, Revised: Lochner and the Origins of Fundamental Rights Constitutionalism*, 92 GEO. L.J. 1 (2003); Barry Friedman, *The History of the Countermajoritarian Difficulty, Part Four: Law's Politics*, 148 U. PA. L. REV. 971 (2000); Tara Leigh Grove, *The Origins (and Fragility) of Judicial Independence*, 71 VAND. L. REV. 465 (2018). Leuchtenburg emphasizes the political underpinnings of the Court's jurisprudence in the 1930s, LEUCHTENBURG, REBORN, *supra*, while Cushman emphasizes legal doctrine and lawyering. CUSHMAN, *supra*. Gillman argues that the *Lochner*-era justices did not radically depart from previous constitutional decision making in order to decide in accord with their conservative

political views. Rather, the justices continued to interpret the Constitution to proscribe class legislation, a proscription with roots in the nineteenth century (and earlier). GILL-MAN, *supra* note 1. David E. Bernstein criticizes Gillman for misconstruing many *Lochner*-era cases. Bernstein, *supra*. I find Gillman more persuasive than Bernstein. Bernstein seems to misunderstand the proscription on class legislation. In particular, Bernstein does not give enough weight to the fact that legislatures could infringe on individual liberties to promote the common good. *See* NOVAK, *supra* note 32 (discussing nineteenth-century cases contrasting the common good and partial or private interests); WHITE, *supra*, at 246–51 (following Gillman's approach).

61. LEUCHTENBURG, *supra* note 1, at 61; *see id.* at 41–62 (on the first hundred days); KENNEDY, *supra* note 1, at 139–59 (same).

62. Home Building and Loan Association v. Blaisdell, 290 U.S. 398 (1934).

63. Nebbia v. New York, 291 U.S. 502, 536 (1934).

64. Stone's comments focused on the common law, but he extended his reasoning to constitutional law, where "more often than in private law, [the issue] is between the conflicting interests of the individual and of society as a whole." Harlan F. Stone, *The Common Law in the United States*, 50 HARV. L. REV. 4, 10, 19–22 (1936).

65. LEUCHTENBURG, REBORN, *supra* note 60, at 214–15.

66. Railroad Retirement Board v. Alton Railroad Company, 295 U.S. 330, 368, 374 (1935); A.L.A. Schechter Poultry Corporation v. United States, 295 U.S. 495 (1935); United States v. Butler, 297 U.S. 1, 62 (1936); Morehead v. New York ex rel. Tipaldo, 298 U.S. 587 (1936); Carter v. Carter Coal Company, 298 U.S. 238, 304 (1936).

67. Robert L. Hale, *Force and the State: A Comparison of "Political" and "Economic" Compulsion*, 35 COLUM. L. REV. 149, 168, 198–99, 200–01 (1935); Morris Cohen, *The Basis of Contract*, 46 HARV. L. REV. 553, 558–62, 565, 585–87 (1933); *see* Morris Cohen, *Property and Sovereignty*, 13 CORNELL L.Q. 8 (1927) (questioning the sharp separation of public and private spheres); Robert Hale, *Coercion and Distribution in a Supposedly Non-coercive State*, 38 POL. SCI. Q. 470, 470 (1923) (emphasizing coercion). Some critics argued the Court was frustrating the democratic will. LOUIS BOUDIN, GOVERNMENT BY JUDICIARY (1932).

68. Felix Cohen, *Transcendental Nonsense and the Functional Approach*, 35 COLUM. L. REV. 809, 811 (1935); KARL N. LLEWELLYN, THE BRAMBLE BUSH 12 (1930); Cohen, *supra*, at 839–40 (explaining how to decide whether a contract existed).

69. Thurman Arnold, *Trial by Combat and the New Deal*, 47 HARV. L. REV. 913, 919–22 (1934). Besides Arnold, radical realists included: JEROME FRANK, LAW AND THE MODERN MIND (1930); Joseph Hutcheson, *The Judgment Intuitive: The Function of the "Hunch" in Judicial Decision*, 14 CORNELL L.Q. 274 (1929).

70. DREW PEARSON & ROBERT S. ALLEN, THE NINE OLD MEN 2–3, 28–32, 36–37, 40 (1936); *Triple A Plowed Under*, N.Y. TIMES, Jan. 12, 1936, at E1 (discussing reactions to United States v. Butler, 297 U.S. 1 (1936)); LEUCHTENBURG, REBORN, *supra* note 60, at 119 (quoting Kentucky newspaper).

71. LEUCHTENBURG, REBORN, *supra* note 60, at 96; *see* Russell Owen Washington, *Nine Justices—and Nine Personalities*, N.Y. TIMES, Jan. 5, 1936, at SM3 (referring to justices as "nine old men in black").

72. CONGRESS OR THE SUPREME COURT: WHICH SHALL RULE AMERICA? 414, 416 (Egbert Ray Nichols ed., 1935) (attributing court-packing idea to Corwin); *Essay*, THE

NATION (Oct. 18, 1933), at 428, 430 (quoted in SHESOL, *supra* note 60, at 57); Lucas Prakke, *Swamping the Lords, Packing the Court, Sacking the King: Three Constitutional Crises*, 2 EUROPEAN CONST. L. REV. 116 (2006) (on Great Britain); AUSTIN, *supra* note 23, at 94, 97 (Table: National Electoral and Popular Vote Cast for President); LEUCHTENBURG, REBORN, *supra* note 60, at 112–31; Friedman, *supra* note 60, at 1019–23.

73. 81 Cong. Rec., 75th Cong., 1st Sess. 877–79 (Feb. 5, 1937).

74. Franklin D. Roosevelt, President, *Fireside Chat* (Mar. 9, 1937), https://perma .cc/64KE-NEDN (81 CONG. REC., appendix at 469–71, 75th Cong., 1st Sess. (March 10, 1937)).

75. *Id.*

76. *Three Senators Score Court Plan Here as Peril to Nation*, N.Y. TIMES, Mar. 13, 1937, at 1; Ira Jewell Williams & Ira Jewell Williams Jr., *What Are a Man's Rights?*, SATURDAY EVENING POST, May 29, 1937, at 17; Thomas Reed Powell, *Authority and Freedom in a Democratic Society*, 44 COLUM. L. REV. 473, 484 (1944) (explaining that the court-packing plan had aroused concerns about the protection of civil liberties); Friedman, *supra* note 60, at 1038; *see* SHESOL, *supra* note 60, at 393–99 (justices defending capabilities).

77. MCMAHON, *supra* note 60, at 69–73, 111.

78. Friedman, *supra* note 60, at 999 (quoting *Purging the Supreme Court*, THE NATION, Feb. 13, 1937, at 173–74); *Labor Strife Laid to Supreme Court*, N.Y. TIMES, Mar. 25, 1937, at 21 (discussing views of Wisconsin Senator Robert M. La Follette); LEUCHTENBURG, REBORN, *supra* note 60, at 135; SHESOL, *supra* note 60, at 514; MARK TUSHNET, TAKING BACK THE CONSTITUTION 216 (2020) (assessing support in House and Senate); Grove, *supra* note 60, at 509. A recent study concluded that more Americans would have preferred a constitutional amendment to FDR's statutory court-packing plan. William D. Blake, *The Law: "Justice under the Constitution, Not over It": Public Perceptions of FDR's Court-Packing Plan*, 49 PRESIDENTIAL STUD. Q. 204 (2019). Even so, Congress might have passed FDR's plan if it had been less ambitious—for instance, if it had sought an additional two rather than six justices. LAURA KALMAN, GHOST OF COURT PACKING PAST (draft; tentative title) (forthcoming Oxford University Press).

79. West Coast Hotel Co. v. Parrish, 300 U.S. 379 (1937).

80. 261 U.S. 525, 544–45, 549, 557, 559, 561 (1923).

81. *West Coast Hotel Co.*, 300 U.S. at 391, 399.

82. *Id.* at 400.

83. *Id.* at 411–12 (Sutherland, J., dissenting).

84. National Labor Relations Board v. Jones and Laughlin Steel Corp., 301 U.S. 1 (1937); National Labor Relations Act (July 5, 1935), 49 Stat. 449.

85. *National Labor Relations Board*, 301 U.S. at 33, 37, 41–44, 46.

86. Steward Machine Co. v. Davis, 301 U.S. 548 (1937); Senn v. Tile Layers Union, 301 U.S. 468 (1937) (upholding state labor law).

87. In one case, for instance, the Court reasoned that Congress must be allowed the "discretion" to pursue the "general welfare" as it deemed fit. *Steward Machine Co.*, 301 U.S. at 583–89, 594. For additional examples of the Court using language reminiscent of the republican democratic era: Thomas v. Collins, 323 U.S. 516, 532 (1945) (states

can regulate to protect "the public interest"), and Brown v. Board of Education, 349 U.S. 294, 300 (1955) (*Brown II*) (invoking "the public interest").

88. Franklyn Waltman, *Politics and People: Wagner Labor Act Decisions Seen as Turning Point in United States History*, WASH. POST, Apr. 13, 1937, at 2; *Supreme Court Upholds Wagner Labor Law; Hailed by Friends and Foes of Bench Change*, N.Y. TIMES, Apr. 13, 1937, at 1.

89. Franklyn Waltman, *Roberts Switch Strengthens U.S. Control in Industry*, WASH. POST, Apr. 13, 1937, 1, 4. The first to refer to the Court's change as the "switch in time that save nine" is disputed, with candidates being Edward Corwin, Abe Fortas, and Thomas Reed Powell. BURT SOLOMON, FDR V. THE CONSTITUTION 162 (2009); OWEN M. FISS, TROUBLED BEGINNINGS OF THE MODERN STATE, 1888–1910, at 8 (1993) (attributing to Powell).

90. *Roosevelt to Quit in 1940, Creel Says*, N.Y. TIMES, Nov. 30, 1936, at 4.

91. *Highlights of Today's Polls*, WASH. POST, Dec. 13, 1936, at B1; CUSHMAN, *supra* note 60, at 18; LEUCHTENBURG, REBORN, *supra* note 60, at 114–31, 143, 310–11 n.17; *see* SHESOL, *supra* note 60, at 96 (discussing earlier reports of administration discussions on controlling the Court).

92. Daniel E. Ho & Kevin M. Quinn, *Did a Switch in Time Save Nine?*, 2 J. OF LEGAL ANALYSIS 69 (2010).

93. SHESOL, *supra* note 60, at 444–46; LEUCHTENBURG, REBORN, *supra* note 60, at 142–43; Grove, *supra* note 60, at 509.

94. *Adverse Report on the Reorganization of the Federal Judiciary*, S. Rep. 711, 75th Cong., 1st Sess. (June 7, 1937); LEUCHTENBURG, REBORN, *supra* note 60, at 146–52; SHESOL, *supra* note 60, at 498–500.

95. Eugene V. Rostow, *Book Review*, 56 YALE L.J. 1469, 1472 (1947).

96. C. HERMAN PRITCHETT, THE ROOSEVELT COURT: A STUDY IN JUDICIAL POLITICS AND VALUES, 1937–1947 (1948).

97. Wickard v. Filburn, 317 U.S. 111, 118, 120, 129 (1942); *see* MCMAHON, *supra* note 60, at 12–22 (FDR's court-packing plan and other related political pressures helped push Court to accept and defend a more inclusive democracy).

CHAPTER 4

1. U.S. Const. art. III, § 1. For discussions of the delegates' debates about the judiciary: RICHARD BEEMAN, PLAIN, HONEST MEN 236–38, 273, 349–50 (2009); MICHAEL J. KLARMAN, THE FRAMERS' COUP: THE MAKING OF THE UNITED STATES CONSTITUTION 164–69 (2016). On Madison's lack of interest: MARY SARAH BILDER, MADISON'S HAND: REVISING THE CONSTITUTIONAL CONVENTION 117–18 (2015). While I focus on three key periods in the history of the law-politics dichotomy and legal formalism, I do not mean to suggest that other eras were unimportant. *E.g.*, MORTON J. HORWITZ, THE TRANSFORMATION OF AMERICAN LAW, 1780–1860, at 253–66 (1977) (legal formalism strengthened during the mid-nineteenth century as a means of protecting wealth).

2. Calder v. Bull, 3 U.S. (3 Dall.) 386, 398 (1798) (Iredell, J.); GEORGE LEE HASKINS & HERBERT A. JOHNSON, HISTORY OF THE SUPREME COURT OF THE UNITED STATES: FOUNDATIONS OF POWER: JOHN MARSHALL, 1801–1815, at 222 (1981) (on judges expressing partisanship).

3. Marbury v. Madison, 5 U.S. (1 Cranch) 137 (1803). On political rancor: STANLEY ELKINS & ERIC MCKITRICK, THE AGE OF FEDERALISM (1993); JAMES ROGER SHARP, AMERICAN POLITICS IN THE EARLY REPUBLIC (1993). On the courts: JENNIFER NEDELSKY, PRIVATE PROPERTY AND THE LIMITS OF AMERICAN CONSTITUTIONALISM 190 (1990).

4. *Marbury*, 5 U.S. at 170, 177.

5. NEDELSKY, *supra* note 3, at 198; *see id.* at 188–99; GORDON SILVERSTEIN, LAW'S ALLURE: HOW LAW SHAPES, CONSTRAINS, SAVES, AND KILLS POLITICS 2, 4 (2009) (law can be "narrowing, formalizing, and hardening" and can "undermine or kill" politics). On the developing concept of judicial review: SYLVIA SNOWISS, JUDICIAL REVIEW AND THE LAW OF THE CONSTITUTION (1990); William Michael Treanor, *Judicial Review before Marbury*, 58 STAN. L. REV. 455 (2005); Gordon S. Wood, *The Origins of Judicial Review Revisited, or How the Marshall Court Made More Out of Less*, 56 WASH. & LEE L. REV. 787 (1999).

6. Citizens United v. Federal Election Commission, 558 U.S. 310 (2010).

7. MAGALI SARFATTI LARSON, THE RISE OF PROFESSIONALISM: A SOCIOLOGICAL ANALYSIS 104 (1977). For discussions of the definition of a profession: Nathan O. Hatch, *Introduction: The Professions in a Democratic Culture, in* THE PROFESSIONS IN AMERICAN HISTORY 1, 1–2 (Nathan O. Hatch ed., 1988); Laurence Veysey, *Higher Education as a Profession: Changes and Continuities, in* THE PROFESSIONS IN AMERICAN HISTORY 15, 15–17 (Nathan O. Hatch ed., 1988) [hereinafter Veysey, *Higher Education*].

8. ANDREW ABBOTT, THE SYSTEM OF PROFESSIONS 2 (1988); LARSON, *supra* note 7, at xvi, 167. On the founding of the ABA: John A. Matzko, *"The Best Men of the Bar": The Founding of the American Bar Association, in* THE NEW HIGH PRIESTS: LAWYERS IN POST–CIVIL WAR AMERICA 75, 75–96 (Gerard W. Gawalt ed., 1984).

9. Veysey, *Higher Education*, *supra* note 7, at 18–19; *see* ABBOTT, *supra* note 8, at 12, 54–58; GEORGE M. MARSDEN, THE SOUL OF THE AMERICAN UNIVERSITY: FROM PROTESTANT ESTABLISHMENT TO ESTABLISHED NONBELIEF 155, 187 (1994); MORTON WHITE, SOCIAL THOUGHT IN AMERICA (1976) (on formalism and reactions against it). On the importance of scientific authoritativeness and objectivity: PETER NOVICK, THAT NOBLE DREAM: THE "OBJECTIVITY QUESTION" AND THE AMERICAN HISTORICAL PROFESSION 16, 31 (1988); DOROTHY ROSS, THE ORIGINS OF AMERICAN SOCIAL SCIENCE 62 (1991). The old colleges focused on the liberal arts, the classics, and teaching "mental discipline," as well as "piety and strength of character." LAURENCE R. VEYSEY, THE EMERGENCE OF THE AMERICAN UNIVERSITY 9 (1965).

10. C. C. Langdell, *Teaching Law as a Science*, 21 AM. L. REV. 123, 123 (1887) [hereinafter Langdell, *Teaching*]. Other writings by Langdell include C. C. LANGDELL, CASES ON CONTRACTS (2d ed. 1879) [hereinafter LANGDELL, CASEBOOK]; C. C. LANGDELL, SUMMARY OF THE LAW OF CONTRACTS (2d ed. 1880) [hereinafter LANGDELL, SUMMARY]; C. C. Langdell, *Preface to the First Edition, in* CASES ON CONTRACTS (2d ed. 1879) [hereinafter Langdell, *Preface*].

11. WILLIAM R. JOHNSON, SCHOOLED LAWYERS: A STUDY IN THE CLASH OF PROFESSIONAL CULTURES 103 (1978) (quoting C. C. Langdell, Record of the Commemoration, Nov. 5–8, 1886, on the 250th Anniversary of the Founding of Harvard College 97–98 [1887]). Not everyone agreed with Langdell's conclusion that law schools

belonged in universities. Thorstein Veblen stated that "[t]he law school belongs in the modern university no more than a school of fencing or dancing." Laura Kalman, *Bleak House*, 84 GEO. L.J. 2245, 2256 (1996) (quoting Veblen).

12. Langdell, *Preface, supra* note 10, at ix; *see* Langdell, *Teaching, supra* note 10, at 124–25; William A. Keener, *Methods of Legal Education (Part II)*, 1 YALE L.J. 143, 144 (1892) (discussing relation of case method of teaching and legal science).

13. Langdell, *Preface, supra* note 10, at viii–ix. For examples of Langdellian case-books: LANGDELL, CASEBOOK, *supra* note 10; WILLIAM A. KEENER, A SELECTION OF CASES ON THE LAW OF QUASI-CONTRACTS (1888); EUGENE WAMBAUGH, A SELECTION OF CASES ON AGENCY (1896).

14. Langdell, *Teaching, supra* note 10, at 124; *see* STEPHEN M. FELDMAN, AMERI-CAN LEGAL THOUGHT FROM PREMODERNISM TO POSTMODERNISM: AN INTELLECTUAL VOYAGE 91–101 (2000) (on Langdellian legal science); Thomas C. Grey, *Langdell's Orthodoxy*, 45 U. PITT. L. REV. 1 (1983) (same).

15. James Barr Ames, *Purchase for Value without Notice*, 1 HARV. L. REV. 1, 3, 7 (1887). For other examples of this type of Langdellian scholarship: Joseph H. Beale Jr., *Tickets*, 1 HARV. L. REV. 17 (1887); William A. Keener, *Recovery of Money Paid under Mistake of Fact*, 1 HARV. L. REV. 211 (1887). This type of scholarship naturally evolved into the writing of Langdellian-style treatises. JOSEPH BEALE, A TREATISE ON THE CONFLICT OF LAWS (1916); SAMUEL WILLISTON, THE LAW OF CONTRACTS (1920).

16. *See, e.g.*, James Barr Ames, *The Disseisin of Chattels*, 3 HARV. L. REV. 23 (1889); James Barr Ames, *History of Assumpsit*, 2 HARV. L. REV. 1 (1888); Samuel Williston, *History of the Law of Business Corporations*, 2 HARV. L. REV. 105 (1888).

17. *See, e.g.*, C. C. Langdell, *Classification of Rights and Wrongs*, 13 HARV. L. REV. 537 (1900); C. C. Langdell, *A Brief Survey of Equity Jurisdiction*, 1 HARV. L. REV. 55 (1887).

18. Gerard W. Gawalt, *Introduction, in* THE NEW HIGH PRIESTS: LAWYERS IN POST–CIVIL WAR AMERICA vii, vii (Gerard W. Gawalt ed., 1984); *see* Robert W. Gor-don, *"The Ideal and the Actual in the Law": Fantasies and Practices of New York City Lawyers, 1870–1910, in* THE NEW HIGH PRIESTS: LAWYERS IN POST–CIVIL WAR AMERICA 51, 56 (Gerard W. Gawalt ed., 1984).

19. ROBERT S. STEVENS, LAW SCHOOL: LEGAL EDUCATION IN AMERICA FROM THE 1850S TO THE 1980S, at 40 (1983) (quoting Ames) (emphasis added).

20. LANGDELL, SUMMARY, *supra* note 10, at 15, 21.

21. STEVE FULLER, PHILOSOPHY, RHETORIC, AND THE END OF KNOWLEDGE 33 (1993); *see* ROBERT FRODEMAN & ADAM BRIGGLE, SOCRATES TENURED 8–9 (2016) (on the purification of philosophy as an academic discipline); BRYAN MAGEE, CONFESSIONS OF A PHILOSOPHER: A JOURNEY THROUGH WESTERN PHILOSOPHY 364–65 (1997) (on professionalization in philosophy); Maxwell H. Bloomfield, *Law: The Development of a Profession, in* THE PROFESSIONS IN AMERICAN HISTORY 33, 42 (Nathan O. Hatch ed., 1988) (on the Langdellians). The discipline of economics assumes "the economy is autonomous from other social institutions." FRED BLOCK & MARGARET R. SOMERS, THE POWER OF MARKET FUNDAMENTALISM 24 (2014).

22. United States v. Carolene Products Co., 304 U.S. 144, 152–53 n.4 (1938); *see* KEVIN J. MCMAHON, RECONSIDERING ROOSEVELT ON RACE 12–22 (2004) (emphasiz-

ing that the Court was implementing one of FDR's goals by protecting a more inclusive democracy). On footnote 4: Louis Lusky, *Footnote Redux: A Carolene Products Reminiscence*, 82 COLUM. L. REV. 1093 (1982).

23. Baker v. Carr, 369 U.S. 186, 208–37 (1962), *overruling* Colegrove v. Green, 328 U.S. 549 (1946). On one person, one vote: Wesberry v. Sanders, 376 U.S. 1 (1964) (focusing on congressional districts); Reynolds v. Sims, 377 U.S. 533 (1964) (focusing on state legislative districts).

24. *Colegrove*, 328 U.S. at 553–56; *id.* at 569–71 (Black, J., dissenting).

25. HENRY M. HART JR. & ALBERT SACKS, THE LEGAL PROCESS: BASIC PROBLEMS IN THE MAKING AND APPLICATION OF LAW (Tentative ed. 1958). Other legal process sources include ALEXANDER M. BICKEL, THE LEAST DANGEROUS BRANCH (1962); Herbert Wechsler, *Toward Neutral Principles of Constitutional Law*, 73 HARV. L. REV. 1 (1959).

26. HART & SACKS, *supra* note 25, at 4, 164–67 (reasoned elaboration); Wechsler, *supra* note 25, at 15–35 (neutral principles); *see* BICKEL, *supra* note 25, at 49–59 (applying Wechsler's concept of neutral principles); Wechsler, *supra* note 25, at 31–35 (questioning the legitimacy of Brown v. Board of Education, 347 U.S. 483 [1954]) (*Brown I*).

27. BICKEL, *supra* note 25, at 16–23 (focusing on countermajoritarian difficulty); U.S. Const. art. III, § 1.

28. C. HERMAN PRITCHETT, THE ROOSEVELT COURT: A STUDY IN JUDICIAL POLITICS AND VALUES, 1937–1947, at xiii (1948); WILFRED BINKLEY & MALCOLM MOOS, A GRAMMAR OF AMERICAN POLITICS 525–26 (1949) (percentage of unanimous opinions); *see* BINKLEY & MOOS, *supra*, at 525–26 (following Pritchett in describing the justices as displaying "a pattern of opposing ideologies"); C. Herman Pritchett, *Dissent on the Supreme Court, 1943–44*, 39 AM. POL. SCI. REV. 42 (1945) (justices and politics). On the link between legal realism and political science: Cornell W. Clayton, *The Supreme Court and Political Jurisprudence: New and Old Institutionalisms*, in SUPREME COURT DECISION-MAKING: NEW INSTITUTIONALIST APPROACHES 15, 16–22 (Cornell W. Clayton & Howard Gillman eds., 1999); Lee Epstein, Jack Knight, & Andrew D. Martin, *The Political (Science) Context of Judging*, 47 ST. LOUIS U. L.J. 783, 786–87 (2003).

29. Fowler V. Harper & Edwin D. Etherington, *Lobbyists before the Court*, 101 U. PA. L. REV. 1172, 1173 (1953); Lee Epstein & Jack Knight, *Mapping Out the Strategic Terrain: The Informational Role of Amici Curiae*, in SUPREME COURT DECISION-MAKING: NEW INSTITUTIONALIST APPROACHES 215, 221–22 (Cornell W. Clayton & Howard Gillman eds., 1999); Samuel Krislov, *The Amicus Brief: From Friendship to Advocacy*, 72 YALE L.J. 694, 713–17 (1963).

30. Williamson v. Lee Optical of Oklahoma, Inc., 348 U.S. 483, 488 (1955); JOHN H. ELY, DEMOCRACY AND DISTRUST 1–104 (1980); *see id.* at 73–75, 136 (emphasizing process).

31. ELY, *supra* note 30, at 106.

32. West Virginia State Board of Education v. Barnette, 319 U.S. 624, 642 (1943); ROBERT A. DAHL, DEMOCRACY AND ITS CRITICS 169–75 (1989); ELY, *supra* note 30, at 105–34; *see* JOHN RAWLS, POLITICAL LIBERALISM (1996 ed.) (articulating the philosophy of political liberalism); MICHAEL J. SANDEL, DEMOCRACY'S DISCONTENT 3–24, 28, 250–73 (1996) (explaining procedural republic).

CHAPTER 5

1. C. HERMAN PRITCHETT, THE ROOSEVELT COURT: A STUDY IN JUDICIAL POLITICS AND VALUES, 1937–1947, at xi, 16, 136 (1948). For another landmark political science publication focusing on judicial behavior: JUDICIAL DECISION-MAKING (Glendon Schubert ed., 1963).

2. On the political science side: JEFFREY A. SEGAL & HAROLD J. SPAETH, THE SUPREME COURT AND THE ATTITUDINAL MODEL (1993). On the law side: Herbert Wechsler, *Toward Neutral Principles of Constitutional Law*, 73 HARV. L. REV. 1 (1959); C. C. LANGDELL, CASES ON CONTRACTS viii–ix (2d ed. 1879) (preface to 1st ed.).

3. On recognizing a connection between law and politics: BARRY FRIEDMAN, THE WILL OF THE PEOPLE (2009) (law professor); HOWARD GILLMAN, THE CONSTITUTION BESIEGED: THE RISE AND DEMISE OF LOCHNER ERA POLICE POWERS JURISPRUDENCE (1993) (political scientist); Lee Epstein et al., *Are Even Unanimous Decisions in the United States Supreme Court Ideological?*, 106 Nw. U. L. REV. 699, 713 (2012) (political scientist, law professor, and judge jointly labeling the Court "a mixed ideological-legalistic judicial institution"); *Symposium: Political Science and Law*, 105 Nw. U. L. REV. 467–787 (2011) (bringing together law professors and political scientists). On the persistence of the law-politics dichotomy: Thomas M. Keck, *Party, Policy, or Duty: Why Does the Supreme Court Invalidate Federal Statutes?*, 101 AM. POL. SCI. REV. 321, 331–34 (2007). On activist judges: ROBERT BORK, THE TEMPTING OF AMERICA 17 (1990); Lino A. Graglia, *Originalism and the Constitution: Does Originalism Always Provide the Answer?*, 34 HARV. J.L. & PUB. POL'Y 73, 74–75 (2011); *see* CASS R. SUNSTEIN, RADICALS IN ROBES: WHY EXTREME RIGHT-WING COURTS ARE WRONG FOR AMERICA 41–44 (2005) (discussing judicial activism); Dan M. Kahan, *Foreword: Neutral Principles, Motivated Cognition, and Some Problems for Constitutional Law*, 125 HARV. L. REV. 1, 4 (2011) (same).

4. Cheney v. U.S. District Court for District of Columbia, 541 U.S. 913, 920 (2004) (memorandum of Scalia, J.); Martin Shapiro, *Judges as Liars*, 17 HARV. J.L. & PUB. POL'Y 155, 156 (1994); JEFFREY A. SEGAL ET AL., THE SUPREME COURT IN THE AMERICAN LEGAL SYSTEM 17–18 (2005); SEGAL & SPAETH, *supra* note 2, at 4, 32; *see id.* at 33–53 (on legal model).

5. HAROLD J. SPAETH & JEFFREY A. SEGAL, MAJORITY RULE OR MINORITY WILL: ADHERENCE TO PRECEDENT ON THE U.S. SUPREME COURT xv (1999); SEGAL & SPAETH, *supra* note 2, at 65; *see* SPAETH & SEGAL, *supra*, at 286–315 (summarizing quantitative evidence regarding the influence of stare decisis on Supreme Court justices).

6. Robert Post, *Theorizing Disagreement: Reconceiving the Relationship between Law and Politics*, 98 CAL. L. REV. 1319, 1320, 1323 (2010) (emphasis added).

7. *E.g.*, Stephen G. Calabresi & Livia Fine, *Two Cheers for Professor Balkin's Originalism*, 103 Nw. U. L. REV. 663, 701 (2009); Steven G. Calabresi & Saikrishna B. Prakash, *The President's Power to Execute the Laws*, 104 YALE L.J. 541, 551–52 (1994).

8. Robert Schwartz, *Like They See 'Em*, N.Y. TIMES, Oct. 6, 2005, at A37 (quoting Sessions); Ilya Shapiro, *For Supreme Court Justices, Only the Law and the Constitution Should Matter*, N.Y. TIMES (Jan. 27, 2015); Thomas Fuller, *"So-Called" Judge Criticized by Trump Is Known as a Mainstream Republican*, N.Y. TIMES (Feb. 4, 2017) (quoting Trump).

9. Matt Shuham, *Trump Criticizes Judges Deciding on His Order: "Courts Seem to Be So Political,"* TPM LIVEWIRE (Feb. 8, 2017) (quoting Trump); Adam Liptak, *Court Refuses to Reinstate Travel Ban, Dealing Trump another Legal Loss*, N.Y. TIMES (Feb. 9, 2017) (same); Julie Hirschfeld Davis, *Supreme Court Nominee Calls Trump's Attacks on Judiciary "Demoralizing,"* N.Y. TIMES (Feb. 8, 2017) (quoting Gorsuch); *see* Paul Butler, *Ginsburg Knows, If Trump Wins, the Rule of Law Is at Risk*, N.Y. TIMES (Jan. 17, 2017).

10. Robert Barnes, *Gorsuch's Speeches Raise Questions of Independence, Critics Say*, WASH. POST (Sept. 27, 2017) (quoting Gorsuch); John Roberts, *Opening Statement during Confirmation Hearings before Senate Judiciary Committee*, CNN.COM (Sept. 12, 2005); Garrett Epps, *America's Red and Blue Judges*, THE ATLANTIC (Sept. 25, 2017).

11. Brett M. Kavanaugh, *I Am an Independent, Impartial Judge*, WALL ST. J. (Oct. 4, 2018); Matt Ford, *The Misleading Chaos of the Kavanaugh Hearing*, NEW REPUBLIC (Sept. 4, 2018); Carolyn Shapiro, *Brett Kavanaugh Said Judges Should Just Follow the Law. Here's Why That's Misleading*, FORTUNE (July 10, 2018); MICHAEL A. BAILEY & FORREST MALTZMAN, THE CONSTRAINED COURT: LAW, POLITICS, AND THE DECISIONS JUSTICES MAKE 6–7 (2011) (during confirmation hearings, Justice Kagan insisted that her political views would not influence her judicial decisions); James L. Gibson & Gregory A. Caldeira, *Has Legal Realism Damaged the Legitimacy of the U.S. Supreme Court?*, 45 LAW & SOC'Y REV. 195, 196–97 (2011) (during confirmation hearings, Justice Sotomayor suggested that judicial decision making was mechanical).

12. SEGAL & SPAETH, *supra* note 2 (political attitudes); SEGAL ET AL., *supra* note 4, at 319 (relying on newspaper editorials); CASS R. SUNSTEIN ET AL., ARE JUDGES POLITICAL? AN EMPIRICAL ANALYSIS OF THE FEDERAL JUDICIARY (2006) (study of court of appeals relying on party of appointing president); *see* Robert E. Goodin & Hans-Dieter Klingemann, *Political Science: The Discipline, in* A NEW HANDBOOK OF POLITICAL SCIENCE 3, 7–9 (1996) (discussing nature of politics). For an extensive discussion of different measurements of political ideology: LEE EPSTEIN ET AL., THE BEHAVIOR OF FEDERAL JUDGES (2013).

13. *See* H. L. A. HART, THE CONCEPT OF LAW 86–88 (1961) (distinguishing internal and external views); Wechsler, *supra* note 2, at 15–35 (judges should decide constitutional issues pursuant to "neutral principles"); Lee Epstein et al., *The Political (Science) Context of Judging*, 47 ST. LOUIS U. L.J. 783, 798 (2003) ("judges make choices in order to achieve certain goals"); Pat K. Chew & Robert E. Kelley, *The Realism of Race in Judicial Decision Making: An Empirical Analysis of Plaintiffs' Race and Judges' Race*, 28 HARV. J. RACIAL & ETHNIC JUST. 91–115 (2012) [hereinafter Chew & Kelley, *Realism*] (empirical study showing that race affects judicial decision making); Pat K. Chew & Robert E. Kelley, *Myth of the Color-Blind Judge: An Empirical Analysis of Racial Harassment Cases*, 86 WASH. U. L. REV. 1117 (2009) [hereinafter Chew & Kelley, *Myth*] (same); Gregory C. Sisk & Michael Heise, *Muslims and Religious Liberty in the Era of 9/11: Empirical Evidence from the Federal Courts*, 98 IOWA L. REV. 231 (2012) (lower court study concluding American Muslims were at a disadvantage in free-exercise cases); Gregory C. Sisk et al., *Searching for the Soul of Judicial Decision-making: An Empirical Study of Religious Freedom Decisions*, 65 OHIO ST. L.J. 491 (2004) (lower court study concluding that a judge's religion is the most salient factor affecting the outcome of religious-freedom cases); Barry Friedman, *The Politics of Judicial Review*, 84 TEX. L. REV. 257, 271 (2005) (defining politics capaciously); Benjamin E.

Lauderdale & Tom S. Clark, *The Supreme Court's Many Median Justices*, 106 AM. POL. SCI. REV. 847 (2012) (suggesting the need for complexity when measuring effects of political ideology on judges).

14. *See* Mark A. Graber, *Constitutional Politics and Constitutional Theory: A Misunderstood and Neglected Relationship*, 27 LAW & SOC. INQUIRY 309, 311–12 (2002) (describing the gulf between law professors and political scientists); Stephen M. Feldman, *The Transformation of an Academic Discipline: Law Professors in the Past and Future (or Toy Story Too)*, 54 J. LEGAL EDUC. 471 (2004) (discussing the development of the professional law teacher).

15. LANGDELL, *supra* note 2, at viii–ix; C. C. LANGDELL, SUMMARY OF THE LAW OF CONTRACTS 21 (2d ed. 1880); *see* STEPHEN M. FELDMAN, AMERICAN LEGAL THOUGHT FROM PREMODERNISM TO POSTMODERNISM: AN INTELLECTUAL VOYAGE 83–105 (2000) (discussing Langdellian legal science). *But cf.*, BRIAN Z. TAMANAHA, BEYOND THE FORMALIST-REALIST DIVIDE: THE ROLE OF POLITICS IN JUDGING 13–66 (2010) (arguing that Langdellians were not pure formalists, but acknowledging that almost all legal historians characterize them as such).

16. HENRY M. HART JR. & ALBERT SACKS, THE LEGAL PROCESS: BASIC PROBLEMS IN THE MAKING AND APPLICATION OF LAW 4, 164–67 (Tentative ed. 1958); ALEXANDER M. BICKEL, THE LEAST DANGEROUS BRANCH (1962).

17. BORK, *supra* note 3, at 5–6, 143–44; Lawrence B. Solum, *We Are All Originalists Now, in* CONSTITUTIONAL ORIGINALISM: A DEBATE 1, 4 (2011) (articulating the "fixation thesis"). To be sure, the meaning of originalism itself is now contested. Thomas B. Colby, *The Sacrifice of the New Originalism*, 99 GEO. L.J. 713 (2011); Peter J. Smith, *How Different Are Originalism and Non-Originalism?*, 62 HASTINGS L.J. 707 (2011).

18. Calabresi & Fine, *supra* note 7, at 701 (words have original meanings); NEIL GORSUCH, A REPUBLIC, IF YOU CAN KEEP IT 110 (2019); American Trucking Associations v. Smith, 496 U.S. 167, 201 (1990) (Scalia, J., concurring) (emphasis in original); Antonin Scalia, *The Rule of Law as a Law of Rules*, 56 U. CHI. L. REV. 1175 (1989); American Legion v. American Humanist Association, 139 S.Ct. 2067 (2019) (Thomas, J., concurring in the judgment); Elk Grove Unified School District v. Newdow, 542 U.S. 1 (2004) (Thomas, J., concurring in the judgment).

19. Herbert M. Kritzer & Mark J. Richards, *Jurisprudential Regimes and Supreme Court Decisionmaking: The* Lemon *Regime and Establishment Clause Cases*, 37 LAW & SOC'Y REV. 827, 839 (2003); Mark J. Richards & Herbert M. Kritzer, *Jurisprudential Regimes in Supreme Court Decision Making*, 96 AM. POL. SCI. REV. 305, 315 (2002); *see* Ryan C. Black & Ryan J. Owens, *Agenda Setting in the Supreme Court: The Collision of Policy and Jurisprudence*, 71 J. OF POLITICS 1062 (2009) (empirical study showing that law matters to Supreme Court justices even at the agenda-setting stage); Howard Gillman, *What's Law Got to Do with It? Judicial Behavioralists Test the "Legal Model" of Judicial Decision Making*, 26 LAW & SOC. INQUIRY 465, 492 (2001) (criticizing Segal and Spaeth's legal model) [hereinafter Gillman, *What's Law*]; Terri Peretti, *Constructing the State Action Doctrine, 1940–1990*, 35 LAW & SOC. INQUIRY 273, 286–87 n.8 (2010) (identifying political science studies concluding that law matters); Barry Friedman & Andrew D. Martin, *Looking for Law in All the Wrong Places, in* WHAT'S LAW GOT TO DO WITH IT? 143, 154–56 (Charles Gardner Geyh ed., 2011) (same); Andrea McAtee & Kevin T. McGuire, *Lawyers, Justices, and Issue Salience: When and How Do*

Legal Arguments Affect the U.S. Supreme Court?, 41 Law & Soc'y Rev. 259 (2007) (on attorneys' legal arguments); Lemon v. Kurtzman, 403 U.S. 602, 612–13 (1971) (specifying the three prongs as purpose, effects, and entanglements).

20. Tom S. Clark, The Supreme Court: An Analytic History of Constitutional Law 19–20 (2019); *id.* at 20, 27 (describing alternative political science approaches to judicial decision making); Michael G. Roskin et al., Political Science: An Introduction 12, 26–28 (9th ed. 2006); John Gerring, *Qualitative Methods*, 20 Annual Rev. of Pol. Sci. 15 (2017) (comparing quantitative and qualitative methods); Colorado State Glossary of Key Terms, http://writing.colostate.edu /guides/research/glossary (on quantitative and qualitative research). "Judicial decision making . . . is a practice that mixes legal, strategic, and attitudinal considerations in ways that cannot be fully isolated by scientific investigation." Mark A. Graber, *Legal, Strategic or Legal Strategy: Deciding to Decide during the Civil War and Reconstruction, in* The Supreme Court and American Political Development 33, 35 (Ronald Kahn & Ken I. Kersch eds., 2006); *cf.*, Cornell Clayton & Howard Gillman, *Introduction, in* The Supreme Court in American Politics: New Institutionalist Interpretations 1, 1–2 (Howard Gillman & Cornell Clayton eds., 1999) (describing the narrow focus of the attitudinal model). On the need for falsifiability: Segal et al., *supra* note 4, at 20–21. The falsifiability thesis, conceptualized by Karl Popper, is itself controversial. Susan Haack, *Federal Philosophy of Science: A Deconstruction— And a Reconstruction*, 5 N.Y.U. J.L. & Liberty 394, 394–97 (2010). For discussions of the human sciences, a term used more frequently in continental studies: Hans-Georg Gadamer, The Beginning of Philosophy 29 (Rod Coltman trans., 1998); Charles Taylor, Philosophy and the Human Sciences (1985). On qualitative evidence: Georg G. Iggers, Historiography in the Twentieth Century 97–100, 139 (1997); Lisa Webley, *Qualitative Approaches to Empirical Legal Research, in* The Oxford Handbook of Empirical Legal Research 926, 940 (Peter Cane & Herbert Kritzer eds., 2010); Ellie Fossey et al., *Understanding and Evaluating Qualitative Research*, 36 Australian & New Zealand J. Psychiatry 717 (2002).

21. Philip Bobbitt, Constitutional Interpretation 12–13 (1991) (specifying six "modalities of argument" judges use to decide constitutional cases); Benjamin N. Cardozo, The Nature of the Judicial Process (1921) (discussing how Cardozo decided cases); Steven J. Burton, Judging in Good Faith (1992) (emphasizing judges' good-faith responsibility to apply the law); Tamanaha, *supra* note 15, at 194 (emphasizing that judges internalize a "commitment to engage in the good-faith application of the law"); Stefanie A. Lindquist & David E. Klein, *The Influence of Jurisprudential Considerations on Supreme Court Decisionmaking: A Study of Conflict Cases*, 40 Law & Soc'y Rev. 135, 137 (2006) (discussing how the justices appear to take law seriously); Paul Wahlbeck et al., *Marshalling the Court: Bargaining and Accommodation on the United States Supreme Court*, 42 Am. J. Pol. Sci. 294 (1998) (justices discussing wording); Jack M. Balkin, *Bush v. Gore and the Boundary between Law and Politics*, 110 Yale L.J. 1407, 1407 n.2 (2001) (justices claim they do not discuss politics); *see* Linda Greenhouse, *Another Kind of Bitter Split*, N.Y. Times, Dec. 14, 2000, at A1 (same); *see, e.g.*, The Supreme Court in Conference (1940–1985): The Private Discussions behind Nearly 300 Supreme Court Decisions 415–17 (Del Dickson ed., 2001) (noting the discussions in *Mueller v. Allen*, 463 U.S. 388 [1983]).

22. SEGAL & SPAETH, *supra* note 2, at 65 (the Supreme Court decides, simply put); SPAETH & SEGAL, *supra* note 5, at xv (overwhelmingly); SEGAL ET AL., *supra* note 4, at 319 (justices who are); Keith E. Whittington, *Once More unto the Breach: Postbehavioralist Approaches to Judicial Politics*, 25 LAW & SOC. INQUIRY 601, 602 (2000) (judicial behavior); *see* SEGAL & SPAETH, *supra* note 2, at 208–60 (quantitative evidence); *see* Robert Cooter, *Do Good Laws Make Good Citizens? An Economic Analysis of Internalized Norms*, 86 VA. L. REV. 1577, 1599 n.24, 1600 n.25 (2000) (summarizing quantitative studies that support the attitudinal model). For an updated version of Segal and Spaeth's influential 1993 book: JEFFREY A. SEGAL & HAROLD J. SPAETH, THE SUPREME COURT AND THE ATTITUDINAL MODEL REVISITED (2002). A law professor, Eric Segall, argues that the Supreme Court does not decide like a traditional court at all. ERIC J. SEGALL, SUPREME MYTHS xvii, 1–9 (2012).

23. Bush v. Gore, 531 U.S. 98, 104–110 (2000); *id.* at 126 (Stevens, J., dissenting) (arguing that a principled application of the majority's equal protection reasoning also would have invalidated the original method of counting votes in Florida); Michael J. Klarman, Bush v. Gore *through the Lens of Constitutional History*, 89 CALIF. L. REV. 1721, 1725 (2001); HOWARD GILLMAN, THE VOTES THAT COUNTED: HOW THE COURT DECIDED THE 2000 PRESIDENTIAL ELECTION 2–5, 141–43, 185–89 (2001); Cass R. Sunstein, *Order without Law*, 68 U. CHI. L. REV. 757, 759 (2001); Balkin, *supra* note 21, at 1426–35; Jeffrey Toobin, TOO CLOSE TO CALL (2001) (detailed political account of the election dispute).

24. Most political scientists would acknowledge the importance of the attitudinal model in the historical development of law and courts research, Julie Novkov, *Understanding Law as a Democratic Institution through U.S. Constitutional Development*, 40 LAW & SOC. INQUIRY 814–15 (2015), yet political scientists disagree about its continuing influence in the field. Back in 2004, one political scientist—himself a historical institutionalist—called the attitudinal model "the most dominant model of judicial decision making in political science." KEVIN J. MCMAHON, RECONSIDERING ROOSEVELT ON RACE 6, 203 (2004). Around the same time, though, another political scientist described attitudinalism as maintaining "predominance" while being "frequently challenged." Nancy L. Maveety, *The Study of Judicial Behavior and the Discipline of Political Science*, *in* THE PIONEERS OF JUDICIAL BEHAVIOR 1, 22 (2002). By 2018, a political scientist could still call the attitudinal model "the dominant theory of judicial behavior and the starting premise for political scientists who study the courts." ROBERT J. HUME, JUDICIAL BEHAVIOR AND POLICYMAKING 16 (2018). Yet other political scientists referred to it as merely "one prominent theory." PAMELA C. CORLEY ET AL., AMERICAN JUDICIAL PROCESS: MYTH AND REALITY IN LAW AND COURTS 13 (2016); *see* CLARK, *supra* note 20, at 20, 27 (describing diverse approaches to law and courts research); Novkov, *supra*, at 815–30 (same).

25. Epstein et al., *supra* note 13, at 798 (judges make choices). The authors note that most rational choice studies assume that judges pursue their policy preferences, but the authors add that judges might sometimes pursue other goals. *Id.* at 798–99; *see* Lee Epstein & Jack Knight, *Mapping Out the Strategic Terrain: The Informational Role of Amici Curiae, in* SUPREME COURT DECISION-MAKING: NEW INSTITUTIONALIST APPROACHES 215, 216 (Cornell W. Clayton & Howard Gillman eds., 1999) (explaining strategic approach). On Thomas: Van Orden v. Perry, 545 U.S. 677 (2005) (Thomas, J., and

Court upholding a display of the Ten Commandments). For an excellent brief history of the historical development of political science, see Novkov, *supra* note 24, at 811.

26. Robert A. Dahl, *Decision-Making in a Democracy: The Supreme Court as a National Policy-Maker*, 6 J. PUB. L. 279, 284, 293 (1957); Peretti, *supra* note 19, at 275; *see* MARTIN SHAPIRO, LAW AND POLITICS IN THE SUPREME COURT (1964) (discussing political jurisprudence). *But see* KEITH E. WHITTINGTON, POLITICAL FOUNDATIONS OF JUDICIAL SUPREMACY 42–45 (2007) (discussing criticisms of Dahl's thesis).

27. On Court and consolidation with new regime: Dahl, *supra* note 26, at 293; Keck, *supra* note 3, at 322; Mark Tushnet, *The Supreme Court and the National Political Order: Collaboration and Confrontation, in* THE SUPREME COURT AND AMERICAN POLITICAL DEVELOPMENT 117 (Ronald Kahn & Ken I. Kersch eds., 2006). "[T]he policy views dominant on the Court are never for long out of line with the policy views dominant among the lawmaking majorities of the United States." Dahl, *supra* note 26, at 285; *see* ROBERT G. MCCLOSKEY, THE AMERICAN SUPREME COURT 224–25 (1960) (presenting similar view).

28. *Brown I*, 347 U.S. 483 (1954). On politics and *Brown*: MARY L. DUDZIAK, COLD WAR CIVIL RIGHTS (2000); Derrick A. Bell, *Brown v. Board of Education and the Interest-Convergence Dilemma*, 93 HARV. L. REV. 518 (1980). Dahl argued that *Brown* might not have actually conferred legitimacy on a policy of a dominant national alliance—because a strong political coalition supporting desegregation had not yet formed—but that *Brown* nonetheless conformed to an explicit or implicit norm widely held by political leaders. Dahl, *supra* note 26, at 293–94.

29. SEGAL ET AL., *supra* note 4, at 35–37; Lee Epstein, *Studying Law and Courts, in* CONTEMPLATING COURTS 1, 5–6 (1995); Keck, *supra* note 3, at 322, 328 (regime as stylized).

30. Peretti, *supra* note 19, at 289 (arrive like orphans); Whittington, *supra* note 22, at 606 (justices behave); Keck, *supra* note 3, at 322, 328; *see* Richard H. Pildes, *Is the Supreme Court a "Majoritarian" Institution?*, 2010 SUP. CT. REV. 103 (arguing that the regimist approach is ambiguous because the definition of the dominant regime and what constitutes following it often seem to change).

31. Frederick Schauer, *Judging in a Corner of the Law*, 61 S. CAL. L. REV. 1717, 1729 (1988); Frederick Schauer, *Easy Cases*, 58 S. CAL. L. REV. 399 (1985); Michael S. Moore, *The Plain Truth about Legal Truth*, 26 HARV. J.L. & PUB. POL'Y 23, 24 (2003) (example of will); *see* Southern Pacific Co. v. Jensen, 244 U.S. 205, 221 (1917) (Holmes, J., dissenting) (arguing that judges make law in the gaps); BENJAMIN N. CARDOZO, THE NATURE OF THE JUDICIAL PROCESS 113–14 (1921) (same).

32. *See, e.g.*, HART, *supra* note 13, at 119 (arguing that legal rules have "a core of certainty and a penumbra of doubt"); EDWARD H. LEVI, AN INTRODUCTION TO LEGAL REASONING 1 (1949) (arguing "for the discussion of policy in the gap of [legal] ambiguity").

33. HART & SACKS, *supra* note 16, at 165 (in the way); Gitlitz v. Commissioner of Internal Revenue, 531 U.S. 206, 219–20 (2001) (tax decision).

34. SEGAL ET AL., *supra* note 4, at 30; SPAETH & SEGAL, *supra* note 5, at 5–7. For a quantitative study of the role of law and political ideology in the lower courts: FRANK B. CROSS, DECISION MAKING IN THE U.S. COURTS OF APPEALS (2007).

35. Forrest Maltzman et al., *Strategy and Judicial Choice: New Institutionalist Approaches to Supreme Court Decision-Making, in* SUPREME COURT DECISION-MAKING:

New Institutionalist Approaches 43, 46 (Cornell W. Clayton & Howard Gillman eds., 1999); *see* Whittington, *supra* note 22, at 612 (describing rational choice new institutionalism).

36. Frank B. Cross & Blake J. Nelson, *Strategic Institutional Effects on Supreme Court Decisionmaking*, 95 Nw. U. L. Rev. 1437, 1492 (2001); *see* Gregory C. Sisk & Michael Heise, *Judges and Ideology: Public and Academic Debates about Statistical Measures*, 99 Nw. U. L. Rev. 743, 774 (2005) (approving the Cross and Nelson study). The law professor Brian Tamanaha draws on multiple sources, including quantitative studies of the lower courts, to support his concept of balanced realism, an oil-and-water approach (he admires Cardozo's description of judging, including the notion that judges generally follow the law but must sometimes fill in gaps). Tamanaha, *supra* note 15, at 125–31.

37. Lucas A. Powe Jr., The Supreme Court and the American Elite, 1789–2008, at viii–ix (2009). Powe considers himself a lawyer—he clerked for Justice William O. Douglas—but holds a joint appointment at the University of Texas in the School of Law and the Government Department. Lucas A. Powe Jr., The Warren Court and American Politics xiii, xv (2000) [hereinafter Politics]. For examples of a law professor and a historian maintaining that law mirrors social and economic interests: Lawrence Friedman, A History of American Law (1973) (law professor); Kermit L. Hall, The Magic Mirror (1989) (historian).

38. Politics, *supra* note 37, at 215, 242; *see id.* at 199–203, 232–55, 260–65; Baker v. Carr, 369 U.S. 186 (1962); Colegrove v. Green, 328 U.S. 549 (1946); Wesberry v. Sanders, 376 U.S. 1 (1964); Reynolds v. Sims, 377 U.S. 533 (1964); Voting Rights Act of 1965, 79 Stat. 437, 42 U.S.C. §§ 1973 et seq.; Civil Rights Act of 1964, 78 Stat. 241, 42 U.S.C. §§ 1971, 1975(a)–(d), 2000(a)–2000(h)(4).

39. Graber, *supra* note 14, at 317 (historical institutionalists); Cornell Clayton & Howard Gillman, *Introduction, in* The Supreme Court in American Politics: New Institutionalist Interpretations 1, 2 (Howard Gillman & Cornell Clayton eds., 1999) (to explore); *see* Rogers M. Smith, Civic Ideals 6, 509–10 n.12 (1997) (discussing historical institutionalism); Rogers M. Smith, *Political Jurisprudence, The "New Institutionalism," and the Future of Public Law*, 82 Am. Pol. Sci. Rev. 89 (1988) (a key article in the emergence of new institutionalism—that is, historical institutionalism); Cornell W. Clayton, *The Supreme Court and Political Jurisprudence: New and Old Institutionalisms, in* Supreme Court Decision-Making: New Institutionalist Approaches 15, 16–22 (Cornell W. Clayton & Howard Gillman eds., 1999) (on "old institutionalism"); Mark A. Graber, Transforming Free Speech (1991); Gillman, *supra* note 3, at 11–12; Peretti, *supra* note 19, at 290; Graber, *supra* note 20, at 35; Whittington, *supra* note 22, at 619, 623, 629; Howard Gillman, *The Court as an Idea, Not a Building (or a Game): Interpretive Institutionalism and the Analysis of Supreme Court Decision-Making, in* Supreme Court Decision-Making: New Institutionalist Approaches 65, 79–80, 86 (Cornell W. Clayton & Howard Gillman eds., 1999) [hereinafter Gillman, *Idea*]. Rational choice scholars are also sometimes characterized as new institutionalists because of their emphasis on institutional constraints, though there are important differences between rational choice scholars and historical institutionalists. Whittington, *supra* note 22, at 608–16.

40. Karen Orren & Stephen Skowronek, The Search for American Political Development x, 6 (2004) (grapples with); Ronald Kahn & Ken I. Kersch, *Introduction, in* The Supreme Court and American Political Development 1, 18–19 (Ronald Kahn & Ken I. Kersch eds., 2006) (conceptualized as; distinctive to; a certain autonomy); Gillman, *supra* note 3; *see* Lochner v. New York, 198 U.S. 45 (1905) (invalidating maximum hours legislation). On the historical development of historical institutionalism and APD: Novkov, *supra* note 24, at 813–19.

41. Politics, *supra* note 37, at xiv (law is); Friedman, *supra* note 3, at 212–25 (discussing FDR's court-packing plan); *id.* at 313–22 (discussing Reagan's efforts to appoint conservative justices).

42. Gillman, *supra* note 39, at 80 (formal responsibility); Gillman, *supra* note 19, at 485–89 (are considered; legal norms; often; political ideology; to the point); Ronald Dworkin, Taking Rights Seriously 31–33 (1978).

43. Gillman, *supra* note 3, at 16–17 (meaning is); Gillman, *supra* note 19, at 489–90 (often; so long) (emphasis added).

44. Gillman, *supra* note 39, at 80; Gillman, *supra* note 19, at 485–86; Whittington, *supra* note 22, at 623.

45. Hans-Georg Gadamer, Truth and Method xxi, 89, 137, 140, 144, 159, 164–65, 295, 309, 462, 477–91 (Joel Weinsheimer & Donald Marshall trans., 2d rev. ed. 1989). For discussions of Gadamer's hermeneutics: Georgia Warnke, Gadamer: Hermeneutics, Tradition, and Reason (1987); Joel C. Weinsheimer, Gadamer's Hermeneutics: A Reading of Truth and Method (1985). Dworkin explains that there is "no algorithm" to ascertain the right answer. Ronald Dworkin, *How Law Is like Literature, in* A Matter of Principle 146, 160 (1985); Ronald Dworkin, *Is There Really No Right Answer in Hard Cases?, in* A Matter of Principle 119 (1985) (right answer exists). For discussions of interpretation: Jürgen Habermas, *The Hermeneutic Claim to Universality* (1971), *in* Josef Bleicher, Contemporary Hermeneutics 181, 183 (1980); Jürgen Habermas, *A Review of Gadamer's Truth and Method, in* Understanding and Social Inquiry 335, 357 (Fred Dallmayr & Thomas McCarthy eds., 1977); Stephen M. Feldman, *The Problem of Critique: Triangulating Habermas, Derrida, and Gadamer Within Metamodernism,* 4 Contemp. Pol. Theory 296, 299–315 (2005); Stephen M. Feldman, *Made for Each Other: The Interdependence of Deconstruction and Philosophical Hermeneutics,* 26 Phil. & Soc. Criticism 51, 53–63 (2000).

46. Gadamer, *supra* note 45, at 133, 282–84, 302, 306.

47. *See id.* at 282–84, 295, 302–09 (discussing interpretation from within the horizon). The Gadamerian concept of the horizon overlaps with Stanley Fish's concept of an interpretive community. Stanley Fish, *Is There a Text in This Class?, in* Is There a Text in This Class? 303, 303–04 (1980); *cf.,* Thomas S. Kuhn, The Structure of Scientific Revolutions 43–51 (2d ed. 1970) (explaining the concept of a paradigm).

48. Dan Simon, *A Third View of the Black Box: Cognitive Coherence in Legal Decision-Making,* 71 U. Chi. L. Rev. 511, 536 (2004); *see* Gadamer, *supra* note 45, at 282, 293, 461–63 (discussing how traditions change); Chew & Kelley, *Realism, supra* note 13 (empirical study showing that race affects judicial decision making); Chew & Kelley, *Myth, supra* note 13 (same). Simon is a professor of law and psychology.

49. CHARLES GARDNER GEYH, COURTING PERIL 8 (2016) ("The norms of the legal culture that are inculcated in law school, entrenched in practice, and perpetuated on the bench, take the role of law as a constraint on judicial behavior seriously"). "All mental processing draws closely from one's background knowledge. A decision to cross a street, for example, is contingent on one's experience-born knowledge about vehicles, motion, and driver behavior." Simon, *supra* note 48, at 536. "The very ability to formulate a [judicial] decision in terms that would be recognizably legal depends on one's having internalized the norms, categorical distinctions, and evidentiary criteria that make up one's understanding of what the law is." Stanley Fish, *Still Wrong after All These Years, in* DOING WHAT COMES NATURALLY 356, 360 (1989); *see* Steven D. Smith, *Believing like a Lawyer*, 40 B.C. L. REV. 1041 (1999) (emphasizing that lawyers and judges remain committed to a traditional view of legal reasoning).

50. On good faith and sincerity: Gillman, *Idea, supra* note 39, at 80; Whittington, *supra* note 22, at 623; BURTON, *supra* note 21, at 35–68 (arguing that judges have a duty to decide in good faith according to the law); TAMANAHA, *supra* note 15, at 194 (emphasizing that judges internalize a "commitment to engage in the good-faith application of the law"). On neuroscience: Anna Spain Bradley, *The Disruptive Neuroscience of Judicial Choice*, 9 U.C. IRVINE L. REV. 1 (2018). On correspondence between politics and interpretation: Stephen M. Feldman, *Do Supreme Court Nominees Lie? The Politics of Adjudication*, 18 S. CAL. INTERDISC. L.J. 17, 31–32 (2008) [hereinafter Feldman, *Politics*]; Stephen M. Feldman, *The Rule of Law or the Rule of Politics? Harmonizing the Internal and External Views of Supreme Court Decision Making*, 30 LAW & SOC. INQUIRY 89, 109–10 (2005) [hereinafter Feldman, *Rule*].

51. JONATHAN CULLER, ON DECONSTRUCTION 110 (1982); Madeleine Plasencia, *Who's Afraid of Humpty Dumpty: Deconstructionist References in Judicial Opinions*, 21 SEATTLE U. L. REV. 215, 247 (1997); *see* RONALD DWORKIN, LAW'S EMPIRE 199–225 (1986) [hereinafter DWORKIN, EMPIRE] (arguing that judges are obliged to adjudicate according to a principle of integrity).

52. Bush v. Gore, 531 U.S. at 104–10; *id.* at 126 n.4 (Stevens, J., dissenting); HOWARD GILLMAN, THE VOTES THAT COUNTED: HOW THE COURT DECIDED THE 2000 PRESIDENTIAL ELECTION 2–5, 185–89 (2001); Sunstein, *supra* note 23, at 759; *see* Gillman, *What's Law, supra* note 19, at 490 n.26 (*Bush v. Gore* is "properly viewed as a rare example of purely partisan decision making"); Sunstein, *supra* at 759. "Florida's decision to leave to each county the determination of what balloting system to employ—despite enormous differences in accuracy—might run afoul of equal protection." *Bush v. Gore*, 531 U.S. at 126 (Stevens, J., dissenting).

53. In theory, a judge could avoid deciding a case in accord with politics writ small in one other way, besides following politics writ large. The judge might opt to decide pursuant to some nonlegal determinant (other than politics writ large). For example, a judge could decide based on coin flips or the spin of a roulette wheel. Of course, in such situations the judge is no longer engaged in judicial decision making—at least as it is commonly understood.

54. Stephen M. Feldman, *Supreme Court Alchemy: Turning Law and Politics into Mayonnaise*, 12 GEO. J.L. & PUB. POL'Y 57, 82–83 (2014); *see* TAMANAHA, *supra* note 15, at 187–89 (distinguishing cognitive framing from willful judging). Jack Balkin and Sanford Levinson distinguish "between the 'high' politics of political principle and the

'low' politics of partisan advantage." Jack M. Balkin, *Bush v. Gore and the Boundary between Law and Politics*, 110 YALE L.J. 1407, 1408 (2001); *see* Jack M. Balkin & Sanford Levinson, *Understanding the Constitutional Revolution*, 87 VA. L. REV. 1045, 1062–63, 1088 (2001) (elaborating distinction between high and low politics in adjudication); Sanford Levinson, *Return of Legal Realism*, THE NATION, Jan. 8, 2001, at 8 (introducing the distinction). In accord with my distinction between politics writ large and writ small, I prefer to distinguish between, on the one hand, the high-level principles embodied *in the text* (part of politics writ small) and, on the other hand, turning away from legal interpretation to focus on politics, whether high or low (politics writ large). *See* LAWRENCE BAUM, IDEOLOGY IN THE SUPREME COURT 2 (2017) (describing Balkin and Levinson's distinction as helpful but "not quite as sharp as it might seem"). Balkin and Levinson's approach appears consistent with Dworkin's later writings, in which he suggests that judges sometimes need to focus on high-level issues of political philosophy. RONALD DWORKIN, JUSTICE IN ROBES 80, 150, 170–71 (2006); DWORKIN, EMPIRE, *supra* note 51, at 90, 255–57; *See* Feldman, *Politics*, *supra* note 50, at 17, 23–27, 32–37 (2008) (explaining and criticizing Dworkin's approach to the connection of law and politics).

55. BAILEY & MALTZMAN, *supra* note 11. Bailey and Maltzman summarize three themes that emerge from their quantitative studies: "First, justices are influenced by more than just the policy preferences emphasized by the attitudinal model. Second, law matters for justices. Third, the influence of specific legal doctrines varies across justices." *Id.* at 143; *see* GEYH, *supra* note 49, at 7–11 (using a legal culture paradigm to explain how both law and politics influence judicial decision making); SUNSTEIN ET AL., *supra* note 12 (quantitative study suggests both political ideology and legal doctrine influence federal court of appeals judges). The political scientist Lawrence Baum explains the "methodological concept, behavioral equivalence, which means that we cannot distinguish between two possible causes of a pattern of behavior when the effects of the two causes would be the same." Lawrence Baum, *Law and Policy: More and Less than a Dichotomy, in* WHAT'S LAW GOT TO DO WITH IT? 71, 76 (Charles Gardner Geyh ed., 2011).

56. Simon, *supra* note 48, at 517, 545–46 (toward a state; coherence-based; do not represent); EILEEN BRAMAN, LAW, POLITICS, AND PERCEPTION 29–30 (2009) (their mental; a judge who); *see* BRAMAN, *supra*, at 157–58 (discussing unconscious influences); Simon, *supra* note 48, at 541–42, 545–46 (discussing the importance of motivated reasoning, and lack of awareness).

57. GEYH, *supra* note 49, at 8 (emphasizing the learning of legal culture in law school and practice); Lindquist & Klein, *supra* note 21, 137 (emphasizing how law students are socialized).

58. Philip Bobbitt argues that judges can draw on six "modalities of argument" to decide constitutional cases legitimately: "historical (relying on the intentions of the framers and ratifiers of the Constitution); textual (looking to the meaning of the words of the Constitution alone, as they would be interpreted by the average contemporary 'man on the street'); structural (inferring rules from the relationships that the Constitution mandates among the structures it sets up); doctrinal (applying rules generated by precedent); ethical (deriving rules from those moral commitments of the American ethos that are reflected in the Constitution); and prudential (seeking to balance the costs and benefits of a particular rule)." BOBBITT, *supra* note 21, at 12–13; *see* PHILIP

BOBBITT, CONSTITUTIONAL FATE (1982) (elaborating the modalities of constitutional argument). I do not agree with Bobbitt's suggestion that the six modalities of argument are, in a sense, a closed set. To me, the sources informing constitutional interpretation can always be contested. Some empirical evidence suggests that traditional legal arguments have greater influence on lower court judges than on Supreme Court justices. James C. Brent, *An Agent and Two Principals: U.S. Court of Appeals Responses to Employment Division, Department of Human Resources v. Smith and the Religious Freedom Restoration Act*, 27 AM. POL. Q. 236 (1999); *see* Gillman, *What's Law, supra* note 19, at 481–82 (mentioning research that suggests precedents have greater influence on lower courts than on Supreme Court). *But cf.*, Emerson H. Tiller & Frank B. Cross, *A Modest Proposal for Improving American Justice*, 99 COLUM. L. REV. 215, 217–18 (1999) (emphasizing that empirical evidence also supports the view that political ideology strongly influences lower court decision making).

59. Feldman, *Politics, supra* note 50, at 32; Dan Simon, *A Psychological Model of Judicial Decision Making*, 30 RUTGERS L.J. 1, 122–23 (1998) (explaining how, from a psychological vantage, judges authentically perceive themselves as reaching the correct decision). Psychology research suggests that "[t]he socialization that starts in law school and continues throughout one's legal career causes those who are trained in this tradition to accept and internalize appropriate norms of decision making." BRAMAN, *supra* note 56, at 28; *see* Feldman, *Rule, supra* note 50, at 103 (emphasizing the learning of legal traditions).

60. Charles W. Collier, *The Use and Abuse of Humanistic Theory in Law: Reexamining the Assumptions of Interdisciplinary Legal Scholarship*, 41 DUKE L.J. 191, 232–33 (1991); Owen M. Fiss, *Objectivity and Interpretation*, 34 STAN. L. REV. 739, 756 (1982). For a criticism of Fiss's conceptualization of interpretation: Stanley Fish, *Fish v. Fiss*, 36 STAN. L. REV. 1325 (1984).

61. Franz Kafka, *The Metamorphosis, reprinted in* THE PENAL COLONY: STORIES AND SHORT PIECES 67 (1948). Litigants might have sufficient resources to seek additional remedies, such as a rehearing. In some instances, a losing party might even seek to initiate the constitutional amendment process to overturn a Supreme Court decision. Feldman, *Rule, supra* note 50, at 105 & nn. 15–16.

62. THE IMPACT OF SUPREME COURT DECISIONS (Theodore L. Becker ed., 1969) (including numerous gap studies, which argued that, empirically, Supreme Court decisions often had limited effect on American society); Neal Devins, *Judicial Matters*, 80 CALIF. L. REV. 1027, 1065 (1992) (acknowledging that "Supreme Court decisions limiting religious observance in the public schools . . . are often disregarded"). *But cf.*, John Brigham, *Judicial Impact upon Social Practices: A Perspective on Ideology*, 9 LEGAL STUD. F. 47 (1985) (criticizing gap studies for being overly positivistic).

63. Brown v. Board of Education, 347 U.S. 483 (1954) (*Brown I*, which resolved the substantive equal protection issue); Brown v. Board of Education, 349 U.S. 294 (1955) (*Brown II*, which resolved that the appropriate remedy was desegregation with all deliberate speed); *see* David W. Romero & Francine Sanders Romero, *Precedent, Parity, and Racial Discrimination: A Federal/State Comparison of the Impact of* Brown v. Board of Education, 37 LAW & SOC'Y REV. 809 (2003) (arguing that empirical evidence shows that, through 1964, state supreme courts did not heed the *Brown* mandate). The overall effect of *Brown* has been subject to vigorous dispute. *See, e.g.*, GERALD N. ROSENBERG,

The Hollow Hope: Can Courts Bring about Social Change? 110–56 (1991) (arguing that *Brown* impeded the Civil Rights Movement by inflaming southern racists, who were able to delay political changes); Richard Kluger, Simple Justice 758–61 (1975) (arguing that although *Brown* alone did not change America, it was central element in social change); Michael J. Klarman, *Brown, Racial Change, and the Civil Rights Movement*, 80 Va. L. Rev. 7 (1994) (arguing that *Brown* indirectly aided the Civil Rights Movement by generating violent southern resistance, which, in turn, aroused apathetic northern whites to support political change). Of course, additional civil or criminal procedures may remain to prolong the litigation. A losing litigant, for instance, can seek a rehearing. But at some point, the adjudication ends, based on the Court's determination. After the Court decided *Engel v. Vitale*, 370 U.S. 421 (1962), a number of groups sought to overcome the decision with a constitutional amendment. Stephen M. Feldman, Please Don't Wish Me a Merry Christmas: A Critical History of the Separation of Church and State 234 (1997).

64. For overviews of many of the various historical and legal positions: Saul Cornell, *"To Keep and Bear Arms," in* Whose Right to Bear Arms Did the Second Amendment Protect? 9, 17–21 (Saul Cornell ed., 2000); Carl T. Bogus, *The History and Politics of Second Amendment Scholarship: A Primer*, 76 Chi.-Kent L. Rev. 3, 3–25 (2000); *Second Amendment Symposium*, 1998 B.Y.U. L. Rev. 1. One of the first articles that helped to spur further debate was Sanford Levinson, *The Embarrassing Second Amendment*, 99 Yale L.J. 637 (1989).

65. District of Columbia v. Heller, 554 U.S. 570, 636 (2008); Bruce Allen Murphy, Scalia: A Court of One 385 (2014) (judicial magnum opus).

66. *See* McDonald v. City of Chicago, 561 U.S. 742 (2010) (extending *Heller* holding to state and local governments).

CHAPTER 6

1. Thomas S. Kuhn, The Copernican Revolution 1–2, 27, 38 (1957). Likewise, certain practical enterprises continue to be based on Newtonian mechanics, even though Einstein's relativity theory has supplanted it scientifically. Bryan Magee, Confessions of a Philosopher: A Journey through Western Philosophy 51–52 (1997).

2. *See* Stanley Fish, *Dennis Martinez and the Uses of Theory*, 96 Yale L.J. 1773 (1987) (arguing that theories of judicial decision making do not affect the practice).

3. Stephen M. Feldman, *Constitutional Interpretation and History: New Originalism or Eclecticism?*, 28 B.Y.U. J. Pub. L. 283, 317–49 (2014).

4. Ogden v. Saunders, 25 U.S. (12 Wheat.) 213 (1827). For that Supreme Court era, under Chief Justice Marshall, the case was unusual because of the multiple opinions. In fact, after reargument Johnson issued yet another opinion on an additional issue. *Id.* at 358 (Johnson, J.). "For the first and only time in his career Marshall had been unable to forge a majority in a constitutional case." G. Edward White, The Marshall Court and Cultural Change 1815–1835, at 651 (1991); *see* Bernard Schwartz, A History of the Supreme Court 39 (1993) (discussing how the Marshall Court usually avoided seriatim opinions).

5. Public meaning: *Ogden*, 25 U.S. at 278–79, 290 (Johnson, J.); *id.* at 329 (Trimble, J.); *id.* at 290 (Johnson, J.) (the sense put; the contemporaries of the constitution);

id. at 329 (Trimble, J.) (contemporary construction). Plain meaning: *Id.* at 274–75 (Johnson, J.); *id.* at 302–03 (Thompson, J.); *Id.* at 302 (Thompson, J.) (if this provision); *id.* at 303 (Thompson, J.) (the plain and); *id.* at 274 (Johnson, J.) (nothing . . . on the face). Textual arrangement: *Id.* at 267–68 (Washington, J.). Fabric of the whole: *Id.* at 275, 288–89 (Johnson, J.); *id.* at 329–31 (Trimble, J.); *id.* at 329 (Trimble, J.) (the principle). In a different case, Marshall, too, found the fabric of the whole significant. McCulloch v. Maryland, 17 U.S. (4 Wheat.) 316, 407 (1819).

6. Framers' intentions: *Ogden*, 25 U.S. at 256, 258 (Washington, J.); *id.* at 274–75, 280 (Johnson, J.); *id.* at 302–05 (Thompson, J.); *id.* at 329, 331 (Trimble, J.); *id.* at 331 (Trimble, J.) (sages); *id.* at 256 (Washington, J.) (I have examined). Purposes: *Id.* at 265 (Washington, J.); *id.* at 274 (Johnson, J.); *id.* at 303 (Thompson, J.) (reason and policy).

7. Natural law: *Id.* at 258, 266 (Washington, J.); *id.* at 282 (Johnson, J.); *id.* at 303–04 (Thompson, J.). History of the political problems: *Id.* at 274, 276–77 (Johnson, J.); *id.* at 339, 354–55 (Marshall, C. J., dissenting). Practical consequences: *Id.* at 276 (Johnson, J.); *id.* at 300, 313 (Thompson, J.); *id.* at 300 (Thompson, J.) (facilitate commercial). Judicial precedents: *Id.* at 272 (Johnson, J.); *id.* at 296 (Thompson, J.).

8. *Id.* at 256 (Washington, J.). Washington added that if the justices were doubtful about constitutional meaning, then they should defer to the legislative judgment, *id.* at 270 (Washington, J.), a viewpoint that James Thayer would famously advocate more than sixty years later. James B. Thayer, *The Origin and Scope of the American Doctrine of Constitutional Law*, 7 HARV. L. REV. 129 (1893).

9. Joseph Story, 1 COMMENTARIES ON THE CONSTITUTION OF THE UNITED STATES 383, 407 (1833) (in 3 volumes); *see id.* at 441 ("we should never forget, that it is an instrument of government we are to construe"); WHITE, *supra* note 4, at 114–18 (discussing Story's interpretive approach); William Michael Treanor, *Against Textualism*, 103 Nw. U. L. REV. 983, 998 (2009) (arguing that the founders' generation did not generally accept a strict interpretative approach).

10. Adarand Constructors, Inc. v. Pena, 515 U.S. 200, 273–74 (1995) (Ginsburg, J., dissenting). Roe v. Wade, 410 U.S. 113, 129–47 (1973). In *Roe*, Blackmun purportedly resolved the case "by constitutional measurement, free of emotion and of predilection." *Id.* at 116. Planned Parenthood v. Casey, 505 U.S. 833, 864–69 (1992). Lawrence v. Texas, 539 U.S. 558, 568–71 (2003).

11. NEIL GORSUCH, A REPUBLIC, IF YOU CAN KEEP IT 10 (2019); *see* Patricia Ewick, *Principles, Passions, and the Paradox of Modern Law: A Comment on Bybee*, 38 LAW & SOC. INQUIRY 196, 199 (2013) (arguing that the combination of rule-oriented and political-oriented views of legality help in "sustaining law's legitimacy").

12. This recognition might help explain how, even after *Bush v. Gore*, Justice Thomas and Chief Justice Rehnquist were able to deny that partisan politics played any role in the Court's decision-making process. *Cf.*, Jack M. Balkin, Bush v. Gore *and the Boundary between Law and Politics*, 110 YALE L.J. 1407, 1407 & n.2 (2001) (noting that Thomas and Rehnquist denied that partisan politics affected their decisions).

13. BENJAMIN N. CARDOZO, THE NATURE OF THE JUDICIAL PROCESS (1921); Roscoe Pound, *Mechanical Jurisprudence*, 8 COLUM. L. REV. 605 (1908); *see* Fish, *supra* note 2 (arguing that theories of judicial decision making do not affect the practice).

14. *Casey*, 505 U.S. at 999–1001 (Scalia, J., concurring and dissenting).

15. *See* Robert Post & Reva Siegel, *Originalism as a Political Practice: The Right's Living Constitution*, 75 FORDHAM L. REV. 545 (2006) (arguing that originalism is a

conservative political practice); Steven M. Teles, *Transformative Bureaucracy: Reagan's Lawyers and the Dynamics of Political Investment*, 23 STUD. IN AM. POL. DEV. 61, 75–78 (2009) (arguing that Edwin Meese's Department of Justice purposefully sought to advocate for originalism as a means of advancing a political agenda).

16. GORSUCH, *supra* note 11, at 10; *see id.* at 114–15 (originalism is not politically conservative). On Scalia: Stephen M. Feldman, *Justice Scalia and the Originalist Fallacy, in* THE CONSERVATIVE REVOLUTION OF ANTONIN SCALIA 189 (Howard Schweber & David A. Schultz eds., 2018); Jamal Greene, *The Age of Scalia*, 130 HARV. L. REV. 144, 155–57, 183–84 (2016); Benjamin Morris, *How Scalia Became the Most Influential Conservative Jurist since the New Deal*, FIVETHIRTYEIGHT (Feb. 14, 2016). On the politics of Supreme Court justices: LEE EPSTEIN ET AL., THE BEHAVIOR OF FEDERAL JUDGES 106–16 (2013); Lee Epstein et al., *How Business Fares in the Supreme Court*, 97 MINN. L. REV. 1431 (2013).

17. Printz v. United States, 521 U.S. 898, 905, 910 (1997); ANTONIN SCALIA & BRYAN A. GARNER, READING LAW: THE INTERPRETATION OF LEGAL TEXTS 93 (2012); *see Printz*, 521 U.S. at 905–11.

18. Eric J. Segall, *Will the Real Justice Scalia Please Stand Up?*, 50 WAKE FOREST L. REV. ONLINE 101, 102 (2015); *see* New York v. United States, 505 U.S. 144 (1992) (invalidating congressional commandeering of state legislatures).

19. American Trucking Associations v. Smith, 496 U.S. 167, 201 (1990) (Scalia, J., concurring) (emphasis in original). On originalism: Lawrence B. Solum, *We Are All Originalists Now, in* CONSTITUTIONAL ORIGINALISM: A DEBATE 1, 4 (2011); Randy E. Barnett, *The Misconceived Assumption about Constitutional Assumptions*, 103 NW. U. L. REV. 615, 660 (2009). Some originalists now distinguish between interpretation and construction. Amy Barrett, *Introduction: The Interpretation/Construction Distinction in Constitutional Law*, 27 CONST. COMMENT. 1 (2010); Thomas B. Colby, *The Sacrifice of the New Originalism*, 99 GEO. L.J. 713, 731–34 (2011). From this perspective, the justices interpret the constitutional text to discern its original public meaning, but they then construct doctrines to implement the meaning. For instance, the justices might read the Establishment Clause to mean that there should be a wall of separation between church and state. Then the justices would construct a doctrine, such as the three-part *Lemon* test, that would facilitate implementing the wall of separation. Lemon v. Kurtzman, 403 U.S. 602, 612–13 (1971). On the one hand, I am agnostic about this distinction between interpretation and construction. The justices interpret both constitutional text and constitutional doctrine (developed in earlier cases). Thus, the crucial component of legal interpretation—the law-politics emulsion—operates whether the justices are focused on text or doctrine. Doctrine, in other words, is just another type of text. On the other hand, I find this distinction misleading because it suggests that the justices can sometimes escape the interpretive process—because construction is differentiated from interpretation—but such escape is impossible. Construction, as the originalists conceive of it, is simply another instance of interpretation. Moreover, the justices themselves rarely distinguish constitutional meaning from doctrine. Rather, they are more likely to perceive their doctrinal statements as manifesting or capturing the textual meaning. Finally, and most important, the distinction between interpretation and construction can lead some theorists to reinscribe the law-politics dichotomy. For these theorists, interpretation is legal, primarily for the courts, while construction is political, primarily for the legislatures. *E.g.*, KEITH

E. WHITTINGTON, CONSTITUTIONAL INTERPRETATION 5–11 (1999). This division of labor between courts and legislatures might also suggest that legal interpretation can be mechanical. *See* Saul Cornell, *The People's Constitution versus the Lawyer's Constitution: Popular Constitutionalism and the Original Debate over Originalism*, 23 YALE J.L. & HUMAN. 295, 298 (2011) (criticizing new originalists who apparently believe that an old dictionary provides an objective meaning for constitutional language).

20. JOHN HOPE FRANKLIN & ALFRED A. MOSS, FROM SLAVERY TO FREEDOM: A HISTORY OF AFRICAN AMERICANS 68–104 (7th ed. 1994) (discussing African Americans, slavery, and the early years of nationhood); ALEXANDER KEYSSAR, THE RIGHT TO VOTE: THE CONTESTED HISTORY OF DEMOCRACY IN THE UNITED STATES 1–60 (2000) (detailing limits on suffrage); RORY DICKER, A HISTORY OF U.S. FEMINISMS 21–24 (2016 ed.) (on coverture and other limits on nineteenth-century women); WOMEN AND THE LAW: COVERTURE IN ENGLAND AND THE COMMON LAW WORLD (Tim Stretton & Krista Kesselring eds., 2013) (on women and coverture); *see* RICHARD BEEMAN, PLAIN, HONEST MEN 310–11 (2009) (discussing slavery at the time of the Constitutional Convention).

21. Antonin Scalia, *The Rule of Law as a Law of Rules*, 56 U. CHI. L. REV. 1175, 1187 (1989); Marc Galanter, *Why the "Haves" Come Out Ahead: Speculations on the Limits of Legal Change*, 9 LAW & SOC'Y REV. 95 (1974) (discussing advantages of the wealthy and powerful in litigation); *see* Donald R. Songer et al., *Do the "Haves" Come Out Ahead over Time? Applying Galanter's Framework to Decisions of the U.S. Courts of Appeals, 1925–1988*, 33 LAW & SOC'Y REV. 811 (1999) (empirical research showing that victory in litigation depends more on access to resources than on formal legal arguments); *see* Paul Gowder, *Equal Law in an Unequal World*, 99 IOWA L. REV. 1021 (2014) (discussing the relationship between formal and substantive equality). Invalidating affirmative action programs: Parents Involved in Community Schools v. Seattle School District No. 1, 551 U.S. 701 (2007); *Adarand Constructors*, 515 U.S. 200. On the political tilt of formalism: Genevieve Lakier, *Imagining an Antisubordinating First Amendment*, 118 COLUM. L. REV. 2117, 2138–39 (2018) (arguing that the Court's formalism causes an emphasis on private power); Tracy E. Higgins, *Democracy and Feminism*, 110 HARV. L. REV. 1657, 1700 (1997) (patriarchy in the private sphere constrains women in the public sphere). I agree with much of Lakier's argument about free-speech formalism, but from my perspective, she attributes too much causal power to legal doctrine and theory without accounting for the dynamic interaction between law and politics. *See* Stephen M. Feldman, *Missing the Point of the Past (and the Present) of Free Expression*, 89 TEMPLE L. REV. ONLINE 55 (2017) (praising and criticizing Genevieve Lakier, *The Invention of Low-Value Speech*, 128 HARV. L. REV. 2166 (2015)).

22. For an example of a formalist decision in which Native Americans win: McGirt v. Oklahoma, _ S.Ct. _ (2020) (holding that large portion of Oklahoma is Indian Country for purposes of criminal jurisdiction). On the convergence of interests and the haves winning in cases involving race: MARY L. DUDZIAK, COLD WAR CIVIL RIGHTS (2000); Derrick A. Bell, *Brown v. Board of Education and the Interest-Convergence Dilemma*, 93 HARV. L. REV. 518 (1980). On the convergence of interests and the haves winning in cases involving religion: STEPHEN M. FELDMAN, PLEASE DON'T WISH ME A MERRY CHRISTMAS: A CRITICAL HISTORY OF THE SEPARATION OF CHURCH AND STATE 175–254 (1997); Stephen M. Feldman, *Empiricism, Religion, and Judicial Decision Making*, 15 WM. & MARY BILL RTS. J. 43 (2006); Stephen M. Feldman, *Religious*

Minorities and the First Amendment: The History, the Doctrine, and the Future, 6 U. Pa. J. Const. L. 222 (2003). On the convergence of interests and the haves winning in cases involving free expression: Stephen M. Feldman, Free Expression and Democracy in America: A History 118–42, 209–40, 420–62 (2008); Stephen M. Feldman, *Broken Platforms, Broken Communities? Free Speech on Campus*, 27 Wm. & Mary Bill Rts. J. 949 (2019).

23. Paul Kane, *The Battle over this High Court Seat Began Decades Ago*, Wash. Post (Oct. 6, 2018); *see* Scott Lemieux, *The Supreme Court Will Never Be the Same*, New Republic (April 7, 2017) (Republicans blame the Democratic defeat of Bork for the eventual end of filibustering Supreme Court nominees, though Bork received a full Senate vote); *Supreme Revenge: Alan Simpson Interview*, Frontline PBS (May 21, 2019) (interview with former Republican Senator Alan Simpson of Wyoming in which Simpson blames Democrats for politicizing the confirmation process, starting with Bork), https://www.youtube.com/watch?v=6ciYXO4V3Y4.

24. Robert Bork, The Tempting of America 144 (1990) [hereinafter Bork, Tempting]; *see id.* at 2, 140–41; Robert H. Bork, *Neutral Principles and Some First Amendment Problems*, 47 Ind. L.J. 1 (1971) [hereinafter Bork, *Neutral*] (Bork's earlier type of originalism); Stephen M. Feldman, Neoconservative Politics and the Supreme Court: Law, Power, and Democracy 75–79 (2013) [hereinafter Feldman, Neoconservative] (discussing Bork's evolving views of originalist methodology).

25. Heather Gilligan, *Borking Is the Conservative Word You Need to Know during Confirmation Hearings*, Timeline (Jan. 12, 2017).

26. Ethan Bronner, Battle for Justice 221 (1989) (quoting Bork: my philosophy); Bork, Tempting, *supra* note 24, at 279 (politicized); *id.* at 298 (Bork quoting Senator Orrin Hatch). On reasonable worries by progressives and moderates: Bronner, *supra*, at 221–60; Norman Vieira & Leonard Gross, Supreme Court Appointments 175–81 (1998).

27. Michael A. Kahn, *The Appointment of a Supreme Court Justice: A Political Process from Beginning to End*, 25 Presidential Stud. Q. 25 (1995). Politics is always in the mix: *Id.* at 32–37. *The Jay Treaty* (Nov. 19, 1794), *reprinted in* 1 Documents of American History 165 (Henry Steele Commager ed., 9th ed. 1973). Before his defeat, Rutledge served in a recess appointment. Henry J. Abraham, Justices, Presidents, and Senators: A History of U.S. Supreme Court Appointments from Washington to Bush II, at 58–59 (5th ed. 2008). For additional helpful sources on the nomination and confirmation processes: James MacGregor Burns, Packing the Court (2009); Dion Farganis & Justin Wedeking, Supreme Court Confirmation Hearings in the U.S. Senate (2014); Paul M. Collins & Lori A. Ringhand, *The Institutionalization of Supreme Court Confirmation Hearings*, 41 Law & Soc. Inquiry 126 (2016) [hereinafter Collins & Ringhand, *Hearings*]. For a discussion of judicial appointments to the lower federal courts: Michael J. Gerhardt & Michael Ashley Stein, *The Politics of Early Justice: Federal Judicial Selection, 1789–1861*, 100 Iowa L. Rev. 551 (2015).

28. Abraham, *supra* note 27, at 104; Farganis & Wedeking, *supra* note 27, at 9–10; Collins & Ringhand, *Hearings*, *supra* note 27, at 129–30.

29. John Braeman, *"The People's Lawyer" Revisited: Louis D. Brandeis versus the United Shoe Machinery Company*, 50 Am. J. of Legal History 284 (2008) (People's Lawyer); Melvin I. Urofsky, Louis D. Brandeis 438 (2009) (quoting Taft); *id.* at 445 (declaring Brandeis unfit); *see* Abraham, *supra* note 27, at 141–44; Farganis &

WEDEKING, *supra* note 27, at 10–11; UROFSKY, *supra*, at 430–59; Collins & Ringhand, *Hearings, supra* note 27, at 130.

30. PAUL M. COLLINS & LORI A. RINGHAND, SUPREME COURT CONFIRMATION HEARINGS AND CONSTITUTIONAL CHANGE 126 (2013) (quoting Zoll) [hereinafter COLLINS & RINGHAND, CHANGE]; *see* ABRAHAM, *supra* note 27, at 172–75; BURNS, *supra* note 27, at 160; Collins & Ringhand, *Hearings, supra* note 27, at 132.

31. COLLINS & RINGHAND, CHANGE, *supra* note 30, at 163 (quoting Eastland); Brown v. Board of Education (*Brown I*), 347 U.S. 483 (1954); Brown v. Board of Education (*Brown II*), 349 U.S. 294 (1955); *see* ABRAHAM, *supra* note 27, at 205–06; FARGANIS & WEDEKING, *supra* note 27, at 12–13; Collins & Ringhand, *Hearings, supra* note 27, at 132.

32. Civil Rights Act of 1964, Title II, 78 Stat. 241 (discrimination); Voting Rights Act of 1965, 79 Stat. 437, 42 U.S.C. §§ 1973 et seq.; Civil Rights Act of 1964, 78 Stat. 241, 42 U.S.C. §§ 1971, 1975(a)-(d), 2000(a)-2000(h)(4); FRANKLIN & MOSS, *supra* note 20, at 525 (more than doubled); MANNING MARABLE, THE GREAT WELLS OF DEMOCRACY 71 (2002).

33. TREVOR PARRY-GILES, THE CHARACTER OF JUSTICE: RHETORIC, LAW, AND POLITICS IN THE SUPREME COURT CONFIRMATION PROCESS 74 (2006) (quoting Rarick); MICHAEL BOBELIAN, BATTLE FOR THE MARBLE PALACE 234 (2019) (quoting STROM THURMOND, THE FAITH WE HAVE NOT KEPT [1968]).

34. PARRY-GILES, *supra* note 33, at 75 (turning to the provision; I think it is); COLLINS & RINGHAND, CHANGE, *supra* note 30, at 169–70 (what committee; why do you think); *id.* at 168 (quoting Ervin); *see* ABRAHAM, *supra* note 27, at 229–30.

35. ABRAHAM, *supra* note 27, at 227–28; FARGANIS & WEDEKING, *supra* note 27, at 14; LAURA KALMAN, ABE FORTAS: A BIOGRAPHY 319–58 (1990); MARK SILVERSTEIN, JUDICIOUS CHOICES 17–32 (1994). Bobelian gives the most complete analysis of the politics that led to Fortas's downfall. BOBELIAN, *supra* note 33.

36. DAVID SAVAGE, 2 GUIDE TO THE U.S. SUPREME COURT 1023–24 (5th ed. 2010) (seeking resolutions); Mark Berman & Christopher Ingraham, *"Supreme Court Justices Are Rock Stars." Who Pays When the Justices Travel around the World?*, WASH. POST (Feb. 19, 2016); Maxwell Tani, *This Supreme Court Justice Made the Most Money on the Side Last Year*, BUSINESS INSIDER (July 10, 2015); Michael Beckel, *Supreme Court Justices' Personal Financial Disclosures Now Featured on OpenSecrets.org*, OPENSECRETS .ORG (Feb. 18, 2011).

37. COLLINS & RINGHAND, CHANGE, *supra* note 30, at 171–73; FARGANIS & WEDEKING, *supra* note 27, at 14–15.

38. Barry J. McMillion & Denis Steven Rutkus, *Supreme Court Nominations, 1789 to 2017: Actions by the Senate, the Judiciary Committee, and the President*, CONGRESSIONAL RESEARCH SERVICE REPORT 13 (July 6, 2018) (1789 to 2017); Lori A. Ringhand, *The Supreme Court Confirmation Process in Historical Perspective*, Testimony before the Senate Judiciary Committee (July 31, 2018); Neal Devins & Lawrence Baum, *Split Definitive: How Party Polarization Turned the Supreme Court into a Partisan Court*, 2016 SUP. CT. REV. 301 (2016).

39. ROBERT J. SHILLER, IRRATIONAL EXUBERANCE ix, 1–2 (2d ed. 2005) (drawing the title of the book from a speech by Alan Greenspan); *see* Eileen Braman & J. Mitchell Pickerill, *Path Dependence in Studies of Legal Decision-making, in* WHAT'S LAW

GOT TO DO WITH IT? 114, 117–18 (Charles Gardner Geyh ed., 2011) (members of disciplines follow their respective disciplinary methods); HA-JOON CHANG, ECONOMICS: THE USER'S GUIDE 3 (2014) (professions develop jargon as means for insiders to communicate); MICHAEL A. BAILEY & FORREST MALTZMAN, THE CONSTRAINED COURT: LAW, POLITICS, AND THE DECISIONS JUSTICES MAKE 3 (2011) (a useful model must be testable); JEFFREY A. SEGAL ET AL., THE SUPREME COURT IN THE AMERICAN LEGAL SYSTEM 20–21 (2005) (in political science, only research based on a model that quantifiable data can falsify is legitimate); MICHELE LAMONT, HOW PROFESSORS THINK (2009) (comparing evaluative criteria in different disciplines); Ross J. Corbett, *Political Theory within Political Science*, 44 PS: POL. SCI. & POL. 565 (2011) (many political scientists try to exclude nonquantifiable or nonfalsifiable methods from the discipline); STEVE FULLER, PHILOSOPHY, RHETORIC, AND THE END OF KNOWLEDGE 33 (1993) (on specialization in disciplines); MAGEE, *supra* note 1, at 364–65 (professionalization in philosophy). "[D]isciplinarity is not simply a matter of individual choice, the pursuit of individual interests, or an individualized search for truth. Rather, it is the product of a set of social forces of normalization and education." Jack Balkin, *Interdisciplinarity as Colonization*, 53 WASH. & LEE L. REV. 949, 954 (1996). For more on the development of professions and disciplines: ANDREW ABBOTT, THE SYSTEM OF PROFESSIONS (1988); MAGALI SARFATTI LARSON, THE RISE OF PROFESSIONALISM: A SOCIOLOGICAL ANALYSIS (1977); DOROTHY ROSS, THE ORIGINS OF AMERICAN SOCIAL SCIENCE (1991).

40. For discussions of the development of law as an academic discipline: BRUCE A. KIMBALL, THE INCEPTION OF THE MODERN PROFESSIONAL EDUCATION: C. C. LANGDELL, 1826–1906 (2009); WILLIAM P. LAPIANA, LOGIC AND EXPERIENCE: THE ORIGIN OF MODERN AMERICAN LEGAL EDUCATION (1994); ROBERT S. STEVENS, LAW SCHOOL: LEGAL EDUCATION IN AMERICA FROM THE 1850S TO THE 1980S (1983); Stephen M. Feldman, *The Transformation of an Academic Discipline: Law Professors in the Past and Future (or Toy Story Too)*, 54 J. LEGAL EDUC. 471 (2004). For discussions of the development of the discipline of political science: JOHN G. GUNNELL, THE DESCENT OF POLITICAL THEORY (1993); Clyde Barrow, *Political Science, in* INTERNATIONAL ENCYCLOPEDIA OF THE SOCIAL SCIENCES 310 (William A. Darity Jr. ed., 2d ed. 2008); Lee Epstein et al., *Ideology and the Study of Judicial Behavior, in* IDEOLOGY, PSYCHOLOGY, AND LAW 705 (Jon Hanson ed., 2012); John G. Gunnell, *Political Science on the Cusp: Recovering a Discipline's Past*, 99 AM. POL. SCI. REV. 597 (2005).

41. HAROLD J. SPAETH & JEFFREY A. SEGAL, MAJORITY RULE OR MINORITY WILL: ADHERENCE TO PRECEDENT ON THE U.S. SUPREME COURT xv (1999); *see* JEFFREY A. SEGAL & HAROLD J. SPAETH, THE SUPREME COURT AND THE ATTITUDINAL MODEL xv–xviii, 65 (1993).

42. Barnett, *supra* note 19, at 660; *see* Solum, *supra* note 19, at 4 (emphasizing "the fixation thesis" of originalism).

43. On path dependence: Braman & Pickerill, *supra* note 39, at 115–18.

44. SEGAL ET AL., *supra* note 39, at 20–21.

45. To be clear, I do not intend to suggest that the attitudinal model is the only or even predominant political science approach to studying Supreme Court decision making. That might have been true in the past but is no longer today. For example, back in 2004, one political scientist—himself a historical institutionalist—called the attitudinal model "the most dominant model of judicial decision making in political

science." KEVIN J. McMahon, Reconsidering Roosevelt on Race 6, 203 (2004). Around the same time, though, another political scientist described attitudinalism as maintaining "predominance" while being "frequently challenged." Nancy L. Maveety, *The Study of Judicial Behavior and the Discipline of Political Science, in* The Pioneers of Judicial Behavior 1, 22 (2002). By 2018, a political scientist could still call the attitudinal model "the dominant theory of judicial behavior and the starting premise for political scientists who study the courts." Robert J. Hume, Judicial Behavior and Policymaking 16 (2018). Yet other political scientists referred to it as merely "one prominent theory." Pamela C. Corley et al., American Judicial Process: Myth and Reality in Law and Courts 13 (2016); *see* Tom S. Clark, The Supreme Court: An Analytic History of Constitutional Law 20, 27 (2019) (describing diverse approaches to law and courts research); Julie Novkov, *Understanding Law as a Democratic Institution through U.S. Constitutional Development*, 40 Law & Soc. Inquiry 811, 815–30 (2015) (same).

46. Marbury v. Madison, 5 U.S. (1 Cranch) 137 (1803); *see* White, *supra* note 4 (discussing Marshall Court); James M. O'Fallon, *Marbury*, 44 Stan. L. Rev. 219 (1992) (discussing Marshall Court and *Marbury*, in particular); William W. Van Alstyne, *A Critical Guide to* Marbury v. Madison, 1969 Duke L.J. 1 (same).

47. United States v. Lopez, 514 U.S. 549 (1995); *see* Nathan Glazer, Affirmative Discrimination (1978 ed.) (a neoconservative criticizing affirmative action programs); *Lopez*, 514 U.S. at 599 (Thomas, J., concurring) (stating that the Court took a "wrong turn" in 1937); Richard A. Epstein, *The Mistakes of 1937*, 11 Geo. Mason U. L. Rev. 5, 20 (1988–89) (arguing that the Court should reverse "the mistakes of 1937"); Segal et al., *supra* note 39, at 70 & n.67 (citing *Lopez* as example of conservative Rehnquist Court decision).

48. *Lopez*, 514 U.S. at 629 (Breyer, J., dissenting) (emphasis in original) (schools that teach); *id.* at 567–68 (what is truly); *id.* at 552–53, 557, 559–68; *see id.* at 627–28 (Breyer, J., dissenting) (criticizing Rehnquist's formalism); *see* Wickard v. Filburn, 317 U.S. 111, 120–29 (1942) (example of case using deferential rational basis test). In the two previous cases invalidating congressional commerce actions, the Court focused primarily on the Tenth Amendment. New York v. United States, 505 U.S.; National League of Cities v. Usery, 426 U.S. 833, 852 (1976), *overruled by* Garcia v. San Antonio Metropolitan Transit Authority, 469 U.S. 528 (1985) (emphasizing that people could vote for new legislators). In *Hammer*, the Court distinguished "a purely federal matter" from "a matter purely local in its character." Hammer v. Dagenhart, 247 U.S. 251, 274, 276 (1918). For examples of cases Rehnquist cited: Heart of Atlanta Motel v. United States, 379 U.S. 241 (1964); Shreveport Rate Cases, 234 U.S. 342 (1914).

49. National Federation of Independent Business v. Sebelius, 132 S.Ct. 2566 (2012) (invalidating individual mandate in Affordable Care Act as beyond Congress's commerce power but upholding it pursuant to Congress's taxing power); United States v. Morrison, 529 U.S. 598 (2000) (invalidating Violence against Women Act as beyond congressional power); Florida ex rel. Attorney General v. U.S. Department of Health and Human Services, 648 F.3d 1235 (11th Cir. 2011) (invalidating individual mandate in Affordable Care Act).

50. Central Hudson Gas & Electric Corp. v. Public Service Commission, 447 U.S. 557, 583–85 (1980) (Rehnquist, J., dissenting); Virginia State Board of Pharmacy v.

Virginia Citizens Consumer Council, 425 U.S. 748, 781–90 (1976) (Rehnquist, J., dissenting); MORTON KELLER, AMERICA'S THREE REGIMES 228 (2007) (discussing criticisms of Warren Court); Bork, *Neutral, supra* note 24, at 17 (judicial restraint).

51. Gonzales v. Raich, 545 U.S. 1, 10–15 (2005); *id.* at 34–40 (Scalia, J., concurring in the judgment); *see* FELDMAN, NEOCONSERVATIVE, *supra* note 24, at 114–39 (on conservatives and moral values); MARK TUSHNET, THE CONSTITUTION OF THE UNITED STATES OF AMERICA: A CONTEXTUAL ANALYSIS 228–29 (2009) (discussing changes in judicial conservatism); Stephen M. Feldman, *Conservative Eras in Supreme Court Decision Making:* Employment Division v. Smith, *Judicial Restraint, and Neoconservatism*, 32 CARDOZO L. REV. 1791 (2011) (distinguishing two eras of conservative judicial decision making).

52. *See* Andrew Coan, *Toward a Reality-Based Constitutional Theory*, 89 WASH. U. L. REV. 273 (2011) (arguing that constitutional theory should become less conceptual and more empirically grounded).

CHAPTER 7

1. Milton Friedman, *Adam Smith's Relevance for 1976*, Selected Papers No. 50, at 15–16.

2. FRIEDRICH A. HAYEK, THE CONSTITUTION OF LIBERTY 94–95 (2011 definitive ed.); Friedman, *supra* note 1, at 18.

3. Arthur Brooks, *Why the Stimulus Failed*, NATIONAL REVIEW (Sept. 25, 2012); Friedman, *supra* note 1, at 24; FRED BLOCK & MARGARET R. SOMERS, THE POWER OF MARKET FUNDAMENTALISM 3 (2014) (explaining market fundamentalism).

4. David Landau & Rosalind Dixon, *Abusive Judicial Review: Courts against Democracy*, 53 U.C. DAVIS L. REV. 1313, 1317 (2020); *see* MARK TUSHNET, THE CONSTITUTION OF THE UNITED STATES OF AMERICA: A CONTEXTUAL ANALYSIS 228–29 (2009) (discussing changes in judicial conservatism); Stephen M. Feldman, *Conservative Eras in Supreme Court Decision Making:* Employment Division v. Smith, *Judicial Restraint, and Neoconservatism*, 32 CARDOZO L. REV. 1791 (2011) (distinguishing two eras of conservative judicial decision making).

5. Commerce Clause: United States v. Lopez, 514 U.S. 549 (1995). Tenth Amendment: Printz v. United States, 521 U.S. 898 (1997); *see* New York v. United States, 505 U.S. 144 (1992) (prohibiting congressional commandeering of state legislatures). Fourteenth Amendment: City of Boerne v. Flores, 521 U.S. 507 (1997) (limiting congressional power under Fourteenth Amendment, sec. 5). Commerce Clause and Fourteenth Amendment: United States v. Morrison, 529 U.S. 598 (2000) (invalidating the Violence against Women Act under both the Commerce Clause and the Fourteenth Amendment, sec. 5).

6. Marc Galanter, *Why the "Haves" Come Out Ahead: Speculations on the Limits of Legal Change*, 9 LAW & SOC'Y REV. 95 (1974) (discussing advantages of wealthy and powerful in litigation); *see* Donald R. Songer et al., *Do the "Haves" Come Out Ahead over Time? Applying Galanter's Framework to Decisions of the U.S. Courts of Appeals, 1925–1988*, 33 L. & SOC'Y REV. 811 (1999) (empirical research showing that victory in litigation depends more on access to resources than on formal legal arguments). *Lopez*, 514 U.S. at 561 (distinguishing between economic and noneconomic activities).

7. City of Boerne, 521 U.S. at 530; Lopez, 514 U.S. at 562–63; *see Morrison,* 529 U.S. at 615 (acknowledging congressional findings but dismissing them as inadequate); A. Christopher Bryant & Timothy J. Simeone, *Remanding to Congress: The Supreme Court's New "On the Record" Constitutional Review of Federal Statutes,* 86 CORNELL L. REV. 328, 356 (2001) (describing "rigorous review of the legislative record" as characteristic of pre-1937 Supreme Court decision making). For an example from the *Lochner* era: Hill v. Wallace, 259 U.S. 44, 68–69 (1922) (invalidating a statute partly because Congress had failed to find specific facts showing that the regulated activity burdened interstate commerce).

8. Richard A. Epstein, *The Mistakes of 1937,* 11 GEO. MASON U. L. REV. 5, 20 (1988–89); *see* Lopez, 514 U.S. at 599 (Thomas, J., concurring) (stating that the Court took a "wrong turn" in 1937); Douglas H. Ginsburg, *Delegation Running Riot,* REGULATION, No. 1, 1995, at 83, 84 (arguing for a return to the Constitution-in-exile). On detrimental consequences: NATHAN GLAZER, AFFIRMATIVE DISCRIMINATION (1978 ed.).

9. National Federation of Independent Business v. Sebelius, 132 S.Ct. 2566, 2581–82 (2012); 42 U.S.C. §1396a(a)(10)(A)(i)(VIII). On the individual mandate: 26 U.S.C. §§5000A, 5000A(c), (g)(1). On Medicaid: 42 U.S.C. §1396d(a). Within this broad category of the poor, the statute includes pregnant women, children, needy families, the blind, the elderly, and the disabled.

10. *Sebelius,* 132 S.Ct. at 2611, 2617 (Ginsburg, J., concurring in part and dissenting in part).

11. *Id.* at 2586–87 (Roberts); *id.* at 2644, 2648–49 (joint dissent).

12. 1 Stat. 271 (Uniform Militia Act of 1792); *Sebelius,* 132 S.Ct. at 2627 n.10 (Ginsburg, J., concurring in part and dissenting in part); *id.* at 2586 n.3 (Roberts).

13. *Id.* at 2586 (Roberts); *id.* at 2644, 2647 (joint dissent).

14. Ginsburg criticized Roberts for relying on formalist reasoning. *Id.* at 2622 (Ginsburg, J., concurring in part and dissenting in part).

15. United States v. Butler, 297 U.S. 1, 53–56, 65–66, 68–73 (1936); Agricultural Adjustment Act, 48 Stat. 31. The Spending Clause states that Congress has the power "to pay the Debts and provide for the . . . general Welfare of the United States." U.S. Const., Art. I, § 8, cl. 1. For another example of a formalist application of the Tenth Amendment: Hammer v. Dagenhart, 247 U.S. 251 (1918).

16. Helvering v. Davis, 301 U.S. 619 (1937); Steward Machine Co. v. Davis, 301 U.S. 548 (1937); South Dakota v. Dole, 483 U.S. 203, 210–11 (1987).

17. Pennhurst State School and Hospital v. Halderman, 451 U.S. 1, 17 (1981) (unambiguously); Oklahoma v. Civil Service Commission, 330 U.S. 127 (1947) (upholding conditions on highway funds); *Dole,* 483 U.S. at 208–09 (1987) (drinking age).

18. *Sebelius,* 132 S.Ct. at 2601–03.

19. *Id.* at 2604–05 (Roberts); *id.* at 2658, 2662 (joint dissent).

20. United States v. Kahriger, 345 U.S. 22 (1953); Sonzinsky v. United States, 300 U.S. 506 (1937); U.S. Const., Art. I, § 9, cl. 4. Undermining the distinction between direct and indirect taxes: New York ex rel. Cohn v. Graves, 300 U.S. 308 (1937); Flint v. Stone Tracy Co., 220 U.S. 107 (1911).

21. *Sebelius,* 132 S.Ct. at 2599–600 (Roberts); *id.* at 2650–55 (joint dissent).

22. *Id.* at 2577, 2579, 2608.

23. Criticizing Roberts for betrayal: MIKE LEE, WHY JOHN ROBERTS WAS WRONG ABOUT HEALTHCARE: A CONSERVATIVE CRITIQUE OF THE SUPREME COURT'S OBAMACARE RULING (2013); Will Dunham, *Justice Scalia Steps Up Criticism of Healthcare*

Ruling, REUTERS (July 29, 2012); Benjamin Hart, *John Roberts Criticism: Conservatives Continue to Attack Justice after Health Care Ruling*, HUFFPOST (June 28, 2012); Luke Johnson, *John Roberts Outrages Conservatives in Health Care Ruling*, HUFFPOST (June 28, 2012). Democrats raised taxes: Moe Lane, *Repeat after Me: The Obamacare Mandate Was Actually a Tax*, REDSTATE, July 1, 2012, http://www.redstate.com/moe_lane/2012/07/01/repeat-after-me-the-obamacare-mandate-was-actually-a-tax (accessed Oct. 5, 2012).

24. Crawford v. Marion County Election Board, 553 U.S. 181 (2008). The Court decided *Crawford* six-to-three, with the generally liberal Stevens joining the conservatives. Stevens wrote a plurality opinion, joined by Roberts and Kennedy, which reasoned that the state satisfied a balancing test, as required by equal protection. *Id.* at 189–203. Perhaps more important, Scalia wrote an opinion concurring in the judgment, joined by Thomas and Alito, that emphasized that the Court should defer to state laws restricting suffrage. *Id.* at 204–09 (Scalia, J., concurring in the judgment). Evidence showed that partisan considerations had played a significant role in the enactment of the voter-identification law, but Stevens reasoned that such partisan influence was irrelevant if there were also "valid neutral justifications." *Id.* at 204. Also, in applying the balancing test, Stevens considered the state's interest in preventing voter fraud, even though the record contained "no evidence of any such fraud actually occurring in Indiana at any time in its history." *Id.* at 194.

25. Shelby County v. Holder, 133 S.Ct. 2612 (2013); Voting Rights Act of 1965, 79 Stat. 437, 42 U.S.C. §§ 1973 et seq. The coverage provision: § 4(b), 79 Stat. 438. On the effects of the Voting Rights Act: MICHAEL K. BROWN ET AL., WHITEWASHING RACE 193–94 (2003); MANNING MARABLE, THE GREAT WELLS OF DEMOCRACY 71 (2002).

26. *Shelby County*, 133 S.Ct. at 2620–21, 2627, 2631. The Court sidestepped the prior challenge: Northwest Austin Municipal Utility District No. 1 v. Holder, 557 U.S. 193, 204 (2009).

27. *Shelby County*, 133 S.Ct. at 2632 (Ginsburg, J., dissenting); *see id.* at 2635–36, 2642–43 (Ginsburg, J., dissenting).

28. *Id.* at 2644 (Ginsburg, J., dissenting).

29. *Crawford*, 553 U.S. 181.

30. Pew Center on the States, *Inaccurate, Costly, and Inefficient: Evidence That America's Voter Registration System Needs an Upgrade* 1, 2, 8 (Feb. 14, 2012). CAROL ANDERSON, WHITE RAGE: THE UNSPOKEN TRUTH OF OUR RACIAL DIVIDE 148–54 (2016) (on the ramifications of *Shelby County*); JONATHAN BRATER ET AL., PURGES: A GROWING THREAT TO THE RIGHT TO VOTE (Brennan Center for Justice 2018) (detailing statistics on purging of voters since the Court decided *Shelby County*); ZACHARY ROTH, THE GREAT SUPPRESSION: VOTING RIGHTS, CORPORATE CASH, AND THE CONSERVATIVE ASSAULT ON DEMOCRACY (2016) (on the Republican attack on democracy). On Texas law: Brennan Center for Justice, *Summary of Voter ID Laws Passed since 2011*, at 13–14 (Nov. 12, 2013) [hereinafter Brennan Center]; Rick Lyman, *Texas' Stringent Voter ID Law Makes a Dent at Polls*, N.Y. TIMES (Nov. 6, 2013). The Fifth Circuit held that this law violated the Voting Rights Act in part but did not constitute an unconstitutional poll tax. Veasey v. Abbott, No. 14–41127 (5th Cir. Aug. 5, 2015). On North Carolina law: Brennan Center, *supra*, at 7–8; Aaron Blake, *North Carolina Governor Signs Extensive Voter ID Law*, WASH. POST (Aug. 12, 2013). On states purging 33 percent: BRATER, *supra*, at 1. Changing election results: Pew Center on the States,

supra, at 1–2; Ben Jealous & Ryan P. Haygood, *The Battle to Protect the Vote: Voter Suppression Efforts in Five States and Their Effect on the 2014 Midterm Elections* (Center for American Progress Dec. 2014); Walter Dean Burnham, *Democracy in Peril: The American Turnout Problem and the Path to Plutocracy*, Roosevelt Institute, Working Paper No. 5, at 25 (December 1, 2010).

31. Rucho v. Common Cause, 139 S.Ct. 2484, 2491–93, 2504 (2019). The Court acknowledged: "The districting plans at issue here are highly partisan, by any measure." *Id.* at 2491. "The plaintiffs alleged that the gerrymandering violated the First Amendment, the Equal Protection Clause of the Fourteenth Amendment, the Elections Clause, and Article I, § 2, of the Constitution." *Id.*

32. *Id.* at 2498, 2500, 2505–07.

33. The Court asserted that "there are no restrictions on speech, association, or any other First Amendment activities in the districting plans at issue," *id.* at 2504, but the Court never analyzed the First-Amendment claims because it reasoned that the rule of the political question doctrine precluded judicial consideration of the claims. *Id.* at 2505.

34. *Id.* at 2509, 2512, 2525 (Kagan, J., dissenting).

35. ERWIN CHEMERINSKY, CONSTITUTIONAL LAW: PRINCIPLES AND POLICIES 140–45 (6th ed. 2019); *see* Martin H. Redish, *Judicial Review and the "Political Question,"* 79 Nw. U. L. REV. 1031, 1031 (1984).

36. Sam Wang, *Gerrymanders, Part 1: Busting the Both-Sides-Do-It Myth*, PRINCETON ELECTION CONSORTIUM (December 30, 2012) (emphasizing asymmetric gerrymandering); Associated Press, *Analysis: Partisan Gerrymandering Has Benefited Republicans More than Democrats*, BUSINESS INSIDER (June 25, 2017). "While Republicans and Democrats both gerrymander, there is no doubt that Republicans do it more and more shamelessly." Zack Beauchamp, *The Supreme Court, Gerrymandering, and the Republican Turn against Democracy*, Vox (June 27, 2019). The political scientists Thomas E. Mann and Norman J. Ornstein emphasize that, in general, Republicans have been breaking traditional norms of democracy far more often and egregiously than Democrats have done. THOMAS E. MANN & NORMAN J. ORNSTEIN, IT'S EVEN WORSE THAN IT LOOKS (2012); *see id.* at 143–47 (focusing on gerrymandering); Joseph Fishkin & David E. Pozen, *Asymmetric Constitutional Hardball*, 118 COLUM. L. REV. 915 (2018) (arguing that constitutional hardball has been asymmetric, with the Republicans pushing more strongly against traditional norms); Thomas M. Keck, *Court-Packing and Democratic Erosion* (February 19, 2020), https://ssrn.com/abstract=3476889 or http://dx.doi.org/10.2139/ssrn.3476889 (with regard to the breaking of norms, Republicans are far worse than Democrats); Samuel S.-H. Wang, *Three Tests for Practical Evaluation of Partisan Gerrymandering*, 68 STAN. L. REV. 1263, 1298–1306 (2016) (examining factors that affect the amount of gerrymandering).

37. *Rucho*, 139 S.Ct. at 2491, 2493; *id.* at 2509–11 (Kagan, J., dissenting). This is the same Thomas Hofeller who recommended the addition of a citizenship question to the census in order to increase Republican political power. Michael Wines, *Deceased G.O.P. Strategist's Hard Drives Reveal New Details on the Census Citizenship Question*, N.Y. TIMES (May 30, 2019); *see* Department of Commerce v. New York, 139 S.Ct. 2551 (2019) (holding that the Department of Commerce did not adequately justify the addition of a citizenship question to the census).

38. The Court tends to be protective of judicial power, even as it is hostile to congressional power. Trump v. Vance, _ S.Ct. _ (2020) (remanding a New York pros-

ecutorial subpoena demand for Trump's income tax returns but recognizing the grand jury's power to demand the returns); Trump v. Mazars, _ S.Ct. _ (2020) (remanding the House of Representatives' subpoena demand for Trump's income tax returns while constraining congressional reach); Boumediene v. Bush, 553 U.S. 723 (2008) (invalidating the congressional act stripping habeas corpus jurisdiction from the federal courts for enemy combatants). For discussions of the Court threatening to undermine democracy, see STEPHEN M. FELDMAN, THE NEW ROBERTS COURT, DONALD TRUMP, AND OUR FAILING CONSTITUTION 199–226, 231 (2017) [hereinafter FELDMAN, FAILING CONSTITUTION]; *see* Jack M. Balkin, *Constitutional Crisis and Constitutional Rot*, 77 MD. L. REV. 147 (2017) (discussing constitutional rot).

39. Barry Friedman, *The Cycles of Constitutional Theory*, 67 LAW & CONTEMP. PROBS. 149, 161 (2004); THOMAS M. KECK, THE MOST ACTIVIST SUPREME COURT IN HISTORY 2 (2004); DAVID M. O'BRIEN, STORM CENTER 31 (8th ed. 2008); ALLIANCE FOR JUSTICE, THE ROBERTS COURT AND JUDICIAL OVERREACH (2013); Keith E. Whittington, *The Least Activist Supreme Court in History? The Roberts Court and the Exercise of Judicial Review*, 89 NOTRE DAME L. REV. 219 (2014); Lee Epstein & Andrew D. Martin, *Is the Roberts Court Especially Activist? A Study of Invalidating (and Upholding) Federal, State, and Local Laws*, 61 EMORY L.J. 737 (2012). Thomas Keck has compiled a list of federal statutes invalidated by the Court from 1981 to 2013. http://faculty.maxwell.syr.edu/tmkeck/Book_1/federal_statutes.htm.

40. Seila Law L.L.C. v. Consumer Financial Protection Bureau, _ S.Ct. _ (2020).

41. *Id.* at _ (citing 12 U.S.C. §§ 5491(c)(1), (3)).

42. Steven Calabresi & Christopher Yoo, *The Unitary Executive during the Second Half-Century*, 26 HARV. J.L. & PUB. POL'Y 667, 668 (2003); Mark Tushnet, *A Political Perspective on the Theory of the Unitary Executive*, 12 U. PA. J. CONST. L. 313 (2010).

43. Morrison v. Olson, 487 U.S. 654, 697–99, 705 (1988) (Scalia, J., dissenting); Sheila Slaughter, *Academic Freedom, Professional Autonomy, and the State, in* THE AMERICAN ACADEMIC PROFESSION 241, 259 (Joseph C. Hermanowicz ed., 2011); Robert Hassan, *Time, Neoliberal Power, and the Advent of Marx's 'Common Ruin' Thesis*, 37 ALTERNATIVES: GLOBAL, LOCAL, POLITICAL 287, 293 (2012).

44. Seila Law, _ S.Ct. at _; *id.* at _ (Kagan, J., concurring and dissenting) (emphasizing "Congress and the President came together to create an agency with an important mission").

45. *Id.* at _ (quoting art. II, § 1, cl. 1) (emphasis added).

46. *Id.* at _.

47. *Id.* at _ (Kagan, J., concurring and dissenting). The Court did not invalidate all agencies with statutory limitations on the president's power to remove agency heads. First, while prohibiting an agency with a *single director* to be independent (in the sense of having the director removable only for cause), the Court continued to allow independent agencies led by multi-member boards. Humphrey's Executor v. United States, 295 U.S. 602 (1935). Second, the Court continued to allow independent inferior officers—reasoning that the CFPB director was a principal officer. *Morrison*, 487 U.S. Finally, the justices realigned on the question of whether the CFPB could continue to operate without the for-cause removal provision. A majority of justices concluded that the removal provision was severable and thus the agency work could continue (with the director now removable at will). Thomas and Alito disagreed with Roberts's conclusion on this point and thus dissented in part, but the progressive justices joined Roberts

on the severability issue. Hence, Kagan was not merely dissenting but concurring in the judgment with respect to severability and dissenting in part (on the merits of the removal power).

48. *E.g.*, American Tradition Partnership, Inc. v. Bullock, 132 S.Ct. 2490 (2012) (invalidating state law restricting corporate political campaign expenditures); Brown v. Entertainment Merchants Association, 131 S.Ct. 2729 (2011) (invalidating state law prohibiting "the sale or rental of 'violent video games' to minors"); Sorrell v. IMS Health Inc., 131 S.Ct. 2653 (2011) (invalidating state law restricting the sale of medical data); Parents Involved in Community Schools v. Seattle School District No. 1, 551 U.S. 701 (2007) (invalidating urban school districts' affirmative action programs).

49. Citizens United v. Federal Election Commission, 558 U.S. 310, 354 (2010) (quoting The Federalist No. 10 [James Madison], at 130 (Benjamin F. Wright ed., 1961)); Citizens United, 558 U.S. at 336–42; Pub. L. No. 107–155, 116 Stat. 81. Buckley, 424 U.S. 1, 19 (1976). First National Bank of Boston v. Bellotti, 435 U.S. 765 (1978). The Court did not always treat free expression as a constitutional lodestar. The Court transformed its conception of free expression only in 1937, when the justices accepted the transition from republican to pluralist democracy. STEPHEN M. FELDMAN, FREE EXPRESSION AND DEMOCRACY IN AMERICA: A HISTORY 291–348, 383–419 (2008) [hereinafter FELDMAN, FREE EXPRESSION]; G. Edward White, *The First Amendment Comes of Age: The Emergence of Free Speech in Twentieth-century America*, 95 MICH. L. REV. 299, 300–01 (1996). For pre-1937 free-expression cases: Gitlow v. New York, 268 U.S. 652 (1925) (upholding state criminal syndicalism conviction); Debs v. United States, 249 U.S. 211 (1919) (upholding Espionage Act conviction); Schenck v. United States, 249 U.S. 47 (1919) (upholding Espionage Act convictions). For post-1937 cases: Thornhill v. Alabama, 310 U.S. 88 (1940) (holding that labor picketing is protected free speech); Schneider v. State, 308 U.S. 147 (1939) (invalidating conviction for distributing handbills); Hague v. C.I.O., 307 U.S. 496 (1939) (upholding right of unions to organize in streets).

50. Citizens United, 558 U.S. at 452 (Stevens, J., concurring in part and dissenting in part); *e.g.*, Brief of Amici Curiae Hachette Book Group, Inc. and HarperCollins Publishers L.L.C. in Support of Neither Party on Supplemental Questions, Citizens United v. Federal Election Commission, 558 U.S. 310 (2010) (No. 08-205), at 13–14 (emphasizing congressional findings); *see* McConnell v. Federal Election Commission, 540 U.S. 93, 207 (2003) (discussing congressional findings). Prevention of corruption constitutes a compelling purpose: Citizens United, 558 U.S. at 356–57.

51. Larry M. Bartels et al., *Inequality and American Governance, in* INEQUALITY AND AMERICAN DEMOCRACY 88, 113–17 (Lawrence R. Jacobs & Theda Skocpol eds., 2005) (determine the pools); Molly J. Walker Wilson, *Behavioral Decision Theory and Implications for the Supreme Court's Campaign Finance Jurisprudence*, 31 CARDOZO L. REV. 679, 684 (2010) (induce suboptimal); *see* LARRY M. BARTELS, UNEQUAL DEMOCRACY 285–86 (2008) (ignoring low-income citizens); CHARLES E. LINDBLOM, POLITICS AND MARKETS (1977) (arguing that empirical evidence shows that corporate wealth dominates politics); Samuel Issacharoff, *On Political Corruption*, 124 HARV. L. REV. 118, 121–25 (2010) (emphasizing different conceptions of corruption). The empirical evidence does not show, however, that the better-financed candidate always wins the election. Sometimes the candidate with less funding wins. BRADLEY A. SMITH, UNFREE

SPEECH: THE FOLLY OF CAMPAIGN FINANCE REFORM 48–51 (2001); Jamin B. Raskin, *The Campaign-Finance Crucible: Is Laissez Fair?*, 101 MICH. L. REV. 1532, 1535 (2003).

52. *Citizens United*, 558 U.S. at 354 (quoting New York State Board of Elections v. Lopez Torres, 552 U.S. 196, 208 [2008]); *id.* at 356–57. The Court soon reiterated the point that anything short of a bribe is unlikely to be corruption: McCutcheon v. Federal Election Commission, 134 S.Ct. 1434, 1441 (2014).

53. *Citizens United*, 558 U.S. at 353; *id.* at 425–32 (Stevens, J., concurring in part and dissenting in part); *id.* at 385–93 (Scalia, J., concurring).

54. *Id.* at 391 (Scalia, J., concurring). Pre-1930s free-expression decisions: *Debs*, 249 U.S. (upholding Espionage Act conviction); Frohwerk v. United States, 249 U.S. 204 (1919) (upholding Espionage Act conviction); Halter v. Nebraska, 205 U.S. 34 (1907) (upholding flag desecration statute). The first 1930s decision that arguably upheld a free-speech claim was not clearly decided under the First Amendment free-speech clause. Stromberg v. California, 283 U.S. 359 (1931); *see* FELDMAN, FREE EXPRESSION, *supra* note 49, at 388–89 (discussing *Stromberg*). On the relation between democracy and free speech: ALEXANDER MEIKLEJOHN, FREE SPEECH AND ITS RELATION TO SELF-GOVERNMENT (1948); *see* FELDMAN, FREE EXPRESSION, *supra* note 49, at 396–401 (discussing self-governance rationale). On the Court's post-1937 protection of free speech: *Thornhill*, 310 U.S. (holding that labor picketing is protected free speech); *Schneider*, 308 U.S. (invalidating conviction for distributing handbills); *Hague*, 307 U.S. (upholding right of unions to organize in streets); WHITE, *supra* note 49, at 300–01.

55. *Citizens United*, 558 U.S. at 391–93 (Scalia, J., concurring). On slavery and capitalism: SVEN BECKERT, EMPIRE OF COTTON 98–135 (2014); DAVID BRION DAVIS, THE PROBLEM OF SLAVERY IN THE AGE OF REVOLUTION, 1770–1823, at 346–54 (1975); ROBERT HEILBRONER & AARON SINGER, THE ECONOMIC TRANSFORMATION OF AMERICA 9–12, 132 (1999). On early corporations: LAWRENCE M. FRIEDMAN, A HISTORY OF AMERICAN LAW 179–81 (2d ed. 1985); JAMES WILLARD HURST, THE LEGITIMACY OF THE BUSINESS CORPORATION 14–17 (1970); Pauline Maier, *The Revolutionary Origins of the American Corporation*, 50 WM. & MARY Q. 51, 51–55 (1993).

56. KATRINE MARÇAL, WHO COOKED ADAM SMITH'S DINNER? A STORY ABOUT WOMEN AND ECONOMICS 61 (Saskia Vogel trans., 2016); Jedediah Purdy, *Beyond the Bosses' Constitution: The First Amendment and Class Entrenchment*, 118 COLUM. L. REV. 2161, 2166–70 (2018). "The neoclassical economists' Homo Economicus has several characteristics, the most important of which are (1) maximizing (optimizing) behavior; (2) the cognitive ability to exercise rational choice; and (3) individualistic behavior and independent tastes and preferences." Chris Doucouliagos, *A Note on the Evolution of Homo Economicus*, 28 J. ECON. ISSUES, No.3 (1994); *see* Christine Jolls et al., *A Behavioral Approach to Law and Economics*, 50 STAN. L. REV. 1471 (1998) (discussing and criticizing concept of homo economicus); Tanina Rostain, *Educating Homo Economicus: Cautionary Notes on the New Behavioral Law and Economics Movement*, 34 LAW & SOC'Y REV. 973 (2000) (same).

57. John Milton, *Areopagitica: A Speech for the Liberty of Unlicensed Printing to the Parliament of England* (1644), http://www.constitution.org/milton/areopagitica.htm; JOHN STUART MILL, ON LIBERTY 21–27 (1859; Liberal Arts Press ed. 1956).

58. Abrams v. United States, 250 U.S. 616, 630 (1919); Zechariah Chafee, *Freedom of Speech in War Time*, 32 HARV. L. REV. 932, 956 (1919).

59. *Citizens United*, 558 U.S. at 354 (quoting McConnell, 540 U.S. at 257–58) (Scalia, J., concurring in part, concurring in judgment in part, dissenting in part); Peter Drucker, The Practice of Management 37 (2006 ed.); Model Business Corporation Act (MBCA) § 3.01 (a); *see* Robert L. Kerr, The Corporate Free-Speech Movement 10 (2008) (emphasizing that "the profit imperative is . . . a fundamental obligation of the corporate charter"); Tamara Piety, Brandishing the First Amendment 31–32 (2012) (emphasizing commercial expression aims for profit). Holmes did not use the precise phrase "marketplace of ideas." *See* Vincent Blasi, *Holmes and the Marketplace of Ideas*, 2004 Sup. Ct. Rev. 1, 13 & n.41, 24 & n.80 (on the first uses of this phrase, more than fifteen years after Holmes's *Abrams* dissent).

60. Thomas M. Keck, *Party, Policy, or Duty: Why Does the Supreme Court Invalidate Federal Statutes?*, 101 Am. Pol. Sci. Rev. 321, 326, 332 (2007); Adam D. Chandler, *Cert.-stage Amicus "All Stars": Where Are They Now?*, Scotusblog (April 4, 2013), http://www.scotusblog.com/2013/04/cert-stage-amicus-all-stars-where-are-they-now; Lee Epstein et al., *How Business Fares in the Supreme Court*, 97 Minn. L. Rev. 1431 (2013) (quantitative study of all postwar business-related cases).

61. *American Tradition Partnership*, 132 S.Ct. at 2491 (quoting Mont. Code Ann. §13–35–227[1] [2011]); *id.* at 2491–92 (Breyer, J., dissenting) (discussing Western Tradition Partnership v. Attorney General, 363 Mont. 220 [2011]). Increase in campaign spending: Timothy K. Kuhner, Capitalism v. Democracy 1–4 (2014).

62. Arizona Free Enterprise Club's Freedom Club PAC v. Bennett, 131 S.Ct. 2806, 2813, 2818, 2821 (2011); *id.* at 2833–34, 2845–46 (Kagan, J., dissenting) (emphasis in original).

63. *McCutcheon*, 134 S.Ct. at 1441, 1449, 1457–58. Justice Thomas maintained that all campaign spending, whether contributions or expenditures, constitutes "[p]olitical speech [that] is 'the primary object of First Amendment protection' and 'the lifeblood of a self-governing people.'" *Id.* at 1462–63 (Thomas, J., concurring in the judgment).

64. Janus v. American Federation of State, County, and Municipal Employees, Council 31, 138 S.Ct. 2448, 2490–91, 2501–02 (2018) (Kagan, J., dissenting); Knox v. Service Employees International Union, 132 S.Ct. 2277 (2012). Harris v. Quinn, 134 S.Ct. 2618 (2014), involved an issue similar to that of *Janus* but was decided on narrower grounds.

65. Sorrell v. IMS Health Inc., 564 U.S. 552, 557–60, 562–64, 570–73 (2011); *id.* at 580–81 (Breyer, J., dissenting); *see* Central Hudson Gas & Electric Corp. v. Public Service Commission, 447 U.S. 557, 566 (1980) (articulating a balancing test for commercial speech cases); Frank Pasquale, The Black Box Society 27–30 (2015) (discussing medical records); Bruce Schneier, Data and Goliath 39–53 (2015) (discussing data mining).

66. Erwin Chemerinsky, *Not a Free Speech Court*, 53 Ariz. L. Rev. 723, 724 (2011). Cases: *Janus*, 138 S.Ct. 2448 (holding that workers cannot be forced to pay union fees related solely to collective bargaining representation even though the workers benefit from the representation); *Knox*, 132 S.Ct. (holding that a public employee union could not impose a special assessment fee to support political advocacy even if union members could opt out); Beard v. Banks, 548 U.S. 521 (2006) (severely limiting prisoners' access to written materials and photographs); Morse v. Frederick, 551 U.S. 393 (2007) (upholding punishment of a high school student for displaying a banner stating,

"BONG HiTS 4 JESUS"); Borough of Duryea v. Guarnieri, 131 S.Ct. 2488 (2011) (limiting a government employee's First Amendment right to petition the government); Garcetti v. Ceballos, 547 U.S. 410 (2006) (limiting free-speech rights of government employees by distinguishing between speech as a citizen and speech as an employee); *Rucho*, 139 S.Ct. (holding that constitutionality of extreme political gerrymandering was a nonjusticiable political question); Citizens United v. Federal Election Commission, 558 U.S. 310 (2010) (invalidating restrictions on corporate campaign spending). For another case denying First Amendment protection: Holder v. Humanitarian Law Project, 130 S.Ct. 2705 (2010) (upholding punishment of speech that might provide material support to foreign terrorist organizations, even without proof of likely harm).

67. McDonald v. City of Chicago, 561 U.S. 742 (2010) (applying the Second Amendment against state and local governments); District of Columbia v. Heller, 554 U.S. 570 (2008) (interpreting the Second Amendment to protect an individual's right to firearms); Comcast Corp. v. Behrend, 133 S.Ct. 1426 (2013) (denying class certification under FRCP Rule 23[b][3] for customers of a cable television corporation); Wal-Mart Stores, Inc. v. Dukes, 131 S.Ct. 2541 (2011) (increasing the burden of proof for class certification under FRCP Rule 23[a][2]); American Express Co. v. Italian Colors Restaurant, 133 S.Ct. 2304 (2013) (holding that the Federal Aviation Administration [FAA] required the enforcement of a contractual waiver of class arbitration); AT&T Mobility L.L.C. v. Concepcion, 131 S.Ct. 1740 (2011) (interpreting FAA to protect the customer contract provision precluding arbitration on a class-wide basis); University of Texas Southwestern Medical Center v. Nassar, 133 S.Ct. 2517 (2013) (requiring a plaintiff-employee alleging employer retaliation to satisfy a more rigorous burden of proof); Vance v. Ball State University, 133 S.Ct. 2434 (2013) (limiting who qualifies as a supervisor under Title VII). Corporations do not win every Roberts Court case. Wyeth v. Levine, 555 U.S. 555 (2009), upheld a state law judgment against a drug manufacturer arising from the amputation of a patient's arm.

68. Ledbetter v. Goodyear Tire & Rubber Co., 550 U.S. 618, 623–32 (2007); *id.* at 643, 650 (Ginsburg, J., dissenting); *see id.* at 623 (citing 42 U.S.C. § 2000e-2(a)(1)); Martha Chamallas, *Past as Prologue: Old and New Feminisms*, 17 MICH. J. GENDER & L. 157, 159–61 (2010) (discussing *Ledbetter*). In this instance, Congress effectively overturned the Court's decision by enacting the Lilly Ledbetter Fair Pay Act of 2009, Pub. L. No. 111–2, 123 Stat. 5 (2009), which changed the statute of limitations for discrimination claims. Later in this chapter (in the section on the Court's protection of Christianity), I discuss another statutory case in which the Court protects corporate power and Christianity to the detriment of women. Burwell v. Hobby Lobby Stores, Inc., 573 U.S. 682 (2014).

69. Roe v. Wade, 410 U.S. 113, 152–55, 162–64 (1973).

70. Planned Parenthood v. Casey, 505 U.S. 833, 861, 870, 872–73, 876–78 (1992); *see id.* at 881–84 (*overruling* City of Akron v. Akron Center for Reproductive Health, Inc., 462 U.S. 416 [1983] [Akron I]; Thornburgh v. American College of Obstetricians and Gynecologists, 476 U.S. 747 [1986]).

71. Stenberg v. Carhart, 530 U.S. 914, 929–30 (2000) (quoting Casey, 505 U.S. at 879; and Roe, 410 U.S. at 164–65).

72. Gonzales v. Carhart, 550 U.S. 124, 147, 159 (2007); *id.* at 183–85 (Ginsburg, J., dissenting).

73. Khiara M. Bridges, *Capturing the Judiciary: Carhart and the Undue Burden Standard*, 67 WASH. & LEE L. REV. 915, 919–20 (2010).

74. Whole Woman's Health v. Hellerstedt, 136 S.Ct. 2292, 2309 (2016).

75. *Id*. at 2302.

76. Neil Gorsuch, *Of Lions and Bears, Judges and Legislators, and the Legacy of Justice Scalia*, 66 CASE W. RES. L. REV. 905, 905 (2016); Garza v. Hargan, 874 F.3d 735 (D.C. Cir. 2017) (en banc) (per curiam); June Medical Services, L.L.C. v. Gee, 139 S.Ct. 663 (2019); NEIL GORSUCH, A REPUBLIC, IF YOU CAN KEEP IT 10, 108–27 (2019) (on originalism); Neil Gorsuch, *Liberals 'n' Lawsuits*, NATIONAL REVIEW (Feb. 7, 2005) (blaming liberal activities for politicizing the judiciary).

77. June Medical Services, L.L.C. v. Russo, _ S.Ct. _ (2020).

78. *Id*. at _.

79. *Id*. at _ (unweighted factors) (quoting Marrs v. Motorola, Inc., 577 F.3d 783, 788 [CA7 2009]). Focusing on abortion: "There is no plausible sense in which anyone, let alone this Court, could objectively assign weight to such imponderable values and no meaningful way to compare them if there were. Attempting to do so would be like 'judging whether a particular line is longer than a particular rock is heavy.'" *Id*. (quoting Bendix Autolite Corp. v. Midwesco Enterprises, Inc., 486 U.S. 888, 897 [1988] [Scalia, J., concurring in judgment]).

80. *Id*. at _ (Gorsuch, J., dissenting).

81. For instance, Gorsuch wrote: "Missing here is exactly what judges usually depend on when asked to make tough calls: an administrable legal rule to follow, a neutral principle, something outside themselves to guide their decision." *Id*. at _ (Gorsuch, J., dissenting). "The Constitution does not constrain the States' ability to regulate or even prohibit abortion." *Id*. at _ (Thomas, J., dissenting).

82. For example, Kavanaugh underscored that five justices rejected any type of balancing test: "Today, five Members of the Court reject the *Whole Woman's Health* cost-benefit standard." *Id*. at _ (Kavanaugh, J., dissenting). The cases in this section do not exhaust the list of decisions hostile to women's interests. *See, e.g.*, Little Sisters of the Poor v. Pennsylvania, _ S.Ct. _ (2020) (upholding the agency's interpretation of the Affordable Care Act allowing employers to avoid paying for insurance coverage for contraceptives based on religious or moral objections; harming women because, in many situations, they will either have to pay for birth control or go without); National Institute of Family and Life Advocates v. Becerra, 138 S.Ct. 2361 (2018) (invalidating state law requiring family planning clinics to provide information about abortion, even though the Court had previously upheld laws requiring family planning clinics to provide antiabortion information).

83. Robert Manduca, *How Economic Inequality Perpetuates U.S. Racial Gaps*, SCHOLARS STRATEGY NETWORK (Aug. 24, 2018) (the average post-tax); Valerie Wilson, *Racial Inequalities in Wages, Income, and Wealth Show that MLK's Work Remains Unfinished*, ECONOMIC POLICY INSTITUTE (January 11, 2018) (the median black worker); Isabel V. Sawhill & Christopher Pulliam, *Six Facts about Wealth in the United States*, Brookings (June 25, 2019). For a fuller discussion of wealth and income inequalities and related racial disparities: FELDMAN, FAILING CONSTITUTION, *supra* note 38, at 207–11.

84. CAROL ANDERSON, ONE PERSON, NO VOTE (2018); Brennan Center for Justice, *The Effects of Shelby County v. Holder* (Aug. 6, 2018); Lawrence Goldstone, *America's Relentless Suppression of Black Voters*, NEW REPUBLIC (Oct. 24, 2018).

85. Adarand Constructors, Inc. v. Peña, 515 U.S. 200, 237–38 (1995); *id.* at 239 (Scalia, J., concurring in part and concurring in the judgment); *id.* at 241 (Thomas, J., concurring in part and concurring in the judgment); *see* ANDREW KULL, THE COLOR-BLIND CONSTITUTION (1992) (arguing that benign racial classifications were inconsistent with the history of the Constitution).

86. *Parents Involved*, 551 U.S. at 720–35; *id.* at 735–48 (Roberts, C.J., plurality opinion); *id.* at 735–48 (Roberts, C.J., plurality opinion) (the way to stop); *id.* at 748 (Thomas, J., concurring) (disfavoring) (citing Brown v. Board of Education, 347 U. S 483 [1954]).

87. Fisher v. University of Texas at Austin, 570 U.S. 297, 314 (2013) (*Fisher I*); *id.* at 327 (Thomas, J., concurring); Grutter v. Bollinger, 539 U.S. 306 (2003).

88. Fisher v. University of Texas at Austin, 136 S.Ct. 2198 (2016); *id.* at 2215–16 (Alito, J., dissenting); *id.* at 2215 (Thomas, J., dissenting).

89. Abbott v. Perez, 138 S.Ct. 2305, 2313, 2324–27 (2018) (*reversing* Perez v. Abbott, 274 F. Supp. 3d 624 [W.D. Tex. 2017]; Perez v. Abbott, 267 F. Supp. 3d 750 [W.D. Tex. 2017]); *see* Washington v. Davis, 426 U.S. 229 (1976) (proof of discriminatory effects alone does not sufficiently prove discriminatory intent).

90. Abbott, 138 S.Ct. at 2336, 2345–46, 2360 (Sotomayor, J., dissenting) (quoting Arlington Heights v. Metropolitan Housing Development Corporation, 429 U.S. 252, 266–268 [1977]). The Court has allowed other discriminatory gerrymandering schemes to stand. Gill v. Whitford, 138 S.Ct. 1916 (2018) (lower court held that a gerrymandered districting scheme violated equal protection and the First Amendment, but the Supreme Court reversed it for lack of standing); Husted v. A. Philip Randolph Inst., 138 S.Ct. 1833 (2018) (upholding, in a statutory decision, an aggressive state program for purging individuals from voter rolls); *cf.*, North Carolina v. Covington, 138 S.Ct. 2548 (2018) (summarily affirming in part and reversing in part a District Court order for redrawing legislative districts because of racial gerrymandering); Benisek v. Lamone, 138 S.Ct. 1942 (2018) (affirming a lower court order denying a preliminary injunction in a political gerrymandering case). In *Husted*, Justice Breyer wrote in dissent: "It is unsurprising in light of the history of such purge programs that numerous amici report that the [state] Supplemental Process has disproportionately affected minority, low-income, disabled, and veteran voters." *Husted*, 138 S.Ct. at 1864 (Breyer, J., dissenting).

91. *E.g.*, McCleskey v. Kemp, 481 U.S. 279 (1987) (upholding capital-sentencing scheme despite strong statistical evidence of discriminatory effects).

92. Kerri Ullucci, *Book Review*, 41 URBAN EDUCATION 533, 538 (2006); EDUARDO BONILLA-SILVA, RACISM WITHOUT RACISTS: COLOR-BLIND RACISM AND THE PERSISTENCE OF RACIAL INEQUALITY IN THE UNITED STATES 52, 56, 59 (5th ed. 2018). The facts in this hypothetical situation resemble those of a Rehnquist Court affirmative action decision. City of Richmond v. J. A. Croson Company, 488 U.S. 469 (1989). The Court invalidated the city's affirmative action program and reasoned that the city's demographic distribution (50 percent black American) and history of awarding construction contracts (0.67 percent of all prime contracts to minority-owned businesses) did not prove intentional discrimination with sufficient particularity. On reinforcing the status quo: Ian Haney-Lopez, *Intentional Blindness*, 87 N.Y.U. L. REV. 1779 (2012).

93. Manhattan Community Access Corporation v. Halleck, 139 S.Ct. 1921, 1927, 1928–34 (2019); *see id.* at 1931–34 (emphasizing private sphere). Justice Sotomayor,

dissenting, persuasively argued that MNN functioned as a state actor in this case. *Id.* at 1934–45 (Sotomayor, J., dissenting). Kavanaugh paraphrased a quotation often attributed to a conservative radio host, Dennis Prager: "It is sometimes said that the bigger the government, the smaller the individual." *Id.* at 1934. Prager has said: "The bigger the government, the smaller the citizen." JEFFERSON REVIEW, https://www.jeffersonreview.com/quotes.

94. Everson v. Board of Education, 330 U.S. 1 (1947) (incorporating establishment clause); Cantwell v. Connecticut, 310 U.S. 296 (1940) (incorporating free exercise clause).

95. Town of Greece v. Galloway, 572 U.S. 565, 572, 576–78 (2014).

96. Lemon v. Kurtzman, 403 U.S. 602, 612–13 (1971) (quoting Walz v. Tax Commission, 397 U.S. 664, 674 [1970]). Applications of *Lemon*: Engel v. Vitale, 370 U.S. 421 (1962) (prayers); Wallace v. Jaffree, 472 U.S. 38 (1985) (moment of silence); McCreary County v. American Civil Liberties Union of Kentucky, 545 U.S. 844 (2005) (Ten Commandments). Three points in Town of Greece, 572 U.S. at 575–82.

97. American Legion v. American Humanist Association, 139 S.Ct. 2067, 2074, 2080–81, 2084–85 (2019); *id.* at 2103–13 (Ginsburg, J., dissenting). "The cross was never perceived as an appropriate headstone or memorial for Jewish soldiers and others who did not adhere to Christianity." *Id.* at 2109 (Ginsburg, J., dissenting).

98. Masterpiece Cakeshop, Ltd. v. Colorado Civil Rights Commission, 138 S.Ct. 1719, 1729 (2018); Colo. Rev. Stat. § 24–34–601(2)(a) (2017). The basic doctrinal approach in free-exercise cases is from Employment Division, Department of Human Resources v. Smith, 494 U.S. 872, 877–83, 890 (1990).

99. *Masterpiece Cakeshop*, 138 S.Ct. at 1723–24, 1729, 1731.

100. *Id.* at 1729.

101. ZYGMUNT BAUMAN, MODERNITY AND THE HOLOCAUST 38 (1989); John 19:12–16; Matthew 23:37–39, 27:25; 1 Thessalonians 2:14–16; WILLIAM NICHOLLS, CHRISTIAN ANTISEMITISM 3, 84, 126–27 (1993); ELAINE PAGELS, THE ORIGIN OF SATAN 10, 103 (1995); PAUL JOHNSON, A HISTORY OF THE JEWS 169–310 (1987); JAMES PARKES, JUDAISM AND CHRISTIANITY 135 & n.35 (1948); *see* LEONARD DINNERSTEIN, ANTISEMITISM IN AMERICA xxii–xxiv (1994) (connecting American anti-Semitism to Christianity); STEPHEN M. FELDMAN, PLEASE DON'T WISH ME A MERRY CHRISTMAS: A CRITICAL HISTORY OF THE SEPARATION OF CHURCH AND STATE 10–27 (1997) (discussing the origins of Christian anti-Semitism); *see, e.g., That Jews Should Be Distinguished from Christians in Dress, reprinted in* THE JEW IN THE MEDIEVAL WORLD: A SOURCE BOOK, 315–1791, at 138 (Jacob R. Marcus ed., 1938) (thirteenth-century decree requiring Jews to wear conical hats or yellow patches). Nazi anti-Semitism was rooted in traditional Christian tropes about Jews, though the Nazis found new ways to subjugate and kill. JOHNSON, *supra*, at 471–74, 482–83; NICHOLLS, *supra*, at xxii.

102. E. N. Elliott, *Introduction, in* COTTON IS KING, AND PRO-SLAVERY ARGUMENTS iii, ix (E. N. Elliott, ed., Augusta: Pritchard, Abbot and Loomis, 1860) (1968 reprint ed.) (we understand the nature); Thornton Stringfellow, *The Bible Argument: Or, Slavery in the Light of Divine Revelation, in* COTTON IS KING, AND PRO-SLAVERY ARGUMENTS 460, 491 (E. N. Elliott, ed., Augusta: Pritchard, Abbot and Loomis, 1860) (1968 reprint ed.) (under the gospel); Albert Taylor Bledsoe, *Liberty and Slavery: Or, Slavery in the Light of Moral and Political Philosophy, in* COTTON IS KING, AND PRO-SLAVERY ARGUMENTS 271, 273 (E. N. Elliott, ed., Augusta: Pritchard, Abbot and Loomis, 1860) (1968

reprint ed.) (the institution of slavery). For additional examples: James Henry Hammond, *Hammond's Letters on Slavery* (Jan. 28, 1845), *in* THE PRO-SLAVERY ARGUMENT: AS MAINTAINED BY THE MOST DISTINGUISHED WRITERS OF THE SOUTHERN STATES 99, 108 (Charleston: Walker, Richards, 1852); Thornton Stringfellow, *A Scriptural View of Slavery* (1856), *reprinted in* SLAVERY DEFENDED: THE VIEWS OF THE OLD SOUTH 86, 86–98 (Eric L. McKitrick ed., 1963). For a discussion of the proslavery reliance on the Bible and Christianity: Drew Gilpin Faust, *A Southern Stewardship: The Intellectual and the Proslavery Argument, reprinted in* PROSLAVERY THOUGHT, IDEOLOGY, AND POLITICS 129, 137–39 (Paul Finkelman ed., 1989). To be clear, abolitionists as well as proslavery advocates invoked religion. Ferenc M. Szasz, *Antebellum Appeals to the "Higher Law," 1830–1860*, 110 ESSEX INSTITUTE HIST. COLLECTIONS 33, 37–47 (1974).

103. Jane Dailey, *Sex, Segregation, and the Sacred after* Brown, 91 J. AM. HIST. 119, 121 (2004) (quoting Burks); *id.* at 125 (quoting Bilbo); Loving v. Virginia, 388 U.S. 1, 3 (1967).

104. *Masterpiece Cakeshop*, 138 S.Ct. at 1729 (the commissioner); *id.* at 1733 n.* (Kagan, J., concurring); Colo. Rev. Stat. § 24–34–601(2)(a) (2017); *see* Peggy Cooper Davis et al., *The Persistence of the Confederate Narrative*, 84 TENN. L. REV. 301 (2017) (arguing that federalism-based emphases on state sovereignty undermine the national protection of civil rights); Steven K. Green, *The Illusionary Aspect of "Private Choice" for Constitutional Analysis*, 38 WILLAMETTE L. REV. 549 (2002) (emphasizing that the Court's protection of private choice undermines the constitutional commitment to equality); K. Sabeel Rahman, *Reconstructing the Administrative State in an Era of Economic and Democratic Crisis*, 131 HARV. L. REV. 1671 (2018) (arguing that attacks on democratic government that encourage privatization simultaneously undermine opportunities for democratic control over certain social interactions); Elizabeth Sepper, *Free Exercise Lochnerism*, 115 COLUM. L. REV. 1453 (2015) (explaining how the Roberts Court uses a market-libertarian approach reminiscent of freedom of contract to invalidate employment and consumer protections); Joseph William Singer, *We Don't Serve Your Kind Here: Public Accommodations and the Mark of Sodom*, 95 B.U. L. REV. 929 (2015) (discussing interrelationship between private property rights and rights to use public accommodations).

105. Espinoza v. Montana Department of Revenue, _ S.Ct. _ (2020).

106. *Id.* at _.

107. *Id.* at _ (Ginsburg, J., dissenting).

108. "Today's ruling is perverse. Without any need or power to do so, the Court appears to require a State to reinstate a tax-credit program that the Constitution did not demand in the first place." *Id.* at _ (Sotomayor, J., dissenting).

109. *Id.* at _.

110. Adam Liptak, *Supreme Court Gives Religious Schools More Access to State Aid*, N.Y. TIMES (June 30, 2020); Nina Totenberg & Brian Naylor, *Supreme Court: Montana Can't Exclude Religious Schools from Scholarship Program*, NATIONAL PUBLIC RADIO (June 30, 2020); Private School Review, *Top Montana Religiously Affiliated Schools*, https://www.privateschoolreview.com/montana/religiously-affiliated-schools (accessed July 2, 2020).

111. *Burwell*, 573 U.S. at 707; *id.* at 757 (Ginsburg, J., dissenting); Obergefell v. Hodges, 135 S.Ct. 2584 (2015) (same-sex marriage); Griswold v. Connecticut, 381 U.S. 479 (1965) (contraceptives); Religious Freedom Restoration Act of 1993 (RFRA), 107 Stat. 1488.

112. The cases in this section do not exhaust the list of decisions favoring Christians' interests and beliefs over others. *See, e.g.*, Our Lady of Guadalupe School v. Morrissey-Berru, _ S.Ct. _ (2020) (expanding ministerial exception under First Amendment religion clauses so that religious schools—which are mostly Christian—can discriminate for any reason against employees; Christian interests over employees); *Little Sisters of the Poor*, _ S.Ct. _ (upholding the agency's interpretation of the Affordable Care Act allowing employers to avoid paying for insurance coverage for contraceptives based on religious or moral objections; Christian interests over women); *Becerra*, 138 S.Ct. (invalidating state law requiring family planning clinics to provide information about abortion, even though the Court had previously upheld laws requiring family planning clinics to provide anti-abortion information; Christian interests over women).

113. Trump v. Hawaii, 138 S.Ct. 2392, 2399 (2018) (listing the eight nations); *id.* at 2438–39, 2442 (Sotomayor, J., dissenting) (taking all; otherwise clear). The dispute was twice at the Court before returning for this final resolution. Trump v. IRAP, 138 S.Ct. 353 (2017); Trump v. Hawaii, 138 S.Ct. 377 (2017). The final ban was Presidential Proclamation No. 9645, 82 Fed. Reg. 45161 (2017).

114. *Masterpiece Cakeshop*, 138 S.Ct. at 2418–20 (describing the ban as "neutral on its face" and deferring to the president); *id.* at 2446–47 (Sotomayor, J., dissenting).

115. Pleasant Grove City v. Summum, 555 U.S. 460, 464 (2009) (the placement; is not a form); *id.* at 481 (recently minted) (Stevens, J., concurring). "The Free Speech Clause restricts government regulation of private speech; it does not regulate government speech." *Id.* at 467. Rosenberger v. Rectors and Visitors of the University of Virginia, 515 U.S. 819 (1995); Good News Club v. Milford Central School, 533 U.S. 98 (2001); *see* Perry Education Association v. Perry Local Educators' Association, 460 U.S. 37, 45 (1983) (streets and parks had been public forums since time immemorial). For another, similar case: Lamb's Chapel v. Center Moriches Union Free School District, 508 U.S. 384 (1993). It is worth noting Alito's dissent, joined by Thomas, Scalia, and Roberts, in another free-expression case, Christian Legal Society v. Martinez, 130 S.Ct. 2971 (2010). The Christian Legal Society (CLS) chapter at the University of California, Hastings College of the Law, argued that the school's "all comers" policy, prohibiting student funded organizations from discriminating against gays and lesbians (and others), violated the First Amendment. *Id.* at 2979–81. Kennedy joined the four progressive justices to uphold the policy. Alito's dissent repeatedly emphasized the importance of protecting CLS, a religious organization dedicated to encouraging a Christian outlook. According to Alito, the only way to explain the school's policy and the Court's decision was that the school and the Court reacted against the Christian identity of the student organization and the content of its message. *Id.* at 3008–09 (Alito, J., dissenting). Citing *Rosenberger* and *Good News Club*, Alito stressed that a public forum analysis should have proscribed government (school) suppression of religious viewpoints. *Id.* at 3009 (Alito, J., dissenting). Alito emphasized that the school had applied its antidiscrimination (all comers) policy in a manner that discriminated against and marginalized religion. *Id.* at 3019 (Alito, J., dissenting). "[R]eligious groups were not permitted to express a religious viewpoint by limiting membership to students who shared their religious viewpoints. Under established precedent, this was [unconstitutional] viewpoint discrimination." *Id.* at 3011 (Alito, J., dissenting).

116. *E.g.*, Holt v. Hobbs, 135 S.Ct. 853 (2015) (Muslim challenger won a statutory claim against Arkansas Department of Correction for a policy prohibiting beards); Wyeth v. Levine, 555 U.S. 555 (2009) (corporate drug manufacturer lost as the Court upheld a state law judgment involving the amputation of a patient's arm).

117. The Court decided the faithless elector case nine-to-zero. Chiafalo et al. v. Washington, _ S.Ct. _ (2020). Polls suggested that Republicans, Democrats, and independents all had similar sentiments about whether an Electoral College elector should be bound to vote for the choice of the people. Adam Liptak, *States May Curb "Faithless Electors," Supreme Court Rules*, N.Y. TIMES (July 6, 2020). In some cases, conservative values might clash. *Brown*, 131 S.Ct., involved a free-speech challenge to state law prohibiting "the sale or rental of 'violent video games' to minors." The case, from one perspective, presented a clash of conservative values: The conservative justices might seek to uphold the law as a matter of moral clarity, but they simultaneously might seek to invalidate the law as interfering with the economic marketplace. The Court invalidated the law as violating the First Amendment.

118. Brandon L. Bartels & Christopher D. Johnston, *On the Ideological Foundations of Supreme Court Legitimacy in the American Public*, 57 AM. J. OF POL. SCI. 184, 196–97 (2013) (arguing that "there are rational bases for citizens perceiving the contemporary Court as a conservative, moderate, and even liberal policymaker"). *But see* James L. Gibson & Michael J. Nelson, *Is the U.S. Supreme Court's Legitimacy Grounded in Performance Satisfaction and Ideology?*, 59 AM. J. OF POL. SCI. 162, 173 (2015) (sharply criticizing Bartels & Johnston, *supra*, and concluding that the Court is "fairly conservative").

119. For rankings of Supreme Court justices based on political ideology: LEE EPSTEIN ET AL., THE BEHAVIOR OF FEDERAL JUDGES 106–16 (2013), which includes comparisons with the Martin-Quinn scores (accounting for changes over time), http://mqscores.wustl.edu/index.php, and the Segal-Cover scores (quantifying Court nominees' perceived political ideologies at the time of appointment), http://www.sunysb.edu/polsci/jsegal/qualtable.pdf (data drawn from Jeffrey Segal & Albert Cover, *Ideological Values and the Votes of Supreme Court Justices*, 83 AM. POL. SCI. REV. 557–565 (1989); updated in LEE EPSTEIN & JEFFREY A. SEGAL, ADVICE AND CONSENT: THE POLITICS OF JUDICIAL APPOINTMENTS [2005]). On being pro-business: J. Mitchell Pickerill & Cornell W. Clayton, *The Roberts Court and Economic Issues in an Era of Polarization*, 67 CASE W. RES. L. REV. 693 (2017); Epstein et al., *supra* note 60, at 1449–51, 1472–73; J. Mitchell Pickerill, *Is the Roberts Court Business Friendly? Is the Pope Catholic?*, in BUSINESS AND THE ROBERTS COURT 35 (Jonathan H. Adler ed., 2016) (empirical study showing that the Roberts Court is business-friendly, though it continues a trend that started years ago with Nixon's appointees); Corey Ciocchetti, *The Constitution, the Roberts Court, and Business*, 4 WM. & MARY BUS. L. REV. 385 (2013). For claims that the Roberts Court is not conservative enough: Ramesh Ponnuru, *Supreme Court Isn't Pro-Business, but Should Be*, BLOOMBERG (July 5, 2011); Jonathan Adler, *Business, the Environment, and the Roberts Court: A Preliminary Assessment*, 49 SANTA CLARA L. REV. 943 (2009); Eric Posner, *Is the Supreme Court Biased in Favor of Business?*, SLATE (March 17, 2008). But according to Mark Tushnet, the "Roberts Court's overall balance sheet in business cases fits the 'pro-business' view of the Court reasonably well." MARK TUSHNET, IN THE BALANCE: LAW AND POLITICS ON THE ROBERTS COURT 213 (2013); *id.* at 187–214 (discussing evidence). The political scientist Michael Bailey

surveyed competing measures of the Court's political leanings and concluded that, as of 2012, the Court was moderately conservative. Michael Bailey, *Just How Liberal (or Conservative) Is the Supreme Court?*, VOX.COM (Feb. 22, 2016). The replacement of Kennedy with Kavanaugh will only move the Court further rightward. On free-speech cases: Lee Epstein et al., *Do Justices Defend the Speech They Hate? An Analysis of In-Group Bias on the U.S. Supreme Court*, 6 J.L. & COURTS 237 (2018). On setting the docket: Chandler, *supra* note 60; Adam D. Chandler, *Cert.-stage Amicus Briefs: Who Files Them and to What Effect?*, SCOTUSBLOG (Sept. 27, 2007) (earlier study).

120. *See* Ryan C. Black & Ryan J. Owens, *Agenda Setting in the Supreme Court: The Collision of Policy and Jurisprudence*, 71 J. POLITICS 1062 (2009) (political science empirical study showing that law matters to Supreme Court justices even at the agenda-setting stage).

121. National Federation of Independent Business v. Sebelius, 567 U.S. 519, 623, 132 S.Ct. 2566, 2629 (2012) (Ginsburg, J., concurring in part and dissenting in part).

122. Bostock v. Clayton County, Georgia, _ S.Ct. _ (2020). For Title VII, see 42 U.S.C. § 2000e–2(a)(1).

123. "Statutes should be interpreted . . . not on the basis of the unpromulgated intentions of those who enacted them . . . but rather on the basis of what is the most probable meaning of the words of the enactment, in the context of the whole body of public law with which they must be reconciled." Antonin Scalia, *Address before the Attorney General's Conference on Economic Liberties in Washington, D.C.* (June 14, 1986), *in* Office of Legal Policy, U.S. Department of Justice, ORIGINAL MEANING JURISPRUDENCE: A SOURCEBOOK 101, 103 (app. C) (1987).

124. Frank Easterbrook, *Statutes' Domains*, 50 U. CHI. L. REV. 533 (1983) (using public choice theory to argue courts should not presume legislative decisions are rational).

125. GORSUCH, *supra* note 76, at 106–07, 131–32.

126. *Bostock*, _ S.Ct.

127. *Id.*; Daniel Hemel, *The Problem with that Big Gay Rights Decision? It's Not Really about Gay Rights*, WASH. POST (June 17, 2020).

128. F. M. KAMM, THE TROLLEY PROBLEM MYSTERIES (2015); Bert I. Huang, *Law and Moral Dilemmas*, 130 HARV. L. REV. 659 (2016).

129. *Bostock*, _ S.Ct. (Alito, J., dissenting) (quoting ANTONIN SCALIA & BRYAN A. GARNER, READING LAW: THE INTERPRETATION OF LEGAL TEXTS 16 [2012]).

130. *Gonzales v. Raich* is another case in which the conservative justices faced a potential conflict between doctrine and results, though it was decided at the very end of the Rehnquist Court era. Gonzales v. Raich, 545 U.S. 1 (2005). If the Court had applied its conservative commerce-power doctrine in a straightforward fashion, it might have reasonably concluded that Congress had exceeded its power in enacting a law that proscribed the possession of marijuana. The conservatives instead found reasons to conclude that Congress acted within its permissible powers, though they avoided the dilution of the conservative doctrine. A less obvious example is *Obergefell*, 135 S.Ct. A five-to-four decision, *Obergefell* held that same-sex couples enjoy a constitutional right to marry. Justice Kennedy joined the four progressive justices to reach the liberal result. But Kennedy's opinion insisted that the Court was remaining politically neutral: The Court did not need to choose between the views and values of same-sex-marriage supporters, on the one side, and the views and values of religious conservatives, on the

other side. *Id.* at 2602, 2606. It was in part that claim to neutrality that facilitated the subsequent decision, *Masterpiece Cakeshop, Ltd. v. Colorado Civil Rights Commission*, in which the Court interpreted the Free Exercise Clause to allow religiously motivated discrimination against a same-sex couple. *Masterpiece Cakeshop*, 138 S.Ct. *See* Stephen M. Feldman, *Having Your Cake and Eating It Too? Religious Freedom and LGBTQ Rights*, 9 WAKE FOREST J.L. & POL'Y 35 (2018) (discussing *Masterpiece Cakeshop* and claims to neutrality); Stephen M. Feldman, *(Same) Sex, Lies, and Democracy: Tradition, Religion, and Substantive Due Process (With an Emphasis on Obergefell v. Hodges)*, 24 WM. & MARY BILL RTS. J. 341 (2015) (discussing the tensions within *Obergefell* opinions).

131. Department of Homeland Security v. Regents of the University of California, _ S.Ct. _ (2020). For the APA, see Pub. L. 79–404, 60 Stat. 237 (June 11, 1946).

132. Department of Commerce v. New York, 139 S.Ct. 2551, 2575–76 (2019).

133. Gundy v. United States, 139 S.Ct. 2116, 2130–31 (2019) (Alito, J., concurring in the judgment) (expressing a desire to resurrect the nondelegation doctrine as means of limiting congressional delegations of power to administrative agencies).

134. *Department of Homeland Security*, _ S.Ct. ("We do not decide whether DACA or its rescission are sound policies"); *Department of Commerce*, 139 S.Ct. at 2576 ("We do not hold that the agency decision here was substantively invalid").

135. *E.g.*, Richard Wolf, *Aligning with Liberals on DACA and LGBTQ Rights, Chief Justice John Roberts Asserts His Independence*, USA TODAY (June 19, 2020). For an example of the conservative reaction to the Court's DACA decision, see Jordain Carney, *Roberts Sparks Backlash from Conservative Senators with DACA Ruling*, THE HILL (June 18, 2020).

136. William Baude, *Foreword: The Supreme Court's Shadow Docket*, 9 N.Y.U. J.L. & LIBERTY 1, 5 (2015). For the most comprehensive discussion of this issue: Stephen I. Vladeck, *The Solicitor General and the Shadow Docket*, 133 HARV. L. REV. 123 (2019). For statistics, see *id.* at 132–34, 161–63 (appendix). For the role of Roberts, see *id.* at 130–32, 135–36, 155–56. For progressive opposition, see *id.* at 138, 148–49, 155–56. On the standards for relief: Trump v. International Refugee Assistance Project, 137 S.Ct. 2080 (2017); Philip Morris USA v. Patricia Henley, 2004 WL 2386754 (U.S.). For additional discussions: Stephen I. Vladeck, *How the Supreme Court Is Quietly Enabling Trump*, N.Y. TIMES (June 17, 2020); Brian Naylor, *Supreme Court Puts Temporary Hold on Order to Release Redacted Mueller Materials*, NATIONAL PUBLIC RADIO (May 8, 2020); Adam Liptak, *Chief Justice Gives Trump Temporary Reprieve in Financial Records Case*, N.Y. TIMES (Nov. 18, 2019).

137. The prominent exception for Roberts is *Sebelius*, but, as explained in this chapter, his *Sebelius* opinion has important conservative elements.

138. *Obergefell*, 135 S.Ct. (Roberts, C.J., dissenting).

139. Whole Woman's Health, 136 S.Ct.; *Fisher*, 136 S.Ct.

140. *See, e.g.*, *Department of Homeland Security*, _ S.Ct. (the administrative law DACA decision); *Department of Commerce*, 139 S.Ct. at 2576 (the administrative law citizenship-census decision).

141. Shelby County, 133 S.Ct.; Rucho, 139 S.Ct.

142. Merrill v. People First of Alabama, No. 19A1063, 2020 WL 3604049 (U.S. July 2, 2020).

143. Republican National Committee v. Democratic National Committee, 140 S.Ct. 1205 (2020) (per curiam); *id.* at 1208 (Ginsburg, J., dissenting). In another case,

the Court refused to vacate a lower court's stay, where the lower court's order would interfere with absentee voting during the pandemic. Texas Democratic Party v. Abbott, No. 19A1055, 2020 WL 3478784 (U.S. June 26, 2020). And in yet another case, the Court refused to vacate a lower court's stay, thus preventing hundreds of thousands of felons from voting in Florida. Raysor v. DeSantis, No. 19A1071, 2020 WL 4006868 (U.S. July 16, 2020). As Sotomayor wrote in dissent, joined by Ginsburg and Kagan, the "Court's inaction continues a trend of condoning disfranchisement." *Id.* (Sotomayor, J., dissenting).

144. Neal Devins & Lawrence Baum, *Split Definitive: How Party Polarization Turned the Supreme Court into a Partisan Court*, 2016 Sup. Ct. Rev. 301 (2016) (emphasizing how polarization has changed the Court).

145. *Sebelius*, 132 S.Ct. at 2577. For additional examples in *Sebelius*: *Id.* at 2579, 2608.

146. *Masterpiece Cakeshop*, 138 S.Ct. at 1732. In *Obergefell v. Hodges*, which protected a constitutional right to same-sex marriage, Kennedy also emphasized the possibility of neutrality, that a constitutional right to marry for same-sex couples can exist without diminishing the views or voices of religious opponents to same-sex marriage. *Obergefell*, 135 S.Ct. at 2602, 2606.

147. Antonin Scalia, *The Rule of Law as a Law of Rules*, 56 U. Chi. L. Rev. 1175, 1187 (1989) (the law of rules); Scalia & Garner, *supra* note 129, at 78, 428 (words must be given); Gorsuch, *supra* note 76, at 10 (offers neutral); *see id.* at 114–15 (originalism is not politically conservative).

CHAPTER 8

1. For example, Justice Alito wants to resurrect the nondelegation doctrine as a means of limiting congressional power, even though the Court has not invoked the doctrine since 1935. Gundy v. United States, 139 S.Ct. 2116, 2130–31 (2019) (Alito, J., concurring in the judgment); *see* Rich Lowry, *Elizabeth Warren's Threat to the Constitution*, National Review (Oct. 11, 2019) (arguing progressive agenda ignores constitutional constraints); Michael Klarman, *Why Democrats Should Pack the Supreme Court*, Take Care (October 15, 2018), https://takecareblog.com/blog/why-democrats-should-pack-the-supreme-court (a progressive worrying about the Roberts Court); Samuel Moyn & Aaron Belkin, *The Roberts Court Would Likely Strike Down Climate Change Legislation* (Sept. 2019) (report from progressive group, Take Back the Court, worrying about Court). The Democrats might need to eliminate the Senate filibuster rule to facilitate enactment of progressive legislation. Molly E. Reynolds, *What Is the Senate Filibuster, and What Would It Take to Eliminate It?* Brookings Policy 2020 (Oct. 15, 2019), https://www.brookings.edu/policy2020/votervital/what-is-the-senate-filibuster-and-what-would-it-take-to-eliminate.it.

2. For ideas about school funding, *see* Carmel Martin et al., *A Quality Approach to School Funding*, Center for American Progress (Nov. 13, 2018); Bruce J. Biddle & David C. Berliner, *A Research Synthesis/Unequal School Funding in the United States*, 59 Educational Leadership 48 (2002). At-risk students would include students with disabilities, low-income students, and students from other at-risk populations. Martin et al., *supra*; David T. Burkam & Valerie E. Lee, *Inequality at the Starting Gate: Social*

Background Differences in Achievement as Children Begin School, ECONOMIC POLICY INSTITUTE (Sept. 2002). To be clear, I am not proposing this statute as a realistically complete or comprehensive attempt to tackle the problems of unequal funding in education. I am merely providing these broad contours of a possible statute in order to demonstrate the constitutional problems that would confront a progressive Congress and president. To make an obvious point, any serious attempt to tackle education-funding problems would need to account for the number of wealthy families that exit the public school systems and invest instead in private education.

3. *$23 Billion*, EDBUILD (Feb. 2019), https://edbuild.org/content/23-billion/full -report.pdf; Clare Lombardo, *Why White School Districts Have So Much More Money*, NATIONAL PUBLIC RADIO (Feb. 26, 2019).

4. United States v. Lopez, 514 U.S. 549 (1995).

5. The key anti-commandeering cases: Printz v. United States, 521 U.S. 898 (1997); New York v. United States, 505 U.S. 144 (1992).

6. City of Boerne v. Flores, 521 U.S. 507 (1997) (limiting congressional power under the Fourteenth Amendment); *see* San Antonio Independent School District v. Rodriguez, 411 U.S. 1 (1973) (disparate funding between school districts does not violate equal protection).

7. *City of Boerne*, 521 U.S. at 530–31; Shelby County v. Holder, 133 S.Ct. 2612, 2620–21, 2627, 2631 (2013) (invalidating a section of the Voting Rights Act, enacted pursuant to the Fifteenth Amendment, sec. 2, power, because of inadequate congressional findings).

8. As discussed in Chapter 7, the conservative justices have been hostile to affirmative action programs that explicitly refer to race. Parents Involved in Community Schools v. Seattle School District No. 1, 551 U.S. 701 (2007). But with this statute, the reference to at-risk students is not an express racial classification. Hence, the Court might be inclined to find it constitutional under equal protection. Yet, as happened in the Affordable Care Act case, the Court has rendered conservative doctrine even more conservative if the original doctrine as applied might lead to a progressive outcome. National Federation of Independent Business v. Sebelius, 132 S.Ct. 2566 (2012).

9. Of course, the conservative bloc might invalidate a Court-expansion statute by deciding pursuant to politics writ large, fabricating a novel and one-time-only rule to maintain conservative control of the Court. But given the long history of congressional changes to the Court's size, the conservative bloc's contravention of judicial-professional norms would be patent. *See* Michael C. Dorf, *How the Written Constitution Crowds Out the Extraconstitutional Rule of Recognition, in* THE RULE OF RECOGNITION AND THE U.S. CONSTITUTION 69, 74–75, 79 (Matthew D. Adler & Kenneth Einar Himma eds., 2009) (acknowledging that text and history support the constitutionality of court packing).

10. MARK TUSHNET, TAKING BACK THE CONSTITUTION 216–18 (2020) (arguing that there are good reasons not to find a norm against court packing); Dorf, *supra* note 9, at 74 (suggesting there is a norm or convention against court packing); Curtis A. Bradley & Neil S. Siegel, *Historical Gloss, Constitutional Conventions, and the Judicial Separation of Powers*, 105 GEO. L.J. 255 (2017) (without reaching a conclusion, the authors recognize that some commentators would argue that there is a constitutional norm against court packing); Tara Leigh Grove, *The Origins (and Fragility) of Judicial*

Independence, 71 VAND. L. REV. 465, 512–14 (2018); *see* STEVEN LEVITSKY & DANIEL ZIBLATT, HOW DEMOCRACIES DIE 130–32 (2018) (arguing norms of forbearance should preclude court packing).

11. TOM S. CLARK, THE LIMITS OF JUDICIAL INDEPENDENCE 5–6, 16 (2010); BARRY FRIEDMAN, THE WILL OF THE PEOPLE 14 (2009). In a forthcoming book, Laura Kalman makes two important points. First, Congress might have passed FDR's plan if it had been less ambitious. Second, the history of FDR's plan does not suggest a clear conclusion regarding court packing today. LAURA KALMAN, GHOST OF COURT PACKING PAST (draft; tentative title) (forthcoming Oxford University Press).

12. *See* FRIEDMAN, *supra* note 11, at 14–15, 367 (explaining constitutional meaning as arising from a dialogue between the people and the justices); Stephen M. Feldman, *The Persistence of Power and the Struggle for Dialogic Standards in Postmodern Constitutional Jurisprudence: Michelman, Habermas, and Civic Republicanism*, 81 GEO. L.J. 2243 (1993) (emphasizing the importance of dialogue in constitutional jurisprudence); Stephen M. Feldman, *Republican Revival/Interpretive Turn*, 1992 WIS. L. REV. 679, 722–31 (on dialogue).

13. KEVIN J. MCMAHON, RECONSIDERING ROOSEVELT ON RACE 61–63, 89, 95–96 (2004) (a more nuanced interpretation of the court-packing plan that acknowledges its successes).

14. Republicans and Democrats are not equally at fault in undermining our democratic culture and system. THOMAS E. MANN & NORMAN J. ORNSTEIN, IT'S EVEN WORSE THAN IT LOOKS xiv–xv, xxiv, 18–19, 102–03 (2012); Joseph Fishkin & David E. Pozen, *Asymmetric Constitutional Hardball*, 118 COLUM. L. REV. 915 (2018) (arguing that constitutional hardball has been asymmetric, with the Republicans pushing more strongly against traditional norms); Norman J. Ornstein, *Yes, Polarization Is Asymmetric—and Conservatives Are Worse*, THE ATLANTIC (June 19, 2014); *see* STEPHEN M. FELDMAN, NEOCONSERVATIVE POLITICS AND THE SUPREME COURT: LAW, POWER, AND DEMOCRACY 43–45 (2013) (discussing increasing polarization).

15. Neal Devins & Lawrence Baum, *Split Definitive: How Party Polarization Turned the Supreme Court into A Partisan Court*, 2016 SUP. CT. REV. 301 (2016) (emphasizing how polarization has changed the Court); Robert Barnes, *Rebuking Trump's Criticism of "Obama Judge," Chief Justice Roberts Defends Judiciary as "Independent,"* WASH. POST (Nov. 21, 2018); Linda Greenhouse, *Who Cares about the Supreme Court's "Legitimacy"?*, N.Y. TIMES (June 6, 2019); Aaron Belkin & Sean McElwee, *Don't Be Fooled. Chief Justice John Roberts Is as Partisan as They Come*, N.Y. TIMES (Oct. 7, 2019). For cases where Roberts refused to uphold a Trump administration action, *see* Department of Homeland Security v. Regents of the University of California, _ S.Ct. _ (2020) (Roberts opinion holding that the Trump administration's rescission of DACA violated APA procedural requirements); Department of Commerce v. New York, 139 S.Ct. 2551 (2019) (holding that the Secretary of Commerce had not adequately justified the addition of a citizenship question to the upcoming census).

16. Roe v. Wade, 410 U.S. 113, 116 (1973); Planned Parenthood v. Casey, 505 U.S. 833 (1992).

17. *Casey*, 505 U.S. at 864 (emphasis added); *see id.* at 864–69.

18. RICHARD H. FALLON JR., LAW AND LEGITIMACY IN THE SUPREME COURT 21–24 (2018). Political scientists have extensively studied the Court's legitimacy,

though their various conclusions sometimes do not harmonize. I draw on BRANDON L. BARTELS & CHRISTOPHER D. JOHNSTON, CURBING THE COURT (2020) [hereinafter CURBING]; CLARK, *supra* note 11; JAMES L. GIBSON & GREGORY A. CALDEIRA, CITIZENS, COURTS, AND CONFIRMATIONS: POSITIVITY THEORY AND THE JUDGMENTS OF THE AMERICAN PEOPLE (2009) [hereinafter GIBSON & CALDEIRA, CITIZENS]; Alex Badas, *Policy Disagreement and Judicial Legitimacy: Evidence from the 1937 Court-Packing Plan*, 48 J. LEGAL STUD. 377 (2019); Brandon L. Bartels & Christopher D. Johnston, *On the Ideological Foundations of Supreme Court Legitimacy in the American Public*, 57 AM. J. POL. SCI. 184 (2013); Gregory A. Caldeira & James L. Gibson, *The Etiology of Public Support for the Supreme Court*, 36 AM. J. POL. SCI. 635 (1992); Tom S. Clark & Jonathan P. Kastellec, *Source Cues and Public Support for the Supreme Court*, 43 AM. POL. RES. 504 (2015); Dino P. Christenson & David M. Glick, *Chief Justice Roberts's Health Care Decision Disrobed: The Microfoundations of the Supreme Court's Legitimacy*, 59 AM. J. POL. SCI. 403 (2015); James L. Gibson & Gregory A. Caldeira, *Has Legal Realism Damaged the Legitimacy of the U.S. Supreme Court?*, 45 LAW & SOC'Y REV. 195 (2011) [hereinafter Gibson & Caldeira, *Realism*]; James L. Gibson & Gregory A. Caldeira, *Blacks and the United States Supreme Court: Models of Diffuse Support*, 54 J. POL. 1120 (1992) [hereinafter Gibson & Caldeira, *Blacks*]; James L. Gibson & Michael J. Nelson, *Reconsidering Positivity Theory: What Roles Do Politicization, Ideological Disagreement, and Legal Realism Play in Shaping U.S. Supreme Court Legitimacy?*, 14 J. EMPIRICAL LEGAL STUD. 592 (2017) [hereinafter Gibson & Nelson, *Reconsidering*]; James L. Gibson & Michael J. Nelson. *Is the U.S. Supreme Court's Legitimacy Grounded in Performance Satisfaction and Ideology?*, 59 AM. J. POL. SCI. 162 (2015) [hereinafter Gibson & Nelson, *Legitimacy*]; James L. Gibson et al., *On the Legitimacy of National High Courts*, 92 AM. POL. SCI. REV. 343 (1998). A recent article introduces another complication into the studies of Supreme Court legitimacy: that the measurement of ideological proximity to the Court is problematic. Michael J. Nelson & James L. Gibson, *Measuring Subjective Ideological Disagreement with the U.S. Supreme Court*, 8 J.L. & COURTS 75 (2020).

19. Moreover, the justices themselves, in their public statements (rather than their judicial opinions), are likely aware of their need to maintain the Court's legitimacy. Colin Glennon & Logan Strother, *The Maintenance of Institutional Legitimacy in Supreme Court Justices' Public Rhetoric*, 7 J.L. & COURTS 241 (2019).

20. LEVITSKY & ZIBLATT, *supra* note 10, at 8–9, 97–117. Mark Tushnet is usually credited with coining the term "constitutional hardball." Mark Tushnet, *Constitutional Hardball*, 37 J. MARSHALL L. REV. 523 (2004).

21. LEVITSKY & ZIBLATT, *supra* note 10, at 130–32; David Kosař & Katarína Šipulová, *How to Fight Court-Packing?*, 6 CONST. STUD. 133, 134–35 (2020) (giving examples of court packing).

22. Bruce Drake, *5 Facts about the Supreme Court*, PEW RESEARCH CENTER FACT-TANK (Sept. 26, 2016), http://www.pewresearch.org/fact-tank/2016/09/26/5-facts -about-the-supreme-court; Gallup, *Supreme Court*, http://www.gallup.com/poll/4732 /supreme-court.aspx (accessed March 6, 2017).

23. Annenberg Public Policy Center, University of Pennsylvania, *Is There a Constitutional Right to Own a Home or a Pet? Many Americans Don't Know* (Sept. 16, 2015), http://www.annenbergpublicpolicycenter.org/wp-content/uploads/Civic-knowledge

-survey-Sept.-2015.pdf. On knowing at least one justice: C-SPAN/PSB Supreme Court Survey: Agenda of Key Findings (Aug. 2018); C-SPAN Supreme Court Survey (July 9, 2009). On Judge Judy: American Council of Trustees and Alumni, *A Crisis in Civic Education*, at 23 (Jan. 2016), https://www.goacta.org/images/download/A_Crisis_in_ Civic_Education.pdf.

24. Clark & Kastellec, *supra* note 18, at 507.

25. For my writings focused on originalism and Scalia: Stephen M. Feldman, *Justice Scalia and the Originalist Fallacy, in* THE CONSERVATIVE REVOLUTION OF ANTONIN SCALIA 189 (Howard Schweber & David A. Schultz eds., 2018); Stephen M. Feldman, *Constitutional Interpretation and History: New Originalism or Eclecticism?*, 28 B.Y.U. J. PUB. L. 283 (2014) [hereinafter Feldman, *Constitutional Interpretation*].

26. CNN Politics, *Election 2016, Exit Polls, National President* (Nov. 23, 2016), http://www.cnn.com/election/results/exit-polls; NBC News, *NBC News Exit Poll: Future Supreme Court Appointments Important Factor in Presidential Voting* (Nov. 8, 2016), http://www.nbcnews.com/card/nbc-news-exit-poll-future-supreme-court -appointments-important-factor-n680381; Pew Research Center, *Top Voting Issues in 2016 Election* (July 7, 2016), http://www.people-press.org/2016/07/07/4-top-voting-is sues-in-2016-election. On the politics of individual viewpoints: Eric A. Posner & Cass R. Sunstein, *Institutional Flip-Flops*, 94 TEX. L. REV. 485 (2016) (arguing that vigorous institutional commitments—for example, to federalism—change when necessary to fit one's political ideology).

27. GIBSON & CALDEIRA, CITIZENS, *supra* note 18, at 17–35.

28. *Id.* at 61. For the distinction between diffuse and specific support, see *id.* at 39–40; CLARK, *supra* note 11, at 17.

29. In fact, a majority of Americans appear to believe in a type of legal realism to some degree. Gibson & Caldeira, *Realism, supra* note 18, at 206–08. That is, "[m]ost [Americans] believe that judges have discretion and that judges make discretionary decisions on the basis of ideology and values." *Id.* at 207. While Bartels and Johnston criticize Gibson and Caldeira on other matters, they agree that many Americans accept a type of legal realism. CURBING, *supra* note 18, at 69–70.

30. GIBSON & CALDEIRA, CITIZENS, *supra* note 18, at 39 (quoting DAVID EASTON, A SYSTEMS ANALYSIS OF POLITICAL LIFE 273 (1965)). For studies generally supporting the resilience of the Court's diffuse support, *see* GIBSON & CALDEIRA, CITIZENS, *supra*; Badas, *supra* note 18; Christenson & Glick, *supra* note 18, at 409; Gibson & Caldeira, *Realism, supra* note 18; Gibson & Nelson, *Reconsidering, supra* note 18; Gibson & Nelson, *Legitimacy, supra* note 18; Gibson et al., *supra* note 18. Bartels and Johnston challenge the conclusion that the Court enjoys a reservoir of goodwill, Curbing, *supra* note 18, at 64–67, 89, but admit that trust in the Court remains high. *Id.* at 70–71. Ultimately, they argue that the Court has public support, but it is not as deep and wide as others maintain. *Id.* at 248–49.

31. GIBSON & CALDEIRA, CITIZENS, *supra* note 18, at 3.

32. *Id.* at 7–9, 121–23; Gibson & Nelson, *Reconsidering, supra* note 18, at 612–15 (reconfirming positivity theory).

33. GIBSON & CALDEIRA, CITIZENS, *supra* note 18, at 61–62, 119–20, 124–25; CLARK, *supra* note 11, at 18; Gibson & Caldeira, *Realism, supra* note 18, at 199–200; Gibson & Nelson, *Reconsidering, supra* note 18, at 595, 604–05, 612.

34. Clark & Kastellec, *supra* note 18, at 505–06, 510–11.

35. Gibson & Nelson, *Legitimacy, supra* note 18, at 173. Gibson and Nelson criticize the conclusions of Brandon L. Bartels & Christopher D. Johnston, who had argued that an individual's political ideology determined his or her diffuse support for the Court. Bartels & Johnston, *supra* note 18, at 196–97. Gibson and Nelson add, though, that for a small group of people, ideological disagreement can affect perceptions of the Court's legitimacy. Gibson & Nelson, *Reconsidering, supra* note 18, at 613. They define legal realists as those individuals who "understand that Supreme Court decisions are based on the justices' ideologies, values, and opinions on the issues at litigation." *Id.* at 597. Then they conclude that a subset of legal realists are most likely to be influenced by perceived ideological differences from the Court—namely, those legal realists who measure highest or strongest (on the measures for belief in realism) and who simultaneously do not view the Court as just another political institution. *Id.* at 607–09. Bartels and Johnston have responded and elaborated their emphasis on political ideology. CURBING, *supra* note 18.

36. Gibson & Caldeira, *Blacks, supra* note 18, at 1140–41; CLARK, *supra* note 11, at 18; Caldeira & Gibson, *supra* note 18, at 640 & n.7; Glennon & Strother, *supra* note 19, at 243.

37. Gibson & Caldeira, *Realism, supra* note 18, at 214. "[M]any Americans believe that the Court is influenced by both political and legal considerations." CURBING, *supra* note 18, at 70.

38. CURBING, *supra* note 18, at 18–28, 35–36, 245, 249 (arguing that empirical studies suggest Americans support court curbing based on policy preferences or political ideology); *id.* at 19–20, 46–50, 253–54 (in times of intense polarization, policy or political differences become even more important in determining support for court curbing); *id.* at 19 (even individuals motivated to support court curbing because of policy or political ideology would likely legitimate such support with process-based claims, such as a failure to follow the rule of law); Clark & Kastellec, *supra* note 18, at 525 (political ideology can influence individual reactions to issues related to diffuse support—such as court-curbing measures—even if diffuse support for the Court itself remains relatively resilient). Based on a survey experiment focused on packing the lower federal courts (not the Supreme Court), Amanda Driscoll and Michael J. Nelson concluded that Democratic court packing would be unlikely to harm the Democratic Party. Democratic voters would likely support Democratic court packing, especially if apolitical justifications were given (such as managing the court's caseload). Amanda Driscoll & Michael J. Nelson, *These Two Arguments Make Americans Less Opposed to Court Packing*, WASH. POST (Monkey Cage) (March 27, 2019) (based on study: Amanda Driscoll & Michael J. Nelson, *The Costs and Benefits of Court Curbing: Experimental Evidence from the United States*, presented at the Social Science Research Council's Anxieties of Democracy Conference (New York, Jan. 30–31, 2019)).

39. Christenson & Glick, *supra* note 18, at 416; *see* CURBING, *supra* note 18, at 18–28 (emphasizing political ideology as key to support for court curbing); GIBSON & CALDEIRA, CITIZENS, *supra* note 18, at 3 (emphasizing positivity bias); TUSHNET, *supra* note 10, at 219–21 (questioning whether Democratic court packing would undermine the Court's legitimacy). Ironically, if Democratic court packing were to engender a threat to the Court's legitimacy, it would likely arise from hyperbolic Republican at-

tacks emphasizing the undermining of the Court's legitimacy rather than from the court packing itself. GIBSON & CALDEIRA, CITIZENS, *supra* note 18, at 61–62, 119–20, 124–25; CLARK, *supra* note 11, at 18. For a recent empirical survey regarding potential court-curbing proposals—albeit taken before Ginsburg's death—see Lee Epstein, James L. Gibson, & Michael J. Nelson, *Public Response to Proposals to Reform the Supreme Court* (Oct. 9, 2020; prepared for the N.Y. TIMES). With regard to empirical studies supporting positivity theory, while some surveys asked about confidence in the Court's leaders, more recent surveys asked multiple questions that indirectly manifest support (or disdain) for the Court. James L. Gibson et al., *Measuring Attitudes toward the United States Supreme Court*, 47 AM. J. POL. SCI. 354 (2003). Some of those questions typically related to support for court curbing, yet those questions are always supplemented by other questions. *Id.* at 358 (Table 2), 366 (appendix B); Gibson & Nelson, *Reconsidering, supra* note 18, at online appendix A. Thus, a high level of support for the Court should not be equated with a necessary opposition to court curbing, much less court packing.

40. David Landau & Rosalind Dixon, *Abusive Judicial Review: Courts against Democracy*, 53 U.C. DAVIS L. REV. 1313 (2020).

41. Gibson & Caldeira, *Blacks, supra* note 18, at 1140–41; CLARK, *supra* note 11, at 18; Caldeira & Gibson, *supra* note 18, at 640 & n.7.

42. Klarman, *supra* note 1.

43. CLARK, *supra* note 11, at 4.

44. Badas, *supra* note 18 (on New Dealers); Marin K. Levy, *Packing and Unpacking State Courts*, 61 WM. & MARY L. REV. 1121 (2020) (on state courts). With regard to the New Dealers, a recent study concluded that more Americans would have preferred a constitutional amendment to FDR's statutory court-packing plan. William D. Blake, *The Law: "Justice under the Constitution, Not over It": Public Perceptions of FDR's Court-Packing Plan*, 49 PRESIDENTIAL STUD. Q. 204 (2019). Moreover, Congress might have passed FDR's plan if it had been less ambitious—for instance, seeking an additional two rather than six justices. LAURA KALMAN, GHOST OF COURT PACKING PAST (draft; tentative title) (forthcoming Oxford University Press).

45. Brief of Senators Sheldon Whitehouse, Mazie Hirono, Richard Blumenthal, Richard Durbin, and Kirsten Gillibrand as Amici Curiae in Support of Respondents, New York State Rifle & Pistol Association, Inc. v. City of New York, New York, 2019 WL 3814388 (U.S.) (No. 18-280) (Aug. 12, 2019); *see* CURBING, *supra* note 18, at 19 (politically motivated individuals would likely legitimate support for court curbing with process-based claims).

46. Clark and Kastellec emphasize the Court's sensitivity to cues about its power. Clark & Kastellec, *supra* note 18, at 524–27. In a similar vein, Clark underscores "the interaction among the public, Congress, and the Court" in understanding judicial power and independence. CLARK, *supra* note 11, at 15.

47. On current threats to democratic government: TOM GINSBURG & AZIZ Z. HUQ, HOW TO SAVE A CONSTITUTIONAL DEMOCRACY 1–5, 237–45 (2018); LEVITSKY & ZIBLATT, *supra* note 10, at 206–12; RICHARD L. HASEN, THE VOTING WARS (2012); Richard L. Hasen, *The 2016 U.S. Voting Wars: From Bad to Worse*, 26 WM. & MARY BILL RTS. J. 629 (2018). On the Court as a threat to democracy: STEPHEN M. FELDMAN, THE NEW ROBERTS COURT, DONALD TRUMP, AND OUR FAILING CONSTITUTION 199–226

(2017) [hereinafter FELDMAN, FAILING CONSTITUTION]. It should be noted that politics and democracy answer the common concern that Democratic court packing will provoke a later round of Republican court packing—tit-for-tat court packing. If and when the Democrats sweep, then the Republican Party will inevitably go through a period of transformation. Meanwhile, a Democratic-controlled national government would be able to protect voting rights to a greater degree than ever before—especially if the Democrats also pack the Court, so the conservative justices cannot block democracy-enhancing legislation. If, subsequently, the Republicans ever control Congress and the presidency, it will likely be a different Republican party from the ultra-polarizing and reactionary Republican party of today. That new (and improved) Republican party might not want to engage in tit-for-tat court packing.

48. McMAHON, *supra* note 13, at 14 (FDR pushed the Court to accept a "more inclusive democracy"); Landau & Dixon, *supra* note 40, at 1383–84 (FDR did not attack democracy). On the ambiguity of court packing in relation to democracy, see GINSBURG & HUQ, *supra* note 47, at 4, 218–22; Aziz Huq & Tom Ginsburg, *How to Lose a Constitutional Democracy*, 65 U.C.L.A. L. REV. 78, 84–86 (2018); Thomas M. Keck, *Court-Packing and Democratic Erosion* (Feb. 19, 2020), https://ssrn.com/abstract=3476889 or http://dx.doi.org/10.2139/ssrn.3476889.

49. ROBERT B. REICH, SAVING CAPITALISM: FOR THE MANY, NOT THE FEW 3–7, 11, 85, 153–54 (2015); *see* THOMAS PIKETTY, CAPITAL IN THE TWENTY-FIRST CENTURY 20–21 (Arthur Goldhammer trans., 2014) (emphasizing that economic inequality arises from political choices rather than unalterable market forces). For earlier arguments against the idea of a free market, free of government: RICHARD T. ELY, STUDIES IN THE EVOLUTION OF INDUSTRIAL SOCIETY (1903; 1971 reprint ed.); Morris Cohen, *The Basis of Contract*, 46 HARV. L. REV. 553 (1933); Morris Cohen, *Property and Sovereignty*, 13 CORNELL L.Q. 8 (1927); Robert L. Hale, *Force and the State: A Comparison of "Political" and "Economic" Compulsion*, 35 COLUM. L. REV. 149 (1935); Robert Hale, *Coercion and Distribution in a Supposedly Non-coercive State*, 38 POL. SCI. Q. 470 (1923). For discussions of neoliberalism: DANIEL STEDMAN JONES, MASTERS OF THE UNIVERSE: HAYEK, FRIEDMAN, AND THE BIRTH OF NEOLIBERAL POLITICS (2012); FELDMAN, FAILING CONSTITUTION, *supra* note 47, at 162–73, 199–219.

50. Vasan Kesavan & Michael Stokes Paulsen, *The Interpretive Force of the Constitution's Secret Drafting History*, 91 GEO. L.J. 1113, 1114 (2003) (arguing that originalism is "working itself pure"). For a comparison of old and new originalisms: Feldman, *Constitutional Interpretation*, *supra* note 25, at 284–86.

51. Citizens United v. Federal Election Commission, 558 U.S. 310 (2010); *see* MICHELLE ALEXANDER, THE NEW JIM CROW (2012 ed.) (mass incarceration); NOLAN McCARTY ET AL., POLARIZED AMERICA (2008) (polarization); KENICHI OHMAE, THE END OF THE NATION STATE (1995) (multinational corporations); FRANK PASQUALE, THE BLACK BOX SOCIETY (2015) (digital technology and the Internet); PIKETTY, *supra* note 49 (inequality); DANI RODRIK, THE GLOBALIZATION PARADOX (2011) (globalization); BRUCE SCHNEIER, DATA AND GOLIATH (2015) (digital technology and surveillance); JOSEPH E. STIGLITZ, THE PRICE OF INEQUALITY (2013 ed.) (inequality); John Cassidy, *An Impulsive Authoritarian Populist in the White House*, NEW YORKER (Jan. 20, 2017) (Trump as authoritarian populist); Pippa Norris, *It's Not Just Trump. Authoritarian Populism Is Rising across the West. Here's Why*, WASH. POST (March 11, 2016)

(authoritarian populism). On the massive changes of the early twentieth century: KARL POLANYI, THE GREAT TRANSFORMATION: THE POLITICAL AND ECONOMIC ORIGINS OF OUR TIME (2001 ed.).

52. Marc Galanter, *Why the "Haves" Come Out Ahead: Speculations on the Limits of Legal Change*, 9 LAW & SOC'Y REV. 95 (1974) (discussing advantages of wealthy and powerful in litigation); *see* Donald R. Songer et al., *Do the "Haves" Come Out Ahead over Time? Applying Galanter's Framework to Decisions of the U.S. Courts of Appeals, 1925–1988*, 33 LAW & SOC'Y REV. 811 (1999) (empirical research showing that victory in litigation depends more on access to resources than on formal legal arguments).

INDEX

STEPHEN M. FELDMAN is the Jerry W. Housel/Carl F. Arnold Distinguished Professor of Law and Adjunct Professor of Political Science at the University of Wyoming. He is the author of *The New Roberts Court, Donald Trump, and Our Failing Constitution*; *Free Expression and Democracy in America: A History*; and *Please Don't Wish Me a Merry Christmas: A Critical History of the Separation of Church and State*, among other titles.